THE
HANDBOOK
OF
GOOD
ENGLISH

THE
HANDBOOK
OF
GOOD
ENGLISH
REVISED AND UPDATED

Edward D. Johnson

Facts On File®

CONTENTS

◇ PREFACE ◇

This book's first edition was published in 1982. Only seven years later I decided to revise it, but not because I thought it had so quickly become out of date. It was based on more than twenty years of experience as a book editor and more than half a life spent largely in well-spoken company, and I didn't think either it or I was substantially dated. I was aware of some new uses and misuses of the language and wanted to comment on them, but my primary intent was to rectify shortcomings that had been exposed by seven years of testing the book against writing I had edited or read for pleasure and speech I had heard. I wanted to expand my discussions of many details, modify my judgments on a few matters, increase the number of cross-references, and enlarge the Glossary/Index—all of which I have done.

In the course of the revision, however, I discovered that English and attitudes toward it have changed more than I had thought, and that I have changed too.

For one thing, the language has made adjustments to complaints that it is sexist, and it continues to adjust. I discuss this change and my accommodations to it under **sexism** in the Glossary/Index; it has affected the diction in this revision considerably. In 1982, I think, avoidance of sexist diction would have weakened my book for many readers, but now, sexist diction would weaken it, because genderless expressions that once were evasive and obtrusive have become straightforward and unsurprising.

Another change—perhaps it is partly an effect of the swift and broad acceptance of nonsexist alternatives to traditional diction, which has demonstrated the adaptability of English—is an increasing awareness among those interested in language and correct use of it that *correct* is not always easy to define. In the 1970s, several widely read writers on language came down heavily on usages and constructions that they considered debased, inane, despicable—and these writers' readers tended to accept such condemnations humbly, even guiltily. As the 1980s began, so did an antithesis in popular writing on language. The best-selling "prescriptivists" of a few years before were rebuked for their bad temper and often jeered at for their bad scholarship. The "permissivists" insisted that English was what it was and would change as it would.

Now we are perhaps in a lull in the war between prescriptivists and permissivists—or in a battle of that war. The war has been going on for centuries, and the current battle may have been evident in the broad world of letters only in the past decade but has been in progress in smaller arenas for some time, certainly since the publication of *Webster's Third New International Dictionary* in 1961 (an event discussed under **usage** in the Glossary/Index). But if there is a lull, nevertheless consciousness has been raised. The broad writing, speaking, and reading public is now not so easily cowed.

The first edition of this book—though "strict," which is to say prescriptive—was considerably more genial in tone than many similar books of its time, and, unusual for prescriptive books, it did its best to explain its prescriptions or admitted that there was no explanation but convention. However, it took it for granted that any reader consulting it would share its author's belief that there was such a thing as "good English" and that it was worth learning.

The present edition is as strict as the first. It assumes that those who use it want to be protected from criticism—and there are still plenty of critics. The general culture may have become more permissive about language, but that does not mean there are no more critics; in fact, the polarizing effect of the prescriptivist-permissivist battle has probably both increased their number and hardened their opinions. And—in my view—a great many of their opinions remain *right*, if there is such a thing as good English.

This edition does, however, take even more pains than the first to explain its rules and to distinguish logic from tradition, tradition from prejudice, prejudice from common sense, common sense from nonsense. It is more thoughtful and, I hope, wiser; it has been through the battle. And as its author, I feel obliged, as I did not in 1982, to explain at some length what I mean by good English, why I feel qualified to expound on its strictures, and why I believe learning those strictures is worthwhile.

* * *

Good English changes over the course of time, and at any given time there is some disagreement about what it is, both as a concept and as an accumulation of usage details. I begin my definition with a statement that may be self-evident but should make it clear that the advice in this book, though "strict," is not based on absolute truths: Good English is English that at present very rarely sparks the expressed or unexpressed reaction "That's not good English," either from those who really do know better or from those who merely think they do. I say "very rarely" rather than "never" because usage arbiters don't always agree, and also because critical reactions of two kinds cannot be avoided. On the one hand, the reactions of those who know almost nothing can be entirely wrongheaded and must sometimes be ignored. For example, I have been criticized for saying *between her and me* on the ground that *between she and I* is more elegant—but elegant or not, and I say decidedly not, *between she and I* is wrong. On the other hand, the reactions of those who know almost everything, the true, and few, serious scholars of language and usage, can be excessively rightheaded. For example, careful avoidance of plural pronouns such as *their* after singular pronouns such as *everyone* is justly criticized by the truly knowledgeable as a rejection of a natural usage that has been common in the best literature for centuries. But a much larger minority, those who are not scholars but do in general "know better," reject the usage, so I think we must reject it too.

To continue my definition, good English is a kind of snobbery. It is not standard English but the English of a minority who are likely to consider themselves superior, and are also likely to be considered superior by others. English that is good enough in one context may not be good enough in another, and thus good English amounts to *savoir faire*, a touchstone of the snob. All of us fail to use it occasionally, and some of us fail to use it frequently. Those who fail infrequently look down on those who fail frequently; those who fail frequently either live in constant fear of embarrassing themselves or find some way of taking pride in their unvarnished expression. Those who fail infrequently make further distinctions among themselves; the famous grammarian H. W. Fowler observed, "Almost every man is potentially a purist and a sloven at once to persons looking at him from a lower and a higher position . . . than his own."

Grammar and usage are therefore touchy subjects, like class distinctions—they *are* class distinctions. We expect occasional correction from a parent or teacher, but any friend who corrects us had better be a good friend indeed; he or she is implicitly criticizing our background, our education, our place in the world, our being. And though many of the strictures of good English promote clear expression and clear thought, many others are merely the prejudices of language snobs. Consequently, those of "good" background are frequently in a position to criticize a speaker or writer who has not shared their advantages but may have superior intelligence and superior overall command of English. Such criticism is unfair and undemocratic, but also far from uncommon; it is simply a fact of society. In this book I usually identify strictures that are prejudices, and so readers who are not snobs and are immune to snobbery can choose to ignore them—but I think few of us are entirely unsnobbish or entirely immune to snobbery; I am not.

Longtime editors like me are, however, at least relatively free of language snobbery. We spend our days and years correcting the written expression of others, some of whom we are forced to recognize as more intelligent, more highly educated, more sophisticated both socially and verbally, and more successful than we are, and unless we are unusually ill-natured we eventually are led to admit to ourselves that our skill is a humble one and that those we correct often have much more to express than we do and often express it with much more flair than we could. We allow superior writers many liberties. It is likely that every so often we have been slapped down by such writers for making ill-considered changes, and we have learned from our humiliations. We have a massive armament of arbitrary prescriptions and niceties, but we bring the big guns to bear chiefly on mediocre and bad writing—which improves markedly when so attacked, partly because editorial routines often expose faulty thought, which can then be attended to; our skills do have an important function in this wordy world.

We find it difficult to explain our weathered, dispassionate, and sometimes permissive attitude to friends who think we should be "guardians" of the language, and who may use English carefully and well but resist its natural evolutions and hold passionately to usage prejudices that they cannot justify. We do very often impose such prejudices on what we edit, since we want to protect those we edit from criticism both right-headed and wrongheaded, but we may not share them. We know the rules, we know the prejudices, but the responsibility we have assumed as professional meddlers, accountable for what we do, has made us respectful of the expression of others.

We also, of course, have our private feelings about English and its proprieties, just as do all users of the language. Our professional experience entitles us, I think, to make public not just our understanding of generally accepted principles of English but some of these private feelings and even private snobberies. I occasionally do so in this book—always, I hope, making it apparent that that is what I am doing.

If good English were merely snobbery, it would still be worth the attention of all except those who are immune to snobbery, but it is more. There are positive reasons for valuing it. Although readers may consult books like mine primarily to avert criticism and save themselves embarrassment, in the long run they are apt to find that they have also increased their pleasure in using language and given others more pleasure in their use of it.

In a sense, a language is an art form; in a sense, it is a game. Those who appreciate or engage in painting or ballet are sensitive to technique; so are those who appreciate or engage in golf or tennis. Occasionally someone untrained in one of these activities does something startlingly unconventional and wonderful, just as a young child or a poorly educated or foreign-born adult occasionally says something wonderful, makes some truly creative use of English. A very few untrained practitioners are even consistently remarkable—certainly this is true in painting. Natural talent and something like luck play an enormous role in art and in sports, and in language too. But amateurs, no matter how talented or lucky they are, do not generally experience or provide much pleasure at first—they do not consistently please themselves or others. It is only as they learn to respect conventions and techniques and begin to master them that they reliably experience and provide pleasure.

Language is an artful game, sometimes casual and sometimes competitive, and those who know its conventions, techniques, and finer points—those who have a command of good English—play it better than those who don't. They are *consistent*—and consistency, even in the details that are the subject of Chapter 3 of this book, is an important secret of their game. They can both please themselves and please others with their play; they give their listeners or readers a good game. They also win their way more frequently.

Good English is not the best English. The best English frequently is good English, but the best users of English—the great writers and poets, the great public speakers and conversationalists—are often innovative and idiosyncratic and therefore often less respectful of the strictures of good English than most of us can dare to be if we want to avoid criticism.

Good English is more than merely adequate or serviceable, however. It is English used well enough to give the user pleasure and to give pleasure to those who hear or read it, and if it falls short of the beauty and grace of the best English, it still reaches for beauty and grace and avoids the unbeautiful and ungraceful.

My definition of good English is as complete as I can make it here—all the rest is in the details. I hope that those who use this book and wrestle with its details not only will avoid criticism but will find that the pleasures of language increase for them and for those who listen to and read their words.

There remain a few comments about the organization and coverage of the book and a suggestion on using it. Its four chapters are a series of rules, each rule followed by examples and explanations. The rules are for the most part the familiar ones taught in primary and secondary schools, but the discussions of them are extended unusually far—far enough to serve sophisticated adult users of the language, those whose thought is complex and whose verbal dilemmas are correspondingly complex. Its coverage of punctuation and styling—that is, matters such as use of capitals and italics—is, I believe, more comprehensive and more detailed than that of any other book intended for general rather than professional use. It includes some basic information on diction and composition.

The Glossary/Index at the back of the book defines and illustrates grammatical terms and indexes the topics discussed in the preceding four chapters. Extending its glossary function, it also provides information and advice on many specific matters of English usage, in the manner of entirely alphabetical handbooks, and thus it is quite long, unlike a typical glossary or index. I have included these items, which in some cases are brief versions of discussions in the preceding chapters and in other cases concern specific words and details that are not discussed or are discussed only glancingly elsewhere, so that the book can have the handiness of an alphabetical guide as well as the coherent structure of the topical guide it primarily is.

When the Glossary/Index does not answer the reader's question directly or completely but refers to a rule, I advise reading the entire discussion of the rule, even though some discussions are rather long. In such references I have often included the wording of the appropriate subheading within the discussion, which will make it easier to find the relevant passage, but reading, or at least skimming, the entire discussion should increase a reader's understanding of the general principles that underlie the answer to a specific question and thus make similar questions less troubling and less frequent in the future. The book is intended to clarify general principles and hence educate the reader, not just answer specific questions, though it does that too.

THE
HANDBOOK
OF
GOOD
ENGLISH

1

GRAMMAR

◆

We learn the basic grammar of our native language, along with its basic vocabulary, at a very early age and without conscious effort. Then as we get older, the adults in our lives become increasingly insistent that we learn *correct* grammar, which seems to be made up of a lot of troublesome details that must be learned consciously. When we get to school, we study grammar more systematically and are exposed to special terms—*conjunction, gerund, predicate,* and so on—used to discuss it. We do learn quite a lot about grammar, but the special terms give many of us difficulty, and almost all of us let them fade from our minds when we leave school behind.

This chapter is concerned with correct grammar. It uses the special terms, because there is no practical way to discuss grammar without using them. However, when I introduce a term that I think some readers may not understand, I define it or give a simple defining example of it, and all grammatical terms used in the book are explained in the Glossary/Index. A reader who has unpleasant memories of struggling with these terms as a child should find them quite easy to understand now and may even get some pleasure from vanquishing *gerund* and other bugbears of grammar school.

One grammatical term is *grammar* itself, and my use of it requires some explanation. Throughout this chapter and this book, when I state that something is ungrammatical or is incorrect or faulty grammar, I am misusing the term *grammar*

1

as it is understood by scholars of language. To them, grammar is not a set of rules that we should obey when using language but a set of observations of how we do use language. If they observe that many fluent native speakers of our language say *between you and I*, they must conclude that English grammar sometimes permits the preposition *between* to have the subjective pronoun *I* as its object, though they may label the usage in some way to indicate that it is not standard and is not in line with broader observations about fluent use of English, such as the observation that fluent users of the language generally use the objective case, not the subjective case, for pronouns that are the objects of prepositions.

This chapter, however, is not a scholarly study of grammar but a guide to avoiding criticism for one's grammar. It assumes that every reader's grammar is fluent, and in that sense correct. Therefore I use the terms *correct grammar* and *incorrect grammar* in their grammar-school senses: Correct grammar employs word relationships and form changes that are accepted as correct by educators and the well-educated, and incorrect grammar employs word relationships and form changes that are condemned by them. Thus I call *between you and I* incorrect grammar, just as our schoolteachers did.

The rules and explanations in this chapter do not amount to anything like a scholarly outline of English grammar. They are merely intended to help fluent writers and speakers of English avoid common errors—avoid faulty grammar—by making them conscious of broad principles of English grammar that they employ unconsciously whenever they use the language. Principles that are understood only on a very deep mental level are difficult to bring to bear on specific problems of expression that we address consciously; we may suspect that something is wrong but be unable to identify and correct the error unless we can bring the principle involved to consciousness. In addition, many errors in grammar do not violate deep principles at all— they merely violate convention. Those who are not aware of the principles and are therefore not aware of the difference between a violation of principles and a violation of convention must face every problem in expression in an almost superstitious way, hoping the jumble of half-remembered and quite likely dubious precepts in their minds—*Don't split infinitives; Don't end a sentence with a preposition*—will see them through.

The chapter includes some advice, such as on parallel construction, that is concerned with effective use of language rather than strictly with grammar, because often it is the choice we make among grammatical structures rather than merely the rightness or wrongness of those structures that determines the overall quality of our expression. Conversely, some matters that could be considered part of grammar are not covered here but in other chapters—especially Chapter 2, on punctuation, which reflects grammar and requires an understanding of grammar if it is to be used well—and in the Glossary/Index. The Glossary/Index should be helpful to those who want quick answers to specific questions. Sometimes it answers a question directly, and sometimes it refers to the appropriate rule in this chapter or one of the others.

It is often difficult for those who do not know the name of the error they may be committing to find the discussion of that error in a reference book. I have done my best to reduce this difficulty by careful listings in the Glossary/Index, but the reader may have to do some skimming of the rules and their discussions. To help the skimming eye, I have subdivided the longer discussions, and when possible I have begun paragraphs with examples of specific constructions that may match the reader's problem.

THE SENTENCE

Most of us don't have to be told what a sentence is. This is fortunate, because it is possible to poke holes in any simple definition. We can say that a sentence is a word group that expresses a complete thought, but *I said yes* is a complete sentence, yet hardly a complete thought; like many sentences, it depends on its context to complete its meaning. We can say that a sentence is a word group that includes a subject and a verb, but *Yes* can be a complete sentence even though it has neither subject nor verb, and *When I came to dinner* can't be a sentence—at least out of context—even though it has both subject and verb. Either the complete-thought definition or the subject-and-verb definition could be expanded enough to make it valid for just about all sentences, but we'd no longer have a simple definition.

Since the subject of this chapter is grammar, we might try the following definition: A sentence is a group of words that are grammatically dependent on one another but are not grammatically dependent on any words outside the group. This definition is not perfect, and it does not uniquely describe

3

sentences—it describes independent clauses too. However, it does emphasize one important property of a sentence: the grammatical dependence we expect the words within it to share.

Grammatical dependence is what determines whether a group of words is a sentence, whether the group contains enough words, too few, or too many, and whether the relationships among the words are easy or difficult for a listener or reader to understand. The following five rules are concerned with basic properties of good sentences—sentences that are both good grammar and good uses of good grammar. (For a discussion of types of sentences and clauses, see Rule 2-1.)

1-1   Write in whole sentences, not in fragments.

I discovered the overalls. When I was ladling out the chowder. The fragment is easy to see. The second "sentence" is merely a dependent clause of the first sentence. The word *When* makes the clause dependent on something outside itself, so the word group *When I was ladling out the chowder* does not meet the definition proposed in the discussion just preceding this rule. It must be joined to the first sentence, on which it depends: *I discovered the overalls when I was ladling out the chowder.*

It may seem unlikely that a writer of any sophistication would be guilty of fragments. Here is a more complicated example: *The President, whose term in office had hardly begun when the opposition in Congress, which included members of his own party, capitulated to public opinion, changing the nature of his party leadership.* The sentence is confusing, and it takes some study to reveal that the confusion results from a fragment. Was it the President or the opposition that capitulated? If it was the opposition, then the whole sentence is a fragment, because *The President*, which is obviously the subject of the sentence, has no verb to be the subject of. If it was the President that capitulated, then *the opposition*, just as obviously intended to be the subject of a dependent clause, has no verb, so the clause is a fragment.

Such fragments are common, particularly in journalism. A hurried writer, or a hurried editor, may feel something is amiss but not see the error—after all, it's hard to see what isn't there, and often it's what isn't there that makes a sentence or clause a

4

fragment. Whenever something seems wrong with a complicated sentence, it helps to make sure that neither the sentence
as a whole nor any clause within it is a fragment.

A proper sentence generally contains a subject and a predicate, but not every proper sentence does. *And what of honor?*
and *So much for noble sentiments* can stand alone as sentences, though their meaning depends on the content of some
preceding sentence or group of sentences. They are not fragments, because they are not grammatically dependent on anything outside themselves and they do not require added words.

Fragments are sometimes deliberately employed to produce
special effects: *I said a year ago that this company was headed
for trouble. Which is where we've arrived, as these figures will
show.* There should ordinarily be a comma after *trouble* rather
than a period, but presenting the dependent clauses as if they
constituted a separate sentence gives them an emphasis that
may be desirable. The device should be used sparingly, and
alternatives should be considered; a dash after *trouble* would
give the clauses similar emphasis.

Sentences beginning with *and* or some other conjunction

And, but, or, for, so, yet, and other so-called coordinating
conjunctions are often used to begin sentences, despite an
older rule, still sometimes heard, that a sentence should never
begin with a conjunction because the conjunction makes the
sentence a fragment. It is true that a sentence that begins with
a conjunction—something joining its thought to the thought of
the preceding sentence—can hardly be anything but a fragment
of the complete thought, but that is no justification for such a
rule. After all, in a well-written paragraph each sentence
should add its thought to the thoughts of preceding sentences
whether or not it begins with a conjunction. Sentences that
begin with conjunctions are now accepted except in very formal writing; I use them frequently in this book. To avoid them
we must either (1) actually connect the sentence to the preceding sentence, which may be undesirable for a variety of reasons; (2) replace the conjunction with a conjunctive adverb or
adverbial phrase (such as *in addition* for *and, however* for *but,
alternatively* for *or,* and *consequently* for *so*), which usually
also requires adding a comma after the adverb and may give
excessive emphasis to the connection to the preceding sentence; (3) just drop the conjunction, which may remove a

helpful indication of the significance of the statement to come; or (4) completely recast the sentence.

It is acceptable to begin an occasional sentence with a conjunction; such a sentence is not a fragment. But remember that some people still condemn such use of conjunctions, and it can lead to inept or confusing sentences (see also *for* in the Glossary/Index).

Elliptical sentences

Many sentences are elliptical—that is, they leave out one or more words that the listener or reader can be expected to supply. The missing word or phrase is called an ellipsis. An elliptical sentence is not a fragment; fragments are faulty grammar, but elliptical sentences are usually quite respectable grammatically. (They are, however, sometimes ambiguous. For example, *John loves money more than Mary* has an elliptical dependent clause, which could be filled out in two very different ways: *more than Mary loves money* or *more than he loves Mary.* See also Rule 1-3.)

Answers to questions are often elliptical. *"When did you discover the overalls?" "When I was ladling out the chowder."* In this dialogue, the answer is severely elliptical, leaving out the entire main clause, which would be *I discovered the overalls.* But any listener or reader could supply the missing words; the answer is still a complete sentence in its context. The context can be more stately than conversation about Mrs. Murphy's chowder: *What is man? A featherless biped.*

1-2   Don't omit grammatically necessary words.

The function of language is to communicate meaning, and grammar is only one of the tools language employs to serve that function. Yet meaning can be entirely clear and grammar still faulty, just as meaning can be entirely clear in a sentence with misspelled words. Good grammar has to be good in itself, not just adequate to communicate meaning. Thus even when a listener or reader would have no real trouble supplying an omitted word, the omission may be an error if the word is essential to the grammar of the sentence.

Omission of parts of phrase pairs

The stock has always performed as well or better than expected attempts to be a compact sentence and does leave out some dispensable words, but the second *as* in the adverbial construction *as well as* should not be omitted; it should be *as well as or better than expected.* The error is common in sentences that include phrase pairs such as *as well as . . . or better than* and *as much as . . . if not more than.* Thus *The stock has gone up as much if not more than IBM* is a similar error. The same errors occur with adjectival comparisons: *Her money is as green or greener than yours.*

The stock has always performed as well as expected or better and *The stock has gone up as much as IBM if not more* are, however, correct. These are elliptical sentences (see Rule 1-1). It is permissible, and often desirable, to let the listener or reader supply the missing words, which would be *than expected* in the first example and *than IBM* in the second example. Thus though the first part of a phrase pair must be complete, the second part can be elliptical. Ellipsis is part of the language, and sometimes an essential part. Note that it occurs elsewhere in these sentences as well. With every ellipsis filled, the first sentence would be *The stock has always performed as well as it was expected to perform or better than it was expected to perform* and the second sentence would be *The stock has gone up as much as IBM has gone up if not more than IBM has gone up.* Ellipsis saves us from such unnaturally tedious sentences.

Omission of words in compared items: false comparison

Like the robbers, the cops' view of law enforcement is complex omits too much, making a false comparison between *the robbers* and *the cops' view of law enforcement.* It is two views, not robbers and one view, that the sentence means to compare. One way to repair the error is simply to make *robbers* an independent possessive (see Rule 1-19), so that cops and robbers share ownership of the phrase *view of law enforcement: Like the robbers', the cops' view of law enforcement is complex.* Another way would be to put the phrase in the first part of the sentence and then repeat a word of it: *Like the robbers' view of law enforcement, the cops' view is complex.* Still another way would be a complete recasting: *The cops, like the robbers, have a complex view of law enforcement.*

Profits were not so high as the preceding year and *Profits were higher than the preceding year* make a false comparison between *Profits* and *the preceding year.* Filled out, the sentences would be *Profits were not so high as they were in the preceding year* and *Profits were higher than they were in the preceding year.* We can leave out *they were*—such an omission is proper ellipsis (see Rule 1-1). And if we don't leave out *they were,* we can even leave out *in;* phrases such as *in the preceding year,* which are called prepositional adverbial phrases, can often be shortened by omitting the preposition, as in *Quarterly earnings will be announced [on] Friday.* But we cannot leave out both *they were* and *in* without creating a false comparison. Since it is usually unlikely that such errors would mislead any reader or listener, they are easy to make and to overlook; they are somewhat disturbing, but it isn't immediately apparent why. We all know that comparisons must be between items of the same nature, and once we summon that very deep principle to our conscious mind, the problem is quite apparent. Although we can't write or speak fluently if our conscious mind is cluttered with grammatical principles, we should be able to bring these principles to consciousness when we need them.

Omission of verb forms

He either will or has already left is wrong. The verb form *left* is appropriate with the second auxiliary verb, *has,* but inappropriate with the first, *will.* This kind of error is sometimes called syllepsis. The sentence should be *He either will leave or has already left.* Similarly, *The country has already and will continue going to the dogs* is wrong; the verb form *gone* should be supplied after *already.* If the form of a repeated verb changes, it cannot be omitted in the first construction and supplied only in the second. The verb can be omitted in the first construction if it does not change form, as in *He either is now or will soon be leaving,* in which *leaving* is the correct form in both constructions, but the omission may not always please the ear.

Changed verb forms can often be omitted in the second construction: *I used the car when my father wasn't; He didn't go but should have; He hasn't gone but will.* When the first application of the verb is omitted, it is an error of grammar, but when the second application is omitted, it is a grammatically permissible syllepsis, though it may be undesirable, as it is to some degree in each of the three examples.

When no auxiliary verb is involved but a verb changes form because of a change in person, the verb can be omitted in the second construction: *I drive more than she; I supply his financial support, his mother his emotional support.* When an auxiliary verb is involved and changes form because of a change in person, the whole compound verb can be omitted as long as the form of the actual verb is the same, as in *I am going to jail, you to your just reward,* in which the omitted auxiliary verb is *are,* but the omitted actual verb is *going,* the same form as in the first clause.

Sometimes an omitted verb has the same form as a supplied verb but a different meaning. *He is crazy already and quickly driving his wife crazy* may look fine—not only is the verb supplied in the first construction but it is unchanged in form in the second construction. However, the omission of *is* in the second construction is at best questionable. In the first construction, *is* is a linking verb—*He is crazy*—but in the second construction, it is an auxiliary verb—*He is . . . driving.* The same word should not be forced to carry two different meanings, so *is* should be repeated in the second construction. Many other verbs can have two or more distinct meanings—*I have gone, I have a gun; He keeps fit, He keeps sheep, He keeps his word*—but *is* is the only one that is likely to be wrongly omitted; no one would write *He keeps fit, sheep, and his word.* Occasionally the multiple meanings of verbs are used deliberately for a humorous effect, a device sometimes also called syllepsis but more precisely called zeugma: *He bolted the door and his dinner; He took his hat and his leave.* See also **zeugma** in the Glossary/Index.

You better do it right now is an odd but very common error; the verb *had* is left out completely. In speech, *You had better* is quite properly contracted to *You'd better,* then improperly blurred to *You better;* people come to consider it some sort of idiom, or perhaps as the correct imperative *You do it right now* with *better* thrown in as an intensifier, and use it even in writing. It is incorrect in either speech or writing, though it may eventually replace the correct form, and it is possible to think up grammatical justifications for it (see **better** in the Glossary/Index). Like any other error, it can legitimately appear in quoted dialogue, but I have seen it often in the dialogue of fictional characters whom the writer did not mean to present as careless speakers.

Omission of relative pronouns

He is the man went to Washington is distinctly folksy. However, *He is the man we sent to Washington* is good standard grammar. We cannot ordinarily leave out a subjective relative pronoun such as *who,* but we can often leave out an objective relative pronoun such as *whom.* In simple sentences, the distinction is clear even with pronouns such as *which* and *that,* which have the same form in subjective and objective cases; we accept *This is the house Jack built* but not *This is the house fell down around Jack*—we have to supply the pronoun *which* or *that* to serve as the subject of *fell.* (When another clause interrupts the relative clause, even a subjective relative pronoun is sometimes omitted, as in *This is the house I thought fell down around Jack.* See Rule 1-6 for more discussion of such interrupting clauses.)

This is the house that Jack built and the weather destroyed, leaving out *that* before *the weather destroyed,* is correct, and in fact the first *that* can be omitted too: *This is the house Jack built and the weather destroyed. This is the house that collapsed in the storm and fell down around Jack* is also correct; the single *that* can serve as the subject of both *collapsed* and *fell down.* However, *This is the house that Jack built and fell down around him* is incorrect. There must be a subject for *fell down around him,* and the *that* earlier in the sentence will not do, because it is already the object of the verb *built.* The same relative pronoun cannot be used both as the object of one verb and the subject of another, with the exception of the pronouns *whoever* and *whomever* (see the discussion of pronouns as part of their own clauses in Rule 1-6). In a complicated sentence, it may take some study to reveal that a relative pronoun is trying to play two grammatical roles. Thus *They were all fully occupied in preparing for the invasion of the mainland, which they had planned as the next stage in Allied strategy and was to follow in less than a month* is troubling—mysteriously so until it is noticed that *which* is both the object of *they had planned* and the subject of *was to follow.* But the error occurs in simple sentences too, such as *Do what you like and makes you feel good,* in which *what* is supplied as the object of *like* but omitted as the subject of *makes.*

This is the house Jack built and that fell down around him is correct, with *that* omitted as the object of *built* but supplied as the subject of *fell down.* It is not, however, a pleasingly balanced sentence; it would be much better with the objective

10

that supplied. Some writers, as well as some editors, like to omit every optional relative pronoun, but such a policy suggests an excessively mechanical approach to language. An optional pronoun often improves readability.

Note that in the examples above in which a relative pronoun is correctly omitted, it always is part of a defining construction rather than a parenthetical construction. A relative pronoun in a parenthetical construction, such as *which* in *This house, which Jack built, fell down,* can never be omitted, and it is unlikely that any fluent user of English would omit it. For discussions of defining and parenthetical constructions, see the Glossary/Index and Rule 2-1.

Omission of a repeated preposition

We disagreed only with regard to what the disaster was due has one too few uses of the preposition *to,* which is needed after *due* as well as after *regard: We disagreed only with regard to what the disaster was due to.* Similarly, *It was a disaster the significance of which no one was entirely ignorant* needs *of* at the end to go with *ignorant;* the earlier *of* after *significance* cannot play two roles.

It must be admitted that the correct versions of these sentences are much harder on the ear or eye than the incorrect versions, and that rewriting them would be advisable. Sentences can end with prepositions, despite the oft-heard dogma that they should not, but a sentence that does is likely to be a sentence in which the word order is not standard, because in standard word order a preposition is followed by its object. Sometimes there is no good reason to depart from standard word order. Certainly *We disagreed only about the cause of the disaster* is easier and pleasanter to read than a sentence so twisted that a preposition can be mislaid among its convolutions.

Omission of a repeated modifier

There is enough time and energy, omitting the adjective *enough* before the second object, is correct, but *There is neither enough time nor energy* is faulty; it should be *There is neither enough time nor enough energy.* The error can be considered faulty parallelism, which is discussed in Rule 1-5.

Body blows are the most reliable, effective, and punishing, omitting the adverb *most* before the second and third adjectives, is correct, but *Body blows are the most reliable, effective, and easiest to learn* is faulty; since *most* does not apply to *easiest to learn*, it should be supplied for *effective*. This error too could be called faulty parallelism.

‖ **1-3   Don't omit words necessary to prevent ambiguity or momentary misreading.**

The preceding rule concerns omissions that leave meaning intact but are grammatical errors. This rule concerns omissions that are grammatically correct but produce ambiguity or permit misreading.

John loves money more than Mary is ambiguous because the *than* clause is elliptical. In most contexts the meaning would be clear and the sentence might therefore be judged acceptable, but in some contexts it might be unclear, and in any context it could be criticized as imprecise. The *than* clause should be at least partially filled out if precision is considered important: *than Mary does* or *than he does Mary.*

He was expelled for failing physics and gambling is ambiguous because of an omitted preposition; it should be *He was expelled for failing physics and for gambling,* to prevent *gambling* from being momentarily taken as a second direct object of *failing.* Few readers would persist in their misreading and believe that gambling was part of the curriculum. We unconsciously and almost instantly correct such misapprehensions when we read. Nevertheless they are annoying, and text that contains many opportunities for misreading can be profoundly irritating; somewhere below the level of consciousness, our comprehension is continually backing out of blind alleys.

The word *that* is often omitted in such constructions as *I believe I'll go home* and *He said I could stay.* These omissions are fine, but sometimes when *that* is left out it is not clear where it belongs. *The expectation is falsely high earnings will be reported* could mean either *The expectation is that falsely high earnings will be reported* or *The expectation is falsely high that earnings will be reported.* Sentences with *that* omitted should be inspected with extra care.

It takes special alertness to catch omissions that are grammatically correct but invite misreading, since we already know what we mean. Ambiguity is always with us; the examples above are merely a few of the many ambiguities that the English language permits. Yet the effort to reduce ambiguity is well worth making and should be part of the process of revising any carefully composed work. See Rules 4-9 to 4-14 for advice about that process.

1-4   Omit redundant or otherwise unnecessary words and phrases— but with some discretion.

The traffic was as usual as ever is a typical careless redundancy; *as usual* and *as ever* mean virtually the same thing. This kind of redundancy repeats the same idea in different words. It seems to be especially common with *as* constructions, as in *Traffic was equally as bad last week*; either *equally bad* or *as bad* should be used. The writer or speaker may be using *equally* merely as an intensifier, like *just,* but to the reader or listener, *equally* and *as* have the same meaning in this context.

I hope that when the parole board votes on my case that it will not fail to consider my recent beatification incorrectly repeats *that.* The first *that* introduces the remainder of the sentence, which is a noun clause with an adverbial *when* clause dependent on it. The second *that* reintroduces the noun clause and should be taken out. The error is common when a noun clause has a preceding dependent clause.

The examples above are true errors. More often, redundancy is not an error but just an unnecessary use of a modifying word or phrase. There are dozens of familiar expressions that cannot be called grammatically incorrect but are redundant: *consensus of opinion* means *consensus; variety of different choices* means *variety of choices; large in size* means *large; plans for the future* means *plans.* One should watch out for such redundant expressions—for one thing, they are overused and consequently bore the reader, like clichés—but they do not have to be exterminated; the cadence of a particular sentence may make *plans for the future* more desirable than *plans.* Writing from which every redundancy has been religiously uprooted is apt to be unnaturally terse and clipped.

Refer back is often condemned as redundant, and it is redundant in *Please refer back to the previous chapter.* But the *re* in *refer* does not necessarily have the same meaning as *back*— obviously it doesn't in *Please refer to the next chapter.* If I am

13

reading Chapter 10, I might expect to be *referred* to Chapter 12 but would not object to being *referred back* to Chapter 8; the *back* might be dispensable, but it would remind me that I am being referred to text I have already read. It is wrongheaded and simpleminded to leap on every redundancy.

Wordiness and flourishes

Because of the fact that I had occasion to be in possession of the money, they were of the opinion that I was the party guilty of having stolen it is wordy for *Because I had the money they thought I had stolen it.* Such wordiness occasionally has a function, emphasizing some part of the meaning or giving it a slight twist, but usually wordiness suggests confusion, pomposity, or both. It is not an error of grammar but an error of composition (see Rule 4-12). One might call it an overuse of grammar—a use of complex grammatical structures to convey a simple meaning.

I venture to say that you wouldn't find me so contemptible if I'd split the money with you begins with a somewhat quaint flourish. However, an occasional flourish is not only permissible but desirable; flourishes can add nuance and expression to otherwise bald statements and convey the feeling of the writer or speaker about the statement. Of course, writers or speakers who use *I venture to say, I would hazard that*, and similar expressions to begin every other sentence—there seems to be at least one such person at every conference table—are adding off-flavor nuances; they are nervous, or pompous, or uncertain, or just clumsy with language.

1-5   If there are elements in a sentence that are parallel in meaning and in grammatical function, make them parallel in grammatical form.

This is a basic rule of clear expression. Violations of the rule are a feature of what one might call deliberately bad writing, committed by writers who consciously vary the grammatical form of parallel elements because they think the variation will make their sentences interesting and impressive. Such variation may violate rules of grammar and will almost certainly make sentences needlessly confusing and clumsy. More often, violations are accidental; writers merely fail to notice a poor choice of phrasing, an omission of a necessary word (see Rule 1-2), or a mispositioning of a word. Correcting faulty parallelism occupies more of an editor's attention than correcting all other grammatical faults put together.

Items in a series not parallel

He liked sailing, swimming, and to fish is a simple example; most of us don't have to be told that the third item in the series should be *fishing*, producing a series of three gerunds rather than two gerunds and an infinitive, or else the first two items should be *to sail* and *to swim*, producing a series of three infinitives. Yet wrong as the example seems, its grammar is technically correct, since either a gerund or an infinitive can be used as an object of *liked*. The error is an error of parallelism.

He liked sailing, beachcombing forays, and swimming is a subtler example of faulty parallelism. Although *sailing, beachcombing, and swimming* are all gerunds, *beachcombing* does not stand alone but merely modifies the noun *forays*, so instead of a series of three gerunds we have a gerund, a modified noun, and another gerund. If we take out *forays*, the series is properly parallel. The faulty parallelism in the example is only faintly troubling, however, and one could even argue that it gives the sentence a vitality that the stolid *He liked sailing, beachcombing, and swimming* lacks. Rule 1-5 should not be applied so zealously that every variation of structure in a series is disallowed, especially in writing that is intended to do more than merely state the facts.

Note that *He liked sailing, swimming, and other seaside activities* is not a case of faulty parallelism. The third item in the series is not parallel in meaning and significance to the other two, but characterizes them and represents a group of unnamed activities. Nor is *He liked sailing, swimming, and girls* faulty parallelism; the series consists of two gerunds and a noun, but there is no way to change the noun without changing the content of the sentence—the series is as close to parallel as it can be. Items in a series should usually be as parallel as their meaning permits, but they don't have to be so parallel that we can't say what we mean. *He liked to sail, to swim, and girls* is faulty, however, because two infinitives and a noun combine in a series much less happily—that is, they are farther from parallel—than two gerunds and a noun.

15

He liked to sail, swim, and to walk on the beach has a series of three infinitives, but they aren't properly parallel. The word *to* should either be eliminated before *walk* or be supplied before *swim*. In putting *to* before the last infinitive but not the middle one, the writer could be hoping to discourage a possible but unlikely misreading; *on the beach* could grammatically go with all three infinitives, as it does in *He liked to sunbathe, read, and sleep on the beach all day*, though it would take a perverse reader to notice the grammatical possibility in the original example. If there is a real possibility of misreading such a series, recasting to avoid the series is a better solution than making the series nonparallel.

He liked to sail, swim, and had a passion for beachcombing is in real trouble, because the last item is not part of the series at all but is the second part of a compound predicate: *He liked . . . and had . . .* The error seems glaring but is very common. *He liked to sail and swim and had a passion for beachcombing* is correct: two predicates to go with *He*, and two parallel objects to go with *liked*. If we want to avoid the run-together look of *sail and swim and had*, we can put a comma after *swim* (a comma is usually unnecessary and undesirable between compound predicates but is permissible to ease reading; see Rule 2-3), or we can put in the comma and also repeat *he* before the second predicate, making it an independent clause: *He liked to sail and swim, and he had a passion for beachcombing*. See also **false series** in the Glossary/Index and the last paragraph of Rule 2-6.

Either . . . or, not only . . . but also: correlative items not parallel

Correlative items in a sentence are ones indicated by pairs of conjunctions such as *either . . . or, not only . . . but also*, and *whether . . . or*.

He has either gone swimming or someone has taken him sailing is faulty parallelism—and faulty grammar—because the second element is not a second predicate sharing the subject *He* with the first predicate, but an independent clause with its own subject, *someone*. The sentence can be made grammatically correct by changing the position of *either*: *Either he has gone swimming or someone has taken him sailing*. Now the correlative elements are both independent clauses. Another solution would be *He has either gone swimming or been taken sailing*. Neither solution produces perfect parallelism—

16

in the first, one verb is intransitive and the other transitive, and in the second, one verb is active and the other passive. However, both solutions are correct, and the parallelism cannot be perfected without changing the meaning. For example, *He has either gone swimming or gone sailing* loses the implication that he can go swimming on his own but wouldn't be expected to go sailing without someone else.

He has either gone swimming or gone sailing is precisely parallel; *gone swimming* and *gone sailing* are grammatically similar and share their relationship with *he has*. The sentence can be made nonparallel all too easily by misplacing *either*: *He has either gone swimming or sailing* omits a repetition of *gone*, and *He either has gone swimming or gone sailing* omits a repetition of *has*. These failures of parallelism are not really offensive in the casual context of the example, but they are noticeable. They could be considered uses of ellipsis (see Rule 1-1), but not every permissible ellipsis is a desirable one. The sentence can also be made nonparallel by leaving *either* where it was but repeating a word: *He has either gone swimming or has gone sailing* unnecessarily repeats *has*. This failure of parallelism is somewhat offensive; the ear and eye are more apt to accept a questionable ellipsis than a questionable repetition.

The properly parallel sentence *He has not only gone swimming but gone sailing* can be made nonparallel in the same ways. With the conjunctive pairs *either . . . or* and *not only . . . but also*, the item following the first conjunction and the item following the second conjunction should be grammatically similar.

Note that this is not true of all conjunctive pairs. With the conjunctive pair *whether . . . or*, the item following the second conjunction usually can be and often should be shorter. *I don't know whether he has gone swimming or he has gone sailing* is precisely parallel but not natural English; the second *he* should come out, and *has* or *has gone* could come out.

He has either gone swimming or gone to town with his father is not strictly parallel—*gone swimming* and *gone to town with his father* are both predicates and hence are grammatically equivalent, but they are structured differently and make different uses of the verb *gone*. That is quite all right; correlative items should be as grammatically similar as their meaning permits, but they cannot always be grammatically identical. *He has gone either swimming or to town with his father* is not all right; since *gone* functions differently with *swimming* and *to town*, it should be repeated (see the discus-

17

sion of omitted verb forms in Rule 1-2), and it can't be repeated without repositioning *either*.

Sentences that are more ambitious than the examples above often fall into misplacement of correlative conjunctions because of an inverted or otherwise unusual word order. The effect is to make serious prose seem somewhat scatterbrained, as in *Not only had classical anticommunism returned to Washington in official rhetoric, but also in military programs and the reassertion of self-confidence.* There is a failure of parallelism, because the item introduced by *Not only* is a clause, but the item introduced by *but also* is merely a prepositional phrase. The latter item could be made a clause, of course: *. . . but it had also returned in . . .* Parallelism could also be achieved by using either standard word order—*Classical anticommunism had returned to Washington not only in official rhetoric but also in military programs and the reassertion of self-confidence*—or a different nonstandard order—*Not only in official rhetoric but also in military programs and the reassertion of self-confidence had classical anticommunism returned to Washington.* See also the discussion of complications in inverted sentences in Rule 2-5.

More than, as much as: adverbial comparisons not parallel

Adverbial comparisons in a sentence are ones joined by phrases such as *more than* and *as much as*. Errors occur with them (and with adjectival comparisons, such as *greener than* and *as green as*) when a necessary *than* or *as* is omitted, as discussed in Rule 1-2. Errors also occur when the second item in the comparison is a pronoun, as in *He sails more than me*, which can be considered an error of parallelism, since *He* and *me* are grammatically parallel and should therefore be in the same case (such errors are discussed in Rule 1-6 as errors in case).

He didn't like swimming as much as to sail is clearly nonparallel and ugly. However, lack of parallelism can be much less apparent in more complicated sentences, and it can be defensible. *He learned to swim that summer, but more than swimming with his friends on the broad public beach he liked to sail to the deserted strands of the islands in the bay* fails to make *swimming* and *to sail* parallel, but then perhaps they are not really parallel in thought anyway—there is an implication that when he got to those deserted strands he liked to swim there, and consequently the parallel in thought is between

18

swimming with friends and swimming alone rather than between swimming and sailing. English is not mathematics, and language can sometimes compare nonparallel things—can compare apples and oranges. Careful parallelism is not the only important property of good English, and sometimes it is a dispensable property.

But not, rather than: antithetical constructions not parallel

Antithetical constructions are used to state that something is true of one thing but untrue of another. *He liked sailing and swimming but not to walk on the beach* is faulty parallelism; *to walk* should be changed to *walking*. When the untrue item is given first, *but not* becomes *not . . . but*, and errors of parallelism can occur in the same way they do in correlative constructions, discussed earlier in this rule: *He has not gone swimming but sailing* omits a desirable repetition of *gone*, *He has gone not swimming but gone sailing* undesirably repeats *gone*, and so on.

He chose to sail to the island rather than swimming there is nonparallel, and it is easily made parallel by changing *swimming* to *to swim* or simply to *swim*—it is often permissible to leave out *to* in an infinitive, though *to* should be either consistently included or consistently omitted in the second and subsequent infinitives in a series, as explained earlier in this rule. However, nonparallelisms with *rather than* are often not objectionable, even in such a straightforward sentence as the example, and sometimes they are necessary. *He sailed to the island rather than swam there* is parallel, and *He sailed to the island rather than swimming there* and *He sailed to the island rather than swim there* are not, but the second and third versions do not mean the same as the first; the first version simply tells us what he did and did not do, whereas the second suggests to us and the third tells us that he made a conscious decision between alternatives. When the negative *rather than* construction precedes the positive construction, parallelism is actually an error: *Rather than swam there, he sailed to the island* is not English, though the nonparallel *swim* and *swimming* would both be English. The normally conjunctive phrase *rather than* is often used, and used correctly, as if it were a prepositional phrase such as *instead of*, and when it is so used, the rule that items joined by conjunctions should be as grammatically similar as possible must sometimes be abandoned.

Like and *unlike*

These words very often occur in introductory constructions: *Like me, she is a teaching fellow; Unlike her classwork, her tutorial duties bore her.* They seem to invite faulty parallelism, and the result is false comparison (discussed in the Glossary/ Index and in Rule 1-2). *Like me, tutorial duties take up a lot of her time* and *Unlike her classwork, she is bored by her tutorial duties* are examples; in the first, *me* is not parallel to *tutorial duties*, and in the second, *classwork* is not parallel to *she*. The frequency of such errors may be partly due to haziness on the proper functions of *like*; see also **like** for **as, as if,** or **as though** in the Glossary/Index.

CASE OF NOUNS AND PRONOUNS: SUBJECTIVE, OBJECTIVE, AND POSSESSIVE

The case of a noun or pronoun is determined by the function of the word within its sentence—by whether it is the subject of a verb, the object of a verb or preposition, or the possessive modifier of another word. English nouns have only two forms for the three cases, since the subjective and objective forms are the same; the possessive case is formed by adding an apostrophe and *s* or sometimes just the apostrophe (see Rule 2-29). Some pronouns, such as *one* and *anybody*, also have only two forms, but some others have not just three but four. *I, me,* and *my* are subjective, objective, and possessive forms, and there is also a special form for the so-called independent possessive, *mine,* which instead of merely modifying another word acts like a noun: *Let's take your car, since mine has bald tires.* The possessive *mine* can even itself be made possessive—*Let's take your car; mine's tires are bald*—though this is not true of other independent possessives, such as *yours* and *theirs.*

Except for independent possessives, possessive nouns and pronouns are actually modifiers, and they are discussed later in this book (Rule 1-19), though Rule 1-7 concerns the use of the possessive case for the subject of a gerund. The three other rules in this section concern the pronouns that have different forms for the subjective and objective cases.

1-6   Put the subject of a verb in the subjective case.

Since nouns have the same form in the subjective and objective cases, violations of this rule occur only with a few pronouns—the personal pronouns *I/me, he/him, she/her, we/us,* and *they/ them,* and the relative or interrogative pronoun *who/whom* and its indefinite form *whoever/whomever.* But because these pronouns are common, errors in case are common.

Pronouns as part of compound subjects

Johnny and me want to go swimming is amazingly difficult to stamp out of a child's speech. This may be one of the times that natural grammar—the grammar we absorb as we learn to speak and long before we go to school—is at real odds with standard English. The child perhaps considers *Johnny and me,* or even *me and Johnny,* to be a single idea that should keep the same form whether subject or object. Eventually, parents and teachers convince the child that the pronoun in a compound subject has to have the same form that it would if it were standing alone—*I want to go swimming*—and we begin to hear *John and I want to buy a motorcycle.*

Pronouns as part of their own clauses

I avoid him who has the plague is correct; *him* is the object of *avoid,* and *who* is the subject of *has,* the verb in its own clause. Those who make it *I avoid he who has the plague* may just be afraid of the objective case, having in childhood been corrected so often about *Johnny and me want to go swimming,* but more sophisticated people make the error too, because it does seem to have some logic going for it. The entire word group *him who has the plague* acts as a unit—in the example, as the direct object of *avoid*—and the *who* in the subordinate clause seems to attract the *him* of the main clause to its own case. It shouldn't; *who* is governed by its own clause, in which it is the subject, but *him* is governed by the main clause, in which it is the object.

It was she I was writing about may seem puzzling at a glance, because there is no objective pronoun and *I was writing about* seems to require one. The temptation is to make it *It was her I was writing about,* thus providing an objective pronoun. This is an error—*It was she* is correct, since a pronoun is governed by its own clause. The missing objective pronoun, *whom*, has simply been omitted, as is entirely permissible (see the discussion of omission of relative pronouns in Rule 1-2). With the ellipsis filled in, the sentence becomes *It was she whom I was writing about.*

I invited people whom I thought would get along together is just as wrong, if less apparently so, as *I invited people whom would get along together.* The pronoun *whom* is the subject of *would*, not the object of *thought*, and it should therefore be *who.* Often a relative clause such as *who would get along together* is interrupted by another clause such as *I thought.* The object of the verb in the interrupting clause is somewhat difficult to pin down. In effect it is the idea, but not the exact words, of the surrounding clause: *I thought they would get along together.* Perhaps this fuzziness about the object of the verb in the interrupting clause explains an odd fact. Even though the relative pronoun in the sentence *I invited people who I thought would get along together* is subjective, it can be dropped: *I invited people I thought would get along together.* Normally we could not omit a subjective pronoun—we could not make it *I invited people would get along together*—but the interrupting clause permits the omission, just as if the pronoun were objective, as it is in *I invited people whom I thought you would like.*

Whom shall I say is calling? is a common error among those who think *whom* is always more genteel than *who* (see **genteelism** and **hyperurbanism** in the Glossary/Index). More sophisticated people make the error too, particularly in passive constructions, such as *Whom did you say was being invited?* Here the interrupting *did you say* camouflages the otherwise glaring wrongness of *Whom was being invited?*

I saw a man who I thought was better dressed than I and *I met a man whom I thought to be better dressed than I* are both correct. In the second example, *whom* is objective as the subject of the infinitive *to be* (see **infinitive** in the Glossary/Index). In *I saw a man whom I thought better dressed than I*, the infinitive is omitted but understood, and *whom* remains correct. (Rule 1-6 would be more precise if I had made it "Put the subject of a *finite* verb in the subjective case"—but I did not want to puzzle readers with the term *finite.* See **finite verb** in the Glossary/Index.)

Whoever, unlike other pronouns, can play two roles in a sentence at once. It can function as the subject of one verb and the object of another, as in *I will invite whoever wants to come*, in which *whoever* is the subject of *wants* and also the object of *invite* (though more precisely it is not *whoever* but the entire clause *whoever wants to come* that is the object of *invite*). *Whomever* can function as the object of verbs in two clauses, as in *I will invite whomever you choose*, or as the subject of a verb and the object of a preposition, as in *Whomever we send invitations to is sure to come* and *For whoever draws the lucky number there will be a prize*. Other combinations of function are possible. As the examples here show, the form of the pronoun—whether it is the subjective *whoever* or the objective *whomever*—is determined by the role it plays in its own clause, which is the clause that completes its meaning, defining who *whoever* or *whomever* is. In speech, occasional errors are almost inevitable, because the role of the pronoun can be so complicated, as in *This invitation is for whoever that is you're with*—the temptation is strong to make it *whomever*, as the object of *for* or the object of *with*. When we are writing, we have time to figure out that *whomever that is* would be an error. See also Rule 1-8 and **who, whom; whoever, whomever** in the Glossary/Index.

Pronouns in elliptical clauses

She sails better than him seems wrong to most of us, and to all of us if the elliptical clause is filled in: *She sails better than him sails*. The word *than* is a conjunction, and conjunctions join words or word groups of similar grammatical significance—two adjectives modifying the same noun, two subjects or two objects of the same verb, two clauses, and so on. In *She sails better than him, than* joins a clause and an objective pronoun, which is not a proper function of a conjunction. Use of objective pronouns with *than* has been exceedingly common for centuries, however, especially with first-person pronouns: *She thinks she's better than me; She sails better than us*. Consequently, some modern dictionaries accept *than* as a preposition, condoning its use with objective pronouns, since the objects of prepositions should be in the objective case (see Rule 1-9). I advise denying oneself this liberty, since there are many who condemn it.

She likes him better than me is a correct use of *than* as a conjunction. *Me* is objective, but that is all right, because it is the objective pronoun *him* that *me* is joined with, and if the elliptical clause is filled in, the sentence becomes *She likes him better than she likes me.* When in doubt about the proper case for a pronoun following *than,* we can just imagine the sentence with the elliptical clause filled in. See also **than** in the Glossary/Index.

He has better friends than I is correct but ambiguous; it could mean either *He has better friends than I am* or *He has better friends than I have.* Elliptical clauses should be checked for ambiguity as well as for grammatical soundness.

Pronouns in apposition

John, he of the big mouth, won't be invited and *Let's not invite John, him of the big mouth* are both correct. In the first sentence, *he of the big mouth* is in apposition to *John,* the subject of the sentence, and the pronoun *he* is in the subjective case. In the second sentence, *him of the big mouth* is again in apposition to *John,* but *John* is the object of the sentence, and the pronoun *him* is in the objective case. The case of a pronoun in apposition is determined by the case of the word that it is in apposition to. (See also Rule 1-19 for special problems with possessives.)

The directors you have chosen, Mr. Smith and me, will do our best is an error; *Mr. Smith and me* is in apposition to *The directors,* the subject of the sentence, and hence should be *Mr. Smith and I.* The intervening *you have chosen* encourages the error—its understood object, the relative pronoun *whom,* seems to offer its invisible self for *Mr. Smith and me* to be in apposition to.

All of us are going may seem puzzling, since *Us are going* is impossible. But in *All of us are going,* the pronoun *us* is the object of the preposition *of,* not a word in apposition to the subject of the verb; there is no apposition in the sentence. The entire phrase *All of us* is the subject, and the case of the pronoun is determined by its role within its phrase.

T. S. Eliot's line *Let us go then, you and I* could be considered an error; *you and I* is in apposition to *us,* and thus it should be *you and me.* However, *you and I* is supported by idiom and to some extent by grammatical analysis. *Let us* and *Let's* are so frequently followed by subjective pronouns that objective pronouns are apt to seem wrong or at least colloquial, as in the correct *Let's you and me have a drink. Let us* and particularly its contraction *Let's* are not perceived as what most grammarians say they are, the imperative *Let* and the objective *us* or its contraction. One of the most scholarly grammarians,

George O. Curme, would consider *Let us go* to be a subjunctive rather than an imperative construction, a modern form of *Go we,* and *Go we then, you and I* could not be attacked for disagreement in case, so perhaps *Let us go then, you and I* should not be attacked either. Nevertheless, I advise not using the subjective after *Let us* and *Let's,* if only because *Let's you and I* has at least a faint whiff of the reeking gentility of *between you and I;* people who use the subjective may be suspected of doing so not because they tolerantly accept idiom but because they intolerantly and ignorantly think the subjective is more elegant.

Let's encourages other apposition errors besides errors of case, such as the colloquial *Let's us go* and *Let's you and him make up,* which when the contraction is expanded become the grossly redundant *Let us us go* and the nonsensical *Let us you and him make up.* Obviously, *let's* has acquired a broader meaning than that of the uncontracted *let us,* but in anything more than casual speech it should not be used where *let us* cannot be used.

It's me or *It's I?* Pronouns as subject complements

A subject complement is a word or phrase that follows a linking verb such as *is* or *seems;* it's the *that* in *This is that,* and it's the *gray* in *All cats seem gray.* A subject complement isn't the object of a verb but something linked to the subject by a verb. The rule for subject complements is very simple: They should be in the same case as the subject they are linked to, which is, of course, the subjective case.

It's me and *It's us* break the rule, a fact that has probably generated more incredulity among grammar-school students than any other precept of "good grammar," because *It's I* and *It's we* seem impossibly unnatural to them. I advise breaking the rule whenever the subjective pronouns *I* and *we* seem stiff or prissy, as they do following the informal contraction *It's* and in many other situations. *That was we singing outside your window last night; When you hear three knocks, it will be I; His chief victim was I*—such sentences may obey the rule, but they are idiomatically objectionable. There are, of course, sentences in which obeying the rule is not idiomatically objectionable. In *It was I who broke your window,* the subjective *who* seems to make *I* preferable even though in principle there need be no agreement in case between a pronoun and its antecedent (see Rule 1-12). The ear has to be the judge.

It's him and *It's her* cannot be defended quite as energetically, because the rule-observing *It's he* and *It's she,* though perhaps slightly stilted, are not outlandish; most careful speakers and writers do use them. *It's them* is perhaps more often defensible, because *It's they* is more than slightly stilted. Again, the ear must be the judge; *That was he singing outside your window* seems fine to me, but *His chief victim was she* seems contrary to idiom, and to a lesser extent so does *That was they singing outside your window.*

1-7   Put the subject of a gerund in the possessive case, if possible.

I dislike that man's wearing a mask and *I dislike that man wearing a mask* are different statements. In the first, the wearing of the mask is disliked; in the second, the man is disliked. In the first statement, *wearing* is a gerund—that is, a special verb form that functions as a noun—and it is the object of the sentence, with the possessive phrase *that man's* modifying it. Such a possessive "owns" the action implied by the gerund and thus is considered the subject of the gerund. In the second statement, *wearing* is a participle—that is, a special verb form that functions as an adjective—and *that man* is the object of the sentence, with the participial phrase *wearing a mask* modifying it.

However, very often the objective case rather than the possessive case is used for the subject of a gerund, especially when it is unlikely that the gerund will be misperceived as a participle, as in *I dislike him wearing a mask.* Many writers and editors, and some of the grammarians whose books they use for reference, consider use of the objective case for the subject of a gerund to be standard idiomatic English, and certainly it is common. Other writers and editors, and the grammarians they prefer, condemn use of the objective case if the possessive case is possible. Since such use of the objective case will not escape criticism, I advise against it. I also believe that it eliminates a useful grammatical signal and permits an annoying fuzziness of syntax. A sharper understanding of what a gerund is may help reduce the fuzziness.

There are two types of gerund. One type is exactly like a noun—it can be the subject or object of a verb, it is modified by articles and adjectives, and it cannot take a direct object. The other type is mostly like a noun but has some of the characteristics of a verb or a participle—it too can be the subject or object of a sentence, but it is modified by adverbs and can take a direct object. In *The inappropriate wearing of a mask is forbidden*, the gerund *wearing* is of the first type; in *Inappropriately wearing a mask is forbidden*, the same gerund is of the second type. Of course, a gerund with no modifier and no object or *of* phrase following it cannot be assigned to either type. We do not mix the types in modern English, though fluent users of the language did mix them in previous centuries. The journals of the eighteenth-century explorer James Cook are full of examples, such as *The trouble and vexation that attended the bringing these animals thus far is hardly to be conceived*, in which *bringing* is modified by *the*, just as a noun would be, but has the direct object *these animals*, just as a verb or participle would have.

Every modern fluent user of English automatically uses the possessive for the subject of gerunds of the first type—*I dislike that man's inappropriate wearing of a mask*—because the "nounness" of the gerund is so evident. But a great many fluent speakers and writers use the objective for the subject of gerunds of the second type—*I dislike that man inappropriately wearing a mask*—because the "nounness" of the gerund is obscured by its adverbial modifier and direct object. When the objective is used instead of the possessive, the gerund can be perceived as a participle modifying *man* rather than a gerund modified by *man*, and the meaning is likely to be different. Sometimes it makes little difference to the sense of a sentence whether a verb form ending in *ing* is understood as a participle or as a gerund. For example, *I don't remember his ever being angry* and *I don't remember him ever being angry* mean very nearly the same thing, and an argument could be made for preferring the latter—the thought is of the man angry more than of the man's anger. But often there is a difference, and if we mean the *ing* word to be a gerund rather than a participle, we should use the possessive case for its subject.

She approves of the teacher handing out extra homework as punishment would probably not be misunderstood; almost certainly the approval is of the handing out of the homework, not of the teacher observed to be handing it out. But a usage that is unlikely to be misunderstood is not necessarily a usage that should be accepted as correct. At least in principle the example is just as wrong as *She approves of the teacher disci-*

pline, in which the gerund phrase has been replaced by a noun. The subject of a gerund "owns" the action of the gerund, and owning is expressed by the possessive case. *She approves of the teacher's handing out extra homework as punishment* is therefore preferable.

When the possessive is impossible or bizarre

When the subject of a gerund is not a simple noun or pronoun but a group of words, it may be impossible or at least bizarre to use the possessive. For example, the plural in *Many of us don't approve of a man whom we voted against's being elected* is bizarre. It may seem reasonable enough to dispense with the possessive in such situations: . . . *a man whom we voted against being elected.* However, we would not write *Many of us don't approve of a man whom we voted against's election* either, and we would not have the alternative of dispensing with the possessive; . . . *a man whom we voted against election* is not English. We would rephrase, using an *of* construction: *Many of us don't approve of the election of a man whom we voted against.* We are not forced to rephrase with the gerund as we are with the noun—but we could choose to rephrase. We accept *a man whom we voted against being elected* only because the objective rather than the possessive is so often used for the subject of a gerund even when the possessive is not impossible; the objective never surprises us. But its failure to surprise us does not make it desirable. I advise not accepting it without some thought; rephrasing to avoid it may be worth the trouble. Sentences in which the possessive is logically called for but is impossible are likely to be clumsy anyway.

Many of us don't approve of this man, whom we voted against, being elected can have no possessive for the subject of the gerund, not even a bizarre one, because the relative pronoun *whom* cannot have a possessive form as its antecedent (see Rule 1-19). But rephrasing remains an option.

Sometimes rephrasing is not a good option and it is wiser to accept the objective subject of the gerund. *There is no law against gambling, but there is a law against people actively involved in a sport betting against themselves* might be such a case. Some words, such as *any*, never or only very rarely have possessive forms, so we use the only form available: *Some players have been hurt, but I've never heard of any dying.* English does accept the objective for the subject of a gerund when there is no reasonable alternative. Yet usually there is an alternative phrasing. For example, *There is no sense in both of us going* cannot be called an error—it is virtually an idiom, and certainly *both of us* cannot be made possessive. The fastidious may nevertheless make it *There is no sense in our both going*, which is just as idiomatic and allows the possessive.

Confusion of gerunds with participles in absolute constructions

John having worn a mask, no one knew he was there begins with an absolute construction (see Rule 1-21 and **absolute construction** in the Glossary/Index). The word *having* is not a gerund but a participle. Past participles can be used in absolute constructions too: *The mask removed, we all recognized John.*

John's having worn a mask, no one knew he was there is a bad error. The possessive should be used for the subject of a gerund, but not for the subject of a participle—that is, for the word the participle modifies. The error is infrequent, but someone trying hard to follow my advice and use the possessive with gerunds might slip into it.

I found a fine example of a gerund construction in an American grammar published in 1863: *Caesar's having crossed the Rubicon spread consternation throughout Rome.* The gerund construction can be made an absolute construction by changing *Caesar's* to the subjective case, inserting a comma, and making *consternation* the subject of the basic sentence: *Caesar having crossed the Rubicon, consternation spread throughout Rome.*

1-8   Put the object or indirect object of a verb or verbal in the objective case.

Like Rule 1-6, this rule is violated only with the few pronouns that have different forms for the subjective and objective cases.

Pronouns as part of compound objects

Our parents sent John and I to Europe and *Our parents gave John and I a trip to Europe* are embarrassing errors, much worse than the childish *Johnny and me want to go swimming.* Not only are they incorrect, they also suggest a self-conscious effort to be correct—they are hypercorrect (see **hyperurbanism** in the Glossary/Index). Once *Johnny and me want to go swimming* is eradicated, some of us go too far and give up the objective case in compound objects, though very few of us would fail to use the objective case for a pronoun standing alone as object—*sent I to Europe* and *gave I a trip* are quite evidently not English.

Pronouns as part of their own clauses

I avoid he who has the plague is incorrect, because the pronoun *he* is the object of *avoid*—the verb in its own clause—and should be *him*. See Rule 1-6 for more discussion of this point.

Pronouns as objects of verbals

I hate saluting him; I hate to salute him; The man saluting him must be his son. The objects of verbals—that is, of gerunds, infinitives, and participles—are always in the objective case. The subjects of verbals are not so consistent—the subject of a gerund should usually be in the possessive case (Rule 1-7), the subject of an infinitive should be in the objective case, as in *I want him to salute me,* and the subject of a participle can be either subjective or objective, depending on its role in the sentence. But the objects of verbals are always objective.

A problem: *who* and *whom, whoever* and *whomever*

Who is the subjective case and *whom* is the objective case, and we can, if we like, apply Rule 1-8 strictly: *Whom are you going to invite? Whom are you going to send invitations?* But for a century and a half, language arbiters from Noah Webster on have been pointing out that educated speakers and writers often use *who* and *whoever* when the objective case is called for: *Who are you going to invite? I'm going to invite whoever I choose.* Certain failures to use the objective are perceived as glaringly wrong, such as *To who will you send invitations?* But most get by, and their correct equivalents can seem labored and prissy. For some reason, *whom* and *whomever* have always had a la-di-da flavor.

In formal writing it is best to follow Rule 1-8 strictly and use *whom* and *whomever* in every objective situation. In less formal writing and in speech it is permissible to use *who* and *whoever* when they seem more natural. This way we are at least less likely to make the foolish error of using *whom* when it should be *who* and ending up both la-di-da and wrong.

Whoever can be, or at least seem to be, both the subject of one verb and the object of another, as in *I'm going to invite whoever wants to come* and *Whomever you invite is likely to refuse*. Its case is determined by the role it plays in its own clause—the clause that explains who *whoever* is. See also Rule 1-6.

1-9   Put the object of a preposition in the objective case.

She wrote the most lovely note to John and I and *I don't understand what's going on between Mary and he* are embarrassing errors, because they suggest an attempt to be elegant. Such errors with objects of prepositions are quite common; for some reason, people who would not break Rule 1-8 by saying or writing *Mary drove John and I home* or *Mary gave John and I a lift* will break this rule, sometimes even when a pronoun directly follows a preposition: *to he and I, between she and he*. The object of *to, between*, or any other preposition must be in the objective case, just as the object or indirect object of a verb must be.

Mistakes with *who* are comparatively rare; few people say or write *For who are you going to vote?* If the preposition does not immediately precede the pronoun it is permissible, as explained in Rule 1-8, to use *who* instead of *whom*: *Who are you going to vote for?*

Everyone but he left and *Everyone left but I* are errors. In many other constructions, the versatile word *but* is not a preposition; for example, in *She left but he didn't* it is a conjunction. But in *Everyone but he left* and *Everyone left but I*, it is preposition, with the same meaning as the preposition *except*, and its object must be in the objective case: *Everyone but him left; Everyone left but me*. Note that *Everyone left but he* cannot be passed off as elliptical for *Everyone left but he didn't leave*, which is a logical contradiction; if he didn't leave, then it is false to say that everyone left.

Don't act like I'm going to bite you is a very common error.

Since *like* is a preposition, the example does violate Rule 1-9, but the error is usually committed not because of ignorance of the rule but because of a misunderstanding of the word *like*, which should not be used to mean *as* or *as if*, which are conjunctions. See also **like** in the Glossary/Index.

Exception

The preposition *of* is sometimes followed by the possessive case, as in *Any friend of John's is a friend of mine*, in which both *John* and *mine* are possessive. See **possessive case** in the Glossary/Index.

AGREEMENT

Long before the schoolteachers get hold of us, we learn that in an English sentence certain words must agree in form with certain other words—that *He don't* and *John and Mary is in love* are faulty grammar. A verb's form may be affected by whether its subject is in the first person (*I*), the second person (*you*), or the third person (*he, she*) and by whether the subject is singular or plural, and we pick up this part of grammar as we learn to talk.

Applying the principles of agreement is not really very difficult, since English, unlike many other languages, does not have separate inflections, or form changes, for every situation. Nevertheless, errors do occur, and disagreement in number, covered in Rules 1-11 and 1-12, is common even in simple situations. Also, the very simplicity of English inflection can be a problem, since a word may be in grammatical agreement with too many other words in the sentence, permitting ambiguity; avoiding such ambiguity is the concern of Rule 1-13.

1-10   Make a subject and its verb agree in person.

You are crazy and *I am not crazy* are straightforward examples of subject and verb agreement in person. But should it be *Either you or I is crazy*, or *am crazy*, or *are crazy?* The verb has two subjects but can agree with only one—a situation called syllepsis (see the discussion of omission of verb forms in Rule 1-2). Syllepsis is sometimes an error, but in *either . . . or* con-

32

structions, the accepted convention is to let the person of the verb be determined by the subject nearer to it: *Either you or I am crazy*, and similarly, *Neither you nor I am crazy*. However, these constructions are forced compromises and are apt to sound clumsy. We may be better off sidestepping the problem, which is usually easy enough: *Either you're crazy or I am*. Note that *Neither of us is crazy* is correct; it is elliptical for *Neither one of us is crazy*, with *one* the real subject and *us* merely the object of the preposition *of*.

You, not I, are crazy is slightly different. When one subject is positive and the other negative, the verb agrees in person with the positive subject, whether or not it is closer to the verb.

It is you that are crazy is more complicated. Some grammarians would argue that the verb in the relative clause beginning with *that* can or should agree with *It*, which is the subject of the sentence, but a subject of a special kind (see **expletive** in the Glossary/Index): *It is you that is crazy*. More grammarians would argue that the verb should agree with the "true" subject, *you*, when the statement is positive, but with *It* when the statement is negative: *It is not you that is crazy, it is I*. This second position seems sensible to me. The subject of the relative clause is the pronoun *that*, and if the sentence states that the antecedent of *that* is *you*, there is a good argument for making the verb in the relative clause agree with *you*, whereas if the sentence states that the antecedent of *that* is not *you*, there seems no argument at all for making the verb agree with *you*—it seems better to let it agree with some not-yet-specified someone. For more discussion of the point, see ***it is, there is, there are*** in the Glossary/Index.

The quandaries above may come up occasionally, but mistakes of person are uncommon among fluent users of standard English. (They are a feature of nonstandard English dialects— *She go home*—and in such dialects they can't really be called mistakes, because a dialect has its own grammar.) There are very few verb forms to choose among. The verb *be* has three forms that vary with person in the present (*am, is, are*) and two forms that vary with person in the past (*was, were*). Almost all other verbs have only two forms in the present (*walk, walks*) and one in the past. A few verbs never vary at all (*can, should, must*).

1-11   Make a subject and its verb agree in number.

The boy swims, the boys swim; John is going, John and Mary are going. We learn the simple grammatical principle of agreement in number as we learn to talk. Since we have very few verb forms to choose among, it would seem unlikely that errors of agreement in number between subject and verb would occur. But they do occur, sometimes because of momentary confusion and sometimes because it can be difficult to determine whether a subject is singular or plural.

Simple confusion

One of those disasters that often occurs when you're traveling befell me contains a typical error of agreement caused by confusion. The subject of *occurs* is the relative pronoun *that*, which can be either singular or plural, depending on its antecedent. In the example, the antecedent of *that* is *disasters*, not *One*, so the verb should be *occur*. Since the relationship of the verb to the antecedent is not direct but via the relative pronoun, and perhaps also since *One* is so strongly singular a word, the error, basic as it is, is not glaring and is easily overlooked.

My suitcase was stolen is unlikely to cause any problem, but if a subject is separated from its verb by several other words, we may lose track of its number. In *My suitcase as well as the briefcase containing all my tax records were stolen*, the long phrase *as well as the briefcase containing all my tax records* is not part of the subject (see the discussion later in this rule of parenthetical subjects between true subject and verb), but it has incorrectly influenced the number of the verb. In *The bellboy or the taxi driver, who were both right here, were probably involved*, the intervening relative clause *who were both right here*, with its correct plural verb, has incorrectly influenced the number of the verb in the main clause (see the later discussion of subjects joined by *or* and *nor*). Such errors may reflect ignorance or inability to analyze a sentence, but I think they far more often reflect momentary confusion; we are all occasionally guilty of them in speech. We can at least avoid them in writing if we attend to details of grammar when we look over what we've written (see Rule 4-13).

Subjects joined by *and*

My suitcase and briefcase were stolen. Simple enough—
though at the moment the theft was discovered we might cry
Hey, where's my suitcase and briefcase? However, some subjects joined by *and* can take singular verbs.

Meat and potatoes, profit and loss, and many other compounds with *and* are likely to have a singular rather than a
plural import and hence correctly take a singular verb. *Profit
and loss are shown in this column,* while not wrong, is apt to
seem an unnaturally rigid application of the basic rule; only a
single figure is probably in the column, in parentheses if it is
loss and without parentheses if it is profit. *Profits and losses
are shown in this column* is natural enough, because the elements of the compound are themselves plural, but this principle doesn't always hold either; we'd correctly say *Pork chops
and potatoes is his favorite snack,* because the subject is still a
singular idea. (Some would argue that the "real" subject of the
verb is *his favorite snack;* see also the comments later in this
discussion on subjects and complements of different number.)

Similarly, when phrases joined by *and* are used as the subject
of a sentence, they may add up to a single idea and thus require,
or at least permit, a singular verb. *Losing my suitcase and
missing my appointment with Smith were my worst mistakes*
has a clearly plural subject and requires its plural verb, but
*Reaching for my suitcase and finding it gone was heartbreak-
ing* has a subject that is plural in structure but singular as an
idea and requires a singular verb.

Often a modifier preceding the subjects joined by *and* combines them into a single idea and thus makes a singular verb
desirable. *Discontent and disenchantment run through his
work* and *Reorganization and reinforcement take time* have
two-idea subjects and plural verbs, but *A pervasive discontent
and disenchantment runs through his work* and *Thorough
reorganization and reinforcement takes time* have one-idea
subjects and singular verbs, though plural verbs would not be
wrong.

Sometimes when the first item of a long, complicated subject is more inclusive or otherwise more important than the
rest, the verb seems willing to agree with just that first item, as
in *This kiss, the hesitations preceding it, and its duration was
noticed by her mother,* in which the second and third subjects
are elaborations on the first, but I think this is going too far; it
is only because the series is a bit precious that the singular verb

seems possible, and it is hardly required—*were noticed* might be preferable.

When singular subjects joined by *and* are merely a wordy or joking way of referring to a single thing, the verb is singular: *My son and heir was supposed to be keeping an eye on the luggage.* Somewhat similarly, fanciful expressions such as *everybody and his grandmother* are usually singular: *Everybody and his grandmother was there.*

When singular subjects joined by *and* are preceded by *each* or *every,* the verb must be singular: *Each suitcase and briefcase has to be checked; Every tourist and business traveler has had similar experiences; Every girl and boy brings his or her own lunch* (see also Rule 1-12). This is true even if *each* or *every* is repeated before the second element: *Each suitcase and each briefcase has to be checked.*

Subjects joined by *and* that come after the verb

In the room was a table and six chairs and *In the garage was a Maserati and two Porsches* are violations of Rule 1-11 but are likely to be accepted in speech and in informal writing. When normal word order is reversed and a compound subject comes after the verb, there is a strong tendency to make the verb agree with a singular first item in the compound subject; the correct plural verb may even seem stiff and studied in a written work that is supposed to have an easy and informal tone. Therefore we can use a singular verb if it seems to fit the tone, but I advise taking infrequent advantage of the privilege. I consider *was a table and six chairs* acceptable, because the items compose the furniture, a basically singular idea, and may even be a dining set. However, I question *was a Maserati and two Porsches,* because even though all three items are cars, they don't combine into a singular idea. Occasionally a singular verb seems preferable, as in *On the porch was a cat and six kittens;* the singular verb suggests the unified group the seven animals probably compose. See also **it is, there is, there are** in the Glossary/Index.

Subjects joined by *or* and *nor*

The bellboy or the taxi driver was probably involved. The subjects are not using the verb together but using it in turn, so the verb is singular, agreeing with each subject individually.

When one of the subjects is singular and the other is plural, the number of the verb is determined by the number of the closer subject: *The bellboys or the taxi driver was probably involved; The taxi driver or the bellboys were probably involved.*

Nor follows the same rule: *Neither the bellboys nor the taxi driver was involved; Neither the taxi driver nor the bellboys were involved.*

Like the rule for determining the person of the verb in such cases (see Rule 1-10), this rule permits sentences that are correct but clumsy. Such sentences can be rewritten to avoid the clumsiness, but note that paired subjects of different number are far more likely to occur than paired subjects of different person, and a policy of not allowing them may be quite onerous. Rewriting may just make a sentence clumsier or change its meaning.

A guest or two was standing near and *One or two was hostile* disobey the usual convention, since the closer subject is *two*, but are idiomatically correct, even in formal writing. The plural *were* would also be correct.

Positive and negative subjects

I think the bellboys, not the taxi driver, were involved; I think the taxi driver, not the bellboys, was involved. The positive subject determines the number of the verb, whether or not it is closer to the verb. This construction does not usually sound too clumsy, and if it does, the negative subject can be repositioned: *I think the bellboys were involved, not the taxi driver.*

Positive subjects joined by *but* or *but also*

I think not only the bellboys but the taxi driver was involved; I think not only the taxi driver but also the bellboys were involved. Both subjects are positive, but the verb occurs only with the subject preceded by *but* or *but also*, and the subject preceded by *not only* does not affect the number of the verb. Of course, if the verb occurs with the subject preceded by *not only*, it agrees with that subject: *I think not only were the bellboys involved but the taxi driver.*

Subjects that look singular but may be plural

Collective nouns, such as *family, group,* and *committee,* can take either singular or plural verbs, depending on whether they are being thought of as singular or plural. *The committee is qualified to decide* makes a statement about the committee as a unit; *The committee are not all qualified to decide* makes a statement about some of the individual members. (The British almost always use the plural—*The committee are qualified*, and even *The government, who were in confusion, were slow to respond*, in which *government* is perceived as meaning the people who constitute the government and is referred to by the pronoun *who*.) *The committee is qualified to decide, but are not all as well informed as they might be* is faulty, because *committee* is first singular and then plural within a single sentence. The number of the subject of a sentence has to be consistent within that sentence. The number of a collective noun should if possible be consistent throughout a written work, though violations of this principle are justified when a term must be used in both singular and plural senses.

About 50 percent of the population is rural and *About 50 percent of the population are farmers* are both correct. Although *rural* and *farmers* in these examples are only subject complements, not subjects, and do not directly determine the number of the verb, they do reflect that *About 50 percent* is, or at least can be, thought of as a singular in the first example and is necessarily thought of as a plural in the second. (See also the comments on subjects and complements later in this discussion.) *About 50 percent of the respondents were rural* and *Half have no insurance* similarly require plural verbs because the subjects have to be thought of as plural.

Some nouns look singular in English but are plural in the language they were adopted from, such as *agenda* and *data*, which are Latin plurals. Whether or not such a noun takes a singular verb is determined by usage rather than rules. *Agenda* has long been accepted as singular, with the plural *agendas*. *Data* has not yet crossed the line but may be on its way. *The data is incomplete* is considered an ignorant error by many, but some handbooks, such as the stylebook of the *Los Angeles Times*, already prescribe the singular for *data*, and others allow the singular when the meaning is essentially singular—that is, when the word means a collection of facts rather than the separate facts. I advise being conservative with *data* and always using a plural verb with it, simply to avoid the appearance of error. When in doubt about the status of a given word, check a recent dictionary.

Any, none, and such combinations of pronouns as *Any of them* and *none of you* are primarily singular; they mean *any one, not one, any one of them, not one of them,* and so on. Formerly the rule was that they always had to be considered singular, but this rule has wisely been loosened, since they are often clearly plural in meaning, as in *None of the citizens vote as often as they are supposed to.* Actually, *any* can mean *any ones* as well as *any one,* and *none* can mean *not any,* and hence *not any ones,* as well as *not one.* Dryden's line is *None but the brave deserves the fair,* but the singular verb seems slightly odd today—and Dryden was not referring to the brave and the fair as categories but to Alexander and Thais.

Subjects that look plural but may be singular

Physics is almost always a singular, as in *Physics was his field,* but *The physics of the device are sophisticated* is correct. Similarly, *statistics* is singular if it means the field of study, plural if it means a collection of information. There are many such words. They can switch back and forth from their singular to their plural meanings quite freely, even in different clauses of the same sentence: *Physics is my field, but the physics of this device baffle me.*

Five boys is certainly a plural—what could be more plural than a plural noun modified by a number larger than one? Yet *Five boys is not enough even for a scrub game* is correct. In that example, the plural *are* could be used too, but sometimes it cannot be. *Five dollars are too much* is wrong, or at best unidiomatic; a sum of money is thought of as singular. Usually we know without thinking about it whether a noun modified by a number is really plural, as in *Five boys were enrolled for soccer,* or just a unit that is plural in form. We can switch back and forth freely: *Seven silver dollars were exposed on his grubby palm, but seven dollars was not enough for a motorcycle.*

More than one can only be plural in meaning but nevertheless often takes a singular verb, either modifying a noun or standing alone: *More than one child was crying; More than one was crying.* This and similar illogical usages (such as *One or two was hostile,* mentioned earlier in this discussion) are idioms.

Subjects and complements of different number

In *The secret is more controls,* the singular subject *The secret* is linked to the plural complement *more controls* by the singular verb *is*. The subject, not the complement, determines the number of the verb.

More controls are the secret has the plural subject *More controls* and the singular complement *the secret*, and the verb is plural. Yet there is an argument for *More controls is the secret*. Although in standard English word order the subject precedes the predicate, not every English sentence has standard word order; fairly frequently the predicate precedes the subject, as in *In this book is the secret* and *Less welcome than increased services were higher taxes*. The reversed word order can't be missed in these examples, because in each case the words preceding the verb can't possibly be the subject. We can claim that *More controls is the secret* has reversed word order too—that is, that the true subject is *the secret* and the true complement is *More controls*—and that the singular verb is therefore correct. Of course, the claim may be met with indignation, since in this case the words preceding the verb can be the subject.

There are times when this idea of out-of-order subject and complement can back up a usage that seems right. For example, in *He had a number of problems, but taxes was the immediate problem*, the singular *was* seems acceptable to me, and perhaps preferable to *were*, and one could claim that it is acceptable because the clause is really *the immediate problem was taxes* with the words out of their usual order. I suggest resorting to this justification cautiously, since it will seem like flimflam to some. I would prefer the vaguer, humbler argument that though *taxes* is plural in form it represents a singular idea in the example, and that the singularity is reinforced, if admittedly not required, by the singular complement *problem*.

All as a subject sometimes mistakenly gets a plural verb when it has a plural complement. *All* is often clearly plural, as in *All are glad to be home*, in which it refers to some group of people. Often it is clearly singular, as in *All is lost*, in which it refers to a totality, not a plural of some kind. In *All I could think of were the children*, it refers to a totality—the totality of what I could think of—but the verb has been attracted to the plural *children*, which is merely the complement, not the subject, and should not determine the number of the verb. *All I could think of was the children* is correct. Even when the complement is multiple, *all* is singular when its own meaning is a totality, as in *All that was in the lawyer's safe was seven gold coins, two wooden candlesticks, and an avocado*. If some plural noun can naturally be imagined after *all*, a plural verb is likely to be correct, as in *There were twenty children on the stage, but all [the children] I could see were mine.* See also ***all*** in the Glossary/Index.

What, as in *What is elusive are rules we can live by,* in which *what* gets first a singular and then a plural verb, often causes difficult problems of agreement. See ***what is*** vs. ***what are*** in the Glossary/Index.

Parenthetical subject between true subject and verb

John, and his parents, was at the zoo yesterday is correct. The pair of commas around *and his parents* takes the word out of the basic sentence, which is *John was at the zoo yesterday,* just as parentheses or dashes would: *John (and his parents) was at the zoo yesterday; John—and his parents—was at the zoo yesterday.* A parenthetical subject has no effect on the number of the verb. If the singular verb seems troublesome, as it well may, the commas can be removed, making a plural verb correct, or the sentence can be recast: *John was at the zoo yesterday, along with his parents.* See also Rule 2-1, and **parenthetical construction** in the Glossary/Index.

The Roman Empire, and subsequent empires, were eventually destroyed is an error of agreement in number if the writer means something like *The Roman Empire, like subsequent empires, was eventually destroyed.* It is an error of punctuation if the writer means *The Roman Empire and subsequent empires were eventually destroyed;* a series of three or more items should be separated by commas (see Rule 2-6), but not a series of two items, and a comma at the end of the series wrongly separates subject and verb (see Rule 2-4). Writers who make the error, whether it is their grammar or their punctuation that is at fault, are apt to have a generally imprecise style, and their meaning may not be entirely clear even in context.

It can be argued that a pair of commas is not necessarily parenthetical in intent—that instead it may emphasize a second subject that is part of the basic sentence and should therefore affect the verb. We do use pauses in speech to give such emphasis. The argument is a good one, and perhaps occasionally it should prevail, but in general it is a poor idea to use a contradiction between grammar and punctuation to imitate speech.

John as well as his parents was entranced by the monkeys and *The zoo in addition to the parks was closed during the war years* are correct. Phrases such as *as well as* and *in addition to* indicate a parenthetical construction—they can be conjunctions, like *and*, but they are not merely wordy versions of *and*, as those who commit errors such as *John as well as his parents were entranced by the monkeys* may assume. Such errors are probably more frequently the result of simple confusion, discussed early in this rule; in the example, the plural *parents* is confused with the distant true subject, *John*, and incorrectly influences the number of the verb. Note that commas could be used around the parenthetical subjects in the examples. The absence of commas is not wrong, but their presence might be helpful—they would make it harder to choose the wrong number for the verb.

Their position, even their lives, was now at risk goes too far, however; it requires the plural *were*. When a second subject is modified by *even*, it seems to take more than a pair of commas to make the subject parenthetical. *Even* does not suggest a tacked-on element in the way that *and* preceded by a comma and phrases such as *in addition to* and *as well as* do; it emphasizes the element and entitles it to affect the verb. The troubling commas can be avoided, of course—*Their position and even their lives were now at risk*—but *Their position, even their lives, were now at risk* is acceptable. We don't have to consider the commas parenthetical; we can consider them an indicator of the omitted *and*, which they sometimes are in a series (see Rule 2-6).

1-12 Make a pronoun and its antecedent agree in number, person, and gender.

The antecedent of a pronoun is the noun or noun phrase that it represents. In *I asked Bill, but he can't go*, the antecedent of the pronoun *he* is the noun *Bill*.

Pronouns do not always have antecedents, and some logically can't have antecedents. In the question *Who can go?* the interrogative pronoun *Who* has no antecedent—how could it? In the statement *Anyone can go*, the indefinite pronoun *anyone* has no antecedent. Frequently when there is an antecedent, it is in an earlier sentence: *I asked Bill. He can't go.*

When there is an antecedent, the pronoun must agree with it in number, person, and gender.

Disagreement in number

Everyone will be responsible for their own welfare is incorrect. The pronouns *everyone* and *everybody, anyone* and *anybody, someone* and *somebody*, and *no one* and *nobody* are all singular, and pronouns that have these words as antecedents must be singular too. Therefore the example should be *Everyone will be responsible for his or her own welfare*—or *his own welfare* if those referred to are all male or if the masculine pronoun is allowed to represent both sexes, or, of course, *her own welfare* if those referred to are all female.

Errors of agreement with *everyone* and the rest of the eight pronouns listed are exceedingly common, for two reasons. The first is that *everyone* and *everybody* actually are plural in meaning—they mean all people in the group referred to. The phrase *almost everyone* is certainly not equivalent in meaning to *not quite one*. When a pronoun with *everyone* as its antecedent occurs in a different clause, we are often unable to make it singular; we cannot say *Everyone booed, and the speaker glared at him indignantly*. We can use *them* in this sentence and claim, perhaps lamely, that its antecedent is not *Everyone* but some plural noun in an earlier sentence. But then sometimes a reflexive pronoun occurs in the same clause, as in *Everyone looked at one another*, forcing us to rephrase or else to accept the anomaly, which is likely to earn us criticism. The other pronouns, though usually genuinely singular, often are essentially plural in meaning, as in *I don't want anyone leaving book bags in my office*, in which the message is to all present and is that all should refrain from leaving their book bags behind.

The second reason that errors with these eight pronouns are common is that a singular pronoun using them as an antecedent must be either masculine or feminine, and many people are now reluctant to use a masculine pronoun to indicate either sex (I do so use it myself a few times in this book, for reasons explained under **sexism** in the Glossary/Index), but at the same time are reluctant to use the cumbersome *his or her, he or she*, and *him or her*. Thus plural pronouns seem a convenient solution even in contexts that must be singular in meaning, such as *Someone seems to have left their book bag in my office*. The error occurs with other words of unspecified sex as well as with the eight pronouns listed above: *The person who left their book bag in my office had better remove it*.

It will be convenient if *their, they*, and *them* are someday accepted as correct with singular antecedents of unspecified

43

sex. Some authorities do now accept them as correct, including, surprisingly, the well-known series of textbooks by John E. Warriner. I have an edition from the 1950s that presents *Did everybody leave the dance early because they weren't enjoying themselves?* as correct, though I suspect the example was carefully chosen to reduce disagreement by avoiding a singular verb such as occurs in *Everybody is leaving the dance early because they aren't enjoying themselves.* (It would be much easier to accept *everybody* and the other pronouns as plurals if they did not invariably take singular verbs.) But for now, such usage cannot be recommended to those who want to avoid criticism, even though it is heard everywhere and from nearly everyone and is condoned by some major scholars and arbiters of usage. It seems ugly, at least in print, to those who are sensitive to it— certainly a minority and perhaps a diminishing one, but I count myself in. In a century, perhaps at least *everyone* and *everybody* will be accepted as plurals and *Everyone in the house were in their beds*, with a plural verb as well as a plural pronoun, will be standard, as, in fact, it was in past centuries; the example is from Fielding's *Tom Jones*, published in 1749. It is certainly likely that nearly all fluent users of the language will continue to flout the careful, and perhaps excessively scrupulous, minority. Probably most members of that minority catch themselves committing the crime in speech, as I do.

The prosecution was required to turn over all their evidence is typical of errors in agreement that result from using a collective noun in both a singular and a plural sense in the same clause (see Rule 1-11). First the prosecution is referred to as one of two sides in a trial, a singular and sexless concept, but later in the sentence the writer is reluctant to use *its* because here the prosecution is more apt to be thought of as made up of people—it's *their* evidence. However, the pronoun should be *its*, or else *was* should be changed to *were*; the writer should stick with the sense of *prosecution* that the sentence began with.

Any, none, and such combinations of pronouns as *Any of them* and *none of you* are primarily singular; they mean *any one, not one, any one of them, not one of them,* and so on. Formerly the rule was that they always had to be considered singular, but this rule has wisely been loosened, since they are often clearly plural in meaning; *any* can mean *any ones* as well as *any one,* and *none* can mean *not any,* and hence *not any ones,* as well as *not one.* Thus *None of the citizens vote as often as they are supposed to,* in which both the verb and the pronoun are plural, is correct. As is often the case in such sentences, the pronoun *they* has a plural noun, *citizens*, available as an antecedent, but the plural pronoun is also correct in *None vote as often as they are supposed to*; if *None* is allowed a plural verb, it must certainly be allowed a plural pronoun.

Disagreement in person

Any of you, none of you, and similar combinations of pronouns are third-person, but they are apt to be followed by a second-person pronoun, as in *I don't want any of you to forget your manners.* Some would claim that this is an error—that the second pronoun must agree with the first in person: *I don't want any of you to forget his or her manners.* Those who make the claim are looking too hard for errors. There is no grammatical necessity for *your,* the possessive pronoun modifying *manners,* to have *any of you* as its antecedent. It doesn't have to have any antecedent at all. A third-person pronoun such as *his* needs an antecedent not grammatically but logically—that is, the person it represents has to be identified—and so in a sentence such as *The boy forgot his manners* the pronoun has an antecedent. But second-person and first-person pronouns such as *your* and *my* do not need an antecedent either grammatically or logically, since the people they represent do not have to be identified. It is implicit in language that the first person is the talker and the second person is the listener. Since they don't need an antecedent, they don't have to be forced to agree with a preceding pronoun combination such as *any of you.* It is wrongheaded to force agreement where none is required. For example, in *Neither of us votes as often as we should,* the third-person pronoun combination *Neither of us* correctly takes a singular verb, but, also correctly, it doesn't force either its number or its person on the pronoun in the next clause, *we.* Although letting it do so and making it *he should* (or *he or she should*) would not be grammatically incorrect, since *Neither of us* is there to serve as antecedent, it would be decidedly unnatural—almost schizophrenic. We don't normally talk about ourselves in the third person.

Each of us brought our own lunch, however, is questionable. *Each of us* means *Each one of us,* and the true subject is the understood third-person pronoun *one,* and thus *our* disagrees with the subject in both person and number. It should be *Each of us brought his or her own lunch.* However, *We each brought our own lunch* is correct; here *each* is not the subject but merely modifies the subject, *We*. (The singular *lunch* is permissible by a principle sometimes called distributive possession; each member of the possessing group possesses one or more of the possessed items.) Note that like the disagreement discussed in the previous paragraph, *Each of us brought our own lunch* is hard to condemn on strictly grammatical grounds, because nothing really requires *our* to agree with the subject—the lunch remains ours whatever the subject of the sentence is. However, more people will perceive this disagreement as an error, so those who want to avoid criticism should avoid it. In addition, one grammatical argument against it can be made. *Our own* is a reflexive formation—the addition of *own* makes it so—and implies that there is a previous noun or pronoun of the same person and number for it to have as an antecedent, or at least to refer to. Sometimes there is no such pronoun, as in *It's our own funeral*, but when there is a pronoun for it to refer to, agreement in number and person seems desirable if not required.

You are the one who wasn't honest with yourself is still more questionable; I consider it truly wrong. The reflexive pronoun *yourself* has the antecedent *who*, which has the antecedent *one*. The pronoun therefore should be *himself* or *herself*, to agree in person with *one*. It is difficult to avoid all such errors in speech, because the emphasized *You* at the beginning of the sentence quite naturally attracts the reflexive pronoun at the end to its own person. The attraction should be resisted when we are writing or choosing our words carefully.

Careless writing and speech often drift from person to person: *He told me to look out for live wires, and if you touch them you'll be sorry, but I thought that as long as you're careful no one could get hurt*. There are grammatical problems here, but the basic problem is a vagueness not just of language but of identity; the writer or speaker doesn't seem quite certain what ingredient he or she is in the pronoun stew.

Disagreement in gender

The dog didn't come when I called him, and the next morning it was still missing is wrong because of the shift in gender from *him* to *it*. We can use a masculine or feminine pronoun for an animal—and usually should if the animal is identified as male or female or has a masculine or feminine name—but we shouldn't then switch to a neuter pronoun. The error is unlikely in most kinds of writing, but it is ubiquitous in pulp fantasy and horror novels; the hurrying author forgets whether the dragon or ghoul is a he, she, or it.

It is nevertheless correct to write *The chickadee, in spite of its ubiquity, is an interesting bird* and a sentence or so later *The chickadee lays her eggs one at a time* and still another sentence or so later *The chickadee has a particular call to announce that in the competition for mates he is a winner.* As long as the reader will not be confused, the gender can be governed by the context and can shift whenever common sense dictates.

Disagreement in case

There is usually nothing wrong with this disagreement. A pronoun doesn't agree with its antecedent in case except by coincidence. (A pronoun should, however, agree in case with a word it is in apposition to; see Rule 1-6.) In the sentence *The dog didn't come, though I called him and rattled his dish, and the next morning he was still missing,* the pronoun is first objective as the object of *called,* then possessive as a modifier of *dish,* and then subjective as the subject of *was still missing.*

The car is really my wife's, who dented the fender is nevertheless an error. A noun or pronoun in the possessive case is usually functioning as an adjective, and an adjective cannot be the antecedent of a pronoun (see Rule 1-19). There are, however, some situations in which a possessive noun or pronoun is not just an adjective and can be the antecedent of a pronoun. *Let's take my car, not my wife's, which has a dented fender* is correct, because *wife's* is not an ordinary adjectival possessive here but a so-called independent possessive, a possessive that can behave like a noun. Some of the personal pronouns have special forms for the independent possessive: mine, *yours, hers, ours, theirs.* See also **possessive case** in the Glossary/ Index.

‖ 1-13   Don't let a pronoun have more than one likely antecedent.

Joan and Sarah are both married to lawyers, but I don't think her husband is a partner in his firm could have several meanings. The first pronoun, *her,* could refer to either Joan or Sarah. The second pronoun, *his,* could refer to *husband* but also could refer to the other husband. In context there may be no ambiguity, and if the words are spoken, the inflections of speech may reduce ambiguity. Still, we often have to correct ourselves and amplify our words in conversation: —*I mean, I don't think Sarah's husband works with Joan's; he must be a partner somewhere, the way they spend.*

Not all sentences that are afflicted with ambiguous pronouns are casually composed. *The resources of the Ruhr were very great, but the capacity of the war industries to take advantage of them was much reduced when they became a prime target of Allied air raids* is a carefully written sentence, but we can't tell whether it was the resources or the war industries that became the prime target. The context might make it clear or it might not; during World War II, the mines and heavy industry of the Ruhr were a prime target, but so were specialized armament and equipment industries both in the Ruhr and elsewhere in Germany. Perhaps the best clue is the word *capacity*—the writer probably wouldn't have used that word unless the war industries, wherever located, were the target. But a reader shouldn't have to work that hard and still end up with a probable meaning rather than a certain one.

Ambiguous pronouns are difficult to catch, because we ourselves know what we mean. Once we've caught one by careful checking for possible misreadings, we may decide to let it go, believing that the misreading is too unlikely to worry about. This decision is sensible enough, especially when changing the sentence would make it less effective.

VERB TENSES: PAST, PRESENT, AND FUTURE

The basic tenses are past, present, and future, but English has a lot more than three tenses—by some counts, it has more than thirty. We have not just *I cooked, I cook,* and *I will cook,* but the present perfect *I have cooked,* the past perfect *I had cooked,* and the future perfect *I will have cooked.* These tenses—now there are six—also have progressive forms: *I was cooking, I am cooking, I will be cooking, I have been cooking, I had been cooking,* and *I shall* (or *will*) *have been cooking.* Some tenses have a special emphatic form: *I do cook, I did cook.* Various other combinations with auxiliary verbs can be considered separate tenses: *I was going to cook, I would be cooking, I would have been going to cook,* and so on.

Foreigners have great trouble with English tenses, especially with the progressive forms, but most native speakers have surprisingly little. Complicated as these forms are, we learned their proper use as young children. We know that *I cried when she appeared* and *I was crying when she appeared* do not mean the same thing. We understand the function of auxiliary verbs—*be, have, will, shall, do,* and other common verbs—in forming tenses even though we sometimes can't give a name to the tenses we form.

We do sometimes have problems with tenses when there is more than one tense required in a sentence and when a sentence includes a participle, infinitive, or gerund. The three rules in this section concern these problems.

1-14   Keep the tense of a verb in proper relation to the tenses of other verbs in the sentence or passage.

In some sentences the tense of a given verb is strictly determined by the tense of another verb, because there is a logical relationship between the times of the two verbs' actions that must be reflected by the verbs' tenses. In other sentences the tense of a given verb may be affected by the tense of another verb but not completely determined by it; we may have a choice of tenses, and the tense we choose may affect the meaning or may not.

A very high percentage of the time, we know without thinking about it when there is only one proper tense for a verb and when we have a choice of tense and we are safe enough just using the tense that seems right. It is usually only when we do think about it, perhaps feeling that we have lost ourselves in a maze of relative times, that we make errors, applying misremembered rules and momentarily losing our ear for the natural tense. Therefore most of the following discussion does not prescribe tenses for specific situations but reminds the reader of the freedom the language permits and of appropriate ways to use that freedom. However, the last section of the rule concerns an error that seems to get by a great many people's ears—an improper sequence of tenses in subjunctive constructions.

Relative time

We say *He assumes she is single* and *He assumed she was single;* the secondary verb follows the main verb into the past

49

tense, a phenomenon sometimes called the normal sequence of tenses. However, we might also say *He assumed she is single.* The main verb does not necessarily force its tense on the secondary verb. Often a subordinate verb that expresses something that is always true, not just true at the time of the main verb's action, is in the present tense, as in *Galileo believed that the earth moves around the sun*—but *moved* would not be wrong, and some would consider it preferable, since a subordinate clause in the present tense is slightly jarring when the main clause is in a past tense.

Thus the generalization that the tense of a main verb determines the tense of a subordinate verb—the kind of generalization we are apt to think we were taught in grammar school—is rather questionable. In fact, sometimes the subordinate verb determines the tense of the main verb. *I walked idly down the street when I heard someone behind me* is incorrect because the *when* clause requires a progressive tense in the main clause: *I was walking idly down the street when I heard someone behind me.*

When a secondary verb does follow the tense of the main verb, it may be unable to go more than part of the distance. We say *He had assumed she was single,* not *He had assumed she had been single,* and we could even say *He had assumed she is single,* though there is a strong tendency for the secondary verb to follow the main verb as far as it can into the past. When the actions of a main verb and a secondary verb take place at different times and this fact is evident because of some modifying word for the secondary verb, the verbs can often be either in the same tense or in the logically appropriate different tenses: *He always goes out after he comes home* or *has come home; He went out after he came home* or *had come home.* Usually the same tense is preferable; see the discussion below of the past perfect.

A secondary verb doesn't follow a main verb into the future tense. We cannot say *He will assume she will be single* but must make it *He will assume she is single.* Similarly, we cannot say *He will go out after he will come home,* though we can say either *He will go out after he comes home* or *He will go out after he has come home.*

Just because we have a choice of tenses in many situations does not, of course, mean that one is always as good as the other. Often each tense has a different implication. For example, when a secondary verb expresses continuing action rather than action that took place specifically at the time of a main verb that is in the past tense, the present progressive or past progressive is likely to be more appropriate than the past for the secondary verb. Thus *I heard that prices went up* suggests that prices had already risen at the time of the hearing, but *I heard that prices were going up* suggests a continuing process that may or may not be incomplete, and *I heard that prices are going up* suggests a continuing process that is incomplete. However, we do not have to invent rules to cover such differences. Fluency in a language means, among other things, an ability to pick the right tense without thumbing through a mental rulebook.

The disappearing past perfect

The basic function of the past perfect is to indicate action that takes place prior to the action of another verb in the sentence or passage that is in the past tense: *He assumed she had married; She discovered he had gone out.* However, more and more often, writers who are generally careful with their grammar do not bother with the past perfect when the time relationship is apparent from the context anyway: *She missed John, who left the party early; John fell in the ditch they dug for the well line.* I advise using the past perfect—*had left* and *had dug* in the examples—as a matter of habit, because not using it does often permit more ambiguity than the writer realizes and does seem incorrect, or at least unpleasantly loose, to many readers.

The situation is somewhat different when the verb in the dependent clause is modified by an adverb or adverbial phrase that makes the time relationship explicit. In *She arrived after he had left the party* and *He had left the party before she arrived*, the past perfect has no necessary function, because the adverbs *after* and *before* express the time relationship. Some grammarians would call the use of the past perfect in these examples redundant, and therefore wrong. Although redundancy is not always an ultimate evil that must be stamped out wherever it appears (see Rule 1-4), there is perhaps something slightly illogical about indicating time differences with both an adverb and a tense; *he left the party* describes an action, and *after he left the party* seems sufficient to describe anything subsequent to that action. Nevertheless, the past perfect is acceptable and to some ears preferable.

Ambiguity with the past and past perfect

She discovered that he had left the party and gone home does not mean the same thing as *She discovered that he had left the party and went home.* Because *go* is an irregular verb, with different forms for the past tense (*I went*) and the past perfect tense (*I had gone*), the first sentence must mean *he had . . . gone home* and the second sentence must mean *She . . . went home.*

If we make it *She discovered that he had left the party and walked home,* we no longer have the grammatical signal provided by *went* or *gone.* The sentence is grammatically correct but can be taken to mean either that she walked home or that he did. If he walked home, we can make the sentence unambiguous by repeating the auxiliary verb: *and had walked home.* If she walked home, we have to change the structure of the sentence by supplying a pronoun for *walked*: *She discovered that he had left the party, and she walked home.* This makes it a compound sentence—that is, a sentence with two or more independent clauses—rather than a simple sentence with a compound predicate (see Rule 2-1).

Past and past perfect in narrative

Smith said he arrived at the bank on time and went to the vault. The verbs *arrived* and *went* are not in the proper tense relative to the verb *said;* since Smith's arrival and his going to the vault took place in time previous to the time established by *Smith said,* the verbs should be *had arrived* and *had gone.*

However, suppose the account of what Smith said goes on for a long paragraph or even for pages. Are we required to let *Smith said* force every subsequent verb into the clumsy and wordy past perfect tense? No. In such a circumstance, it is not only permissible but desirable to let the tense slide to the simpler past tense, and the sooner the better. If we pick the right time to let the tense of the narrative change from the past perfect to the past—not in the middle of the narrative but near its beginning, and usually not in the middle of a sentence—the reader or listener will have no difficulty following and will be spared a long succession of past perfect verbs. Of course, once the narrative has switched to the past tense, there may be further uses for the past perfect: *Smith said he had arrived at the bank at the usual time and had gone to the vault. When he opened the vault, he discovered that someone had filled it with money.*

Some kinds of narrative constantly involve two levels of pastness. A book about a famous trial, for example, is likely to be an account of what witnesses and lawyers *said* about what *had happened,* and so the situation described above recurs every time a new witness or lawyer comes onstage. Writers of such narrative often become impatient with the past perfect and try to do without it: *The defense next called Mary Jones to the stand. She said that Smith left for work at the same time she did and spoke to her in the street, and he was not carrying any bags of money.* This leaves it to the reader to figure out the levels of pastness—not, perhaps, an overwhelming task, yet it becomes something of an irritation when it is presented to the reader hundreds of times over the course of a book. In addition, excessive avoidance of the past perfect can make narrative seem flaccid and crude. The slight extra wordiness of the past perfect seems to me by far the lesser evil.

Problems with subjunctive tenses

If they swim well, their father smiles contains two indicative verbs in the present tense, *swim* and *smiles.* If they don't swim well and we want to state what the effect on their father would be if they did, we use subjunctive verb forms: *It's too bad they don't swim well. If they swam well, their father would smile.* The verb *swam* looks like a past tense and the verb *would smile* looks like a special form of the past tense used to show habitual action, and that is what they would be in a different context: *The children sometimes swam well. If they swam well, their father would smile.* But in the original context, there is no "pastness" to the meaning of the verbs; the sentence is a statement about an imaginary present rather than an actual past, and the verbs are subjunctive. Subjunctive forms used to make statements about an imaginary present typically are identical with indicative forms used to make statements about an actual past. (See also the discussion of the subjunctive preceding Rule 1-17.)

If they had swum well, their father would have smiled is a statement about an imaginary past. The subjunctive verb forms are like indicative forms used for statements about an actual past perfect; they are a step farther back into the past than the forms discussed in the preceding paragraph. This seems simple enough, but very often the wrong tense is used for the *if* clause: *If they would have swum well, their father would have smiled.* The error seems to be more and more common. In the first edition of this book, I used the incorrect *If you'd have paid me, I'd have been grateful* as an example. I assumed that the error was camouflaged by the contractions, and I pointed out that *you'd* had to mean either *you had* or *you would* and that neither was possible in the sentence. I wrote confidently, "Expanding the contraction should make the error apparent: *If you would have paid me, I would have been grateful* is obviously wrong." Not so obviously wrong, I have discovered—I now see sentences like it almost daily, free of contractions or any other camouflage. The error is an ugly one, and I hope its rude health declines.

The *would have . . . would have* error may be appealing partly because using the same tense in the *if* clause and the main clause seems a neat and balanced way of arranging things. But an if-this-then-that statement is necessarily not balanced—one part of it is a condition and the other part is a conclusion based on that condition—and therefore the tenses should not be balanced. The subjunctive sequence of tenses is *If A were, then B would be; If A had been, then B would have been.* A subjunctive form occurs in both the first clause and the second, but the forms are of different tenses. (Note that if-then statements about the future, which in American English are usually indicative rather than subjunctive in both clauses, show the same pattern of different tenses: *If A happens, then B will happen.* The British often use a subjunctive form for the *if* clause: *If A should happen, then B will happen.*)

If you would pay me, I would be grateful is correct, which may seem to contradict the point I have just made. However, the *would* in the first clause is not just an auxiliary verb, as it is in the second clause—it is the subjunctive of the independent verb *will*, meaning to wish or to be willing. A plainer version of this sentence, with no use of the independent verb *will*, is *If you paid me, I would be grateful.* Both versions actually conform to the standard sequence mentioned above, *If A were, then B would be.*

I wish you would have paid me is another common error; it should be *I wish you had paid me.* The mistaken urge to balance verb forms cannot explain this error, at least directly; perhaps the rise in *would have . . . would have* errors has led to a general loss of sensitivity to incorrect *would* forms of the subjunctive, or perhaps *will* is reacquiring the strong identity as an independent verb that it once had and *I wish you would have paid me* is felt to mean *I wish you had been willing to pay me*—though I don't think that is likely. Subjunctive forms are peculiarly sensitive to changes in taste from generation to generation, doubtless partly because it is very difficult to explain why they are what they are without getting far deeper into language theory and history than most people are willing to go. Perhaps the usages condemned here will eventually be considered acceptable, but at present they are rather serious errors.

I wish I were rich and *I wished I were rich* are both correct. In this construction—the indicative verb *wish* followed by a subjunctive clause—the tense of the subjunctive verb is not affected by the tense of the indicative verb. (The special subjunctive form *were* is discussed in Rule 1-17). Similarly, *He wishes he had been elected, He wished he had been elected,* and *He will wish he had been elected* have identical subjunctive clauses.

He acts as if he were rich, He acted as if he were rich, and *He will act as if he were rich* are also correct, and so are *He acts as if he had been elected, He acted as if he had been elected,* and *He will act as if he had been elected.* A clause beginning with *as if* or *as though,* unlike a clause beginning with *if,* is typically dependent on an indicative clause, and the tense of the indicative verb in that clause has no effect on the tense of the subjunctive verb in a subjunctive dependent clause. I occasionally see odd errors such as *He had acted as if he had been rich,* committed, I expect, because the writer thinks the verb in the dependent clause is obliged to agree in tense with the verb in the main clause.

Some clauses beginning with *as if* or *as though* are not subjunctive: *It looks as if it will rain; He acted as though he was angry.* These clauses express what the speaker believes is true or probably true and hence are not truly subjunctive in meaning. Nevertheless the subjunctive is often used for them; *He acted as though he were angry* is not wrong, and we are likely to say *The engine is coughing as if it were out of gas* even if we are almost certain that it is out of gas. See also Rule 1-17 and the discussion preceding it.

1-15   Use the present participle and present infinitive to indicate time that is the same as the time of the main verb, whatever the tense of the main verb is; use the perfect participle and the perfect infinitive to indicate time previous to the time of the main verb.

Being a thief, he knew how to open the safe; Being a thief, he knows how to open the safe; Being a thief, he will know how to open the safe. In all these sentences, the man is a thief at the same time that he knows how to open the safe. Suppose we change the present participle *Being* to the perfect participle *Having been* and make it *Having been a thief, he knew how to open the safe* and so on. In all the resulting sentences, the man was a thief at some time previous to the time when he knows how to open the safe; although he may remain a thief, the implication is strong that he has gone straight.

The infinitive works the same way: *He was proved to be a thief, He is proved to be a thief, He will be proved to be a thief; He was proved to have been a thief, He is proved to have been a thief, He will be proved to have been a thief.*

Sometimes a verb that is in the past tense unnecessarily attracts a participle or infinitive to the perfect tense, as in *The prosecutor accused him of having been the guilty one* and *The prosecutor assumed him to have been the guilty one.* These are not true errors of grammar but simply examples of careless thinking and pointless wordiness; he was guilty, or not guilty perhaps, at the time of the accusation and the assumption, and *The prosecutor accused him of being the guilty one* and *The prosecutor assumed him to be the guilty one* are better. I have frequently seen exceedingly unnatural uses of perfect participle or perfect infinitive, such as *The witness said she had allowed him to have gone into the vault,* which is grammatically incorrect; I believe a good many writers doggedly follow what they think is a rule and force participles and infinitives into the wrong tense. Sometimes, of course, the perfect participle or infinitive is precisely correct, as in *The judge ruled that the prosecution could not show Smith to have been a thief except by his own testimony,* which means that the prosecution was not allowed to reveal Smith's previous record.

The present infinitive very frequently has a future meaning, as in *I am to go tomorrow.* In this construction, it is like the present progressive tense, which is formed with the present participle and can also indicate future time, as in *I am going tomorrow.*

Tenses of gerunds

Cooking the meal pleases him and *Cooking the meal pleased him* are the same statement, first in the present and then in the past. *Having cooked the meal pleases him* and *Having cooked the meal pleased him* are a quite different statement, first in the present and then in the past. The tense of a gerund is part of the gerund's meaning—it does not affect and is not affected by the tense of verbs in the sentence. *Cooking* and *Having cooked*, as gerunds, are like two nouns with different meanings; one means the process or activity of cooking, the other means the fact of having cooked.

1-16   Don't use the present participle to indicate action just previous to the action of the main verb.

Crossing the room, he sat down is poorly phrased unless he really did sit down while in the act of crossing the room, in which case one would expect a less matter-of-fact statement. *Having crossed the room, he sat down,* with the participle in the past tense, keeps the actions in order but may give the act of crossing an inappropriate significance.

The simplest way to indicate consecutive actions is to use consecutive verbs: *He crossed the room and sat down.* Someone who has just written several sentences of similar construction may want to provide some variation and thus may fall into the *Crossing the room* trap. In fact, many careful and respected writers spend a good deal of time in this trap; they may be fine writers, but they abuse the special modifying effect of a participle.

The time of the participle is bound to the time of the main verb (Rule 1-15). Some flexibility is allowable when the participle and the main verb describe actions of markedly different types. *Noticing that his knees were shaking, he sat down* is all right, because the noticing and the sitting are different types of action, and the noticing can go on throughout the act of sitting and even beyond. *Knowing that the market would drop, she sold out* is all right, because the knowing can go on before, during, and after the selling. *Hearing that the market would drop, she sold out* begins to be questionable, and *Hearing that the market would drop, she called her broker* is well along the path to not all right, with its implication of simultaneous listening and talking. *Hearing that the market would drop, she learned that selling out quickly would save her* is definitely not all right; the hearing and learning couldn't be simultaneous.

Even when the time of the participle agrees with the time of the main verb, sentences such as those used above as examples can be annoying. They are convenient for writers, with their two-for-the-price-of-one narrative function, but excessively convenient; they are much overused. Unsurprisingly, they are a feature of mass-market fiction.

VERB MOODS: INDICATIVE, IMPERATIVE, AND SUBJUNCTIVE

The indicative mood is the familiar, standard mood of verbs: *She touches the lamp; He eats his breakfast.* The imperative mood is used less frequently but is just as familiar, perhaps because we hear it so often in infancy: *Don't touch that lamp. Eat your cereal.*

The subjunctive mood may seem comparatively difficult and rare, though it is actually common. It is not used to express what something is or what something does, as the indicative mood is, or to make a direct command, as the imperative mood is. It is used to express what something might be or do, should be or do, or must be or do. In a way, it is the most distinctively human of moods, because it expresses possible being or action rather than actual being or action. Animals can exist only in the real world, but we exist in imaginary ones as well, and we need the subjunctive mood to think about and talk about our imaginary worlds.

Usually the subjunctive form of a verb is identical to a past-tense indicative form, which makes it possible for grammarians to claim that the subjunctive is passing out of the language. They can say, for example, that a common construction such as *I should go* just happens to use the past tense of the verb *shall*, and thus they can avoid using the term

58

subjunctive, which seems to frighten people. But this doesn't make sense. There is no "pastness" to the meaning of *should* in *I should go;* the verb form is subjunctive. The subjunctive is still very much a part of English, and we use it effortlessly all the time.

It is true that certain distinctive subjunctive forms seem to be passing out of English. The subjunctive form *were* used with a singular subject, as in *I wish I were rich,* is one of them, and it is the subject of the one rule in this section. Some tense problems with other forms of the subjunctive are discussed in Rule 1-14.

1-17 Use the subjunctive forms *I were* and *he, she,* or *it were* in clauses that describe a desired situation that is contrary to fact or set forth a condition that is contrary to fact, but do not use them in other clauses.

I wish I were rich expresses a desire for something contrary to fact. *I wouldn't wear these clothes if I were rich* and *I try to dress as if I were rich* set forth a condition that is contrary to fact. The clause *I were rich,* which looks very strange standing alone, is a subjunctive construction used for statements that are known to be untrue or at least highly unlikely and that are presented just as desires or hypotheses. Note that in the second example the verb in the main clause, *wouldn't,* is a subjunctive form too, because it states an imaginary situation rather than a real one.

Was is often used instead of *were* in all these constructions. *I wish I was rich* and similar uses of *was* are now considered somewhat informal but not incorrect; the distinctive subjunctive form *were* is no longer prescribed by all grammarians and is not the preference of many educated writers and speakers. However, in the example, *was* is still a subjunctive form even though a variant one. The indicative would be *I wish I am rich,* which is clearly wrong. A sentence in the past tense, such as *I wished I was rich,* may seem to be using *was* as an indicative past, as in *I discovered I was rich,* but it is really still a subjunctive. *I wish I were rich* and *I wished I were rich* are better usage at present. Perhaps in another few generations both these examples and *I wish I was rich* will seem affected, and all but the rich will be saying *I wish I am rich*.

Clauses that begin with *if* or *as if* are not always subjunctive. *If he is rich he will be welcome* is indicative; the *if* clause presents a condition that may be true. *He acts as if his life is in danger* and *He acts as if his life were in danger* are both correct; the indicative *as if* clause in the first sentence implies that his life may well be in danger, and the subjunctive *as if* clause in the second sentence implies that it is unlikely that his life is in danger—it states a condition that is, or at least is believed to be, contrary to fact. *He acts as if he thinks his life is in danger* and *He acts as if he thought his life is in danger* are also both correct but different; now it is his thinking that is presented as probable by the indicative *think* and improbable by the subjunctive *thought*. In sentences such as these, in which the *as if* clause has another clause as its object, the verb in the object clause often becomes subjunctive, regardless of whether the *as if* clause is subjunctive: *He acts as if he thinks his life were in danger; He acts as if he thought his life were in danger*. I am not aware of any criticism of this use of *were*, but it is rather hard to understand, especially when the *as if* clause is indicative. It does seem acceptable to the ear, and perhaps one could claim that it implies that his life is not actually in danger just as it would without the interrupting *he thinks* or *he thought*. In the last section of this discussion are comments on some other cloudy uses of *were*.

Incorrect uses of *were* in past-tense sentences

I wondered if she were single and *If he were rich you couldn't tell it by his clothes* are errors; in both cases the verb in the subordinate clause should be *was*. The subordinate clauses are not subjunctive, they are merely in the past tense to agree with the main verbs, *wondered* and *couldn't*, which are indicative and in the past tense. If we put the main verbs in the present tense, the verbs in the subordinate clauses also change to the present tense and are clearly indicative: *I wonder if she is single; If he is rich you can't tell it by his clothes*. A statement that is subjunctive, such as *If he were rich he wouldn't wear those clothes*, cannot be put in the present tense this way—it already is in the present.

She knew that if she were to graduate she would have to study harder is an error; *were* should be *was*. Again, the sentence can be tested by seeing if it can be put in the present tense—if it can be, it must be an indicative sentence, not a subjunctive one. And it can be: *She knows that if she is to graduate she will have to study harder.*

If he were disappointed he did not show it is an error; *were* should be *was.* The example can be put into the present tense: *If he is disappointed he does not show it.*

The errors discussed above all yield to a single logical test—trying to put them in the present tense and seeing what becomes of *were.* If it becomes *am* or *is,* one can conclude that *were* is wrong in the past tense.

If he were disappointed he would not have shown it is also an error, but of quite a different kind. The *if* clause should indeed be subjunctive, because it expresses a contrary-to-fact condition, but the subjunctive tenses in the two clauses are not in the correct sequence. It should be either *If he had been disappointed he would not have shown it* or *If he were disappointed he would not show it,* depending on whether the statement is about the past or about the present. See Rule 1-14 for a discussion of the sequence of subjunctive tenses.

Many well-educated people use *were* when the indicative past *was* is called for. Some of them may be trying too hard to be elegant, like those who use *between you and I,* but I suspect most of them are merely perpetuating a usage that is considered incorrect now but was considered correct a generation or so ago and has survived in their own circles. The subjunctive was formerly used in most *if* and *as if* clauses, not just those that are contrary to fact, and in Britain it is still widely so used. A well-educated Englishman directed to put *She asked if I were single* into the present tense might produce *She asks if I be single,* using a distinctive *be* subjunctive form that is alive in Britain but sounds odd and old-fashioned in the United States except in a few constructions, such as after the verb *insist: I insist that he be polite.* Thus an Englishman might just be commendably consistent in saying *She asked if I were single.* It is merely current usage, not logic and not historical usage, that in American English confines *were* to contrary-to-fact clauses. Nevertheless, I advise being careful with *were.*

Were in future conditional clauses

In August 1981, President Reagan said, *If there were some kind of international crisis, we would correct that with new legislation,* using the distinctive *were* form of the subjunctive for a conditional sentence about the future, which cannot logically be a condition contrary to fact. This use of the subjunctive is one of those that grammarians have been waving farewell to for decades, but it has remained alive and seems to be becoming more common, perhaps partly because the contrary-to-fact implication makes the unthinkable closer to thinkable. *If there were an all-out nuclear attack, we would correct that with new legislation* seems to imply greater doubt about the possibility of nuclear attack than the also subjunctive alternatives *If there should be an all-out nuclear attack* and *If an all-out nuclear attack took place;* it is certainly less scary than the indicative *If there is an all-out nuclear attack, we will correct that with new legislation.*

Use of the distinctive *were* forms for the future conditional is defensible; it permits expression of a special degree of doubt about the future condition. It has always been common among the well-educated. It is perhaps a bit fussy, but it does not invite derision the way *It is I* and *Whom do you want to invite?* may.

Dilemmas with *were*

Sometimes it is not easy to justify uses of the subjunctive *were* that seem right to the ear and are generally accepted. For example, *If I thought that were true, I would be lost* is not incorrect but does seem to make unnecessary use of the subjunctive *were,* which is not the verb of the *if* clause itself but merely the verb in a noun clause that serves as the object of the *if* clause. We might argue that *that were true* does express something assumed to be contrary to fact and therefore deserves the subjunctive, but not every statement that is contrary to fact is subjunctive—we say *I thought that was true and it isn't* and *He thinks that is true and it isn't. If I thought that was true, I would be lost* is not incorrect either; we might argue either that *was* is subjunctive, a variant of the subjunctive *were,* or that the noun clause *that is true* has been drawn into the past tense by the attraction of *thought,* which is not actually a past tense but looks like one. *If I thought that is true, I would be lost,* which seems defensible logically, is wrong to the ear.

If I thought that were all I were, I would be lost also bothers the ear, but *that were all I was, that were all I am, that was all I was,* and *that was all I am* all seem possible. Again, *that is all I am,* the logical phrasing, seems wrong; at least the first verb must be past or subjunctive. If all the verbs are made present indicative, the sentence becomes *If I think that is all I am, I will be lost*, which suggests that *If I thought that was all I was, I would be lost* would be a good choice, as I think it is, but note that the original sentence is a subjunctive one—it is not like the past-tense sentences discussed earlier but is about the present, and its meaning is quite different from that of the indicative version, so the test recommended for past-tense sentences is not applicable.

Other quandaries with *were* come up. There is little point in trying to resolve them by logic alone. It is apparent that in subjunctive sentences of any complexity, verbs that seem to have no reason to be in the subjunctive are attracted to it, just as in past-tense indicative sentences, verbs that logically should be in the present are attracted to the past (see Rule 1-14). Those who are accustomed to making correct uses of *were* in simple constructions are likely to have an ear reliable enough to trust in complicated constructions. I advise using *was* whenever the choice between *was* and *were* seems difficult, because *was* is acceptable as a subjunctive or a past, whereas *were* is only a subjunctive. Whatever choice one makes, there is some security in knowing that if it is difficult to defend logically, it also is likely to be difficult to attack logically.

VERB VOICES: ACTIVE AND PASSIVE

The active voice is simple and direct: *Smith hired Brown*. The passive voice reverses the position of the agent of the verb and makes the object of the verb its subject: *Brown was hired by Smith*. The passive voice takes more words than the active voice, and it can be cumbersome and pointlessly roundabout. However, it also has important advantages, which are discussed in the one rule in this section.

1-18   Don't be afraid to use the passive voice.

First we were shown the wall paintings in the main part of the house, and then we were taken by the guide, who was a very friendly man, over to a refreshment area to wait while the grown-ups went to see some other paintings in a room where we children weren't permitted. Poor little guy—he used the passive for all the *we* clauses, reserving the active for the clauses in which adults were the subject, and some school-teacher is going to tell him to avoid the "weak" passive voice and make him rewrite it: *First we saw . . . then we went . . .* The comparatively swashbuckling account that will result from the rewriting will not be as good, as a child's expression, as the original tale of being taken rather than going to Pompeii.

When we are children, we often perceive ourselves as objects of action more than as subjects of it, and we use the passive voice even though it takes more words and requires more complicated constructions. The passive voice is a feature of childish expression. It does make childish expression weak compared to adult expression, and therefore teachers try to get us to make more use of the active voice. This is not stupid or wrong of teachers, though a teacher may be insensitive about the problem. We do have to become adults, do have to learn to think of ourselves as the subjects of action as well as the objects of it.

However, once we become adults and the reason for proscribing the passive disappears, the proscription itself is likely to remain in memory, and when we use the passive we feel we're breaking a rule. We are not. The passive voice is respectable, is capable of expressing thoughts and shades of meaning that the active voice cannot express, and is even sometimes more compact and direct than the active voice.

The trouble-saving passive

Smith was arrested, indicted, and found guilty, but the money was never recovered has four passive verbs. Yet it is simpler and more direct than *The police arrested Smith, the grand jury indicted him, and the trial jury found him guilty, but the bank never recovered the money,* which has four active verbs. The use of the active voice requires naming the agent of the verb, because in the active voice the agent and the subject are the same, and a verb must have a subject. The passive voice permits not naming the agent of the verb, because the object of the active verb becomes the subject of the passive verb. If the agent is too obvious, too unimportant, or too vague to mention, the passive is usually better.

The passive to emphasize the agent

The money was stolen by a man, judging from those footprints emphasizes the agent, *a man*, more than does the active sentence *A man stole the money, judging from those footprints.* The passive sentence positions the agent at the end of the clause and automatically gives it emphasis. In the active sentence, *a man* does not automatically get this emphasis, although it could be deliberately emphasized in speech.

The pussyfooting passive

The money was stolen while Smith was in the vault states the crime and the circumstances but avoids making a direct accusation. This tact would be difficult to achieve were it not for the passive voice.

The pussyfooting passive is admittedly often overused. *These arrears cannot be overlooked, and if payment is not made promptly, our legal staff will be notified and rigorous action will be taken* is an offensive, falsely polite way of saying *We cannot overlook these arrears, and if you do not make payment promptly, we will take rigorous legal action.* In the passive sentence, the writer seems to pretend that the recipient of the letter is being threatened by abstract forces beyond the writer's control—the credit system, perhaps. By not naming the agent of the threats, the writer avoids admitting responsibility as the agent. The active sentence is forthright and as inoffensive as a dunning letter can be.

The pussyfooting passive is essential in journalism—often the writer does not know who did something or is not free to say who did it, but wants to say it was done.

MODIFIERS

Adjectives and adverbs are the parts of speech that the term *modifier* brings to mind—adjectives modify nouns and sometimes pronouns, and adverbs modify verbs, adjectives, and other adverbs. However, the term also includes phrases and dependent clauses that define or elaborate on words or other phrases and clauses.

Modifiers are misused in various ways. They can be forced into double duty as both modifier and noun (Rule 1-19), they can be badly positioned in a sentence so that it is not clear what they modify (Rule 1-20), they can occur in sentences in which they have nothing to modify or must modify the wrong thing (Rule 1-21), and they can just be the wrong type of modifier—an adjective where an adverb is called for, or vice versa (Rule 1-22).

1-19   Consider a possessive form to be a modifier, not a noun; don't use it as an antecedent for a relative pronoun, and don't let a noun be in apposition to it.

The hat is John's, who forgot it is incorrect, because it uses the possessive form *John's* as the antecedent for the relative pronoun *who*. *The hat belongs to John, who forgot it* is correct; *who* now has a real noun, not a modifier, as its antecedent. *The hat is John's; he forgot it* is another solution, permissible because the personal pronoun *he*, unlike the relative pronoun *who*, does not require a definite antecedent. Though *John's* does identify *he*—as is, of course, desirable—it is not grammatically required to be an antecedent.

The hat is John's, the young man who is so forgetful is incorrect, because *the young man who is so forgetful* is in apposition to the possessive form *John's*. A word or phrase in apposition has to agree in case with the word or phrase it is in apposition to (see Rule 1-6). If we try to make the appositional phrase agree with *John's* by using the possessive *man's*, we just move the error farther along in the sentence; in *the young man's who is so forgetful*, the possessive *man's* incorrectly serves as the antecedent for *who*. We can avoid that error by moving the possessive form all the way to the end—*The hat is John's, the young man who is so forgetful's*—but we have moved the sentence right out of the English language. In a simpler sentence, making an appositive noun a possessive may work: *Is that John's, my husband's, hat?* In the original example, avoiding the possessive form is the only solution: *The hat belongs to John, the young man who is so forgetful.*

My husband John's hat is nevertheless acceptable. The name *John*, though not a defining appositive, since a woman has only one husband, is tightly combined with *My husband* into a single phrase, which is then made possessive. This is often possible when the second term is more specific than the first term and hence is defining: *his friend John's hat*, but not *John his friend's hat*. Some grammarians do permit *John, his friend's, hat*, but if we take out the parenthetical *his friend's*, as we should be able to do without affecting the grammar of what remains, we have *John hat*. See the discussion of parenthetical and defining appositives in Rule 2-1.

Exception: the independent possessive

If you need a hat, take John's, which has been hanging here all week uses the possessive *John's* as antecedent for the relative pronoun *which,* but it is nevertheless correct. The antecedent of *which* is not John himself but the thing he owns, his hat, and we might consider the example an elliptical sentence, with *John's* representing *John's hat. John's* is actually functioning as an independent possessive—a possessive that can function as a noun and hence can be the antecedent of a relative pronoun.

The distinction between ordinary possessives and independent possessives is clearly seen when we use pronouns, some of which have distinctive forms for the independent possessive: *I needed a hat and took yours, which you had left behind; If you need a hat take mine, the gray one.* The forms *yours* and *mine* are possessives but can act like nouns, unlike the forms *your* and *my,* which act only as modifiers.

1-20   Position modifiers in a sentence so that they modify the right word and only that word.

Since word order is the most significant indication of the meaning of an English sentence, a misplaced modifier can make a sentence unclear or at least momentarily confusing.

Adjectives and adjective chains

Adjectives almost always either directly precede the word they modify, as in *gray cats,* or directly follow it and a linking verb, as in *Cats are gray.* Errors in position of an adjective and the word it modifies are uncommon.

However, when two or more adjectives modify the same word, there is often some doubt about the correct order for the adjectives. Sometimes all the adjectives stand in the same direct relation to the modified word, and the order does not greatly matter. For example, *a gray, cold, fretful sea* has a string of three descriptive adjectives that could be put in any order. Usually adjectives that all directly modify the same word are separated by commas. We can test whether or not the adjectives all modify the same word by seeing if *and* can be put between the adjectives—*a gray and cold and fretful sea*—

without changing the meaning. The commas can be thought of as representing *and*.

On the other hand, sometimes there is a progression in the order of adjectives from the most specific to the least specific, as in *my three beautiful furry rabbits*. Each adjective modifies the whole word group that follows, and tampering with the order of the adjectives makes the phrase sound wrong or changes the meaning. In the example, the first adjective is the possessive *my*, which is classified as a definitive adjective. (Other definitive adjectives are the articles *the* and *a* and the demonstrative adjectives *this*, *that*, *these*, and *those*.) After definitive adjectives come numerical adjectives—*three* in the example—modifying what remains of the word group. Then there are adjectives implying judgment or opinion of some kind, such as *beautiful*. Then there are purely descriptive adjectives, such as *furry*.

When there are two or more descriptive adjectives in a series, usually adjectives expressing size come first, then adjectives expressing shape, and then adjectives expressing other qualities: *large round furry rabbits*, or more commonly, *large, round, furry rabbits*, since even though the adjectives have an order they each modify the noun directly.

Admittedly, the line between judgmental and descriptive adjectives can be hard to draw and the best order for a string of descriptive adjectives hard to determine. A good deal must be left to the ear. However, the fact that such a series of adjectives does progress can be tested by trying to insert *and* as we did above in the random series *a gray and cold and fretful sea*. We can't; *my and three and beautiful and furry rabbits* is not English. Yet we can double the adjectives in each category and join the pairs with *and*, and the result is English even though clumsy: *your and my third and fourth beautiful and courageous soft and furry rabbits*.

Note that when a string of adjectives forms a progression, commas are usually not desirable to separate the adjectives. Since each adjective modifies the whole word group that follows, a comma would separate the modifier from the modified phrase, which is a misuse of the comma (see Rule 2-5).

Adverbs

Adverbs are prone to wander. In *The young man swims badly*, the adverb *badly* immediately follows the verb, and in *The young man almost failed to finish*, the adverb *almost* immediately precedes the verb. This closeness is common, but it is also common to find the adverb well separated from the verb: *The young man swam all but the 100-meter freestyle race badly.*

In sentences in which the position of an adverb is critical, we are unlikely to make mistakes. In the following five examples, the adverb *harshly* migrates from the beginning of the sentence to the end: *Harshly, he asked how they could be punished; He asked harshly how they could be punished; He asked how harshly they could be punished; He asked how they could be harshly punished; He asked how they could be punished harshly.* There is some overlapping of intended meanings in the five examples, but no two are precisely the same in meaning, and almost everyone would unerringly pick the best word order for the intended meaning.

However, because adverbs can wander and because they can modify adjectives, other adverbs, and whole sentences as well as verbs, there may be several words or phrases in a given sentence that an adverb can modify, and this makes confusion and ambiguity possible even in sentences that are grammatically correct.

Not is often ambiguous. *She is not famous for her books* may mean either that her books have not made her famous and nor has anything else, or that she is famous but not for her books, as, for example, are many former government officials who publish memoirs. If the ambiguity is present even in context, the sentence should be rewritten.

We can't accept completely abstract logic is ambiguous. The adverb *completely* could modify either the verb preceding it or the adjective following it. Such a modifier is sometimes called a squinting modifier—it seems to look in two directions at once. Squinting modifiers can be hard to find when we're looking over what we've written, because we ourselves, of course, know what we mean, and the grammar is not incorrect, just ambiguous. The example could be made unambiguous by making it either *We can't completely accept abstract logic* or *We can't accept logic that is completely abstract.* For the second meaning, we have to make the sentence more complicated and use a relative clause, because in the original sentence there is no position for *completely* that will make it unambiguously the modifier of *abstract.*

I'm almost having the best time of my life is not ambiguous, except by very perverse misreading, but it is careless and graceless; it should be *I'm having almost the best time of my life.*

The adverb usually should not be separated from the word it does modify by any other word that it is grammatically possible for it to modify, though adverbs are too slippery to permit this principle to be stated as a definite rule.

I'm only going to tell you once has a misplaced modifier—it should be *I'm going to tell you only once*—but it is not ambiguous, and it is not graceless either; it is almost an idiom. The "correct" version may sound a little stiff. Sometimes taste must determine when positioning a modifier precisely is desirable and when it is too fussy. I recommend allowing *only*—an especially vagrant word even among the adverbs—to wander with some freedom in speech, but positioning it precisely in anything but the most casual writing. The habit can have a surprisingly pervasive beneficial effect on overall expression, because it is by just such attention to detail that prose becomes truly good instead of merely workmanlike and adequate.

You must be a bit more in tune with your intentions earlier than you're in the habit of being—an example drawn from self-help literature, which is often rich in sentences that need professional help—shows a special kind of confusion that can result from the ability of adverbs and adverbial constructions to be separated from the word or phrase they modify and to be placed in the middle of other constructions. The adjectival clause *a bit more in tune with your intentions . . . than you're in the habit of being* is a subject complement—it is linked to *you* by the verb phrase *must be.* The overlapping adverbial clause *earlier than you're in the habit of being* modifies everything that precedes it in the sentence, including *more in tune.* Both the adjectival clause and the adverbial clause are comparative, and because the adverbial clause acts on the adjectival clause, it compares something that already is comparative. Some kind of semantic calculus might permit the simultaneous plotting of one varying quantity varied by another varying quantity against a baseline of habit, but language does not; you can be more in tune and you can be in tune earlier, but you cannot be more in tune earlier. The solution is to provide something other than the comparative *more in tune* for the comparative *earlier* to modify: *You must be a bit more in tune with your intentions and in tune earlier than you're in the habit of being.* The sentence could be further improved, but it is no longer nonsense.

Split infinitives

It was impossible to completely follow his logic contains a split infinitive, but it is far better than either *It was impossible to follow completely his logic*, which is unnatural, or *It was impossible completely to follow his logic*, which is both unnatural and ambiguous. As is frequently the case, we do have a good alternative to splitting the infinitive: *It was impossible to follow his logic completely.*

The rule against the split infinitive is an arbitrary one, a hangover from the nineteenth century, when grammarians attempted to make English grammar conform to Latin grammar. The Latin infinitive cannot be split, but only because it is all one word, not because there is any rule against splitting it. Fewer and fewer writers, and few grammarians, subscribe to the rule against the split infinitive. And yet there is some virtue in obeying it. Arbitrary it is, but arbitrariness alone is no reason to violate a rule; many rules of grammar and particularly of usage are arbitrary. To me—perhaps because I was made to follow the rule as a student—split infinitives retain some implication of ignorance and sloppiness. I suspect I have a good deal of company. Also, the rule against the split infinitive seems to be the one rule that everyone remembers. If we sophisticated users of the language break it, we may find our grammar being criticized by less sophisticated users, which is infuriating.

Nevertheless, splitting an infinitive is better than putting its modifier in an unnatural or ambiguous place. If we choose to avoid split infinitives, we should also take the trouble to recast sentences to avoid putting the modifier in an unnatural place. Occasionally writers seem to go out of their way to put the modifier in an unnatural place, perhaps as a kind of showing off—they want their readers to notice that they know enough not to split infinitives.

Participles and participial phrases

He was the only man in the group dancing is ambiguous; it could mean either *He was the only man dancing in the group* or *He was the only man in the dancing group.* Participles are used as adjectives, but they wander more like adverbs.

He was the only man in the group wearing makeup has the same ambiguity; it could mean either *He was the only man wearing makeup in the group* or *In the group wearing makeup*

71

he was the only man. Similarly, *I met her going to the store* is ambiguous; the participial phrase *going to the store* must modify either *I* or *her,* but we can't tell which. If it modifies *I,* we can make the sentence unambiguous by repositioning the participial phrase—*Going to the store, I met her*—but that is hardly natural. Often it is better to recast and avoid the participial phrase: *I met her on my way to the store* or *on her way to the store.*

Participles and participial phrases must be watched carefully; like adverbs, they can cause confusion and ambiguity.

Prepositional phrases

At the age of five, Piaget insisted children were too young to vote can be corrected simply by putting the prepositional phrase *At the age of five* somewhere after *children.* However, quite often the context of a sentence makes it desirable to begin with such a prepositional phrase. The error in the example is actually an error in punctuation. As the sentence stands, the introductory prepositional phrase *At the age of five* modifies everything that follows, and so it seems to indicate Piaget's age, not the children's. We can prevent the introductory phrase from applying to Piaget by inserting a comma after *insisted,* which makes *Piaget insisted* a parenthetical construction that does not disturb the grammatical relationships of the words in the basic sentence, which is *At the age of five, children were too young to vote.* See also the discussion of parenthetical constructions in Rule 2-1.

Dependent clauses

When the election was over, he planned to abolish the electoral system is intended to mean *He planned to abolish the electoral system when the election was over,* but because the dependent clause beginning with *when* is introductory, it seems to modify the main verb in the sentence, *planned,* not the infinitive construction *to abolish the electoral system,* and hence to mean that he didn't make his plans till after the election. Similarly, *After he was elected, he knew he could declare himself king* is intended to mean *He knew he could declare himself king after he was elected*—that is, he had it all planned from the start—but the misplaced dependent clause seems to indicate that it was only after his election that he

72

knew he could coronate himself. Here an added comma, making *he knew* parenthetical, could achieve the intended meaning: *After he was elected, he knew, he could declare himself king.* In both examples, the dependent clauses are adverbial, and like adverbs themselves, adverbial clauses can all too easily be mispositioned.

He was flown to Miami for combat training, where he was commissioned is not ambiguous and not truly an error, but it does annoyingly separate the *where* clause from the word it modifies, *Miami.* When a dependent clause modifies a specific word or phrase in a sentence, it is best to put the clause directly after the modified word or phrase: *He was flown for combat training to Miami, where he was commissioned.* If this makes the sentence seem awkward, it should be recast to avoid the dependent clause: *He was flown to Miami for combat training and was commissioned there.*

1-21   Don't let modifiers dangle with nothing appropriate to modify.

The function of a modifier is to modify, and if we give one nothing it can modify, it is said to dangle. The dangling participle is a famous dangler, but some other dangling constructions are just as common.

Dangling participles

Inspecting the books, the error was immediately apparent contains a dangling participial phrase. The sentence does not contain too many words that the participle *Inspecting* could grammatically modify—the concern of Rule 1-20. However, the only word the participle can grammatically modify is *error,* which cannot be the intended meaning, because an error can't inspect. The word the participle should modify must be some word signifying whoever inspected the books, and it is not in the sentence at all. The error is almost always just that simple. A participle, like any adjectival word, must have something to modify.

Inspecting the books, the error was immediately apparent to us may seem to correct the problem by providing *us* for the participle to modify, but it too is wrong. When a participle or participial phrase begins a sentence, it should modify the subject of the rest of the sentence (or the subject of the following independent clause, if the sentence has more than one clause). Thus *Inspecting the books* is still a dangling participle; *us* is not the subject, and the participle can't modify it. *The error was immediately apparent to us, inspecting the books, but not to him, inspecting his royalty statement* is correct, because the participial phrases do not begin the sentence and they immediately follow the words they modify.

Shown the books, the accountant's hands began to tremble also has a dangling participle. The participial phrase *Shown the books* is intended to modify *accountant*, but *accountant* is in the possessive case—*accountant's*—and thus is not a noun but an adjective, and the participle phrase cannot modify it (see Rule 1-19). The only noun available for the participle to modify is *hands*, which obviously is not the intended meaning. This error is quite common, especially with possessive pronouns, as in *Mulling over the options, his perplexity only increased.*

Permissible dangling participles

Considering the state of the books, the error was found surprisingly quickly contains a dangling participle, because *Considering* has nothing appropriate to modify. However, this and many similar common expressions are accepted as correct. Actually they do have something to modify—the whole rest of the sentence. They are essentially sentence modifiers, as *however, therefore,* and similar adverbs usually are. *Regarding, looking, judging, allowing, excepting,* and other participles that indicate some kind of generalized mental activity permit such sentence-modifying phrases. Dictionaries are apt to identify the most common of these participles, such as *considering* and *regarding,* as prepositions and conjunctions, which gets them off the hook; it lets us call *Considering the state of the books* a prepositional phrase rather than a dangling participial phrase. This may seem a bit weasely of the dictionaries, but the participles in such phrases do indeed play the role of prepositions and conjunctions. *Considering the state of the books* is the same as the prepositional phrase *In view of the state of the books.* In *Considering the books were incomplete, the error was found surprisingly quickly,* the participial *Considering* is equivalent to the conjunctive phrase *inasmuch as.*

Providing, as in *Providing the books are complete, we will find the error,* is also accepted by dictionaries as a conjunction, but it is nevertheless much condemned. I advise using *provided* instead—an option not available for *considering* and the other participles discussed above. *Provided,* being a past participle, is passive in relation to what it modifies (see **participle** in the Glossary/Index), and in *Provided the books are complete,* it properly modifies *the books are complete*—it is like the absolute constructions discussed just below.

Absolute constructions: not danglers

The books having been inspected, the error was apparent is correct; there is no dangling participle. *The books having been inspected* is a so-called absolute construction. The phrase itself includes the word the participial form *having been inspected* modifies: *books.* Absolute phrases do not have to modify any specific word in the rest of the sentence. They modify the whole rest of the sentence, just as an introductory dependent clause does: *When the books had been inspected, the error was apparent.*

Danglers other than participles

By being prepared and giving a brief show of your best work, your family and friends will think you are quite a photographer is not a case of the dangling participle, because *being prepared* and *giving* are not participles but gerunds, but it does have a dangling construction. The gerunds are part of an adverbial phrase, *By being prepared and giving a show of your best work,* and this adverbial phrase should relate to the subject and verb of the main clause—that is, it should modify either the verb or the whole sentence. It is intended to modify *you,* which occurs late in the sentence as the subject of the noun clause *you are quite a photographer* and is in no position to be modified. Therefore the adverbial phrase dangles, with nothing appropriate to modify. To correct the sentence, the main clause must be rewritten to make *you* the subject: *you will make your family and friends think you are quite a photographer.*

A proved incompetent, they made him head of the department contains a dangling appositional phrase. *A proved incompetent* and *him* are intended to be in apposition, but when an appositional phrase begins a sentence—which it can, though in

75

standard word order it follows the word it is in apposition to—
it must be in apposition to the subject of the sentence, which
in the example is *they*, not *him. They made him, a proved
incompetent, head of the department* is correct; the appositional phrase does not begin the sentence but is in its natural
position, directly following the word it is in apposition to. *A
proved incompetent, he was made head of the department* is
also correct.

*Modest and reticent, his Mohawk haircut nevertheless gave
him a certain presence* contains the dangling adjectival phrase
Modest and reticent, which is intended to modify *him* but as
the sentence is constructed modifies *his Mohawk haircut*.

It pays to be suspicious almost anytime a sentence begins
with a subordinate element, whether the element is a modifier,
a prepositional phrase, or some other construction. *At the age
of five, his father died* is a classic example; the sentence doesn't
contain anything that *At the age of five* can both appropriately
and grammatically modify, since *his* is merely adjectival (see
Rule 1-19) and the father couldn't be a father if he died at five.
(*When he was five, his father died* does not dangle, though it
does permit misreading.) A similar example is *In no real need
of money, nevertheless greed proved his undoing*. Sometimes
the problem is just that the subordinate element comes first,
and the sentence can be made grammatically correct simply by
shifting order: *Fat and wheezy, the run was too much for John*
can be changed to *The run was too much for fat and wheezy
John* or *The run was too much for John, fat and wheezy*, in
which the adjectives are not in the standard position but still
modify *John*. Shifting order may at least make the basic problem of a bad sentence more evident and hence easier to correct.

Not all dangling modifiers are found at the beginning of a
sentence. *Like many of his mannerisms, he had learned to
wink from his father* contains the dangling prepositional
phrase *Like many of his mannerisms*. If the phrase is repositioned—*He had learned to wink, like many of his mannerisms, from his father*—it still dangles. The dangling prepositional phrase perhaps cannot be attacked on strictly
grammatical grounds, yet the words in this sentence are not
happy together; there is a failure of parallelism (see Rule 1-5,
especially the discussion of *like* and *unlike*). The infinitive *to
wink* could not be the object of a preposition—we could not say
*He had learned to wrinkle his nose, like to wink, from his
father*—and the sentence needs something that *like* can have as
an object so that *like many of his mannerisms* can parallel it.

The infinitive *to wink* is linked very awkwardly with the noun phrase *many of his mannerisms,* although sometimes an infinitive does accept such a role, as in *To go, like many of his options, seemed fruitless.* We could improve the sentence by changing the infinitive to a gerund, because gerunds can be the objects of prepositions and can be compared with nouns and noun phrases: *He had learned winking, like many of his mannerisms, from his father.* There are, of course, other acceptable ways of changing the sentence; my intention here is simply to show that it can be considered to contain a dangling construction and that changing it is desirable.

1-22   Don't misuse adverbs as adjectives, and don't misuse adjectives as adverbs.

Adjectives that should be adverbs

She drives really good is wrong because *good* modifies the verb *drives* and thus should be the adverb *well. She drives real well* is wrong because *real* modifies the adverb *well* and thus should be the adverb *really. She drives real good* is, of course, a double error. Most of us are unlikely to use adjectives as adverbs except when being deliberately slangy.

Note that *I drive slow in town* is not an error. Some common adverbs have two forms; both *slow* and *slowly* can be adverbs, though the only adjectival form is *slow.* Don't automatically correct an "adjectival" form that seems idiomatic as an adverb; check the dictionary—it may be a legitimate adverb too. In fact, *real* is very frequently an adverb in casual speech and is accepted as such by dictionaries—it means *very* rather than *genuinely* or *veritably* and hence is distinct from *really*—and therefore *she drives real well,* condemned in the preceding paragraph, has been granted some license.

Adverbs that should be adjectives

I feel badly about it is such a common error that some authorities accept it as idiomatically correct, though no one would say *I feel well about it.* The verb *feel* is a linking verb in these examples, not an ordinary verb as it can be in other sentences, such as *I feel strongly about it* and *We feel similarly about it.* A linking verb links its subject to the following word or phrase. *I* is a pronoun and cannot be modified by or linked to an adverb, but it can be modified or linked to an adjective. Thus it should be *I feel bad about it.*

An occasional expression such as *I feel badly about it* may infiltrate the speech and writing of those who are careful of their grammar and know something about grammar but not quite enough; they think the verb *feel* has to be modified by an adverb, so they tack on the *ly.* It's an embarrassing error, because it suggests a self-conscious effort to be correct. To avoid such errors we have to pay special attention to sentences that contain linking verbs. The most common linking verb is, of course, *be.* Other common verbs that can be linking verbs include *seem, appear, look, become, grow, taste, smell, sound, remain,* and *stay.* Most of them are not always linking verbs. The verb *smell* is not a linking verb in *He vigorously smells the wine* or in *He smells less acutely than the winemaster,* but it is a linking verb in *He smells winy after his sessions in the cellar.*

You have to hold the camera vertically for close-up portraits is incorrect. It is the camera, not the holding of it, that has to be vertical; the sentence should read *You have to hold the camera vertical for close-up portraits.* The error is similar to the error in *I feel badly,* but instead of a linking verb it involves an object complement—a noun or adjective that follows the actual object of a verb to complete the meaning. In *They elected him president,* the noun *president* is an object complement; in *They called him crazy,* the adjective *crazy* is an object complement. Sometimes a sentence can be phrased either with adverbs or with object complements with no significant change in meaning: *Slice the steak thinly* or *Slice the steak thin; Let us see it clearly and plainly* or *Let us see it clear and plain.* But *You have to hold the camera vertically* is just as wrong as *She climbed vertical up the cliff,* in which the modifier modifies *climbed* and must be an adverb.

Precision with adjectives and adverbs can be important. In opening his poem on his father's dying with the line *Do not go gentle into that good night,* Dylan Thomas was being precise. He wanted his father to remain himself as he faced death, not to be gentle and resigned, but he did not want his father to die ungently and painfully, which is what *Do not go gently* would mean. To communicate his meaning, Thomas used *gentle* as what is called a predicate complement—a construction that is quite common, as in *I came home tired* and *Don't go away mad*, and is not likely to give any fluent user of the language trouble, but that does surprise us and make us pay attention when we find it in Thomas's line where we would expect an adverb.

◇ **2** ◇

PUNCTUATION

◆

Punctuation can be thought of as a means of indicating in writing the pauses and changes of tone that are used in speech to help communicate the meaning of sentences. The marks of punctuation evolved partly as indicators of pause and tone—a comma usually indicates a pause, a question mark usually indicates a rising tone, and so on—and they retain this significance. Consequently, in this chapter I often point out that a comma, question mark, or some other mark of punctuation can be "heard" at a given point in a sentence.

However, we cannot rely completely on our sense of proper spoken delivery when we are punctuating sentences. For one thing, often when we are trying to punctuate a difficult sentence and mutter it a few times to determine how we would say it, its meaning somehow disintegrates and we find we can't say it naturally at all. More important, punctuation represents both less and more than the pauses and changes of tone in speech.

It represents less because an infinite variety of pauses and tone changes are available to the speaker but only a few marks of punctuation are available to the writer. It represents more because it has ways of indicating syntax—that is, the grammatical relationships each word in a sentence has with the words before and after it—that spoken language does not.

Syntactical punctuation, which was introduced quite deliberately into the English language in the seventeenth century by

Ben Jonson and others, is somewhat independent of the spoken language and has allowed the written language to acquire some special capacities. For example, the apostrophe and quotation mark of modern written English have no parallel in spoken English. Furthermore, marks of punctuation that do have parallels in speech, such as the comma and the dash, are perceived by the eye as *direct* signals of syntax—we don't perceive them as actual time lapses and then feel the effect of those lapses. Unless we are just learning to read or are muttering over a sentence we are having difficulty punctuating, we feel a comma's effect without filtering it through the spoken language. Reading and listening are distinctly different mental activities, and written and spoken language are correspondingly different.

Punctuation can suggest only roughly the infinite variety of pauses and tones available in speech. On the other hand, speech can indicate only rather imprecisely the syntactical relationships that the marks of punctuation make evident in written English, and therefore spoken sentences, even when carefully composed rather than extemporaneous, cannot contain much complexity of syntax or they become unintelligible. Some complicated sentences can be clear and balanced in writing, but cannot be spoken, or even read aloud, without extreme awkwardness and ambiguity. Spoken language, rich and beautiful as it can be in other respects, must often be less compact and complex than written language, because it does not have the precise syntactical signals that marks of punctuation represent.

But precise syntactical signals must be precisely used. Imprecise punctuation, which is a feature of the writing of the badly educated and is by no means uncommon in the writing of the well educated, can be worse than no punctuation at all, because it gives false signals. It also gives the writer away. It doesn't just suggest ignorance of "good English," as might an occasional grammatical lapse; it exposes muddled ideas and faulty connection of ideas, an impairment not only of expression but of thinking.

There is often more than one valid way to punctuate a sentence. Also, punctuation practices change more quickly than grammatical rules, and there is more disagreement about them from authority to authority, from stylebook to stylebook. Nevertheless, punctuation can be absolutely wrong.

Like the preceding chapter, on grammar, this chapter focuses on common errors and problems. However, it covers its topic relatively thoroughly, both because punctuation is a less complex topic than grammar and can be covered in a single long chapter and because basic punctuation errors are much more frequent than basic grammatical errors.

The chapter is divided into obvious major sections. The first section, which contains just one rule with a very long discussion, concerns sentence structure; the rest of the sections concern the individual marks of punctuation. Points of ellipsis (which look like periods) are discussed, but I have not provided a sentence on the period itself, because it has only one use—to end a declarative sentence. However, the problems that come up when the period is used with other marks of punctuation are covered in the discussions of the rules for those marks, and the various conventional uses of the point, loosely called a period, such as to indicate an abbreviation, are covered in Chapter 3.

SENTENCE STRUCTURE

Punctuation within a sentence is largely determined by the structure of the sentence. Structure includes grammar, but it is not just another word for grammar; several of the terms used in this chapter to discuss structure are not necessary at all in the preceding chapter, which is specifically on grammar.

There is only one rule in this section, but the discussion of it is very long. Readers who want a quick solution for a specific problem may find themselves growing impatient with this discussion, because even though it does solve specific problems, its primary intent is to promote an analytical approach to sentences that will make specific problems much rarer. It must therefore be absorbed, not just consulted for quick solutions. It also includes a review of terms that are used elsewhere in the chapter. These terms are defined separately in the Glossary/Index, but they will be more conveniently learned within the discussion of the rule.

While revising this book, I considered splitting Rule 2-1 up into several rules and including most of it in the section on commas, since commas—both those that are present and those that are omitted—are by far the most common signals of sentence structure. Splitting up the rule might make the punctuation chapter handier for the reader. However, I believe that leaving it whole makes the chapter far more useful to the reader in the long run, because the whole rule communicates certain major differences among sentences, and hence certain major purposes of punctuation, better than its split-up parts would. Readers consulting other rules will find themselves referred to Rule 2-1 frequently—and I hope that eventually every reader will get through it.

2-1   Consider the structure and meaning of a sentence when punctuating it.

Sentence structure is a basic part of language, and ordinarily we don't have to think about it very much. However, when we are not sure how to punctute a sentence, we do have to think about its structure, and usually in terms of three basic questions:

1. Is it a simple sentence, a compound sentence, or a complex sentence?
2. If the sentence includes a dependent clause or phrase, is the dependent clause or phrase parenthetical or defining?
3. Does the sentence begin with the main clause or with an introductory word, phrase, or dependent clause?

Each of the terms used in these questions is discussed below.

Simple sentences

Mary writes is the simplest sort of simple sentence, containing just a subject, *Mary,* and a verb, *writes. Mary writes me letters* is still a simple sentence, though now the verb has the direct object *letters* and the indirect object *me. Mary and John write* is also a simple sentence, though it has the compound subject *Mary and John.* And *Mary writes and telephones* is a simple sentence, though it has the compound predicate *writes and telephones.*

A sentence can get quite long and complicated and still remain a simple sentence. *Until recently, Mary and John, my grandchildren, wrote me letters twice a month and telephoned every Sunday afternoon* is a simple sentence, even though it includes an introductory adverbial phrase, a compound subject with an appositive, a compound predicate, a direct and an indirect object for one of the verbs, and an adverbial phrase for each of the verbs. It is simple because in spite of its complexity and its three commas, it still merely connects one subject or set of subjects to one action or set of actions.

The following discussion of other types of sentence should help clarify the nature of the simple type.

Compound sentences

John writes, and Mary telephones is a compound sentence. It consists of two clauses, either of which could stand alone: *John writes. Mary telephones.* They are independent clauses—that is, not only does each have its own subject and predicate (the minimum any clause must have), but neither one is dependent on the other. A compound sentence is merely a group of two or more simple sentences (or complex sentences, discussed below) that have been made one sentence by punctuating them appropriately and often by using a conjunction such as *and.*

Complex sentences

John, who is my grandson, doesn't write anymore contains the dependent clause *who is my grandson. Mary still gets the urge to telephone just before the rates go up on Sunday* contains the dependent clause *just before the rates go up on Sunday.* Both are complex sentences—that is, sentences with one or more dependent clauses. The clause *who is my grandson* is obviously not an independent clause (unless one makes it a question); it is an adjectival clause modifying *John.* The clause *just before the rates go up on Sunday* is not independent either; it is an adverbial clause modifying *gets the urge to telephone.* Each dependent clause merely modifies something in the main clause.

Compound/complex sentences

They wanted to go on writing and telephoning, but after they moved into my house I told them to stop has an independent clause extending up to the comma and then another independent clause, *I told them to stop,* at the end, so it is a compound sentence. The second independent clause is modified by the dependent clause *after they moved into my house,* so the sentence is also a complex sentence. Thus we have a compound/complex sentence—a compound sentence in which at least one of the independent clauses is modified by a dependent clause.

The meaning of the parts and the meaning of the whole

As can be seen in the examples above, a simple sentence may have quite a lot of internal punctuation and a compound or complex sentence may have very little, although usually a compound sentence has at least a comma (see Rule 2-2). We may now be able to identify a sentence as simple, compound, or complex, but to punctuate it properly we must answer the second and third of the three questions listed at the beginning of the rule—we must determine whether any dependent constructions are parenthetical or defining and whether the sentence begins with the main clause. Essentially this requires us to consider the meanings of the separate parts—the phrases and clauses—that form the sentence and the relationships among these meanings that give the sentence its overall meaning. Writers who punctuate improperly very likely do not always understand what their sentences mean and perhaps do not always understand even what they want them to mean; if they inspected their writing carefully enough to punctuate it properly, they might actually improve their ability to think.

One part of a sentence may be like a parenthetical remark—helpful, perhaps even very important, but not essential to the meaning of the rest of the sentence. Another part may actually define the meaning and hence be essential. A primary purpose of punctuation is to indicate this distinction, as explained below.

Parenthetical constructions

His son, who is a good swimmer, made the rescue contains the parenthetical dependent clause *who is a good swimmer.* The pair of commas around the clause are, in their effect on the structure of the sentence, exactly like a pair of parentheses: *His son (who is a good swimmer) made the rescue.* Omitting one comma or the other would be just as bad an error as omitting one of the parentheses.

Parenthetical constructions are often called nonrestrictive, because they do not restrict the meaning of the word or words they relate to but only expand on that meaning; they could be removed from the sentence without changing the basic meaning of the subject-predicate combination that makes up the basic sentence. In the example above, *His son made the rescue* is the basic sentence, and its meaning is not changed by the parenthetical *who is a good swimmer.*

Note, however, that a parenthetical construction is not necessarily of less importance to the overall meaning, the overall effect on the reader, than other parts of the sentence containing it. In *The former senator, who will be spending his weekends in prison for the next two years, no longer attends St. Michael's,* the basic sentence is *The former senator no longer attends St. Michael's,* and the parenthetical clause does not affect the meaning of the basic sentence, but it certainly affects the overall meaning of the complete sentence. Parentheses themselves often do suggest that what they enclose is a digression or a bit of incidental information that should not distract the reader from the main point of the sentence, but pairs of commas, and especially pairs of dashes, frequently emphasize what they enclose.

The rescue was made by his son, who is a good swimmer contains the same parenthetical clause as the first example. We don't use the second comma, because we have reached the end of the sentence and use a period instead, but if we replace the commas with parentheses, it is apparent that the clause is still parenthetical: *The rescue was made by his son (who is a good swimmer).* When a parenthetical clause begins a sentence, the first comma is, of course, omitted: *Although he swims well, he has no lifesaving training.* The second comma—in the example, the one after *well*—is optional but often desirable, as explained in the discussion of introductory constructions below.

Parenthetical elements don't have to be clauses; they can also be phrases or even single words, as explained more fully below in the discussion of appositives. *His son, John, made the rescue* has the parenthetical element *John. John, swimming strongly, reached the child in time* has the parenthetical element *swimming strongly.*

The examples of parenthetical constructions above might lead one to conclude that such constructions must always be set off by punctuation. However, sometimes they are not. In *John as well as his brothers has received lifesaving training,* the phrase *as well as his brothers* is parenthetical. The phrase has no effect on the basic meaning, *John has received lifesaving training* (and it has no effect on the verb *has*; see Rule 1-11). We can set the phrase off if we wish, giving the sentence a somewhat different effect, but we don't have to. The phrase *as well as* and some others can be so clearly parenthetical, so clearly an interruption, that the signal of enclosing punctuation is not needed.

Defining constructions

His son who is a good swimmer made the rescue is quite different from the earlier example with commas. When the sentence has no commas, the subject is no longer just *His son*, but a specific son who is a good swimmer, as distinguished from other sons who aren't. There are no commas because *who is a good swimmer* is now a necessary, integral part of the sentence, essential to the meaning. Read aloud, the sentence would have no pauses. Similarly, *His son John made the rescue* singles that son out from others with different names—but see also the discussion of appositives below.

Defining constructions are often called restrictive, because they restrict the meaning of the word or phrase they relate to. Like nonrestrictive elements, restrictive elements can be single words or phrases as well as clauses. Because they are an essential part of the meaning, they should not ordinarily be separated from the words they relate to by commas—though, as will be explained, they sometimes can and sometimes should be so separated when they begin a sentence and in certain special situations.

It is apparent that only the person who is writing about the water rescue can know whether *who is a good swimmer* is intended to be restrictive or nonrestrictive, defining or parenthetical. If we punctuate the phrase properly, we make our meaning unmistakable; if we don't, it is uncertain what we mean. In speech, we can hear slight pauses for the parenthetical construction and a run-together failure to pause for the defining construction. In writing, the presence or absence of commas (or other marks of punctuation that can play the same role, such as dashes or parentheses) makes the distinction.

His son John who is a good swimmer made the rescue is good news but bad punctuation. The lack of punctuation clearly tells the reader that both *John* and *who is a good swimmer* are defining elements, but that can't be the case, because surely only one son is named John. The clause *who is a good swimmer* must be considered a parenthetical element and thus be set off with a pair of commas or other marks. The word *John* may be either parenthetical or defining, depending on whether there is only one son or more than one. If it is defining, it should not be set off: *His son John, who is a good swimmer, made the rescue.* If it is parenthetical, it ordinarily should be set off—*His son, John, who is a good swimmer, made the rescue*—but see the discussion of appositives below.

In *His son, the one who is a good swimmer, made the rescue* the interrupting construction is obviously defining—it pins down which son is meant—but it just as obviously requires the commas, unlike the defining constructions in earlier examples. The reason is that *the one who is a good swimmer* is actually an alternate subject of the sentence; *The one who is a good swimmer made the rescue* is as grammatically valid a sentence as *His son made the rescue.* The complete sentence has two beginnings and one ending, and the commas are necessary signals of the second beginning. Although careful writers generally avoid having to begin sentences twice to make their meaning clear, alternate subjects are sometimes employed for rhetorical effect: *This sentence, this much-punctuated sentence, this self-interrupting syntactical situation, this tedious example, is a tedious example.*

Parenthetical and defining appositives

An appositive is a noun, or a group of words acting as a noun, that immediately follows another noun to define it or further explain it. *My friend Mary is getting married* uses *Mary* as a defining appositive, narrowing down *friend* to a specific friend, and no commas are used. *Mary, my friend from school, is getting married* uses *my friend from school* as a parenthetical appositive, and parenthetical commas are used. Note that a defining appositive restricts the meaning and makes the word it is in apposition to more specific, whereas a parenthetical appositive, though it may clarify and elucidate meaning, does not really restrict it. *Mary* in itself means a specific person; *my friend from school* may supply helpful additional information, but it doesn't make *Mary* any more specific.

When a noun and another noun in apposition to it are both completely specific, the noun in apposition is considered parenthetical: *My husband, John, is at work; John, my husband, is at work.* Both *John* and *my husband* are completely specific.

My sister Mary is getting married indicates by the absence of commas that *Mary* is defining—that is, that there is more than one sister. *My sister, Mary, is getting married* indicates by the

89

presence of commas that *Mary* is not defining but merely parenthetical—that is, that there is only one sister, whose name is provided as additional but not essential information.

The principle of setting off parenthetical appositives and not setting off defining appositives is very important. We cannot punctuate correctly without understanding it. Nevertheless, we do not always have to observe it to punctuate correctly.

Parenthetical commas can often be omitted in phrases such as *my husband John* and *my sister Mary*, even though there could be only one husband and there may be only one sister. *My husband John* can be considered a unit, somewhat like *my Uncle Bob*, rather than an ordinary case of noun and appositive; it often would be spoken without pauses. *My sister Mary* can also be considered a unit when the existence of other sisters is unknown or irrelevant; and conversely, *my sister, Mary*, with *Mary* treated as parenthetical, may be quite all right even if there are a dozen other sisters as long as Mary is the only possible one meant in the context. Some writers and editors always try to make the punctuation conform to the genealogical facts, but forcing such conformity may be a violation of common sense. Usually we can insert or omit commas in such phrases by ear—but only if we understand the principle we are observing or not observing. If we don't understand the principle, we don't have a trustworthy ear.

In other situations, failure to follow the principle is indefensible. *In his essay, "Self-Reliance," Emerson celebrated individualism* is a gross error. Since Emerson wrote more than one essay, *"Self-Reliance"* is defining, not parenthetical, and it should not be set off by commas (though the second comma is desirable, as explained below). Similarly, *An old saying, "Haste makes waste," was stamped on his forehead* is correct, but *The old saying, "Haste makes waste," was stamped on his forehead* is grossly wrong. The error is particularly common when the appositive is in quotation marks, perhaps because people with a hazy grasp of punctuation confuse apposition with direct quotation, which, as explained in Rule 2-11, is usually preceded by a comma: *Emerson said, "Self-reliance is an American characteristic."* However, errors with titles also occur frequently when the title is in italics rather than enclosed by quotation marks, as in *Faulkner's novel, The Mansion, is part of a trilogy.* The converse error, omitting commas when the subject of the sentence is already completely specific and the appositive is therefore necessarily parenthetical, as in *Smith's only poem "My Dog" was never published*, seems to be rare.

90

Introductory constructions

An introductory construction is anything that precedes the main clause, or the first independent clause, of a sentence. It may be a single word, such as *However*; it may be a phrase, such as *In view of the circumstances*; it may be a dependent clause, such as *When I'm ready*. It may be either defining or parenthetical. Frequently an introductory construction is followed by a comma, which serves as a signal that the main clause is about to begin.

I'll call you when I'm ready contains the defining dependent clause *when I'm ready*. *When I'm ready, I'll call you* puts the dependent clause first, as an introductory construction; *When I'm ready* is still a defining clause, restricting the meaning of *I'll call you*, but because it is introductory it can be set off with a comma. Thus after an introductory construction, a comma is not the signal of a parenthetical element but simply a clarifying pause.

A comma is not always required following an introductory construction—*When I'm ready I'll call you* is fine, since the introductory clause is short and very closely related to the main clause. The comma can sometimes be omitted even when the introductory clause is parenthetical, as in *Although he swims well he has no lifesaving training*, which might benefit from a comma after *well* but does not strictly require it. Commas or omitted commas are clear indications of parenthetical or defining constructions only when the constructions are not introductory.

We can usually "hear" whether the comma is desirable or necessary following an introductory construction. *When we're eating local politicians are not to be discussed* requires a pause after *eating* in speech and a comma after *eating* in writing, to keep *local politicians* from being momentarily misunderstood to be the direct object of *eating*. *Dinner being over we began to quarrel* requires a comma after *over* to separate the absolute phrase *Dinner being over* from the main clause; an absolute phrase, even though it is not an independent clause, is independent of the sentence containing it (see **absolute construction** in the Glossary/Index), and its independence is honored in speech with a distinct pause.

We can also hear when the comma is not permissible, as in *In the dining room, were twelve quarrelsome people*, which should not have the comma after *room*. In such cases the opening words are usually not an introductory construction at all but a displaced part of the predicate of the main clause (see the discussion of inverted sentences in Rule 2-5). Listening a little harder, we can hear when a permissible comma is not desirable, as in *A moment later, he left the room, and we discussed the issue more openly;* omitting the comma after *later* would make it more apparent that the introductory phrase modifies only *he left,* not *we discussed,* for which it is not a very suitable modifier—it indicates a point in time, and *we discussed* indicates an activity that extends over time. Without such conscious analysis, in saying the sentence we would tend not to pause after *later* but to pause after *room,* and good punctuation can be similarly unconscious—though we should expect to devote more conscious attention to writing than to speech, and analysis never hurts.

Therefore, however, in addition, and many similar words and phrases are usually followed by a comma when they are used to introduce a sentence: *Therefore, let's talk about something else.* There is some flexibility when such words and phrases are used in a compound sentence to introduce a second clause: *Tempers were beginning to rise, and therefore we changed the subject.* A comma after *therefore* would not be incorrect, but it would give the sentence a loose look, with no distinction made between the major pause after *rise* and the minor or missing pause after *therefore. Tempers were beginning to rise; and therefore, we changed the subject* uses a semicolon for the major pause and a comma for the minor one, which is correct but gives the sentence more punctuation than it really needs. (Grammar books of a century ago would require a comma between *and* and *therefore* as well—an example of the changes that "proper punctuation" has endured; we use lighter punctuation today.)

When we use introductory constructions in speech, we are often almost forced to pause after them if the following word is important to the grammar and meaning—a noun or an adjective, say—and is therefore stressed: *After Munich / war seemed unlikely.* We often aren't forced to pause if the following word is unstressed, as the articles *a* and *the* nearly always are: *After Munich a war seemed unlikely; After Munich the war preparations abated.* We can keep this fact in mind when we are deciding whether to set off introductory phrases, but it can't be the only basis for the decision; *When we're eating a local politician is not to be discussed* requires a comma after *eating* just as much as the slightly different earlier example does.

The most important thing to remember about introductory constructions is simply that they *are* introductory—they precede the beginning of the main clause—and whether they are defining or parenthetical and no matter how vital they are to the overall meaning, they may require or at least benefit from a comma to set them off.

The goal: punctuation that reinforces structure

This long rule is intended to increase the reader's awareness of the structure of sentences—of the ways in which the parts of a sentence combine their meanings to build the meaning of the complete sentence. Along the way, it has demonstrated ways in which punctuation, particularly the comma, can clarify and sometimes change sentence structure and meaning.

Punctuation does not always indicate structure, and many of the other rules in this chapter are concerned with its other functions. However, bad punctuation—not just the occasional error with an apostrophe but truly bad punctuation, consistently bad punctuation, such as one is apt to see in the letters column of a small-town newspaper, in committee reports, in almost any written effort that has not been professionally edited—is nearly always, I think, the result of failure to consider how sentences are structured and how punctuation can strengthen rather than contradict structure.

It seems a pity that only professional editors, and not all of them, can be expected to punctuate well. Professional editors have no monopoly on intelligence, on analytic ability, or on "communication skills"—on language. Nor should they have a monopoly on punctuation, which is a vital part of the written English language.

Editors have acquired their monopoly because many people who write, even many who write professionally, do not take punctuation seriously. They are quite willing to admit that they don't know much about it; they even make a virtue of their ignorance—they're concerned with important matters, with the broad picture, with the main thrust, and they gladly leave punctuation to the drudges who concern themselves with fussy details. They would be less willing to admit that they don't know much about relating ideas to one another, about language, about thinking. But in boasting of ignorance of punctuation, they may unknowingly also be admitting to a significant deficiency in these broader areas.

COMMA

The comma is by far the most frequent mark of punctuation within the sentence, and it is the most frequently misused. Its function is very simple: to separate one word, phrase, or clause from another. What is not always simple is determining whether such separation is correct. Also, the comma is not the only mark of punctuation that has this function. Semicolons, colons, parentheses, and dashes are separators too. Errors with commas frequently occur because the writer is unsure whether the comma or one of the other separators is required.

The ten rules that follow cover the most common proper and improper uses of the comma. For advice on when commas are desirable in a series of adjectives, as in *gray, cold, fretful sea* and *my three beautiful furry rabbits*, see Rule 1-20.

2-2   Separate independent clauses joined by *and*, *or*, *but*, *for*, and similar coordinating conjunctions with a comma or a semicolon.

We're going to discuss it, and then we'll decide what to do is a compound sentence—that is, it has two independent clauses. *We're going to discuss it* can stand alone as a complete sentence, and so can *Then we'll decide what to do*. When joined by *and*, the clauses are separated by a comma. A semicolon could be used instead, and if *and* is omitted, a semicolon should be used (see Rule 2-12). When *and* is supplied, a semicolon is usually an unnecessarily strong mark of punctuation; the comma is better.

Often when the second independent clause begins with an introductory construction (see Rule 2-1), the comma is misplaced: *We're going to discuss it and, when we've worked it out, we'll let you know* should have a comma after *discuss it* and no comma after *and*. The comma after *out* is optional in this example. See Rule 2-8 for similar problems with introductory constructions.

Exceptions

Let's sit down and I'll tell you a story is a compound sentence and could have a comma after *down*, but it is better without

94

the comma. This is often the case when the clauses of a compound sentence are short; the syntactical signal a comma would provide just isn't needed, because even though there are two clauses, the sentence can be absorbed as a unit. However, *We sat down and he told a strange story*, even though its clauses are short, would benefit from a comma after *down*, because the clauses are not as closely related and a pause between them seems natural—or at least it does to me. The distinction is subtle, and probably many writers would not use a comma in the second example either. Some writers punctuate lightly, omitting nearly all such optional commas; others punctuate more heavily, inserting nearly all optional commas. Whatever a particular writer's habit is, when a comma between compound clauses seems tedious and unnecessary it can be omitted.

I'll tell her that we're going to have lunch and then we'll discuss it also omits the comma between the clauses—but notice that they are no longer independent clauses but together make up the object of *I'll tell her*; they are noun clauses, a special type of dependent clause. Omitting the comma makes the sentence clearer in the example; if a comma is inserted after *lunch*, the reader can't be sure whether *then we'll discuss it* is one of the things *I'll tell her*—it might be an independent clause.

It's an unusual problem and no one knows much about it, but we're going to discuss it and then we'll decide is a double compound sentence—two independent clauses joined by *and* connected to two other independent clauses joined by *and*. We could put commas after *problem* and *discuss it*, but if we do, we had better change the existing comma after *about it* to a semicolon to avoid a loose string of three commas: *It's an unusual problem, and no one knows much about it; but we're going to discuss it, and then we'll decide*. This would have been considered the best way to punctuate the sentence a generation or so ago, and in formal prose it remains a good way, but the trend today is to use light punctuation. With only one internal mark, the comma after *about it*, the sentence is smoother and just as easy to understand.

When the board met yesterday, the topic came up and I discussed it with John has an introductory *when* clause followed by two independent clauses that are not separated by a comma. The meaning is clearly that the discussion with John took place at the meeting—that is, the introductory *when* clause modifies both the following clauses, not just the first

95

one. If we make it *When the board met yesterday, the topic came up, and I discussed it with John,* the meaning is no longer so clear; the discussion with John may have taken place before or after the board meeting. If it did not take place at the meeting, the sentence could be made unambiguous by adding a modifier—*and later I discussed it with John,* or *and I discussed it with John over lunch,* or whatever is the case. If it did take place at the meeting, the omitted comma between the independent clauses makes it clear enough.

As a general principle, it is sensible to omit a comma between independent clauses that are both modified by the same dependent clause or introductory phrase. *Tomorrow morning, I'll come over, and we'll see the lawyers in the afternoon* is not such a case—the second independent clause is not modified by *Tomorrow morning.* But *Tomorrow morning, I'll come over and we'll see the lawyers* is such a case, and though the comma omission is not required for clarity in this example, it is nevertheless desirable to indicate the shared relationship with the introductory phrase. (The comma after *morning* could be omitted in both examples; see the discussion of introductory constructions in Rule 2-1.) If in a given example of a shared introductory phrase the sentence begins to seem unwieldy and to require a comma between clauses just for ease of reading, it is likely that the sentence has outgrown its structure and should be divided or recast.

2-3   Do not separate two predicates with a comma unless the comma has a valid function.

We checked the books, and notified the lawyers contains two predicates: *checked the books* and *notified the lawyers.* The comma after *books* has no function. In this simple sentence the functionless comma does no harm, but nevertheless, commas that have no function should be omitted, just as words that have no function should be omitted (see Rule 1-4).

In some sentences, such an unnecessary comma can cause confusion. *I told her that we'd checked the books and notified the lawyers* is unlikely to be misunderstood—I told her two things, that we'd checked the books and that we'd notified the lawyers. *I told her that we'd checked the books, and notified the lawyers* could mean that too, or it could mean I told her we'd checked the books and, in a separate action of mine, I notified the lawyers; the comma makes it uncertain whether the subject of *notified* is *I* or *we*. The reader expects the comma to signal something and is likely to invent a signal if none was actually intended. In the example, the reader may pick up the false but quite plausible signal that *notified the lawyers* is unlike *checked the books*—it does not connect to *told her that we'd* but to *I*. The reader then will consider the sentence equivalent to the unambiguous compound sentence *I told her that we'd checked the books, and I notified the lawyers.* Omitting the comma does not completely prevent misreading, but it makes misreading much less likely.

Valid commas between predicates

We'll check the books, and let you know next week justifiably uses the comma to make it clear that the adverbial phrase *next week* modifies only *let you know*, not *check the books*. Often a comma is helpful to counter the tendency of modifiers to link themselves to the wrong word or phrase.

He left, and mixed a tray of drinks justifiably uses the comma to keep the first verb from momentarily seeming to share the object *a tray of drinks* with the second verb, as in *He mixed and served a tray of drinks*. Verbs joined by *and* are likely to be perceived as having equal effects on the rest of the sentence containing them.

He mixed the drinks, then served them necessarily uses the comma, because the *and* that would normally join the predicates is missing. The comma often is used in place of a missing word (see Rule 2-9), and even though its primary function is to separate—to prevent conjunction—it can replace the conjunction *and*; the slight pause it represents leaves mental room for the omitted word.

He said, "I'll make some drinks," and left the room necessarily uses the comma after *drinks* to mark the end of the quotation and to balance the comma after *said. He said, "I'll make some drinks" and left the room* violates the standard pattern for punctuating dialogue, and though many writers do invent their own patterns, this particular violation seems pointless. Another mark of punctuation can be used if appropriate, as in *He said, "Would you like a drink?" and left without waiting for an answer* or even *He said, "I'm sure we're all thirsty"—and passed out*, but some mark should be used.

The comma is also standard between predicates when *he*

said or a similar attribution follows a quotation: *"I'll make some drinks," he said, and left the room.* The comma after *said* might be omitted, and it often is in such sentences, but it reflects a pause in speech and helpfully separates quote-and-attribution from verb-and-object, countering the tendency to perceive joined verbs as sharing whatever object is handy. See Rule 2-11 for a discussion of other complications with quotations and attributions.

He left the room, and a moment later reappeared with a tray of drinks justifiably uses the comma to indicate a lapse in time. *He left the room, and reappeared with a tray of drinks* is even more justifiable, since the explicit time-lapse indication *a moment later* isn't there. If the sentences were spoken, we would probably hear a pause after *room* in the first sentence and would almost certainly hear a pause in the second.

A moment later he left the room, and reappeared with a tray of drinks also justifiably uses the comma; without it, the reappearance would seem instantaneous—more the behavior of a magician than of a good host. Note that a comma after the introductory adverbial modifier *A moment later* would be undesirable; omitting it helps link the modifier to *he left* and separate it from *reappeared.* *A moment later he left the room and reappeared only after dinner* gives the reader a serious jolt; the contradictory time indications *A moment later* and *only after dinner* seem to quarrel over the two verbs. A comma after *room* is required to signal that only the first verb is modified by *A moment later*, and it would be desirable to go further and repeat the subject, making a compound sentence: *A moment later he left the room, and he reappeared only after dinner.* Introductory adverbial modifiers are particularly likely to extend their effect further than intended.

He is doing well, and will rise to the top if he keeps it up justifiably uses the comma to separate predicates that are quite different in significance—one is a statement about the present and the other is a prediction. When the verbs in a compound predicate are in different tenses, as they are in the example, a comma is often justifiable. Somewhat similarly, *He was not doing well, and was eaten by a bear* has a justifiable comma; the verb in the first predicate is active, the verb in the second predicate passive.

He had little money, and was deficient in looks as well is justifiable because the second predicate, *was deficient in looks as well*, is being presented as a parenthetical construction (see Rule 2-1). The comma after *money* could be eliminated, but the sentence would then have a different effect; the second predicate would no longer seem a humorous addition but just a second fact.

Often a sentence with a compound predicate can be made to conform strictly to the rules by inserting a pronoun and making it a compound sentence, as in the above example *A moment later he left the room, and he reappeared only after dinner.* However, to reuse another example, *He left the room, and he reappeared with a tray of drinks* is a very tedious sentence; that sentence is better without the second *he.*

Note that *He left the room, mixed a tray of drinks, and returned* has commas simply because there are three predicates, not just two; see Rule 2-6.

2-4   Do not separate subject and verb, verb and object, or preposition and object with a comma.

The cavalry, artillery, and light infantry, were drawn up in order incorrectly has a comma after *infantry,* as if the writer began inserting commas to separate the elements of the compound subject, forgot to stop, and separated the compound subject from its verb as well. Rarely, *and* is omitted from such a series and it is followed by a comma for a deliberate rhetorical effect, as in *Cavalry, artillery, infantry, were drawn up in order;* this special case is discussed further in Rule 2-6. Also note that *All the troops, cavalry, artillery, and light infantry, were drawn up in order* requires the comma after *infantry;* the subject of the sentence is *troops* alone, and *cavalry, artillery, and light infantry* is a parenthetical appositive, which, as explained in Rule 2-1, requires commas before and after.

The sun shining through the unshuttered window, woke her early incorrectly has a comma after *window,* separating the subject from the verb. For some reason this error is very common. Note that instead of removing the comma after *window* we could add a comma after *sun,* changing the meaning slightly by making *shining through the unshuttered window* a parenthetical phrase rather than a defining phrase (see Rule 2-1). A parenthetical construction and its enclosing commas can come between a subject and its verb, since the parenthetical construction is outside the grammar of the basic sentence, which in the example is *The sun woke her early.*

The figures do not prove but merely suggest, that trouble is ahead incorrectly has a comma after *suggest,* separating it from its object, which is the noun clause *that trouble is ahead. The figures do not prove, but merely suggest that trouble is ahead* is also incorrect, because it separates *prove* from its object, which is also *that trouble is ahead;* the verbs share the same object. The sentence must have either two commas or none. Two commas make a proper parenthetical interruption, but a single comma cuts one verb or the other from its object.

He praised and gave recommendations to, Smith, Brown, and Jones incorrectly has a comma after *to,* separating the preposition from its compound object. The example could represent a failure to insert the second comma to embrace a construction intended to be parenthetical—a comma after *praised* would make the comma after *to* correct—or a mistaken feeling that a list such as *Smith, Brown, and Jones* needs some sort of punctuation to introduce it. No such introductory punctuation is needed when the list fits into the grammar of the sentence (see Rule 2-16).

Exceptions

Whatever is, is right is right enough, because the comma helpfully separates *is* from *is.* With the comma omitted, the sentence is not wrong but is more difficult to read. The comma is sometimes desirable to separate repetitions of a word: *Whoever feels, feels sorrow now; Those who vote only infrequently, infrequently are satisfied with their representation.* Such repetition of words is usually a rhetorical device to give special force to speech, and as we might expect, the rule-flouting comma is very clearly heard if the examples are read aloud. Note that repetitions of a word don't always require separation to be clear, either in writing or in speech, and sometimes separation is wrong. *I said that that man must go* and *The pollsters hoped to determine what kind of women women would vote for* would be incorrect with a comma between the repeated words.

We who breathe, love benefits considerably from the comma, because *love* could be misread at least momentarily as a noun rather than a verb—that is, as the direct object of *breathe.* Again, the comma would be clearly heard in speech, separating the two stressed verbs.

The fact is, you're wrong is right, though the comma could be omitted too. The comma substitutes for the missing word *that:*

The fact is that you're wrong. It could also be interpreted as an instinctive way of countering the strong tendency of *is*, and any form of the verb *to be*, to link itself with whatever immediately follows, as in *The expectation is falsely high earnings will be reported*, which most readers would have to read twice to get the meaning—which is falsely high, expectation or earnings?—and they couldn't be sure of it then. Inserting a comma after *is* would make the meaning clear, though inserting *that* there instead would be better (see Rule 1-3). Of course, *that* should be inserted after *high* if that is the intended meaning.

Exceptions to Rule 2-4 tend to fall into the two categories discussed—the rhetorical (*Whatever is, is right*) and the casually elliptical (*The fact is, you're wrong*). If what we're writing is neither rhetorical nor casual, we probably won't need to make exceptions.

The question is, what are we to do now? is, however, an exception that can occur in straightforward formal writing. The enclosed direct question is a subject complement, linked to the subject of the sentence, *question*, by the verb *is* (see **linking verb** in the Glossary/Index), and normally it is as wrong to separate a verb from its complement as it is to separate a verb from its object. However, the comma, or else some more elaborate punctuation, is desirable to introduce the question. Note that the sentence is difficult to read aloud without a pause. (As it happens, a pause after *question* instead of after *is* would work too, but punctuating the sentence to indicate such a pause would contradict its syntax; see the introduction to this chapter.) There is further discussion of such enclosed questions in Rule 2-20.

2-5 Do not ordinarily put a comma between an adjective or adverb and a following word or phrase that it modifies. When an adjective or adverb follows the modified word, usually set off the adjective, but not the adverb, with a pair of commas.

A sunny, day is too obvious a mistake for almost anyone to make, but *Day broke on a gray, cold, fretful, sea* is an example of a surprisingly common pattern. It may sometimes be an absentminded error; the writer may simply forget when to stop inserting commas to separate a series of adjectives (see Rule 1-20) or may have it in mind to add a fourth adjective but be unable to think of one. If the modified element is not a single word but a compound noun, such as *merchant ship* or *dishwater blonde*, the first word of the compound may be mistakenly treated as part of a series of adjectives and preceded by a comma, as in *Ours was a solid, old-fashioned, merchant ship* and *Our captain was a blowsy, profane, dishwater blonde*, which should not have their second commas.

Similarly, *We were becalmed—foully, despicably, damnably, becalmed* incorrectly has a comma between the last adverb and the modified verb.

Parenthetical modifiers

A single comma separates a modifier from what it modifies, but two commas make it parenthetical: *It was my third, and last, voyage around the Horn.* This is quite all right (see Rule 2-1). The adjective *last* still modifies the following noun, *voyage*, but it is given a special emphasis by the parenthetical commas.

The same optional use of parenthetical commas is correct with adverbial modifiers. In *I had lately, and gladly, assumed the post of second mate*, the adverb *gladly* gets special emphasis from the commas and still is linked to the following word, *assumed*. But parenthetical commas are sometimes essential around adverbial modifiers just to keep them from modifying the following word. *We were incredibly becalmed in January* and *We were, incredibly, becalmed in January* are quite different in meaning; the first sentence states that the degree to which we were becalmed was incredible, the second that the whole situation, being becalmed in January, was incredible. In the second sentence, the adverb *incredibly* modifies the whole sentence, not just the following verb (see the discussion of sentence modifiers below and the discussion of adverbs in Rule 1-20). It could, of course, be put at the beginning of the sentence—*Incredibly, we were becalmed in January*—but it gains some emphasis by interrupting the basic sentence *We were becalmed in January* (see the discussion of parenthetical constructions in Rule 2-1).

When the modifier follows the modified word

The sea, fretful, lashed the ship is the typical pattern for adjectives that follow the word they modify. The comma after *sea* is not really separating adjective from noun, it is one of a pair of commas that make the adjective parenthetical. The adjective is added almost as if it were an afterthought, but also gains some emphasis just from being displaced from its "normal" position. However, sometimes adjectives that follow the noun are not parenthetical; see the discussion of inversions below.

When an adjectival modifier is not a simple adjective but a participle or an adjectival phrase or clause, it is set off by commas if it is parenthetical but not if it is defining (see Rule 2-1): *The boy, swimming rapidly, reached the child in time; The boy swimming rapidly is the captain's son.* Such modifiers rarely precede the modified word, except for defining participles: *The swimming boy is his son.*

The sea lashed fretfully at the ship is the typical pattern for adverbs that follow the word they modify. A single comma after *lashed* would be incorrect, and parenthetical commas around *fretfully* would be pointless. However, parenthetical commas do occasionally have a function in adverbial constructions: *The wind blew, fitfully but energetically enough for some progress, until late afternoon; The afternoon lull was expected and therefore accepted, gratefully by the crew and sullenly by their captain.*

Sentence modifiers

Imperceptibly, the becalmed ship lost ground to the current separates adverb from verb not only with the comma but with the subject of the sentence, *the becalmed ship.* The comma is desirable but optional; removing it would slightly affect the tone of the sentence but not its grammatical relationships or basic meaning. Adverbs can wander from the words they modify (see Rule 1-20), but *Imperceptibly* has not actually wandered. It is a modifier for the entire sentence, not just the verb, as in the comparatively flat *The becalmed ship imperceptibly lost ground to the current,* in which the adverb is closely linked to the verb by its position. In the example, the meaning is not much changed. This is not always the case. *Incredibly, we were becalmed in January,* an example used above in the discussion of parenthetical modifiers, changes its meaning entirely if the adverb, instead of modifying the whole sentence, is bound to the verb by changing its position and omitting commas: *We were incredibly becalmed in January.*

However, therefore, and similar words often begin sentences. They are considered adverbs, but they usually modify everything that follows—they are sentence modifiers, not just word or phrase modifiers, and they are somewhat like conjunctions, linking what follows to what precedes. Usually a comma after such introductory adverbs is desirable, and often it is necessary to prevent misreading: *However the captain shouted orders and organized the men into work parties* reads at first like a sentence fragment (see Rule 1-1), with *However* meaning *in whatever fashion* rather than *but.*

Inversions

Sunny and warm, September is the best month has a comma between adjectives and noun but is nevertheless correct. It is an inversion of *September, sunny and warm, is the best month,* in which *sunny and warm* is parenthetical, and when the word order is changed, the comma after *warm* is retained to show that *sunny and warm* is still parenthetical—descriptive rather than defining.

Days sunny and warm gave way to days dank and cold omits parenthetical commas for the following adjectives for the excellent reason that the adjectives are not parenthetical—they are very strongly defining. Commas would signal that they were parenthetical and would make nonsense of the sentence.

Complications in inverted sentences

Toward the hazy cape, rowed the weary whalers is an inverted sentence, with the subject, *the weary whalers,* at the end instead of the beginning. The inversion is not wrong, but the comma after *cape* is wrong. *Toward the hazy cape* is a prepositional phrase with a clearly adverbial function—modifying *rowed*—and it should not be separated from *rowed* by a comma. When the subject of a sentence follows the verb—that is, when the usual word order has been inverted—we are apt to supply too much punctuation, thinking readers need some kind of help. They may need help, but excessive punctuation can't provide it.

Toward the hazy cape, the weary whalers rowed, with subject and verb in normal order but the adverbial *Toward the hazy cape* at the beginning rather than at the end, is only partially inverted. The comma after *cape* is still wrong, though less obviously so; in fact, older grammars advise setting off such adverbial phrases with commas, as if they were ordinary introductory constructions (see Rule 2-1). In standard order, the basic sentence is *The weary whalers rowed toward the hazy cape,* and when the adverbial *toward the hazy cape* is moved to the beginning, it is still part of the basic sentence, not an introductory construction.

In the weathered whaleboat, were the weary whalers is an extreme example of the same error. *In the weathered whaleboat* is not only a defining phrase and part of the basic sentence, it is a grammatically necessary part of the predicate, which, untangled, is *were in the weathered whaleboat.* The verb *were* has no meaning by itself. There should, of course, be no comma.

Toward the hazy cape, the weary whalers spied a far-off sail can have the comma, though it could be omitted too. *Toward the hazy cape* has become somewhat hazy itself, however; it is not clear what the phrase modifies, and Rule 2-5 can't make it clear, though awareness of the rule and the principle behind it—that it should be clear what a modifier modifies—increases awareness of the weakness of the sentence. It probably indicates the direction in which the rowers spy the sail, but if so, it does not directly modify *spied* but an understood participle: *Looking toward the hazy cape, the weary whalers spied a far-off sail.* Or it could be taken as an adjectival phrase, modifying *sail,* rather than an adverbial one: *The weary whalers spied a far-off sail toward the hazy cape.* Or it may indicate the progress of the whalers, as the participial phrase does in *Nearing the hazy cape, the weary whalers spied a far-off sail*—in which case, considering the rearward-facing position of rowers, the sail is not in the direction of the cape but somewhere in the opposite quadrant. *Toward the hazy cape* has such an ambiguous connection to the rest of the sentence that it doesn't matter whether it is followed by a comma. Sometimes inverted sentences need more than careful punctuation to eliminate ambiguity—they must be recast, usually by reversing the inversion and linking the modifying phrase clearly to the word it modifies.

Inverted sentence are by no means always bad. An inverted sentence that is ambiguous in isolation may be unambiguous in context. Even if it isn't, the ambiguity may somehow make the sentence more effective and thus be justifiable. Deliberate ambiguity is a common and useful literary technique. Accidental ambiguity, however, even when the context clarifies it, is hard to justify, and accidents are frequent in inverted sentences.

2-6   Use a comma before *and*, *or*, or *nor* preceding the last of a series of three or more words or phrases.

The safe contained coins, jewelry, and documents has a series of three nouns. *He emptied the safe slowly, carefully, and completely* has a series of three adverbs. *He came in, sat down, and began to tell his story* has a series of three predicates. *His manner was not shifty, shy, or sheepish, but his flying, fluttering, and flouncing hands suggested some deep anguish* has a series of three adjectives and a series of three adjectival participles. In all such cases, I advise using a comma before the *and* that connects the last item in the series to the preceding items.

This rule is old-fashioned. Most newspapers and magazines do not use the comma before *and*—called the final serial comma—and a few book publishers recommend not using it. Don't use it if you don't want to. However, Rule 2-6 is splendidly simple, and I think it is defensible on two grounds.

First, the comma is clearly heard in a spoken series. We say *coins and jewelry* with no pause, but we say *coins, jewelry, and documents* with a pause after *coins* and an equal pause after *jewelry*. Omitting the comma ignores one of the functions of the comma—to indicate a pause in speech.

Second, even those who prefer not to use the final serial comma should use it sometimes.

I opened with the last of my red chips, he began to bring out his blue ones, and you folded is a series of three clauses. Even if one of the clauses is removed from the sentence—*I opened with the last of my red chips, and you folded*—it is still a compound sentence and the clauses should be separated by a comma (Rule 2-2). Thus those who customarily omit the final serial comma should make an exception for a series of clauses.

I remember the gleam of the rain-washed pavement, the distant clatter of streetcars, the garlicky aroma wafting from the restaurant downstairs and the simple dress she wore is one of those jocose examples invented by writers like me to bully readers and attempt to amuse them. But such sentences do occur. Thus those who customarily omit the final serial comma must take special care to make an exception when the final item in the series can be misread as part of the preceding item. Misreading is likely when the items in the series are not just single words.

Other well-known references are Skillin and Gay, Fowler and Strunk and White does not indicate which of the last three names are joint authors and which is a lone author. It requires a comma after *Fowler* to make it clear that *Fowler* is one book and *Strunk and White* another. Thus those who customarily omit the final serial comma must make an exception when the last or next-to-last item in the series contains *and.*

Why bother making exceptions? Play it safe and use the final serial comma.

Use of the final serial comma does not, unfortunately, always guarantee that a series will be read correctly. *They invited Smith, the chief of police, and me* could mean that three people were invited or that only two were invited, with the appositive *the chief of police,* correctly set off by commas, identifying Smith. Such ambiguity is common. In the example, it could be avoided by using dashes instead of commas if only two people were invited or by rewording—perhaps replacing *the chief of police* with *Chief of Police Brown*—if three were invited.

When *and, or,* or *nor* occurs more than once in the series

The safe contained coins and jewelry and documents needs no commas. When *and* is repeated after every item but the last, no punctuation is necessary, just as no pause would be necessary in speech. Similarly, *His manner was not shifty or shy or sheepish* and *His manner was neither shifty nor shy nor sheepish* need no commas. Commas can be used, however, to produce a deliberate cadence: *His manner was not shifty, or shy, or sheepish.* Usually if the commas are used, they should be used consistently after every item, including the last if the sentence continues—*His manner was not shifty, or shy, or sheepish, but seemed strained*—because they make each item after the first a parenthetical addition, and by Rule 2-1 the commas should be in pairs.

Various complexities are permissible. *His manner was not shifty, or shy or sheepish, or even much of a manner at all; yet his hands, flying, fluttering and flouncing, and flirting with each other, suggested some more than ordinary concern* uses the commas and absence of commas with deliberate intent to connect some items in the two series more closely than others.

When *and, or,* or *nor* does not occur at all

The safe contained coins, jewelry, documents and *The beach swarmed with men, women, children* must have the comma between the last two items of the series they contain, since the conjunction *and* is missing. Omission of the conjunction is a rhetorical device with a rather vague effect. Perhaps most often it suggests that the series could continue but the writer doesn't want to trouble the reader by naming every item. In the second example, however, the series seems complete—*Men, women, children* exhausts the apparent category, humanity—and although omitting *and* does have an effect, it is difficult to define.

Sometimes a comma is used after a series that contains no conjunction: *Coins, jewelry, documents, covered the floor; Men, women, children, lay asprawl on the sand; No man, woman, child, dared defy the lifeguard.* This deliberate violation of Rule 2-4 perhaps heightens the effect of the omitted conjunction, whatever that may be, and it does reproduce a deliberate effect in speech, a sort of caesura in the middle of a statement. Thus usually we can "hear" the comma if it is desirable. If we cannot hear it, perhaps we should not only omit it but put the conjunction in and make the series straightforward.

False series

I opened with the last of my red chips, began to bring out my blue ones, and you folded is punctuated as if it contained a single subject and a series of three predicates. However, it contains two subjects—the last predicate has its own subject, *you.* The comma after *chips* should be replaced by *and* (Rule 2-3), and the comma after *ones* should remain (Rule 2-2): *I opened with the last of my red chips and began to bring out my blue ones, and you folded.* The error is very common; it is basically an error of parallelism, discussed in Rule 1-5. Before punctuating something as a series, make sure that it really is a series—that is, a listing of parts that have identical grammatical significance. Two predicates and a clause do not make a series. Nor do two objects and a predicate: *He picked up a king, a jack, and added another king* should be corrected to either *He picked up a king, a jack, and another king* or *He picked up a king and a jack and added another king.*

2-7   Don't automatically use commas to set off a negative element from a following positive element in *not . . . but* constructions.

He opened the book, not to read it, but to seem occupied is, in my opinion, overpunctuated. The comma after *book* would rarely be heard in speech; the comma after *it* might not be heard either.

Most punctuation guides do prescribe commas around a negative element such as *not to read it* in the example above. I don't know why they do. The infinitive phrase *not to read it* is not a parenthetical element (see Rule 2-1); if it were, then *He opened the book but to seem occupied*, with *not to read it* omitted, would be a good sentence, and it isn't, unless one claims that the conjunction *but* has mysteriously transformed itself into an adverb meaning *only*, as in *Life is but a dream.* The commas have no necessary function at all, either as indications of spoken delivery or as signals of grammatical structure.

There is a strong tendency to punctuate such sentences as they would be spoken: *He opened the book not to read it, but to seem occupied.* The comma—or pause—after *it* doesn't signal the end of a parenthetical element, it signals that what follows is in some way opposed to what precedes. I hope this tendency prevails, but meanwhile I must point out that it breaks the accepted rule.

However, it is permissible to omit both commas: *He opened the book not to read it but to seem occupied* is acceptable according to at least some major modern punctuation handbooks, and it follows the current trend toward light punctuation. The omission is virtually required by idiom when the negative element is very short: *They advised making not war but love; He gave not time but only money to the cause; I think not she but he is to blame.* I recommend omitting both commas whenever the sentence reads better without them, and would not condemn anyone who omitted just the first comma.

When a negative element follows a positive element

He opened the book to seem occupied, not to read it requires the comma to separate the positive element from the following negative element. The comma is clearly heard if the sentence is spoken. In certain constructions the comma can be omitted: *He came to conquer not to serve; He will leave in shame not in honor.* Commas could be used in these examples, but the omission gives them a rhetorical effect—it reflects the ringing way they might be spoken.

He opened the book to seem occupied, not to read it, and to conceal the spot on his tie requires two commas to set off the negative element between two positive elements. The negative element can be considered a parenthetical construction, since if it is removed the sentence remains a good one and the basic meaning is unchanged.

Confusion with *not only . . . but*

He opened the book, not only to read it, but to seem occupied is wrongly punctuated; it is a misapplication of the common rule—disputed by me—that negative elements should always be set off. The sentence has no negative element; both *not only to read it* and *but to seem occupied* are positive. There should be no comma after *book,* and the comma after *it* is optional.

Not only did he hope to seem occupied, but he wanted to read the book is a different situation; the comma is correctly used to separate two independent clauses, though it would not be incorrect to omit it in this example (see Rule 2-2).

2-8   Don't ordinarily put a comma after a conjunction just because what follows is an introductory word, phrase, or clause. This rule applies not only to coordinating conjunctions such as *and*, *but*, and *or* but to subordinating conjunctions such as *that*, *if*, and *when*.

The wind had risen, and, throughout the night, the rain beat against the windows and *The storm was over, but, in its aftermath, the heavy rain continued* are overpunctuated. The *and* in the first sentence and the *but* in the second are coordinating conjunctions, connecting independent clauses. There is no reason to have commas after them; a conjunction should not have its joining function contradicted by a comma.

I often see such unnecessary and illogical commas in carefully edited books and magazines. They are a hangover from past centuries, when commas were used much more heavily; they violate the overriding general principle of modern punctuation—to use punctuation lightly and omit it when the signal it would give is false or unnecessary.

The commas after *night* in the first sentence and *aftermath* in the second are optional to set off the introductory phrases (see Rule 2-1). It would be somewhat better to omit them, since in each case the introductory phrase is short and reads smoothly without a pause into the final clause. Moreover, it is the presence of these commas that makes the definitely undesirable commas after *and* and *but* seem to belong—the phrases *throughout the night* and *in its aftermath* are made to look like parenthetical constructions, and the commas are apparently properly paired; we don't have the much more obvious error of a lone, orphaned comma, as in *The storm was over, but, in its aftermath the heavy rain continued*. But the phrases are not parenthetical. We can test this by removing the initial clause of each sentence and putting the phrase in question after rather than before the remaining clause. If the phrase is parenthetical, a comma will appropriately signal the fact (see Rule 2-1). In *The rain beat against the windows, throughout the night* and *The heavy rain continued, in its aftermath*, the commas are obviously false signals, unless an odd effect, an unnatural pause, is intended.

111

When *that, if, when*, and similar words introduce subordinate clauses, they are acting as subordinating conjunctions. *That* is also considered a conjunction when it introduces a noun clause that is the object of *said* or a similar verb, as in *He said that he would go*. Rule 2-8 applies to these conjunctions just as it applies to *and* and *but*, and thus *He said that, if it rained, he would stay home* is excessively punctuated. The clause *if it rained* is set off as if it were parenthetical, but it is not—it is a defining clause, as is clear if the order of clauses is changed: *He said that he would stay home if it rained.* In the original sentence, the comma after *that* should definitely be omitted; the comma after *rained* is optional, but it would be better to omit it too, since the introductory clause is very short and the omission makes it a bit clearer that the entire word group *if it rained he would stay home* is the object of *He said*.

If, in the first part of the year, the market rallies, we'll be rich is also excessively punctuated. Omitting the first two commas improves the sentence. It could be further improved by a straightforward word order: *If the market rallies in the first part of the year, we'll be rich.*

He said that, although he couldn't stay long, he would come differs from the preceding examples in that the dependent clause *although he couldn't stay long* is not defining but parenthetical (as is any clause beginning with the subordinating conjunction *although*, since the word can't restrict the meaning of anything but can only elaborate on the meaning). Nevertheless, there is no justification for the comma after *that*. The entire word group *although he couldn't stay long, he would come* is the object of *He said*, and putting a comma in front of it is like improperly separating verb and object (see Rule 2-4), though the intervening *that* makes it less obvious that the separation is being committed. The comma after *long*, marking the end of the introductory clause of the two-clause word group, is optional but quite desirable, both because the clause is not very short and because the meanings of the clauses it separates are opposed.

We had thought that, considering your woeful position, we might buy you out is a similar case, with an undesirable comma between *that* and the parenthetical phrase *considering your position* (which looks like a dangling participle but is nevertheless acceptable—see Rule 1-21).

When a comma is necessary or acceptable

It had better rain, or, he thought, he would have to go is not a violation of Rule 2-8. The pronoun and verb *he thought* are like an attribution such as *he said* and require a comma before and after (see Rule 2-11). In structure the sentence is equivalent to *"It had better rain, or,"* he said, *"I will have to go."* Although the sentence looks odd as a direct quotation because the attribution isn't where one would expect it, the punctuation is correct.

He was relieved when, the weather having turned bad, he didn't have to go is correctly punctuated; the absolute phrase *the weather having turned bad* requires the commas.

There are times when an introductory construction that follows a conjunction is so much an interruption in the sentence that a comma is needed both before and after the interruption. *The storm was over, but, apparently because of the heavy rain, the river was in flood* benefits from the commas around *apparently because of the heavy rain* because it allows *but* to carry its force, after the interruption, to *the river was in flood; but* does not apply to the interrupting phrase at all, and the insulating comma indicates that. *She thought that, boss or not, the man was a swine* benefits from the commas setting off *boss or not,* because the interruption is elliptical—with the ellipsis filled out, the sentence would be *She thought that whether he was the boss or not the man was a swine*—and the commas somehow give the reader time to make sense of the ellipsis. *Smith, Jones, and, somewhat later, Brown arrived* benefits from the commas because *somewhat later* interrupts an otherwise very regular series, and the commas apologize for the interruption. These and similar exceptions can be justified and therefore do not contradict the rule: Don't *ordinarily* put a comma after a conjunction *just because* what follows is an introductory word, phrase, or clause.

2-9   Don't use a comma to indicate an understood word unless the sentence requires it for clarity.

His office gave him little satisfaction, and his wife, none requires the comma after *wife* so that the reader can be certain that something has been omitted there—a repetition of *gave him.* Without the comma, the sentence could easily be taken to mean *His office gave him little satisfaction and gave his wife none.* (The comma after *satisfaction* in the original sentence does not prevent this misreading, because it may be there just to give the second predicate a parenthetical effect; see Rule 2-3.) Note that the comma after *wife,* required as it is, is really rather a nuisance; *His office gave him little satisfaction, and his wife gave him none* gives more satisfaction as a sentence.

He quit his job, and his wife, her excessive social engagements does not require the comma after *wife,* because the only possible meaning is *his wife quit her excessive social engagements.* We can take out the comma and still be sure both where a word is missing and what the word is. Since the comma has no function, it should be taken out.

He had always had a secret yearning for a more contemplative life, she for a life of toil and accomplishment requires no comma after *she,* even though the omission—*had always had a secret yearning*—is quite long.

He now has ample time to dream, she the self-respect of the breadwinner, they the loving marriage both had longed for, and I the suspicion that their solution would not work for us requires no commas to indicate the omissions, even though the omitted word changes form: *she has; they have; I have.* (See also Rule 1-2.)

The use of a comma to indicate an understood word or group of words is apt to make a sentence seem old-fashioned and fussy. If a sentence does seem to require such a comma for clarity, perhaps the sentence can be improved by supplying the omitted word or words or by otherwise changing the basic sentence to make the comma unnecessary.

2-10   Use commas to set off names and similar words in direct address.

I am writing, Mr. Smith, to confirm our agreement and *Tell me, my friend, whether this is a sensible course* are typical examples of forms of address that interrupt the course of a sentence. If the commas are omitted in the first example, *Mr. Smith* becomes the indirect object of *writing* and the meaning of the sentence changes completely. If the commas are omitted in the second example, there is no change in meaning, but the pauses that would be very clearly heard before and after *my friend* are not indicated and the sentence is quite hard to read; *Tell me my friend whether this is a sensible course* looks like gibberish at first glance. The interjection of a form of address is actually a parenthetical construction (see Rule 2-1), so commas should be used.

If the name or other form of address occurs at the beginning or end of the sentence, it is, of course, set off with only one comma: *Mr. Smith, I am confirming our agreement; Tell me whether this is a sensible course, my friend.*

Exception

But officer, I wasn't speeding and *Oh my friend, what a fool I've been* omit the first of the parenthetical commas. The omission indicates the way the sentences would be spoken. Similarly, *Yes sir* and *No sir*—sometimes *Yes sir* is spelled *Yessir*, and considerably less often *No sir* is spelled *Nosir*—indicate a failure to pause in speech before the form of address. It is quite proper to omit the first comma when quoting speech and in some cases when trying to give written words some of the immediacy of speech, but in writing that is meant to be read rather than imagined as spoken, Rule 2-10 should apply.

2-11   Use a comma, or some other mark of punctuation, before or after direct quotations to set off *he said* and similar attributions.

"I'm looking for a job," John said (or *said John*) and *John said, "I'm looking for a job"* show the standard form for attribution. We might consider the comma a violation of the rule against separation of verb and object (Rule 2-4), since the quotation is essentially the object of *said*. However, the comma represents a pause that is very clearly heard if the examples are spoken, and it is required by convention if not logic. (Of course, conventions are very often deliberately flouted in fiction, particularly conventions that apply to dialogue. Many novelists invent their own conventions.)

The most common verb in attributions is *said*, but there are many others—*he wrote, he shouted, he asked, he whimpered*—and they all follow Rule 2-11. Sometimes the verb is poorly chosen: *"Don't come any nearer," he hissed* is poor because there are no sibilant sounds in *Don't come any nearer* to be hissed. Sometimes the verb has nothing to do with spoken or written expression at all but indicates manner or some accompanying action: *"Please come closer," he smiled; "I've never seen you before," he frowned.* This is a kind of shorthand for *he said with a smile* or *he said, frowning;* it is a convenient shorthand and has been in use for generations, but it is not logical and it annoys some readers. One repair is to replace the comma with a period, making what was an attribution an independent sentence: *"I've never seen you before." He frowned.*

Other marks of punctuation

John said: "I'm looking for a job" replaces the comma with a colon. This is correct, and some writers always use the colon rather than the comma when the attribution precedes the quotation. However, the colon is a strong mark of punctuation, and it holds the reader up more than the comma does. It may be desirable, particularly in nonfiction, to hold the reader up— perhaps to emphasize the importance of what follows or to introduce a quotation that runs for several sentences—but otherwise the comma is smoother.

"I'm looking for a job!" John said; "I'm going to look—" John began; "Should I look for a job?" John asked; and *"I think maybe I'll . . ." John began* do not have commas because other marks of punctuation have displaced them—an exclamation point in the first example, a dash in the second example, a question mark in the third example, and points of ellipsis in the fourth example. It would be logical to use the comma as well as the other mark of punctuation—*"I'm looking for a job!," John said; "I think maybe I'll . . . ," John began*—but this is contrary to American conventions of punctuation; the comma is not used with the exclamation point, dash, quotation mark, or ellipsis but is displaced by the stronger mark. One does see such retained commas in published material; they shouldn't be there. (However, the comma can be used with points of ellipsis in scholarly quotation, as explained in Rule 2-27. See also the discussions of titles ending with the question mark or exclamation point in Rules 3-20 and 3-21.)

The position of commas and quotation marks is also governed by convention rather than logic; see Rule 2-24.

When the sentence continues after the quotation

"I'm looking for a job," John said, and smiled broadly and *John said, "I'm looking for a job," and smiled broadly* are the standard patterns. In the first, a comma follows *said* even though it separates two predicates (see Rule 2-3). In the second, a comma occurs at the end of the quotation to balance the comma preceding the quotation; *John said, "I'm looking for a job" and smiled broadly* is unbalanced and ignores a pause that the sentence would require if spoken.

John exclaimed, "I'm looking for a job!" and smiled broadly; John said thoughtfully, "I wonder if I should try . . ." then gazed into space; John asked, "Could you lend me four hundred dollars for a new suit?" and smiled radiantly"; and John began, "I think I'll—" but looked up angrily as I began to laugh make the best of a difficult situation. The exclamation point, the points of ellipsis, the question mark, and the dash do not satisfactorily balance the comma before the quotation, but we should not add a balancing comma to them. I usually accept dialogue punctuated as in the examples when I find it in manuscripts I am editing—it is common enough, and it breaks no rules—but I consider it clumsy. I suggest avoiding it; it is hard enough to compose good, graceful dialogue without bucking the strictures of punctuation conventions.

When the attribution interrupts the quotation

"I," John said, "am looking for a job" shows the standard form when the attribution comes in the middle of a quoted sentence: comma before and comma after, making the attribution parenthetical. (If the interruption of the quotation is not an attribution, dashes should be used, not commas: *"I"—John paused and seemed to glow with self-esteem—"am looking for a job."* See Rule 2-17.)

"I'm looking for a job," John said, "will you let me marry your daughter?" is, however, incorrect, because the attribution comes between sentences, not in the middle of one. If we take out the attribution, we have *"I'm looking for a job, will you let me marry your daughter?—*two independent clauses joined only by a comma, which is an error (see Rule 2-12). There could be a semicolon instead of a comma after *said*, but this is rarely seen; the simplest and clearest punctuation is a period after *said*, with *will* then capitalized as the beginning of a new sentence.

"I'm looking for a job," John said, and then, "Will you let me marry your daughter?" is correct, with the comma and *and then* connecting the independent quotations.

Exception: when *that* appears between *said* and the quotation

He said that, "regardless of cost" he would pay is a serious error of punctuation. So is *He said, that "regardless of cost" he would pay.* There should be no comma either before or after *that* when it is used in this way as a subordinating conjunction (see Rule 2-8). This is true both when the quotation is just a fragment, as in the example, and when it is a complete sentence: *He said, "Britain will pay for this"* but *He said that "Britain will pay for this."* (Usually it is pointless and clumsy to introduce a directly quoted complete sentence with *that* unless the enclosing sentence continues, as in *He said that "Britain will pay for this" and that he would send a bill.*) The construction *he said* is a straightforward attribution that requires the conventional comma, but *he said that* is not a straightforward attribution. The conjunction *that* makes what follows a noun phrase or noun clause, and thus this exception to the rule is really an example of the larger class discussed below.

He said that, "regardless of cost," he would pay seems to escape the serious error of *He said that, "regardless of cost" he would pay* because it makes the quotation parenthetical; the basic sentence is thus *He said that he would pay,* and the parenthetical quotation is enclosed by commas. However, the comma after *that* should not be there whether or not *regardless of cost* is enclosed in quotation marks (see Rule 2-8). The punctuation looks all right because one is so accustomed to seeing superfluous commas after *that,* and there is a second comma that seems to balance the first (actually its legitimate function is to separate the introductory *regardless of cost* from *he would pay;* the separation is optional, as explained in Rule 2-1). But it is not all right. At best the sentence is overpunctuated, unless for some reason the quotation is really intended to be parenthetical—a possibility in some contexts.

Exception: when quotations are noun phrases

Sometimes a quotation is used as a noun within the grammar of a sentence: *His battle cry is "More benefits and fewer taxes";*

His reply was "No comment." This can be the case even with verbs such as *say* that are normally used in attribution: *He never said "I agree" when he did not; He was a poor pickpocket, for as he passed on he always said "Thank you."* In each of these examples, the quotation is not an ordinary one but a group of words acting grammatically as a noun—the quotations in the first pair of examples are acting as subject predicates, and those in the second pair are acting as direct objects, which are grammatical functions of nouns. When a quotation is so used—as a noun phrase—it should not have a comma before it, nor should there be one between it and the attributive construction: *"No comment" was his reply.* Similarly, *The Quaker maxim "Do well before you do good" was his motto* should have no commas; the quotation is a defining appositive (see Rule 2-1).

Quotations are frequently in a gray area between true quotations and noun phrases, allowing us to reason in either direction. It is often convenient to reason in the direction of considering them noun phrases, because otherwise we may have to insert not just one comma but two, cluttering up the sentence and obscuring the way it would probably be spoken. Thus *Not until he said "Thank you kindly, ma'am" did she realize that her wallet was gone from her purse* would have to be *Not until he said, "Thank you kindly, ma'am," did she realize that her wallet was gone from her purse*—a comma is required after *ma'am* to balance the comma after *said*. My preference is to omit the commas.

In the preceding example, the attribution is complicated by its grammatical relationship to the rest of the sentence—it is an adverbial clause modifying the verb in the main clause, *realize.* In general, complication may make it desirable to consider a quotation a noun clause and omit a comma. Any attribution that is a subordinate clause introduced by *not until, when, as soon as,* or some other adverbial conjunction is likely to present such complication. *He paused politely when she cried, "Stop thief!"* would be better without the comma. Note that although *She cried, "Stop thief!"* would be spoken with a pause after *cried,* there would be no pause, or only a very slight one, after *cried* in the original sentence, in which the subordinating conjunction *when* makes everything that follows a modifier of *paused.* Similarly, *The man who wrote, "We are all thieves at heart," must have kept unusual company,* in which the attribution is in a subordinate clause introduced by the relative pronoun *who,* would benefit greatly from removal of the commas.

119

Negation is a complication. *She did not say "Please stop"* seems much better to me than *She did not say, "Please stop."* When a quotation is something not said rather than something said, it really isn't dialogue, and a comma preceding it—a convention specifically of dialogue—seems more hindrance than help. The effect of the negation may even carry over to a quotation in a following clause or sentence, making it appropriate to omit a comma before that quotation too: *She did not say "Please stop." She said "Stop thief."*

Sometimes one can think of a good reason to omit the comma, sometimes only a tenuous one. In *He muttered something like, "Don't take the Constitution too seriously"* the comma jarringly separates the preposition *like* from its object, the quotation—good reason, I think, to omit it (see Rule 2-4). In *I heard people in the crowd say, "I thought this was a republic," and "The king should live so long"* I would omit both commas, which clutter the sentence, and perhaps argue that the quotations aren't really dialogue but just samples of overheard utterances, so the standard convention can be suspended. Variations on conventional attribution do put strains on conventional punctuation; the simplest solution, of course, is to keep variations to a minimum.

On the other hand, sometimes a quotation that is quite clearly presented as a noun phrase may more naturally be preceded by a comma. For example, in *The big question to him was always "Did my novel hold your interest?"* the quotation is clearly functioning as a noun would—it is used as a subject complement—and there should not be a comma. But in *I asked, "So how do you like my new office?" but all he wanted to know was, "Did my novel hold your interest?"*—in which the quotation is again a subject complement—the comma is defensible; the grammar of the sentence may make the quotation a subject complement, but it is still being presented as an item of dialogue. Sometimes novelists, perhaps not the finest ones, seem to tire of he-said-she-said attributions and vary them with *His somewhat risky gambit was* and *her incredulous rejoinder was* and *The gentle ultimatum that after careful deliberation he chose to deliver was* and so on. Since these elaborations play the role of attributions, they might as well be punctuated like attributions and followed by a comma (or by a colon, a mild violation of Rule 2-16). The same goes for such attributions following the quotation: *"But you're only ten years old," was her incredulous rejoinder.*

The famous grammarian Henry W. Fowler did not like Rule

2-11; he wished that the convention did not exist and that any quotation could be treated as a direct object of the verb of attribution. If he had had his way, there would be no gray area between true quotations and "nounlike" quotations to puzzle the punctuator. However, human language does contain gray areas, and perhaps the more gray matter a human writer has, the more time he or she must expect to spend in those gray areas, trying to make words and punctuation better serve shades of meaning.

Just one further complication should be noted. Sometimes a noun phrase is presented as a quotation in a sentence, but without quotation marks: *The question is, which was ruder?* In this example the comma is needed to set off the question even though it is a subject complement. (Some writers would capitalize *which* here, just as one would if the question were in quotation marks; capitalizing is defensible, but a capital after a comma usually is an unnecessary surprise.) If the example is ended with a period instead of a question mark, however, the question becomes indirect (see Rule 2-20) and does not need setting off: *The question is which was ruder.*

SEMICOLON

The semicolon has two main uses: to separate independent parts of a sentence, and to separate elements of a series when some of the elements already contain commas. It can be thought of as a very strong comma, though it has some special powers too—it can connect as well as separate.

Some writers use semicolons when commas would be sufficient, and the result is apt to be an unnecessarily choppy style that slows the reader down. Others don't use the semicolon enough, and their sentences are apt to seem run-on and toneless. Still others don't use the semicolon at all, and unless they confine themselves to short and simple sentences, they commit real errors of punctuation by using commas where semicolons are required.

2-12   Use a semicolon to separate independent clauses that are not connected by *and*, *but*, or some other conjunction.

It's an unusual problem, no one knows much about it is an example of the so-called comma fault—using a comma to connect two independent clauses. The comma is not a connector; it is a separator. The semicolon, however, can function as both a connector and a separator, and at the same time: *It's an unusual problem; no one knows much about it.* If we use a comma, then we have to supply a connector—that is, a conjunction such as *and*: *It's an unusual problem, and no one knows much about it.*

We're going to discuss it, then we'll decide what to do may seem less obviously a comma fault, because *then* seems to be performing the role of a conjunction. But *then* here is an adverb, modifying *decide*; it is not a conjunction (see Rule 2-13). The comma should be a semicolon, or else it should be followed by *and*. Note, however, that *We discussed it, then decided* is correct. It is not a compound sentence. It merely has a compound predicate, and the comma indicates the missing conjunction *and*—an odd role for a comma, which normally prevents conjunction, but the pause it indicates represents the missing word.

Exception: the comma to emphasize

The problem was simple, the solution was difficult uses a comma instead of a semicolon to emphasize the contrast—in this case an antithetical contrast—between the two independent clauses. The comma is especially desirable if the second clause is made elliptical: *The problem was simple, the solution difficult.* If we make it *The problem was simple; the solution was difficult,* we lose some of the energy and pithiness of the original contrast.

We could quibble with this example and claim that it is not really an exception to Rule 2-12 but an elliptical sentence, with *but* understood after the comma: *but the solution was difficult.* An understood word—that is, a missing word—is often more conspicuous in its absence than it would be if it were present, because the reader has to supply it.

In any case, the comma is occasionally desirable when the rule calls for a semicolon. *He was not twenty, he was twenty-one* uses the comma to emphasize the contrast between a negative statement and a parallel positive one. *She was twenty, he was twenty-one* uses the comma not to emphasize contrast but to emphasize the slightness of contrast. *The problem was simple, the solution was simple* uses the comma to emphasize the absence of contrast. In all the examples of exceptions given here, the comma is not only justifiable but preferable.

If the independent clauses are considerably longer than they are in the examples above, if they do not balance so neatly, or if for any other reason the comma does not seem a sufficient signal to the reader that another independent clause is coming up, it is better to follow Rule 2-12 and use the semicolon.

Exception: the comma to indicate a continuing series or to heighten parallels in a series.

Smith couldn't vote because she was out of town, Jones couldn't vote because she was sick, Brown couldn't vote because he didn't know it was election day. Only 50 percent of the electorate turned out. This is an acceptable use of commas. A seemingly desirable *and* is omitted after *sick* chiefly to indicate that the series could go on (see Rule 2-6). Semicolons might not be quite as good, since the implication of an unfinished series wouldn't be as strong. At the same time, the commas make the parallel structure of each clause more evident. In a sense, a semicolon tells a reader to forget the grammar (if not the content) of what precedes, because a new independent clause is about to start. The comma makes it more likely that the reader will still be aware of the preceding grammar and will better appreciate the parallelism.

2-13   Use a semicolon to separate independent clauses that are connected by *however*, *thus*, *therefore*, *nevertheless*, and similar emphatic conjunctions.

The problem is difficult, however, we will solve it and *The problem is difficult, therefore we couldn't solve it* are far too loosely punctuated. In both examples the comma after *difficult* should be a semicolon.

Emphatic conjunctions such as *however* and *therefore* are not really conjunctions—they are adverbs. When they introduce clauses, they are classed as conjunctions or so-called conjunctive adverbs, but they don't lose their adverbial function and they don't gain all the powers of a true conjunction— that is, a coordinating conjunction such as *and* that connects elements of equal grammatical value. Therefore, use of the comma instead of the semicolon can be considered a violation of Rule 2-12, because the clauses are not connected by a true conjunction.

Most conjunctive adverbs—*however* is an exception—can be preceded by a true conjunction, making the comma correct: *The problem is difficult, and therefore we couldn't solve it.* (The semicolon would also be correct, if a stronger separation is wanted.) We can't double up true conjunctions, such as *and* and *but*, but we can pair a true conjunction and a conjunctive adverb, which suggests that conjunctive adverbs aren't very conjunctive.

Note that there is a third type of conjunction, the subordinating conjunction. In *Please attend the annual conference, where we will address the problem* and *We will hold the conference when I can attend*, the subordinating conjunctions *where* and *when* make the clauses they introduce subordinate—that is, dependent. Rule 2-13 doesn't apply, since it affects only independent clauses. Dependent clauses at the end of a sentence are usually preceded by a comma if they are parenthetical in meaning and not preceded by any punctuation if they are defining, as explained in Rule 2-1.

‖ **2-14 Use a semicolon to separate items in a series when some of the items already contain commas.**

The committee included Smith, Jones, and Brown is a straightforward series of three people. If we make it *The committee included Smith, the treasurer; Jones, the production supervisor; and Brown, the security officer*, we need semicolons to separate the items. Otherwise the series could be understood to list four or five people (not six, since *and Brown, the security officer* has to signify a single person).

I spoke to the chairman, I notified the treasurer, and I wrote an account of the action into the company record is a straightforward series of three independent clauses. If we add a dependent clause to one of the independent clauses, we may still be able to get away without using semicolons: *I spoke to the chairman, I notified the treasurer, who hadn't been at the meeting, and I wrote an account of the action into the company record.* But if we keep adding complications, we soon need semicolons to help the reader grasp the structure of the sentence: *I spoke to the chairman, who told me that he, like other members of the board, disapproved; I notified the treasurer, who hadn't been at the meeting; and I wrote an account of the action into the company record.* If only commas were used, the sentence would still mean the same but would be difficult to read.

Using a comma instead of a semicolon before *and*

Some stylebooks, including *The New York Times Manual of Style and Usage*, prescribe a comma rather than a semicolon before *and* in a series that otherwise uses semicolons: *The committee included Smith, the treasurer; Jones, the production supervisor; Brown, the security officer, and Green, the legal counsel.* It is true that the semicolon is not needed before *and* to prevent ambiguity, but the switch from semicolon to comma is pointless and jarring. I recommend using semicolons all the way through, just as I recommend using the final serial comma (see Rule 2-6), which newspapers in general do not use.

COLON

The specific function of the colon is to introduce whatever follows: a list, a statement, an example, or anything else that the earlier part of the sentence has led the reader to expect. The use of the colon in the preceding sentence is typical. Sometimes the colon is mistakenly used when no punctuation is necessary—the subject of Rule 2-16.

This is not the only common function of the colon: many writers also use it instead of the semicolon or the dash to link independent clauses when the second clause restates, explains, or expands on the first clause. The colon in the preceding sentence is an example. This use has long been standard in British writing, and it is becoming more common in American

125

writing. However, American writers sometimes seem not quite certain which use they are making of the colon and are consequently not certain whether the following word should be capitalized—the subject of Rule 2-15.

The colon also has various conventional uses, such as to separate hour from minutes when figures are used for time of day (see Rule 3-5) and to separate chapter from verse in biblical citations and volume from page in scholarly citations. Some writers use it instead of a comma to introduce a quotation after an attribution such as *he said* (see Rule 2-11).

2-15   Do not capitalize a normally lowercase word after a colon unless what follows the colon is a grammatically complete sentence and the colon is being used primarily to introduce rather than to link.

This rule is often difficult to apply when a grammatically complete sentence follows a colon, because it is not always easy to decide whether the colon is primarily introducing or linking. Some older punctuation guides, including the first edition of this book, advise always capitalizing after a colon when what follows is a grammatically complete sentence—a very easy rule to follow, but changing American punctuation practices have made it a poor one.

The colon before a list or other fragment

Three people stood before us: the chairman, the treasurer, and the security officer has a lowercase word after the colon. The words following the colon do not form a grammatically complete sentence; standing alone, they would be a fragment. The colon is used quite formally to introduce the list of officials. The dash could be used instead (see Rule 2-17); it would make the sentence less formal and put less stress on the introduced words, as if they were being offered almost as incidental information. A semicolon should not be used; the semicolon cannot introduce a list, and it would give the clear, and false, signal that an independent clause was about to begin.

We knew what sort of man our chairman was: honest, able, vindictive has a lowercase word after the colon; again, the following words do not form a sentence. *We knew when to pay attention: when his nostrils began to flare* has a clause after the colon, but it is a dependent clause, not a grammatically complete sentence, so again the word following the colon is lowercase.

We can confidently not capitalize any normally lowercase word when the words following the colon do not constitute a grammatically complete sentence.

The colon to introduce a grammatically complete sentence

The chairman offered us the following choice: We could jail the treasurer or fine the security officer has a capitalized word after the colon. The words following the colon are a grammatically complete sentence, and the colon clearly introduces that sentence. In a sense, the colon divides the example into two separate sentences, just as a period would, but the colon also indicates that the first sentence introduces the second. Note that the phrase *the following* almost always leads to a colon; in the example, neither a semicolon nor a dash can take the place of the colon.

The chairman offered us a shocking choice: We could jail the treasurer or fine the security officer is quite similar. Again the independent clauses are almost as separate as a period between would make them. However, in this case the colon can be replaced by either the semicolon or the dash. The dash would perform the same introductory function as the colon but in a less formal way. The semicolon would obscure the introductory effect of the colon and suggest instead that what follows merely explains or expands on what precedes; this may be appropriate if earlier sentences have made it quite clear what the choice is and if the example sentence is not really introducing the choice but merely summing up. If either the dash or the semicolon is used, we must lowercase *We*, because neither mark of punctuation can join two sentences—they can only join parts of a single sentence.

The chairman raised a question: Should we jail the treasurer or fine the security officer? uses the colon to introduce a question. A dash could be used in place of the colon, for a distinctly informal effect; *should* would then, of course, be lowercased.

Theoretically, at least, a semicolon could be used, since one of the primary functions of the semicolon is to join independent clauses, but it is hard to imagine a context that would make it desirable for the example. The semicolon does not introduce, and introduction of the question seems to be the intent of the sentence.

Sometimes a colon is used to introduce more than one sentence. *We had several choices: We could jail the treasurer. We could fine the security officer. We could do both. We could do neither.* This should be avoided, because unless there is a new paragraph after the colon, the introductory effect of the colon does not carry well beyond the first sentence. In the example, a period would be preferable to the colon. A colon that ends a paragraph, of course, is understood to introduce everything that follows, and usually there must be some clear indication of where the introduced material ends, perhaps several paragraphs later.

The introducing colon after a fragment

Jail the treasurer or fine the security officer: those were our choices has a grammatically complete sentence following the colon, but only a fragment preceding the colon. It is an inversion of *Those were our choices: to jail the treasurer or fine the security officer*, or perhaps of *Our choices were to jail the treasurer or fine the security officer*, in which no colon is needed or permissible (see Rule 2-16). If in the inverted sentence we capitalize *those* as the beginning of a grammatically complete sentence, we seem to put behind us the words up to the colon; they are somehow orphaned. It is better to lowercase *those*, maintaining a closer connection with the opening words.

The colon to link a grammatically complete sentence

The chairman offered us a shocking choice: several of us gasped has a lowercase word after the colon. The words following the colon are a grammatically complete sentence, but the colon is not introducing that sentence, it is merely linking it to the preceding sentence.

This use of the colon is very common in British writing and is becoming more common in American writing, though most

Americans continue to favor the dash and the semicolon, either of which would be correct in the example. What, one may ask, does the linking colon do that a dash or semicolon would not do?

In the example, the clause *several of us gasped* has a specific logical connection to the earlier word *shocking;* it supports the idea that the choice was shocking. In *Not one of the men showed up: they all claimed to be sick* and in *Not one of the men showed up: two of them claimed they'd never even been notified,* the second clauses expand on and give additional detail to the first clauses. The semicolon would do the job in all these sentences, but since the semicolon commonly links clauses that not only have no grammatical interdependence but have no close logical interdependence, we would lose the signal of a logical connection that the colon provides, perhaps as a remnant of its introducing function. The dash would do the job too, and it would signal a logical connection. However, the dash is apt to suggest that what follows is incidental, even parenthetical, as in *Not one of the men showed up—they all claimed to be sick—so the women made the decision alone.* Also the dash is perhaps excessively versatile, able to play too many roles; the linking colon is more precise.

When the linking colon is properly used, it signals not just the structure of the sentence but a relationship between the meanings of its parts. It has its place in modern American punctuation, at least for writers who understand its rather subtle advantages. As an editor, I find it a nuisance; I must decide whether to capitalize the word following each colon and therefore whether the colon's intent and effect is primarily to introduce or to link, and colons in other people's real-world sentences are rarely as easy to make decisions about as the colons in my made-up examples. As a writer, I am leery of it; I prefer to use semicolons and dashes for linking and reserve the colon for introducing. Yet as a reader, I like it.

I do think that the linking colon can be overused. It checks the reader, and repeated tiny checks are irritating, especially when the logical connection that the colon signals could be more smoothly and exactly made by supplying a subordinating word or phrase between the clauses. Thus while *The women were angry: they believed the men had been deliberately rude* is acceptably punctuated, *The women were angry, for they believed the men had been deliberately rude* is more explicit; the connection only implied by the colon is established by *for,* and the subordination of ideas—first the anger, then the reason for it—is perhaps better made by a main clause and a subordinate clause than by two independent clauses. The colon is a very strong mark and should be used with restraint.

The colon may not seem so strong to the British, who sometimes use it in long sentences in which semicolons indicate the strongest separations: *The men were embarrassed; the women were angry: they believed the men had been deliberately rude; the children knew they would have to provide a diversion.* American readers may have a little trouble with such punctuation, since they perceive the colon as stronger than the semicolon; they would be happier with a dash.

An alternative: always lowercase

Some writers, and especially some editors, may object to the apparent inconsistency in capitalization that Rule 2-15 requires; sometimes grammatically complete sentences after a colon will begin with a capital and sometimes they won't. If consistency is considered essential, I suggest always lowercasing rather than always capitalizing. In sentences in which the colon is clearly introducing, the colon will not lose that effect. On the other hand, always capitalizing will interfere with the intended effect of the linking colon; the capital will give the false signal that the following clause was intended by the writer to be a separate sentence rather than an expansion of or comment on the thought of the preceding clause.

2-16   Do not use a colon to introduce words that fit properly into the grammar of the sentence without the colon.

The forbidden activities included: smoking, drinking, and smiling should not have the colon. The colon violates a principle stated for commas in Rule 2-4; there should be no punctuation separating the verb *included* from its object.

However, mild beer was permitted in: one's own quarters, the back kitchen, and the sacristy should not have the colon. This colon violates the same principle; there should be no punctuation separating the preposition *in* from its object.

The abbot later added to the list of proscriptions: lechery, blasphemy, and murder should not have the colon. Again, the colon should not separate verb from object; the intervening phrase *to the list of proscriptions* makes no difference.

The forbidden activities included the following: smoking, drinking, and smiling is correct. If the colon is removed, the words that follow do not fit properly into the grammar of the sentence. The phrase *the following* always calls for a colon if the sentence continues.

Sometimes the colon takes the place of a phrase such as *for instance* or *namely*. *Some unanticipated misbehavior occurred in the first week: lechery, blasphemy, and murder* is the same as *Some unanticipated misbehavior occurred in the first week, namely, lechery, blasphemy, and murder*. The dash could be used instead of the colon, with very little difference in effect in the example.

DASH

The dash is almost excessively versatile. It can interrupt the grammar of a sentence in the same way a colon can, and in a few other ways as well. A pair of dashes can enclose a parenthetical construction, as a pair of commas or parentheses can. The dash can separate independent clauses, as a semicolon can. And it can do some things no other mark of punctuation can. Any castaway on a desert island who is allowed only one mark of punctuation could do worse than choose the dash, which might even be useful for spearing fish. However, the rest of us should not habitually neglect other marks of punctuation in favor of the dash.

The dash is often badly typed. It should be typed as two hyphens, with no space before or after it, except that there can be a space after it to indicate an interrupted statement followed by a completely new statement—one of the many uses discussed in Rule 2-17.

2-17   Don't overuse the dash; consider using other marks of punctuation.

We've been spending the summer pretty much as usual—partly in Vermont—partly on Long Island—usual problems with jellyfish out there—and it's been a cold summer in Vermont—but that must make you New Yorkers laugh—or cry—we certainly don't have much to complain about—

This letter could continue indefinitely with no punctuation but dashes; it probably would end with *that's about all the news—see you soon— Love—*

There is really nothing wrong with a heavy use of dashes in casual correspondence. The dashes make such correspondence like friendly conversation: disjointed and elliptical, but easy and even pleasant to absorb. Many of us are fussier about our letter-writing style, but few of us are offended by someone else's dashed-off letter.

Not all writing, however, is friendly correspondence; writing that is not casual should not be casually punctuated. Dashes have a place in even the most formal writing, but they should not displace other marks of punctuation that are more appropriate.

Appropriateness is often a matter of judgment. The following discussion of specific uses of the dash reflects my own judgment, which is harsher than my self-discipline; I tend to overuse the dash myself.

Dashes for parenthetical constructions

He was seen—not for the first time—in the bar downstairs before eleven o'clock could be punctuated with either commas or parentheses instead of dashes. Commas would make the sentence blander, giving *not for the first time* about the same importance as the rest of the sentence. Parentheses would tend to make *not for the first time* seem less important than the rest of the sentence. The dashes, breaking sharply into the progress of the sentence, give what they enclose some emphasis. In a given context, the emphasis might be appropriate or inappropriate.

It was obvious—could there be any question?—that he had a serious problem could be punctuated with parentheses instead of dashes, but not with commas; commas cannot enclose a grammatically complete sentence as parentheses and dashes can, and in any case a comma should not be used with a question mark (see Rule 2-21). Since the intrusion of a complete sentence, and a question at that, in the middle of another sentence must represent a sharp break in thought, dashes are usually better than parentheses.

The dash to connect independent clauses

I felt I had to speak to him—he was setting a bad example for the other salesmen could be punctuated with a semicolon or even a colon (see Rule 2-15) instead of a dash, since either can be employed to link independent clauses. However, note that in the example the dash is not just linking the clauses but taking the place of an understood word, *because* or *for,* that would make the second clause dependent on the first in grammar as it is in thought. This use of the dash is correct but can make sentences seem not just casual and informal but lazy and loose. *I felt I had to speak to him, because he was setting a bad example for the other salesmen* is a tighter sentence.

It is by no means always poor to connect independent clauses with a dash. *I called him into my office before lunch—he had just reappeared* is quite all right, at least in the informal account in progress. The dash is not taking the place of a subordinating word; the clauses are truly independent. The dash is probably better for this sentence than the semicolon, which doesn't have the added-on, parenthetical effect of the dash. The second clause could, in fact, be enclosed in parentheses instead of connected with the dash, but the dash does the job as well as they would, and generally it is best to save parentheses for times when they are really needed.

The dash to connect a phrase to the rest of a sentence

Tardiness, insolence, and drunkenness—these are things a manager must nip in the bud could have a colon instead of a dash, but the dash is far more common to connect a beginning phrase or other fragment to a main clause. The fragment may come at the end of a sentence too: *Certain things a manager must nip in the bud—tardiness, insolence, drunkenness.* In this example the colon has an edge over the dash, since introducing such a list is one of its precise functions. However, *I was surprised at his manner—open, innocent, and friendly* seems better with the dash, perhaps because the list of adjectives directly modifies the word preceding the dash, and a colon would make too great a separation. In effect, the dash or colon takes the place of a subordinating construction, which it would be better to supply in less casual writing: *I was surprised at his manner, which was open, innocent, and friendly.*

Usually it's possible to save the employee—with firm

enough action does not use the dash to connect the ending phrase—no connection is needed, since the ending phrase fits into the grammar of the sentence anyway—but to separate it and hence emphasize it. This is a special and useful function of the dash. A comma would provide a similar but much weaker emphasis.

The dash to indicate interruption

"I must speak to you about your midmorning boozing," I began politely. "We can't put up with—"
"But I don't drink," he interrupted.
"I— But you— You were seen—" I stopped, at a loss.

The dash is properly used to show interruptions in dialogue, whether another speaker does the interrupting or the original speaker cuts off abruptly.

Note that in the last item of dialogue in the example, the speaker has interrupted himself and begun new sentences. There are spaces after the first two dashes, and each new sentence begins with a capital letter. The dialogue could be treated as all one incomplete sentence; *"I—but you—you were seen—"* is perhaps less fussy, if also less precise, than the original example. A writer of dialogue can use either convention and trust that readers will accept it, but shouldn't use both indiscriminately.

Some writers use points of ellipsis—three dots—to indicate interruptions. Points of ellipsis are better used to indicate pauses in midsentence or sentences that trail off; they are not emphatic enough to indicate interruption and in fact almost contradict the intended effect. They should certainly not be used to indicate an interruption in the middle of a word; the dash is needed: *"But this morning you were obser—" I began.*

Dashes to set off material within a quoted sentence that is not part of the quotation

"I don't drink, but I do sell insurance," he went on. "If you don't like the way I sell it"—now his face was flushed, but with anger, not drink or shame—"I'll tear up this million-dollar policy I've just sold the bartender downstairs." Some writers use commas instead of dashes in this situation, just as they would for an attribution such as *he said* (see Rule 2-11), but interruptions should not be made to appear to be attributions.

In the example, beginning the interruption with *and* would make the commas acceptable, because it would make it immediately evident that what follows is not an attribution: *"If you don't like the way I sell it," and now his face was flushed, but with anger, not drink or shame, "I'll tear up this million-dollar policy."* This punctuation tends to even out the tone of the sentence, whereas dashes make the interruption quite emphatic; a writer may prefer one effect or the other.

Note the position of the dashes in relation to the quotation marks in the original example. Sometimes one of the dashes has to go within the quotation: *I said, "Even if you don't drink—and I'm not saying I believe you—" I was pretty angry myself now—"you're fired for insolence."* The punctuation is a somewhat clumsy compromise; it would be logical to put a dash on both sides of the second quotation mark, but that would be much clumsier. One can simply avoid such complications, of course, and many good writers of dialogue do—their dialogue is sharp and natural enough so that they do not have to interrupt it constantly to tell the reader how it is spoken.

Dashes—dashes—dashes—

As may have been noted, the examples throughout this rule make up a story. Each use of the dash is defensible, and some of the uses are better than any alternative punctuation. However, try reading all the examples consecutively. There are just too many dashes, even for this casual, informal account, and even if it is intended as a transcript of an oral account.

A worthwhile general principle is to avoid using more than two dashes in a sentence. *The next time I saw him in the bar he was drinking, all right—I'd never believed him about that— but he wasn't mourning, he was celebrating—because he'd taken that policy—the one he'd sold the bartender—across the street to Liberty Unilateral and gotten himself another job—at a guaranteed ten grand more a year.* Too many dashes.

It is also wise to avoid using too many sentences with dashes in the same paragraph. Useful as the dash is, it is basically an interrupting mark of punctuation and is always something of a hitch for readers, bringing them up short, jabbing them in the ribs. A paragraph should have an overall smoothness; it shouldn't repeatedly interrupt itself.

The dash with other marks of punctuation

The dash can be used with the question mark (Rule 2-21), the exclamation point (Rule 2-22), and the quotation mark (Rule 2-24 and this rule), and sometimes it occurs after a closing parenthesis (Rule 2-18).

In modern practice, the dash is not used with the comma, the semicolon, the colon, or points of ellipsis. This sometimes puts it at a disadvantage. For example, *He was with his new boss, whom I know—she's my ex-wife—and they pretended not to see me* has a comma after *boss* that would normally be balanced by a later comma, setting off the parenthetical subordinate clause beginning with *whom*, but that subordinate clause has its own subordinate clause, set off with dashes, and the second comma has been supplanted by the second dash. The punctuation in the example is correct, but *He was with his new boss, whom I know (she's my ex-wife), and they pretended not to see me*, with parentheses instead of dashes, is perhaps better, with both subordinate clauses properly set off.

Sometimes one sees the comma supplanting the dash rather than the dash supplanting the comma: *He was with his new boss, whom I know—she's my ex-wife, and they pretended not to see me.* This is wrong; the dash is a much stronger mark of separation than the comma, and in the example it makes the sentence fall apart. One could, however, uses dashes in place of the commas and a semicolon instead of the original dash: *He was with his new boss—whom I know; she's my ex-wife—and they pretended not to see me.* The second dash is doing double duty again, because normally one would put a comma between the independent clauses *He was with his new boss* and *and they pretended not to see me*, but the dash can do double duty, and in any case the comma could be omitted between the two short clauses (see Rule 2-2).

PARENTHESES AND BRACKETS

Parentheses have the obvious function of isolating some words from other words within a sentence, or some sentences from other sentences within a paragraph. They usually have the effect of making the material they enclose seem less important than the rest of the sentence or paragraph; they often imply that what they contain is incidental or digressive and could almost be skipped by the reader. They are indispensable to set off entire sentences from other sentences, but not to set off parts of sentences; there are much gentler ways of indicating that part of a sentence is parenthetical, in the sense discussed at length in Rule 2-1 and used throughout this book (see **parenthetical construction** in the Glossary/Index).

The most common problem with parentheses is not how or when to use them but how to use other punctuation—commas, periods, question marks, dashes, quotation marks—with them. This is covered in Rule 2-18.

Brackets are sometimes used within parentheses to enclose parenthetical material within parenthetical material. I have not included a rule about this use. (It is obvious enough [at least to likely readers of this book], and in any case should usually be avoided.) Usually it is better to use a pair of commas or a pair of dashes within parentheses rather than brackets. Aside from their use with parentheses, brackets do have certain necessary uses, and these are explained in Rule 2-19.

2-18   Put parentheses in the proper position when they are used with other marks of punctuation, and don't use other marks of punctuation in some circumstances.

The word *proper* in the rule above is significant. The placement of parentheses is governed by their function and is entirely logical. For example, a comma can never directly precede either an opening parenthesis or a closing one and can never directly follow an opening parenthesis, because there can be no logical function for such placements.

Before using parentheses in a given sentence or paragraph, consider whether they are really desirable. Perhaps they could be avoided by reorganizing the ideas in the sentence, the paragraph, or the whole written work. Frequent parentheses give the usually accurate impression that the writer has not put his or her thoughts in order and must constantly correct, explain, and qualify. Within the sentence, pairs of commas or dashes are very often preferable.

When parentheses enclose an entire sentence

The Smiths were giving a loud party. (We hadn't been invited.) At about two o'clock, I began to get annoyed. The enclosed sentence is independent of the sentences before and after. It begins with a capital letter. It requires a period, which must go within the closing parenthesis; putting the period outside the parenthesis is a very common error, probably more often careless than ignorant.

I called the police (they've heard from me before about the Smiths) and made a complaint; not too long afterward (my prominence gives me some clout in this town), a cruiser appeared. Each pair of parentheses encloses a complete sentence, but the enclosed sentences fall within another sentence, so no periods are used with them and they do not begin with a capital letter. In the example, pairs of dashes could be used instead of pairs of parentheses. The comma would have to be omitted, because the dash and comma cannot be used together (see the last paragraph of Rule 2-17), but it is an optional comma anyway (see the discussion of introductory constructions in Rule 2-1).

Both policeman got out (why should it take two for a minor complaint?) and went up to the house. If the enclosed sentence requires a question mark or an exclamation point, it gets one. Dashes could be used instead of parentheses, and the question mark would remain.

When parentheses enclose more than one sentence within another sentence

The policemen knocked on the door awhile (someone had started playing the bongos. How the policemen thought anyone could hear the knocking I don't know) and then banged on it with their nightsticks. There is a period between the two sentences enclosed by the parentheses, but no period after the second enclosed sentence. The first enclosed sentence begins lowercase, but the second begins with a capital. Dashes should not be used; only parentheses or brackets can make two or more sentences parenthetical.

It is inevitably somewhat clumsy to put multiple sentences in the middle of other sentences. Sometimes accepting this clumsiness may permit a sentence some desirable effect, perhaps forcing the reader to assimilate a complicated and twisted thought as a whole rather than in stages. More often there is little justification for the clumsiness, as in the example.

When the material enclosed by parentheses comes at the end of a sentence

Someone finally answered the door (after at least ten minutes of banging). The period is outside the closing parenthesis, since it's the period for the whole sentence, not just the part in parentheses. Putting the period inside the parenthesis in this situation is as common an error as putting it outside when the parentheses enclose an independent sentence, as discussed above. Even if the words in parentheses make a complete sentence, there is no period inside the parenthesis: *Someone finally answered the door (the police had been banging for at least ten minutes).*

If the enclosed material is a question, a question mark should usually be inserted, though sometimes it is optional: *I don't know what the Smiths had to celebrate (and who cares?).* Here the question mark could be omitted (see the exceptions to Rule 2-20). If the enclosed material is an exclamation, an exclamation point can be inserted. If the enclosed material ends in an abbreviation, there is a point both before and after the closing parenthesis: *The noise never stopped, though, and I almost called my private security firm (Noyse, Dynne and Co.).* Points of ellipsis can also be enclosed, though the clutter of punctuation is annoying: *I decided that would be too much (but if they keep this up . . .).*

When there is parenthetical material within parenthetical material

The next day, I hear—I didn't see it for myself because I had to go to work (it was a Sunday, but I'm a clergyman)—the police chief found the cops sleeping it off outside in the cruiser is correct.

The next day, I hear (I didn't see it for myself because I had to go to work—it was a Sunday, but I'm a clergyman), the police chief found the cops sleeping it off outside in the cruiser is also correct.

The parentheses and dashes in the examples are in principle interchangeable. Note, however, that the choice of which is used to enclose which affects the overall punctuation in the examples. There are really not just two but three parenthetical constructions. The comma after *day* signals the beginning of a parenthetical construction that encloses the other two and extends up to the subject of the main clause, *the police chief,* and we would normally expect a comma to signal the end of the parenthetical construction (see Rule 2-1). But in the first example there is no comma after the terminal dash, because the comma should not be used with the dash (see the end of Rule 2-17); the terminal dash is doing double duty, ending two of the parenthetical constructions. In the second example there is the expected comma after the terminal parenthesis, because the comma can be used with a closing parenthesis. However, now the dash before the parenthetical *it was a Sunday, but I'm a clergyman* is not balanced by a terminal dash. The terminal parenthesis replaces the terminal dash, just as a period would in a simpler sentence that ended there: *I had to go to work—it was a Sunday, but I'm a clergyman.* Parentheses always come in pairs, but a single dash (like a single comma) is often employed to make the end of a sentence parenthetical, and in the example it clearly makes the end of a larger parenthetical construction parenthetical. Though neither example is admirable as composition, the second example could be considered better punctuated, because it permits the comma—but as often as not the writer of such overly parenthetical prose loses all sense of the structure of the sentence and omits the comma anyway.

Brackets and parentheses could be used instead of dashes and parentheses to mark the structure of the examples, but brackets are best avoided except for the uses explained in Rule 2-19.

When parentheses are used with quotation marks

The cops didn't have much of an explanation (all they said was "We were keeping an eye on the Smiths' party"). The parentheses enclose the entire quotation, so the quotation mark goes inside the closing parenthesis. Note that there is no period after *party* and there is a period after the parenthesis.

The newspaper reported, "A strange illness overcame Mr. and Mrs. John Smith and their guests last Saturday evening (a form of food poisoning, Mr. Smith surmised)." The parentheses enclose only the last part of the quotation, so the quotation mark goes outside the closing parenthesis (and outside the period as well; see Rule 2-24).

When the material within parentheses is a source note following a quotation

Emerson said, "I hate quotations" (Journals, May 1849). There is no period after the quotation, even though Emerson put a period there. There is a period after the closing parenthesis of the source note.

Dickens has a character say, "I don't believe there's no sich a person!" (Martin Chuzzlewit). If an exclamation point or question mark ends the quotation, it is retained, but there is still a period after the closing parenthesis.

There is some disagreement about this convention—a few handbooks advise putting the terminal punctuation wherever it would go if there were no source note, then using just parentheses and no period for the source note. I have used the University of Chicago Press's *A Manual of Style*, which is particularly handy when principles of punctuation and conventions of typography overlap, as my authority.

2-19   Use brackets primarily within a quotation to enclose material that is not part of the quotation.

Parentheses within a quotation enclose material that is part of the quotation. Brackets are the only mark of punctuation that indicate that the enclosed material is not part of the quotation.

The mayor said, "John is my choice for treasurer" may not be clear if John has not been identified or if more than one John has been mentioned. *The mayor said, "John [Smith] is my choice for treasurer"* uses brackets to give the surname without misquoting the mayor.

The mayor said, "He is my choice for treasurer" can be clarified by replacing the pronoun with the bracketed name: *The mayor said, "[John Smith] is my choice for treasurer."* The pronoun could be allowed to stay—*The mayor said, "He [John Smith] is my choice for treasurer"*—but it is rarely necessary to hold the reader up this way; it is usually better to omit a pronoun.

Smith said, "The Bard of Amherst [Emily Dickinson, 1830–86] is my favorite poet" uses the bracketed material after *The Bard of Amherst* rather than in place of it, because it is not just a pronoun that would be displaced; the writer does not want to lose the epithet Smith used but does want to explain it.

The mayor said, "Smith [who is now out on bail] may not seem the obvious choice" uses brackets to supply material that may not be essential to clarify what the mayor said but that the writer thinks readers will find relevant.

Smith said, "I base my oratorical style on that of Pliny the Elder [actually, Pliny the Younger; the elder Pliny was a naturalist] and expect to overwhelm the electorate with my eloquence" uses brackets to enclose a correction. Such bracketed corrections are apt to seem snide and often are snide—which is all right when writers are being frankly derisive, but objectionable if they are just slipping in a little dig to make themselves appear superior to whomever they are quoting. The overuse of *[sic]* indicates such a smart aleck—*[sic]* is useful when it is important to point out an error, but it should not appear after every minor error; minor errors should either be allowed to stand for readers to notice for themselves or else be quietly corrected, except in works of literary, historical, or legal significance in which such correction would be an unacceptable violation of the text.

Excessive users of *[sic]* sometimes expose themselves: *"Who [sic] shall I say is calling?" she warbled* indicates that the writer, ignorant of Rule 1-6, thinks *Whom* would be correct.

Scholarly uses of brackets

The hand-printed first edition contained the epigraph "Vulnera[n]t omnes, ultima necat" ("All things wound, the last thing kills") uses brackets to enclose a single letter mistakenly left out of the Latin tag. A scholar discussing the epigraph would not want either to let the error stand or to correct it without comment, so would use brackets. Otherwise several extra words would be required to point out and correct the faulty Latin.

Sometimes several letters of a word are supplied in brackets, as to complete names that are given partly in initials in a quotation: *Smith claimed, "Chekhov was not seriously influenced by A[leksey] K[onstantinovich] Tolstoy."* Note that the points that would follow the initials in the unadorned quotation are omitted.

Brackets have special uses in various areas of learning. For example, in mathematics they enclose material that already includes items in parentheses, which is the opposite of their relationship with parentheses in English punctuation: $a = c[b + b(b-c)]$. Anyone in a special field of study needs a special handbook of usage within that field.

QUESTION MARK

The question mark usually indicates a full stop—that is, the end of a sentence. Occasionally it is used as an internal mark of punctuation, as in *Whatever it was that drove him—honor? greed?—he was a man driven.* It is also used within parentheses to express doubt about an immediately preceding phrase or fact: *Chaucer's dates are 1340(?)–1400.* This use within parentheses is overdone by amateurish writers, as in *The beds in the Grand Hotel (?) had no mattresses,* in which the question mark unnecessarily and annoyingly calls attention to the irony. Another habit of the amateur is using multiple question marks: *What, no mattresses???*

Aside from amateurish misuses, common errors with question marks include using them with indirect questions (discussed in Rule 2-20) and positioning them improperly when they are used with other marks of punctuation (discussed in Rule 2-21).

2-20   Use the question mark after direct questions but not after indirect questions.

Do you like zucchini? is a direct question, and it ends with a question mark. *She asked if I liked zucchini?* is not a question—it is a statement that contains an indirect question—and it should not end with a question mark. Usually an indirect question is phrased differently from a direct question: *He asked, "What is zucchini?"* is direct; *He asked what zucchini was* is indirect. Sometimes the phrasing is the same: *What is cooking? I wonder what is cooking.*

"Do you like zucchini?" she asked? and *"Do you like zucchini," she asked?* are both wrong. There should be a question mark after *zucchini* but a period after *asked*; the quotation is a question, but the full sentence is a statement, not a question. The errors are frequent, perhaps because when such a sentence is vocalized the voice tends to rise on *asked*, and a rising

inflection in speech almost always signals a question. In this case the ear cannot be trusted.

Does he like zucchini? she wondered is correct; there are no quotation marks around the question because it is not voiced, only thought, but it is still a direct question. *The question was, did he like zucchini?* is also correct; the past tense of the question may seem to make it indirect, but it is still direct. Note that *did* is not capitalized; it could be, and some editors routinely capitalize in such a situation, but a capital is a surprise after a comma and in the example would give the question more independence and emphasis than the writer may want it to have. Note also the comma after *was*, needed to set up the question, almost as a weak colon. We could, of course, actually use the colon and, in accordance with Rule 2-15, capitalize after it: *The question was: Did he like zucchini?* Or we could add quotation marks—which makes changing the tense desirable—and then would need no punctuation before the question, in accordance with one of the exceptions listed in Rule 2-11: *The question was "Does he like zucchini?"* These alternatives make the sentence rather stately, almost dramatic; the writer may prefer the smoother, more casual *The question was, did he like zucchini?*

Does he like zucchini? I wondered and *Does he like zucchini? Mary wondered* are correctly punctuated. Unfortunately, since *I* and *Mary* are necessarily capitalized, each example is apt to be perceived by the reader as two sentences instead of one, a misreading the writer may be tempted to prevent by mispunctuating: *Does he like zucchini, Mary wondered?* If the words are read aloud, the voice rises on *wondered* at least as strongly as on *zucchini*, adding to the temptation. In general, I advise not giving in, but see the discussion of dialogue in fiction below.

But did he like zucchini, I wondered, with a comma instead of a question mark (and a period at the end), is acceptable to avoid the ambiguous question mark; the past tense of the question lessens its urgency to the point that it hardly is a question. Even *But does he like zucchini, I wondered* may be acceptable in a narrative that has a deliberately flat, understated tone.

Exception: dialogue in fiction

In nonfiction, questions are likely to be infrequent, and Rule 2-20 can be strictly applied. But fiction typically contains

many questions—most conversations and even interior mono-
logues are apt to be full of them—and may also contain statements that the writer wants to inflect as questions. Strict
application of Rule 2-20 would make it hard to write good
dialogue.

A character in a novel is more likely to say *Does he like
zucchini, I wonder?* than to say *Does he like zucchini? I wonder.* That is, the "incorrect" punctuation in the first version
gives a better impression of the character's intonation than the
"correct" punctuation in the second. *I wonder if he likes zucchini?* is similarly defensible.

She thought I might not like zucchini and *You thought I
might not like zucchini?* are both statements, not questions,
but the question mark in the second example is nevertheless
appropriate to show a rising tone that expresses incredulity or
surprise, or perhaps anguished disingenuousness. The statement *I wonder if you could take away this zucchini?* uses the
question mark to indicate that the speaker is being plaintive,
not peremptory. Similarly, *How can I thank you for the zucchini!* may be a question in form, but is unlikely to be one in
intent; it is intended as an exclamation, and the exclamation
point gives a better sense of the spoken words than a question
mark would.

Some novelists take considerable freedom with punctuation
in dialogue. *"Did you know you were doing eighty," the trooper
said* uses the comma instead of the question mark to indicate
the bored, perhaps bullying tone of the trooper, who is making
a charge rather than asking a question; the reader may be jarred
a bit by the unusual punctuation, but does get the message. A
novelist should be permitted deliberate effects, although such
freedom can be abused; constantly odd punctuation is
tiresome.

*"He said he was Judge Crater," the trooper said. "He said he
was Judge Crater?" the desk sergeant said.* Obviously the first
statement really is a statement and the identical second statement really is a question, a request for confirmation, and the
punctuation is no surprise to the reader. Statements are frequently inflected as questions in dialogue.

Other exceptions

Often an instruction or command is phrased as a question, but
no question mark is used: *Would you attend to this immediately.* The intent is not to ask but to order, and the absence of

the question mark can be "heard"; the voice does not rise if the words are spoken as an order.

Statements are sometimes punctuated as questions for rhetorical effect. *They want to end the cold war? Maybe they'd like a hot one* uses the question mark to communicate the writer's attitude toward the statement—dubious and querulous, which is to say questioning—and also to mark the thesis-antithesis, blow-counterblow structure of the thought that the two sentences together communicate. Such rhetorical questions tend to harangue the reader, of course, but sometimes writers want to do that.

There are occasions in fiction when narrative sentences begin as questions but evolve into something else: *What woman could compare with Mary, the childhood playmate who glowed in his memory like a ruby, a distant fire at which he knew he would never warm himself, for each year he ran faster and faster from the ways of the gypsy camp.* A question mark at the end would be no service to the reader; the purple torrent has washed away the question. The writer can avoid such occasions, of course, but some good writers do not. An editor might as well accept whatever punctuation the writer has chosen.

2-21 Position question marks properly when using them with other marks of punctuation.

The position of question marks is always logical, though sometimes a compromise is necessary to avoid two question marks close together, and sometimes the convention prohibiting its use with the comma ignores logic.

The question mark should never be used with a period, except, of course, when the period is not a true period but merely a point indicating an abbreviation: *Is the proper form Ms. or Mrs.?* It can be used with points of ellipsis, too—points of ellipsis are not true periods.

The question mark should not be used with the comma. This causes a problem when the question mark ends a quotation and the sentence continues. *He asked, "Why me?" which seemed an odd question* seems underpunctuated, because if the quotation were not a question a comma would signal both the end of the quotation and the beginning of the second clause, as in *He said, "I suppose I deserve it,"* which seemed an odd remark. Nevertheless, *He asked, "Why me?,"* which seemed an odd question is wrong, and *He asked, "Why me?",* which seemed an odd question, with the comma after the closing quotation mark, is doubly wrong. The comma should not be used even though using it would be quite logical (see Rule 2-11). An exception is sometimes made when the question mark actually has no function in the sentence but is part of a title: *His first poem, titled "Why Me?," was dedicated to his mother.* This exception has some merit; it is discussed in Rules 3-20 and 3-21. Other exceptions are made in certain scholarly, legal, and other special contexts that are beyond the scope of this book.

Combining the question mark with the exclamation point—*Why me?!* or *Why me!?*—is usually frowned on as childish.

The question mark with the dash

He told me—who would have expected it?—that he had married again logically puts the question mark within the dashes that enclose the parenthetical question.

But do you suppose—? is an acceptable use of the dash and question mark to indicate a question that is cut off abruptly. However, the dash alone is sufficient if the phrasing indicates a question, as in the example. A novelist who too frequently combines dash and question mark in dialogue may leave readers feeling that all the characters are in a constant state of wild conjecture, psychotic indecision, or speechless wonder.

The question mark with the parenthesis

I think the company is bankrupt (who can think otherwise?). The question mark is part of the parenthetical question, so it goes within the closing parenthesis. Note the terminal period outside the parenthesis.

Are we bankrupt (as these figures suggest)? The question mark is outside the parenthesis, since the whole sentence is a question; the material within the parentheses is not a question at all.

Are we bankrupt (or do these figures lie?)? is permissible—a question mark for the parenthetical question and another for the whole sentence—but the clumping of punctuation is ugly. *Are we bankrupt (or do these figures lie)?* is also acceptable, and I think preferable, if for some reason one cannot go further and eliminate the parentheses: *Are we bankrupt, or do these figures lie?*

Are we bankrupt (or do these figures lie?), and if we are, what now? This is correct; the question mark is not directly followed by a comma because the closing parenthesis intervenes.

The question mark with the quotation mark

They raised the question "Are we bankrupt?" The question mark is inside the closing quotation mark, where it logically belongs. Note that no period is used. A period cannot go outside a closing quotation mark (see Rule 2-24) or directly after a question mark, so the period is just omitted.

Did they announce, "We're bankrupt"? The question mark is outside the closing quotation mark, since the whole sentence is a question and the material within the quotation marks is not a question.

Did they ask the question "Are we bankrupt?"? is logical, but here logic must give way to compromise; the very ugly clumping *?"?* is condemned. Some handbooks of punctuation would advise *Did they ask the question "Are we bankrupt?"* and others would advise *Did they ask the question "Are we bankrupt"?* Still others suggest deciding each case on its own merits, which I think is the best advice. There is usually some ground for making a decision. For example, *The chairman warned, "Don't you think the stockholders will ask, 'Are we bankrupt?' "* could also be punctuated with the question mark between the single and double quotation marks—*'Are we bankrupt'?"*—but I would argue that the former is better because *Are we bankrupt?* is a stronger question than the question it is part of.

The question mark with points of ellipsis

The committee's report then raised several questions: "What is the present status of the company? . . . When does the treasurer plan to return from Paraguay?" The points of ellipsis following the question mark indicate that something has been omitted following the completed question that ends with the word *company.* If we transpose question mark and points of ellipsis—*"What is the present status of the company . . . ? When does the treasurer plan to return from Paraguay?"*—the points of ellipsis indicate that part of the first sentence has been omitted; it did not originally end with the word *company* but went on.

For more on points of ellipsis, see Rule 2-27.

EXCLAMATION POINT

The exclamation point is essentially an indicator of emotion—anger, pleasure, surprise, strong resolve. When it is used too frequently, it loses its force and is annoying to the reader. Certain sentences require it because they are worded as exclamations: *What a sunset! How we despised your annual report!* Other sentences are given it to change them from declarations to exclamations: *The sunset was magnificent! We despised your annual report!* Frequently exclamations are not grammatically complete sentences, and they can be single words.

The principles governing the position of the exclamation point when it is used with other marks of punctuation are almost the same as those governing the position of the question mark; they are explained in Rule 2-22.

2-22 Position exclamation points properly when using them with other marks of punctuation.

Like the question mark, the exclamation point is always positioned logically but sometimes forces one to forgo a logically desirable comma.

The exclamation point should not be used with a true period—one that ends a sentence—but it can be used with a point indicating an abbreviation: *She insists on being addressed as Mrs.!* It can also be used with points of ellipsis, which are not true periods.

The exclamation point should not be used with the comma. This causes a problem when the exclamation point ends a quotation and the sentence continues. *He shouted, "Crown me!" which made us all laugh* seems underpunctuated, because if the quotation were not an exclamation a comma would signal both the end of the quotation and the beginning of the second clause, as in *He said, "I deserve to be chairman," which made us all laugh.* Nevertheless, *He shouted, "Crown me!," which made us all laugh* is wrong, and *He shouted, "Crown*

149

me!", which made us all laugh, with the comma after the closing quotation mark, is doubly wrong. The comma should not be used even though using it would be quite logical (see Rule 2-11). An exception is sometimes made when the exclamation point actually has no function in the sentence but is part of a title: *His first poem, titled "Crown Me!," was dedicated to his mother.* This exception has some merit; it is discussed in Rules 3-20 and 3-21. Other exceptions are made in certain scholarly, legal, and other special contexts that are beyond the scope of this book.

Combining the question mark with the exclamation point— *Why won't you crown me?!* or *Why won't you crown me!?*—is usually frowned on as childish.

The exclamation point with the dash

He told me—we could have expected it!—that he had married again logically has the exclamation point within the dashes that enclose the parenthetical exclamation.

But he told me—! logically has the exclamation point after the dash to indicate an exclamation abruptly cut off. One might ask if it is really important to indicate the exclamatory tone so positively; the dash alone is adequate to break off the sentence, and it suggests an energetic, if not actually exclamatory, tone. (A less energetic musing tone could be suggested by points of ellipsis: *But he told me . . .*)

The exclamation point with the parenthesis

I think we're bankrupt (and we are!). The exclamation point is part of the parenthetical exclamation and thus goes within the closing parenthesis, with a terminal period outside the parenthesis. *I think we're bankrupt (and we are!), and we'd better decide what to do* shows the exclamation point followed by a parenthesis and a comma; this is correct, but the exclamation point should not be directly followed by a comma.

It is hard to produce a credible example of an exclamation point after a closing parenthesis, because parentheses lower the urgency of the words they enclose unless there is an exclamation point within them. *I think we're bankrupt (and we are)!* is not incorrectly punctuated if the whole sentence is intended to be exclamatory, but the urgency of the exclamation point contradicts the diminishing urgency of the sentence suggested by the parentheses. *I think we're bankrupt, and we are!*

and *I think we're bankrupt (and we are)* are obviously better; each has it own uncontradicted effect.

The exclamation point with the quotation mark

The chairman shouted, "We're bankrupt!" has the exclamation point inside the closing quotation mark, where it logically belongs. Note that there is no period to end the sentence. A period should not be placed outside a closing quotation mark (see Rule 2-24) or directly after an exclamation point, so the period is just omitted.

They just announced, "We're bankrupt"! has the exclamation point at the end of the sentence, making the whole sentence exclamatory.

Other uses with the quotation mark similar to those described for the question mark in Rule 2-21 should be avoided. Question marks often cannot be avoided, but exclamation points almost always can be, and should be if using them produces clumps of punctuation.

The exclamation point with points of ellipsis

One furious stockholder wrote the chairman: "I want my money! . . . Get that treasurer back from Paraguay!" The points of ellipsis following the exclamation point indicate some omission after the completed exclamation ending with *money.* If we make it *"I want my money . . . ! Get that treasurer back from Paraguay!"* the points of ellipsis preceding the exclamation point indicate that part of the exclamation has been omitted; it did not originally end with *money* but went on. In this latter case the exclamation point can often be omitted, with just the three-point ellipsis remaining or, if the truncated exclamation is a grammatically complete sentence, as here, a period added: *"I want my money. . . . Get that treasurer back from Paraguay!"*

Novelists sometimes use points of ellipsis with the exclamation point in dialogue: *His eyes widened. "You mean . . . !"* Perhaps they pick it up from the balloon dialogue in comic strips.

QUOTATION MARKS

The rules that follow cover the most common and most obvious uses of quotation marks—to enclose words or sentences that are quotations or that are borrowed in some similar way from a source outside the writer's own composition, and to set off words that are being used in some special way.

Some other uses of quotation marks, such as to enclose the titles of short musical and literary works, are covered in Rule 3-21.

2-23 Use quotation marks for direct quotations, but do not use them for indirect quotations and paraphrases.

Samuel Johnson wrote, "Language is the dress of thought." This is a direct quotation of the simplest kind, with the straightforward attribution *Samuel Johnson wrote.* Note that the period falls within the quotation mark. The comma after *wrote* could be a colon (see Rule 2-11).

Quotations as part of the writer's own sentence

When Samuel Johnson wrote that "language is the dress of thought," it was in reference to Abraham Cowley, not Aleister Crowley. When *that* is used to introduce the quoted words, they become part of the grammar of the writer's own sentence, and so there is no comma (see Rules 2-8 and 2-11) and the first word of the quotation is not capitalized even though Johnson began his own sentence with it. Even if Johnson's words had been *I believe that language is the dress of thought,* the word *that* should not be within the quotation marks; it is an essential part of the writer's sentence to introduce the quoted words, and it is just by coincidence the word preceding the words the writer wants to quote. Note that this kind of quotation is something like a paraphrase; the quotation marks could be omitted if the writer does not think it important to indicate by them that Johnson's exact words are being incorporated into the writer's own sentence.

Some writers are very skillful at working quotations into the grammar of their own sentences. *Johnson criticized even Shakespeare, claiming that though "we owe everything" to Shakespeare, Shakespeare "owes something to us," for although some of our admiration for him is well deserved, some is also "given by custom and veneration"; we consider only Shakespeare's "graces," not his "deformities," and we overlook "what we should in another loathe and despise."* All the words within quotation marks in the sentence above are exactly Johnson's words, and the sentence is an accurate statement of Johnson's opinions. Unskillful writers may encounter terrible problems because the tenses and other inflections within a quotation don't fit their own grammar, and they may be tempted to corrupt the quotation just a bit to make it fit: *Johnson was aware of his debt to earlier writers; he said he "owed everything" to Shakepeare.* This is dishonest quoting, and it may accompany, as it does in the example, a willingness to corrupt the thought as well as the text of the quotation; Johnson was not expressing a feeling of personal debt to Shakespeare in the passage in question.

As Johnson said, *"Language is the dress of thought"* may look at a glance like another simple direct quotation. However, the tricky word *as* complicates it considerably. *Johnson said* is a straightforward attribution, but *As Johnson said* is not. It could just as easily introduce a paraphrase: *As Johnson said, words are the clothes that thoughts wear.* The quotation marks could be omitted in the original wording, because *As Johnson said* makes no promise that what follows will be a direct quotation: *As Johnson said, language is the dress of thought.* Note that *language* now is not capitalized. In fact, there is a good argument for not capitalizing it even when the quotation marks are present, because *As* has made the quoted words part of the writer's sentence (just as *that* does when the quoted words are introduced by *Johnson said that*), and we don't expect ordinarily lowercase words to be capitalized in the middle of sentences. The writer can decide whether the quotation should be perceived as a complete utterance as well as part of the sentence including it and can capitalize or not capitalize accordingly, but could avoid this often troublesome decision by avoiding *as*.

An additional complication is that *As Johnson said* indicates that the writer is in agreement with the words quoted or paraphrased—the writer is not just quoting them but using them to express the same meaning. Careless writers, apparently unaware of this, begin attributions with *as* because they think it is just a handy all-purpose connective between sentences or clauses: *Gibbon enjoyed hard work, unlike many scholars; as Johnson said, "Every man is, or hopes to be, an idler."* If the writer agrees with Johnson, and *as* explicitly indicates such agreement, how can he or she believe at the same time that Gibbon enjoyed hard work? Some use *as* in introducing a quotation of several sentences, which contradicts its legitimate function of indicating the incorporation of someone else's turn of phrase or thought into the writer's own sentence or thought. I advise being very careful with *as*.

According to Johnson, "Every man is, or hopes to be, an idler," but Gibbon enjoyed hard work avoids indicating that the writer agrees with the quoted words, but there is still the problem of deciding whether the first word of the quotation should be capitalized. The introductory *According to Johnson* has to be perceived by the reader both as part of the writer's sentence and as an attribution, and as a general principle any word or phrase should have only one function within its sentence. Such formulas are useful and are thoroughly established in the language—there is no point in condemning them—but they are inherently troublesome.

Direct quotations of thoughts

Thoughts can be treated like other quotations and enclosed in quotation marks. They can also be italicized, without quotation marks. Both of these conventions are common. It is more common to dispense with both quotation marks and italics: *Johnson thought, Now why did I say that?*; *Now why did I say that? he brooded.* I recommend this third convention, although one has to be careful to keep thoughts and narrative from mingling, usually by paragraphing appropriately and inserting enough attributions to keep the reader straight. Using quotation marks is likely to be confusing when there is ordinary dialogue nearby. Using italics gives an unintended intensity to all thoughts and makes italics unavailable to show intended intensity.

Telepathic thought is often italicized. Some writers invent their own conventions to meet their needs—asterisks instead of quotation marks for the telepathic alien, small capitals for the computer speaker, italic capitals for the oversoul who providentially straightens out the mess, and so on.

Direct quotations of more than one paragraph

When a direct quotation runs more than one paragraph, no closing quotation mark is used at the end of the first paragraph, but an opening quotation mark is used at the beginning of the second paragraph. This pattern continues; the closing quotation mark appears only when the quotation finally ends.

In nonfiction, long quotations of written material can also be presented without quotation marks by indenting them a few spaces from the left margin of the regular text. Indenting sets off long quotations better than quotation marks do, and so it is a service to the reader. In books, such quotations, often called block quotations, are usually set in smaller type than the regular text.

Direct quotations from more than one speaker or source

In fiction, the standard American convention is to have no more than one speaker in a paragraph; each time a different person speaks, there should be a paragraph break. The convention can be relaxed occasionally: *The usual squabble was going on in the playroom. "Give me that!" bellowed Amy; "It's mine!" countered her brother. "It isn't!" "It is!" "It isn't!" "It is!"*

Similarly, random quotations from a group can be in the same paragraph: *The crowd began to turn ugly, and angry shouts were heard: "Come on out and fight!" "You dirty skunk!" "Give us back our money!"* Note that each shout requires its own enclosing quotation marks; if we put quotation marks only before the first and after the last shout, it would appear that only one person in the crowd was shouting or that the crowd was, improbably, shouting in unison.

In nonfiction, especially scholarly nonfiction, quotations from several properly identified sources may occur in the same paragraph. The main function of paragraphing in nonfiction is to organize the writer's argument or narrative, not to separate quotations from different sources. However, if there are passages of dialogue in nonfiction, they usually should be paragraphed in fiction style, with a new paragraph for each speaker. It is much easier for a reader to follow an exchange of words when there are paragraph breaks.

Indirect quotations and paraphrases

"Have I made myself clear?" he asked is a straightforward direct quote, correctly punctuated. *"Had he made himself clear?" he asked* is not correctly punctuated. The sentence *Had he made himself clear?* is a direct question (see Rule 2-20) and therefore deserves the question mark, but it is not a direct quotation and therefore cannot have quotation marks. Both the

tense of the verb and the person of the pronoun are different from what they are in the direct quote *"Have I made myself clear?"* We must take out the quotation marks: *Had he made himself clear? he asked.*

He said he hoped he'd "made himself clear" is also wrong; the quotation marks indicate that what they enclose are the man's exact words, but obviously they are not. *He said he hoped he'd "made myself clear"* is correct in principle, but the switch from third person to first person is annoying and quite unnecessary; incorporated quotations of this kind should fit neatly into the grammar of the sentence incorporating them. The quotation should be made an indirect quotation, without quotation marks: *He said he hoped he'd made himself clear.* It could, of course, be made a straightforward direct quotation: *He said, "I hope I've made myself clear."*

If "language were the dress of thought," as Samuel Johnson claimed it is, your brain would be arrested for indecent exposure should not have the quotation marks, because *language were the dress of thought* is not a direct quotation—Johnson's words are *Language is the dress of thought*—but a paraphrase. A paraphrase is a writer's rewording or recasting of someone else's words to suit the requirements of the writer's own sentence, or sometimes to simplify a difficult passage. Paraphrases are legitimate and very useful, since they free the writer from the grammar and diction of the actual quotation, but the writer must be careful not to distort the meaning. In the example, the writer could paraphrase part of the quotation and leave the rest in quotation marks: *If language were "the dress of thought," as Samuel Johnson claimed.*

Exceptions

I told the judge yes, you said maybe, and the policeman said no. The words *yes, maybe,* and *no* are presumably direct quotations, but they do not need to be enclosed in quotation marks. These short words of agreement, indecision, or disagreement can function as part of the sentence without any surrounding punctuation, though they can also, of course, be treated as regular quotations: *You said, "Maybe."* Often they may be a kind of indirect discourse: *I told the judge yes, I had stopped at the light* indicates that it is indirect quotation by the tense of the verb *had stopped*, and *The policeman said no, I hadn't* indicates that it is indirect not only by the tense but by the person of *I hadn't*—the policeman must actually have said *he didn't.*

I spoke to the chairman, and he said do you think it's your business to ask such a question, and I said of course it's my business. This is a compromise between direct and indirect quotation; the quotations are direct but are run into the enclosing sentence as if they were indirect. It is used by many novelists and occasional writers of nonfiction, especially for quotations of dialogue within other dialogue. It reflects natural speech, because when we are speaking rapidly, we tend to omit the usual slight pause before direct quotations; conventional punctuation would be likely to make the overall sentence seem unnaturally precise and studied. Like other narrative liberties, this one can be used well or badly.

2-24   Position quotation marks according to typographical conventions, even though these conventions sometimes violate logic.

With dashes, parentheses, question marks, and exclamation points, quotation marks are placed where they logically belong (see Rules 2-17, 2-18, 2-21, and 2-22). They are also placed logically with semicolons, colons, and points of ellipsis, as is explained below. But they are not always placed logically with commas and periods, which are the marks of punctuation most often associated with them.

Do not confuse the single closing quotation mark with the apostrophe. They may be identical in appearance, but they are quite different in function, and different rules govern their position. An apostrophe at the end of a sentence goes inside the period: *I don't know where I'm goin'.*

The quotation mark with the comma and the period

He said, "I have to go home now." The punctuation happens to coincide with logic; the period ends the quotation and is inside the closing quotation mark. Perhaps it would be even more logical to have a period outside the quotation mark as well, to end the complete sentence, but that is never done; the period inside the quotation mark ends both the quotation and the sentence containing it.

"I have to go home now," he said. The attribution has been moved to the end of the sentence, and the quotation is separated from the attribution by a comma, as required by Rule 2-11. But why is the comma inside the closing quotation mark? Certainly the comma is not part of the quotation; the speaker naturally ended his sentence with a period. The answer has nothing to do with logic. In the days of handset type—so the story goes—printers discovered that a period or comma hanging out at the end of a sentence after a quotation mark was easily knocked awry, and they solved the problem by putting the period or comma within the closing quotation mark regardless of logic. Now this arbitrary positioning of the quotation mark is the universal American convention. For some reason, an apostrophe at the end of a sentence was permitted to stay inside the period, perhaps because apostrophes were considered part of the spelling of words and inseparable from them.

I'm not sure what is meant by "fail-safe". This is logical punctuation, since *fail-safe* is just an isolated term, not a statement or question; only the complete sentence deserves a period. Nevertheless it is wrong; it should be *I'm not sure what is meant by "fail-safe."* It isn't logical, it's just the way it is. Commas and periods always go within closing quotation marks.

The quotation mark with the semicolon and the dash

He keeps using the word "fail-safe"; I'm not sure what it means has the semicolon after the closing quotation mark; *He gave me a definition of "fail-safe": a system of safeguards that hasn't failed yet* has the colon after the closing quotation mark. This is logical, since the semicolon and colon are punctuation for their respective sentences, not for the quotations within the sentences; neither a semicolon nor a colon can have any legitimate function at the end of a quotation, since the one is supposed to connect what precedes to what follows and the other is supposed to connect or introduce what follows, and there is no more quotation to connect or introduce. The only way the semicolon or the colon can be used with the quotation mark is outside a closing quotation mark; neither should ever be within a closing quotation mark or, of course, immediately after an opening quotation mark.

This is true even if there happens to be a semicolon or colon at the point where the quotation ends. If something to be quoted reads in full *I didn't like World War II; it was dull* and the writer wants to quote only the first clause and then continue with a clause of his or her own, it should be *The duke wrote in his memoirs, "I didn't like World War II"; he found it dull.* If it is important—as it might be in a study of a literary classic—to preserve the semicolon and indicate that the quoted sentence continued, it can be done by inserting points of ellipsis: *The duke wrote in his memoirs, "I didn't like World War II; . . ."; he found it dull.* The ugly clumping of punctuation could be improved by making *he found it dull* a separate sentence instead of tacking it to the preceding sentence with a semicolon.

The quotation mark with points of ellipsis

". . . regardless of the precedents," read the Chief Justice's dissent, "a wrong is not being righted." Points of ellipsis (three points) can be used after an opening quotation mark to show the omission of the first part of a quoted sentence. Often the points of ellipsis are unnecessary (see Rule 2-27).

The dissent continued, "The failure of this Court to address the basic injustice dismays me. . . ." Points of ellipsis (a period plus three points here, because the quotation is a grammatically complete sentence) are used before a closing quotation mark to show the omission of the last part of a quoted sentence.

It concluded, *"This is worse than 'blind justice.' . . . It is a callous averting of our eyes."* The closing single quotation mark follows the period here, to indicate that in the full text the sentence ends; the points of ellipsis follow the single quotation mark to indicate an omission before the next sentence.

Exceptions

The British usually position quotation marks logically even with commas and periods: *He keeps using the word "fail-safe", and I'm not sure what is meant by "fail-safe".* Here the quotation marks are being used not to enclose a specific direct quotation but to set off a term that is being discussed. The British do usually put the comma inside the closing quotation mark before an attribution: *"I'm going to ask what it means," he said.* (The British are likely to use single instead of double quotation marks; see also the exceptions to Rule 2-25.)

In certain scholarly and scientific disciplines, American practice is closer to the British. Those who write within such disciplines need an appropriate specialized handbook.

2-25 Use single quotation marks only within double quotation marks.

The Ayatollah said, "I well remember the words of your Western philosopher Nietzsche: 'Distrust all in whom the impulse to punish is powerful.'" This is the standard American punctuation for a quotation within a quotation. Note that the closing single quotation mark follows the same rules that the double quotation mark does (Rule 2-24)—it goes outside the period.

One newspaper reported, "The ambassador was heard to mutter, 'Who can trust the quotations of those whose prophet advises, "Whatever verse we abrogate or cause to be forgotten, we bring a better in its like"?'" This is the standard American punctuation for a quotation within a quotation within a quotation. The alternation of double and single quotation marks could go on indefinitely. Note that the question mark is positioned where it logically belongs within the collection of closing quotation marks, as required by Rule 2-21, and that it also serves to end the whole sentence.

Exceptions

The British usually, but not always, use single quotation marks first, then double quotation marks, the reverse of the American sequence.

Many British writers and some American writers use single quotation marks when the words they enclose are not dialogue or regular quotations from some specific written source but words that are set off for other reasons, such as those discussed in Rule 2-26: *The expression 'What's up, Doc?' is a vulgar, leporine Americanism; I did not immediately understand the pejorative 'wascally wabbit', perhaps partly because the creature it referred to seemed to be a hare.* In the second example, note the logical rather than conventional position of comma and quotation mark (see exceptions to Rule 2-24); those who use the single quotation mark in this manner are also likely to follow the British practice of positioning the quotation mark according to logic rather than convention. An American has little to gain from following this British practice; most other Americans won't understand the distinction, and American editors will change such single quotes to double quotes if they get the chance—not because they don't understand the distinction but because they don't think it's worth making, which is true for most writing.

However, certain scholarly disciplines have assigned special functions to single quotation marks. In linguistics, a word that is being discussed is italicized and its meaning follows directly after in single quotation marks, with no other punctuation:

> *Cleave* 'to adhere' and *cleave* 'to split' are the same in English but have different derivations.

In philosophy and theology, terms of special significance are commonly enclosed in single quotation marks, with other punctuation following the British logical pattern: *There is some question whether 'nonbeing' can have an 'essence'.* Those who write within such a discipline should observe its conventions and need a specialized handbook of usage for it.

2-26   Make judicious use of quotation marks for purposes other than to enclose quotations; consider alternatives.

The setting-off function of quotation marks is often indispensable. However, sometimes no setting off is necessary, and sometimes other means of setting off are preferable.

Quotation marks following *signed*, *marked*, and similar words

I signed the letter just "Gloucester," since I happen to be a duke is correct. But note that *I signed the letter sincerely his, Gloucester*—admittedly a quirky way of putting it—has no quotes, since *sincerely his* makes it an indirect quotation; the actual words would have been *Sincerely yours.*

The crate was stenciled "This side up" is correct. However, stenciled words are usually in capitals. Most book publishers would prefer to use small capitals and no quotation marks: *The crate was stenciled* THIS SIDE UP. On an ordinary typewriter, of course, only full capitals could be used.

The copperplate inscription read "For meritorious service" is correct. However, an inscription is likely to be in script; certainly a copperplate one would be. A book publisher might well use italics for the quotation, with no quotation marks:

The copperplate inscription read *For meritorious service.*

When capital letters or italics are used to set off special material, quotation marks may be used as well, but they are usually superfluous; the distinctive typography is sufficient. The advantage of distinctive typography is that it makes the words more vivid for the reader; it indicates not just their meaning but their appearance. It can be overused for this purpose, too; a page spotted with many capitals and italics (or typewritten underlines) is unattractive and somewhat forbidding. The pages of this book are an unavoidable example; it is impossible to write about the language itself without making heavy use of italics, quotation marks, or the sort of indenting that most readers associate unhappily with textbooks, and I settled on italics.

Quotation marks for words under discussion

The word "grammar" has different meanings in different contexts and to different people. This is the conventional American way of setting off words under discussion. The word *word* doesn't have to appear before the discussed word to justify the quotation marks: *I don't think "grammar" is quite the right term here; "diction" or "usage" might be better.*

Words such as "grammar," "diction," "usage," "syntax," and "inflection" are defined in the Glossary/Index shows the occasional problem that occurs when quotation marks are used for words under discussion—there are so many quotation marks that a passage may look as if grass were growing on it. We cannot get away with just an opening quotation mark before *grammar* and a closing quotation mark after *inflection*; each term needs its own enclosing quotation marks. If this problem can be expected to come up frequently in a given written work, it makes sense to use italics (or underlines on a typewriter or printer that cannot produce italics) rather than quotation marks:

Words such as *grammar, diction, usage, syntax,* and *inflection* are defined in the Glossary/Index.

It is conventional in printing to put most or sometimes all marks of punctuation following such uses of italic in italic too. I have not done so in this book because I believe it would make it more difficult to perceive the punctuation as part of the enclosing sentence rather than part of the italic example. The careful distinction between italic and roman punctuation is unlikely to be noted consciously by readers, but I nevertheless expect it to make reading easier for them.

Once a convention has been decided on, the writer should stick to it throughout the written work, departing from it only when it doesn't work—as my convention wouldn't work just above; I use italics for words I discuss and for the words and sentences I present as examples, but to present an example of that convention I must use indenting instead.

Note that when a word under discussion is made a whimsical plural, it is better not to use either quotation marks or italics. *This writer uses "however" too often* is fine—the quotation marks, or italics if that convention is preferred, are necessary; the sentence would be quite puzzling without them. But *This writer uses too many buts and howevers and maybes and ifs* is best left alone. The whimsical plurals make it clear enough that the words are not playing their typical roles but are being discussed. If we put them in quotation marks, we should leave out the *s,* producing the awkward *"but"s.* Occasionally one sees *"buts";* this is illogical, since the *s* is not actually a part of the word. Similarly, if we italicize them, the final *s* logically should not be italicized, producing the somewhat fussy-looking *buts.*

Quotation marks for unfamiliar terms

Ideally, the curve of a suspension bridge's main cable is a "catenary curve," the shape formed by a flexible chain or cord loosely suspended from both ends is a typical use of quotation marks to set off an unfamiliar term. The meaning of the set-off term should either be clear from the context or else, as in the example, be explained as soon as possible. Subsequent uses of the term should not have quotation marks, unless there is a long stretch until the next use and the writer judges that the term needs redefining.

Quotation marks for this purpose are adequate when unfamiliar terms are rare. If such terms come up frequently, as they are apt to in technical material, italics are preferable. Italics make it much easier for readers to fix the unfamiliar terms in their minds and, if necessary, to skim over what they have read to find a previously defined but forgotten term.

Quotation marks should not be used following such expressions as *so-called* and *known as*, because the expressions have the same function as quotation marks would: *The cable's shape is a so-called catenary curve.* However, italics can be used, if the writer's policy is to italicize all such terms on first mention.

Quotation marks for nicknames and epithets

"Joe" Louis is a thoroughly unnecessary use of quotation marks. *"Jersey Joe" Walcott* is not quite so unnecessary a use, but it certainly isn't a necessary use either; quotation marks are superfluous when a nickname is very well known.

Admiral William Halsey retired after more than forty years of service. "Bull" Halsey is best remembered for his part in the South Pacific campaign in World War II. This is a desirable use of quotation marks for a nickname. If the nickname is used again as the passage continues, the quotation marks should be dropped; they are needed only when the nickname is introduced.

William "Bull" Halsey retired in 1947 shows the standard method of giving both a first name and a nickname. If both first and middle names are given, the nickname follows the middle name: *Charles Dillon "Casey" Stengel was born in 1891.* Once the nickname has been supplied this way, if it is used again without the first name no quotation marks should be used.

Alfonso the Chaste, grandson of Alfonso the Catholic, sired no successor shows the form for royalty, great conquerors, and similar historical figures. No quotation marks are used. Whimsical modern epithets based on the same pattern, but sometimes with conventional word order and often with the last name instead of the first, don't ordinarily need quotation marks either: *Jeeves the Inimitable; the Magnificent Montague.*

Epithets without given names or surnames, such as *the Iron Duke, the Swedish Nightingale,* and *the Sun King,* may or may not be familiar enough to a writer's readers to make quotation marks unnecessary. Each case must be decided for itself. *Louis*

XIV, the Sun King, succeeded to the throne in 1643 may require the real name as well as the epithet to be clear to all readers, but it doesn't require quotation marks around *the Sun King* for any reader. On the other hand, *Jenny Lind, "the Swedish Nightingale," earned Barnum one of his greatest triumphs* may benefit from the quotation marks; they do suggest to the reader who is completely in the dark that maybe Jenny Lind was not a bird. *Wellington, the Iron Duke, was the hero of Waterloo* requires no quotation marks. However, if the epithet is not immediately after the name but is used for the first time in a separate sentence, quotation marks may be desirable: *When he returned from Verona there were further honors heaped on "the Iron Duke."* Yet in a similar situation, *the Sun King* probably would need no quotation marks. My advice is to lean toward not using quotation marks.

Quotation marks to indicate raised eyebrows

I felt constrained to award a modest "gratuity," though gratitude was not the emotion I felt. After the "bellboy"—actually a ragged urchin of no distinguishable sex—left the room, I inspected the "bathroom"—a hole in the floor bracketed by crude concrete footprints. I later found the "dining facilities" to be a noisome alcove off the lobby where deep-fried pig innards were dispensed.

Raised-eyebrow quotation marks can be the most irritating of all mannerisms in written English. In the example, the supercilious writer just steps on the intended jokes; each pair of quotation marks telegraphs the bad news that some pedestrian irony is coming up. The writer's mean-spiritedness would be less blatant without the quotation marks.

Nevertheless, raised-eyebrow quotation marks are not always foolish, and they can be useful to indicate that a word is being used in some special way or with some reservation. I have often in this book written sentences such as *The comma in this construction can be "heard."* The quotation marks indicate that *heard* is not being used in its literal sense. We must each judge for ourselves when raised-eyebrow quotation marks are genuinely useful, when they are pointless, and when they are foolish; my advice is to be a harsh judge.

POINTS OF ELLIPSIS

Points of ellipsis look, of course, like periods. However, they are not periods; a period is a mark that indicates the end of a sentence. I call points of ellipsis *points*, or sometimes *dots*, to emphasize the distinction. They are sometimes called *suspension points*. They are also sometimes called *ellipses*, as if each point were an ellipsis and three of them together made three ellipses. But an ellipsis is an omission, and three dots signal only one omission and therefore are only one ellipsis.

Points of ellipsis have two main functions: to indicate the omission of words within something that is being quoted, as discussed in Rule 2-27, and to indicate lengthy pauses and trailed-off sentences, as discussed in Rule 2-28.

2-27   Use three points to indicate ellipsis at the beginning or in the middle of a quoted sentence. Also use three points to indicate ellipsis at the end of a quoted sentence if the quotation is not a grammatically complete sentence either by itself or in conjunction with the words that precede the quotation.

Use a period plus three points to indicate ellipsis at the end of a quoted passage if the quotation is a grammatically complete sentence either by itself or in conjunction with the words that precede the quotation. Also use a period plus three points to indicate an omission within a quotation between a grammatically complete sentence and another complete or incomplete sentence.

I apologize for this very long rule. The principles governing points of ellipsis are not difficult, but it is difficult to state them compactly.

Points of ellipsis can indicate quite a lot about how a writer has shortened a quotation. They cannot indicate everything; the reader won't know how much of the full text is omitted and sometimes won't know where sentences in the full text begin or end. They can be used correctly as punctuation and still be misused; the writer who changes another writer's *This novel is no good* to *This novel is . . . good* is obviously misusing them, and it is surprisingly easy to misuse them accidentally. The shortened text should not misrepresent the full text.

The following quotation, given in full (that is, without ellipsis), is from an essay by Lionel Trilling. It is used throughout this discussion for examples.

Matthew Arnold was born in 1822, on the 24th of December. He was the son of a remarkable father. Thomas Arnold was at this time a young clergyman of the Church of England, who, in the little village of Laleham on the upper Thames, made a modest livelihood by taking young gentlemen into his home and preparing them for the universities. He was not long to remain thus obscure. In 1827, at the age of thirty-two, he was elected headmaster of Rugby School, an ancient but much deteriorated foundation. The story of Thomas Arnold's reform of Rugby, of his raising it from the shabby slackness in which he found it to the position of one of the most famous and influential of schools, has become one of the legends of Victorian England, and even today people who do not know another name in the long history of scholastic education know the name of Dr. Arnold.

Ellipsis at the beginning of a quoted sentence

Trilling writes, ". . . even today people who do not know another name in the long history of scholastic education know the name of Dr. Arnold." It would also be correct to begin, less formally, *Trilling writes that "even today*, with the points of ellipsis omitted; the running in of the quotation by *that* and the lowercase *even* suggest, though they do not unmistakably indicate, that Trilling's sentence does not begin with *even*. If the writer considers it unimportant to indicate the opening ellipsis, it would be permissible to begin *"Even today," Trilling writes, "people who*, with *even* capitalized to suit the requirements of the writer's own sentence and no suggestion that Trilling's sentence did not begin there. A writer must decide how important it is in a given piece of writing to indicate ellipsis and then follow a consistent policy.

Ellipsis in the middle of a quoted sentence

"Thomas Arnold . . . made a modest livelihood by taking young gentlemen into his home and preparing them for the universities," Trilling writes. Three points indicate ellipsis within a sentence. Such ellipsis should always be indicated, even in informal writing. Sometimes if there is punctuation in the full text just before or just after the ellipsis, it is left in: *Trilling writes, "In 1827, . . . he was elected headmaster of Rugby school, an ancient but much deteriorated foundation."* There is no point in leaving in the comma here, but sometimes leaving punctuation in makes the shortened quotation more readable. For example, if there is an ellipsis just before or just after a colon or semicolon, the shortened quotation is likely to benefit from leaving the colon or semicolon in.

Ellipsis at the end of a quoted sentence

One wonders if Trilling does not exaggerate the school's de-crepitude when he writes, "The story of Thomas Arnold's reform of Rugby, of his raising it from the shabby slackness in which he found it . . ." Here the ellipsis leaves a fragment only, not a grammatically complete sentence. There should be no period, just three points; the writer's complete sentence actually has no terminal punctuation, a rare situation but accepted here. (Note that a period is closed up to the word it follows, and if there is no period, the first point of an ellipsis is spaced from the word it follows.)

Trilling begins, "Matthew Arnold was born in 1822. . . ." Trilling's sentence has been cut short, but there is a period as well as three points, because what is left of the sentence is by itself a grammatically complete sentence. The period serves to end the writer's sentence as well.

Trilling writes that Thomas Arnold's rise to prominence began "In 1827, at the age of thirty-two. . . ." The period is used with the three points because though the quotation is not a grammatically complete sentence it blends with the writer's words to make a complete sentence. This particular use of points of ellipsis is, however, overly fussy for anything but a very close analysis of the quoted material. It is acceptable and almost always preferable to assume that the reader will understand that the quotation is a fragment—what else could it be?—and to omit the points of ellipsis and also lowercase the word *In*. If the writer does not want to lowercase a capital letter without indicating the change, brackets can be put around the changed letter: *"[i]n 1827.*

Of Matthew's father, Trilling writes, *"He was not long to remain thus obscure. . . . The story of Thomas Arnold's reform of Rugby . . . has become one of the legends of Victorian England. . . ."* There is a period with the first ellipsis, because an entire sentence has been dropped between complete sentences. There is no period with the second ellipsis, because the ellipsis is in the middle of a sentence. There is a period with the final ellipsis, because a grammatically complete sentence ends there, even though Trilling's sentence continues in the full text.

Ellipsis of the end of one sentence and the beginning of another

Trilling begins, "Matthew Arnold . . . was the son of a remarkable father." Here the end of one sentence and the beginning of another have been omitted, creating a single grammatically complete sentence. This is quite acceptable, and it is done just as if the two sentences were one. The danger is that such a double ellipsis will distort the meaning of the quoted passage, but there is no problem in the example. Note that the ellipsis could have come after *was* instead of before it, since the word occurs both places in the full text. The writer can choose which *was* to omit; here it seems a little better to keep the entire predicate together.

Of Matthew's father, Trilling writes, *". . . he was elected headmaster of Rugby School. . . . his raising it from the shabby slackness in which he found it . . . has become one of the legends of Victorian England."* The first, third, and fourth uses of ellipsis have been explained already. The second ellipsis is a new situation—the ellipsis includes the end of one sentence and the beginning of another, and each of the two shortened sentences is grammatically complete. The lowercase *his* makes it apparent that the second sentence does not begin there in the full text. The reader will note the period with the preceding ellipsis and thus be aware that a new sentence is beginning even though *his* is lowercase. However, the writer can capitalize *his* to add to the readability of the passage by giving a clearer signal of a new sentence, and can bracket the capital—*[H]is*—if it is important to indicate that the change has been made.

Ellipsis around obvious fragments

Matthew Arnold's father ". . . *made a modest livelihood . . .*" *as a tutor* is not incorrectly punctuated, but it is obviously an unnecessary use of points of ellipsis; the quotation couldn't be anything but a fragment. Points of ellipsis may still be needed in the middle of an obvious fragment—*Matthew Arnold's father* "*made a . . . livelihood*" *as a tutor*—but they aren't needed before or after it.

Ellipsis with the question mark and exclamation point

The question mark and exclamation point are used logically with points of ellipsis, as explained in Rules 2-21 and 2-22. For example, suppose that a quoted sentence ends with a question mark, and then there is an ellipsis, and then the quotation continues. The question mark follows the first sentence just as in the full text, and three points follow the question mark. If a quoted sentence is a question and the last part of it is omitted, the part that is quoted is followed by three points and then a question mark. If there is then a further ellipsis before the quotation continues, there are three more points to indicate it, so one can have the lengthy clumping . . . ? . . . in the middle of a quotation—not attractive but sometimes necessary. Sometimes the question mark or exclamation point can be omitted to simplify the punctuation; it depends how important the writer feels it is to indicate the punctuation of the full text and how readable the omission will leave the quotation.

Ellipsis at the end or beginning of a paragraph or between paragraphs

Points of ellipsis, with a period if the last quoted sentence is grammatically complete, should appear when the end of a paragraph has been omitted and the quotation then continues with a new paragraph. This is sufficient even if several paragraphs have been omitted, and it is also usually the convention when the end of the paragraph has not been omitted but one or more complete paragraphs have been skipped before the quotation resumes.

Points of ellipsis should appear when the beginning of a second or subsequent paragraph has been omitted. If both the end of one paragraph and the beginning of the next have been omitted, points of ellipsis should appear in both places.

Note that quotations of more than one paragraph or even a single long paragraph are usually better set as block quotations—that is, indented and without quotation marks (see Rule 2-23). The first line of each paragraph is given an additional paragraph indent. However, if the quotation is a single paragraph, the first line need not be given a paragraph indent; the quotation will look neater without one.

2-28   Use points of ellipsis sparingly to indicate pauses, and use them correctly.

"Well, let's see. . . . We have . . . yes, eleven cents. . . . I'm afraid those candy bars are fifty-nine cents, son," the storekeeper said. The period and three points are used when a sentence ends before a pause; just three points are used when there is a pause in the middle of a sentence.

"I don't have enough? Well . . ." Just three points are used when a sentence trails off unfinished.

"Yes," the storekeeper said, "you're exactly forty-eight cents short. . . ." A period and three points are used when a complete quotation trails off. This use of points of ellipsis is troublesome, however. The points of ellipsis can't indicate a pause, since the quotation doesn't continue. Can a complete quotation really trail off? A sentence may have a trailing-off intonation, but punctuation usually does not attempt to indicate such minor subtleties of speech. Points of ellipsis at the end of dialogue may be taken to indicate a pause while the speaker waits for an answer. This saves the writer the trouble of writing *The storekeeper waited smugly for the child to realize his embarrassment* or *About as much time elapsed as it takes a mediocre typist to hit the period key three times.*

Some writers of fiction seem to punctuate mostly with points of ellipsis. It's annoying. Well-composed dialogue, combined with well-composed narrative, does not need constant signals of pauses and trailings-off.

One side of a telephone conversation

"Hello? . . . Yes, this is she. . . . Oh. . . . I'll come right down and get— Shut up a minute. I'll pay for the damn window. . . . Look, I wonder if you're aware that I'm with the health department here, and that my office issues licenses to the food retailers in this city. . . . That's better. If you've even frightened that boy, you'll be sorry. . . . Yes, I'll be right there. Goodbye."

There are several ways of presenting one side of a telephone conversation. The above is what I advise. The unheard side is represented by a period and three points, even if the heard side is not speaking in complete sentences. An interruption is indicated by a dash, followed by a space.

When both sides of a telephone conversation are given, the conversation can be presented as ordinary dialogue. Italics, or switches from roman for one speaker to italics for the other, are unnecessary.

APOSTROPHE

The apostrophe is not actually a mark of punctuation but a part of the spelling of a word; it occurs as part of a word, not as something between words. Its primary functions are to form the possessive case and to indicate contractions and dropped letters.

Errors occur frequently when plurals are confused with possessives and when plurals are possessive. These errors and many complications of the possessive form are covered in Rule 2-29. Other errors, such as misplacing the apostrophe in a contraction, are frequent in careless or hasty writing; they are discussed in Rule 2-30.

See also Rule 3-6 for advice on use of the apostrophe with numbers.

2-29   Form the possessive case of singular words, including words ending in *s* or *z* sounds, by adding an apostrophe and *s*; form the possessive of plural words ending in *s* by adding the apostrophe alone.

This is the simplest rule that can be given for forming the possessive, and still it has its complications. It is not the only possible rule—some handbooks of punctuation advise forming the possessive of singular words that end in *s* or *z* sounds with the apostrophe alone, some make a distinction between words that end in *s* and those that end in *x* or *z*, some make a distinction between short and long words (usually prescribing an *s* after the apostrophe for words of one or perhaps two syllables but not for longer words), some make a distinction between words that end in *s* and those that end in *ss*, some advise using only the apostrophe after a silent *s* (as in *Descartes' work*), some advise using the *s* only if it would be pronounced in speech (tricky because not everyone pronounces some possessives the same way, though the longer the word is the less likely it is that the *s* will be pronounced), and so on.

Since there is such disagreement among the authorities about words ending in *s* or *z* sounds, each writer is entitled to make his or her own decision about certain possessives, but each should try to have a consistent policy and avoid inconsistencies such as *Charles's garage is bigger than Miles' house.*

A generation or so ago, many authorities advised against using the possessive case with any word that does not denote an animate thing. Thus one could write (or say) *the dog's dish* but not *the dish's contents*; it would have to be *the contents of the dish.* The distinction is no longer made except by very fastidious writers; when it is made, few readers are aware of it, though they may wonder why unidiomatic phrases such as *a vacation of a week* occasionally appear. It does seem to survive sometimes when phrases denoting inanimate things are made possessive: *the pot of coffee's position on the table* and *the wine from Greece's resinous taste* are awkward. But *the coffeepot's position* and *the Greek wine's taste* are not.

See also **possessive** in the Glossary/Index.

Singular and plural possessives

The candle's glow and *the candles' glow* show the simplest possessive situations; in the first phrase there is one candle, in the second more than one.

The boss's office and *the bosses' salaries* show the use of the apostrophe plus *s* that I advise for singular words ending in *s* and of the apostrophe alone for plural words (which are usually formed by *es* when the singular ends in *s*). There are very few common nouns in English that end in a single *s* in the singular; those that do exist are apt to be direct borrowings from other languages, such as *pus* from Latin and *catalysis* from Greek. Many of these words have plurals that are nonstandard but do end in *s*, and they usually form the possessive plural in the standard way—*catalyses* is the plural, and *catalyses'* is the possessive plural. There are quite a few common nouns that end in *x*, such as *box*, and some that end in *zz*, such as *buzz*, and these words follow the same pattern as *boss* for the possessive: *box's, boxes'; buzz's, buzzes'*.

The children's room, the people's choice, and *women's rights* are examples of an important exception to Rule 2-29. Some of the most common nouns in English are many centuries old, adopted before the added *s* became the standard method of forming plurals. These so-called irregular plurals that don't end in *s* form the possessive in the same way singular words do, by adding an apostrophe and *s*. *The childrens' room, the peoples' choice,* and *womens' rights* are wrong. One sees such errors frequently; I think they are usually careless rather than ignorant errors.

Other venerable English words, such as *deer*, some evident borrowings from other languages, such as *species*, and many proper nouns such as *Chinese* are the same in the singular and the plural, and the possessive forms are also the same in the singular and plural: *this deer's huge antlers; these deer's wintering grounds; this species' habitat; these species' habitats.*

Some words that have been directly adopted from Latin or other languages form their plurals as they do in the original language: *alumnus, alumni; alumna, alumnae.* These plurals too form the possessive in the same way singular words do: *alumni's, alumnae's.*

Possessives of personal pronouns

Personal pronouns have special possessive forms, none of which use the apostrophe. The singular forms are *my* and *mine*; *your* and *yours*; *his*; *her* and *hers*; and *its*. The plural forms are *our* and *ours*; *your* and *yours*; and *their* and *theirs*. Some of these forms end in *s* (see the discussion of the independent possessive in Rule 1-19), tempting one to commit errors such as *your's*, *her's*, and especially *it's*, which is not immediately bothersome to the eye because it is the correct contraction of *it is*. These are bad errors; they may often be careless rather than ignorant, but somehow they strongly suggest ignorance.

Possessives of names of people

Smith's house means a house owned or occupied by someone named Smith, who is either the sole owner or the head of the family, or possibly is just the only person under discussion. *The Smiths' house* means a house owned or occupied by a family named Smith; the surname is made a plural by adding an *s*, and an apostrophe is added to make the plural possessive. Note that when the family members are named, the surname is not made plural: *Mr. and Mrs. Smith's house*; *John, Mary, and little Jennifer Smith's house*. There is, however, a special form of reference that combines *the* with the names and requires the surname to be plural: *the John and Mary Smiths, the John and Mary Smiths' house*.

Errors are common when the name ends in *s*. *Curtis's house* is correct, meaning a house owned or occupied by someone named Curtis; so is *Curtis' house* if the writer prefers not to add an *s* in such cases. Problems start when the Curtis family is involved. More often than not one sees *the Curtis's house*, which is wrong. The plural of the surname *Curtis* is *Curtises*, so it must be *the Curtises' house*. Similarly, *Jones, Jones's house, the Joneses' house*; *Mr. Cross, Mr. Cross's house, the Crosses' house*. I think errors are usually the result of a hazy understanding of how to make names plural—many people think the plural of *Curtis* is *Curtis's*.

Individual possession and joint possession

Smith's and Brown's cars are in the parking lot has an apostrophe and *s* for each person; each has a car. *Smith and Brown's tennis match was postponed* has an apostrophe and *s* only for *Brown;* the match "belongs" to Smith and Brown jointly—they were going to play it together. In these examples, the plural *cars* and the singular *match* make the logic quite obvious, but sometimes one has to think a bit: *Mary's and John's behavior at the office party was disgraceful* is correct if the two misbehaved separately; *Mary and John's behavior* is correct if they misbehaved together. This convention does sometimes permit perverse misreadings: *Mary and John's theatrics were disgraceful* could mean that both were guilty of the same disgraceful theatrics or that only John was guilty of theatrics and that Mary disgraced herself in some other way—Mary herself was disgraceful.

The Smiths' and Browns' parties were on the same night; The Smiths and Browns' joint party was not a success. Plurals follow the same rules that singulars do for individual possession and joint possession.

This is my and John's car does not follow the usual rule for joint possession. Personal pronouns are in the possessive case even in joint possession, and so are any other possessors in a series that includes personal pronouns, regardless of their position: *This is John's and my car; This is my sister's, my cousin's, and my room.*

Possessives of singular names that are plural in form

Des Moines, Los Angeles, and *Three Rivers* are plural in form but singular in meaning. So, of course, is *the United States.* Someone doggedly applying Rule 2-29 may form the possessive *Des Moines's, Los Angeles's,* and even *Three Rivers's* and *the United States's.* These are wrong; one must observe the plural form rather than the singular meaning and omit the final *s*— which, after all, is a common way of forming the possessive of any word ending in *s,* even though it is not Rule 2-29's way. Many of these names are foreign or foreign in origin, and the writer may not know whether they are singular or plural in form; everyone knows that *Paris* is singular in form and that *Paris's* is therefore proper, but what about *Nantes?* Half an hour with my own reference books has not given me an answer. In dubious cases, I suggest assuming the form is plural and adding just an apostrophe for the possessive.

In newspaper and periodical names, *Times's* and *News's* are acceptable possessive forms. *The New York Times Manual of*

Style and Usage specifies *Times's;* some newspapers, including the *Los Angeles Times,* do not use the final *s.*

Some surnames are plural in form: *Snopes, Carruthers, Brooks,* and so on. Since we routinely pluralize these plurals—*Snopeses, Carrutherses, Brookses*—we can routinely make them possessive as if they were singular in form: *Snopes's tricks, Carruthers's wife, Brooks's job.* Those who object to such possessives can make an exception for surnames, but apparent inconsistencies may occur: *The boss's son is going to marry John Brooks' secretary.* An inconsistency may be justifiable if a particular name seems excessively odd with *s* after the apostrophe. *Fields's* seems all right to me, but *Meadows's,* for some reason, does not. A nickname such as *Bubbles,* which strongly retains its identity as a plural word, is probably better off with just an apostrophe.

Other occasions when the final *s* can be omitted

Names from the Bible and from classical history and legend that end in *s* often take only the apostrophe to form the possessive: *Moses', Jesus', Aristophanes', Hercules'.* Adding the *s* is not wrong, but most handbooks of punctuation advise omitting it, and in many cases when it is added it looks odd, especially with long names: *Aristophanes's.*

Most handbooks also advise dropping the *s* in certain common phrases, especially with *sake: for convenience' sake; for conscience' sake; for goodness' sake.* The reason usually given is that a succession of *s* sounds should be avoided, but some people do pronounce all the *s* sounds in at least some of these phrases. I have seen the forms without the *s,* but rarely, and then mostly in older books, particularly older British books. Usually they appear as *convenience's sake, conscience's sake,* and *goodness sake,* the last with no signal of the possessive—the *s* is very unlikely to be pronounced. I recommend this newer practice.

Possessives with *Jr.* and *Sr.*

By convention, *Jr.* and *Sr.* are set off as if they were parenthetical: *John Smith, Jr., was there.* They are not actually parenthetical but defining (see Rule 2-1); in the example, *Jr.* indicates which John Smith is meant. Their function is the same as that of *II, III,* and so on—to indicate where a person belongs in a line of people with the same name—but the Roman numerals are not set off: *John Smith II was there.* Many newspapers and some other publications have forsaken the convention and treat *Jr.* and *Sr.* just as they do Roman numerals: *John Smith Jr. was there.* Very sensible! But unfortunately the convention persists in most private and public writing, and it causes terrible problems in possessive constructions.

John Smith, Jr.'s, daughter was there is correct, annoying as it is to make the parenthetically punctuated *Jr.* bear the burden of the possessive. I think it is acceptable to drop the convention in such cases and make it *John Smith Jr.'s daughter was there;* if I found the example in a book I was editing, I would almost certainly let it stand, and if I ever write something in which the problem recurs frequently, I will probably drop the convention and may even go further and always omit commas, as the newspapers do. But I hesitate to recommend this bold step in this book, which is intended to enable its readers to avoid criticism. The convention is alive, and those who flout it may be criticized.

John Smith, Jr.'s daughter occurs sometimes but has no merit; the comma between the possessive and the word it modifies is eliminated, which is good (see Rule 2-5), but the single comma that is left splits up the phrase much more than two commas do. I don't believe I have ever seen errors such as *John Smith's, Jr.'s, daughter* and *John Smith's, Jr., daughter.*

Possessives in names of companies, organizations, and institutions

Official names follow no rules; one simply must find a reliable authority for the proper form, though an assiduous researcher may find that a company's name is treated two ways on its letterhead stationery and a third way in its advertising, and that no one at the company has any idea what the proper form is. Often an apostrophe that seems necessary or desirable isn't there. One would expect Columbia University's subdivision to be Teachers' College, but it is Teachers College—the plural noun directly modifies *College*, without being made possessive. (The current edition of the Merriam-Webster unabridged dictionary lists *teachers college* as the generic compound noun, but the previous edition had *teachers' college.* Teachers College, founded in 1888, is only belatedly supported.) According to the *Los Angeles Times* book of style and usage, Childrens Hospital is the Los Angeles institution, even though *childrens* is a distinctly unhealthy English formation. The Bricklayers, Masons and Plasterers' International Union of America follows the joint-possession rule explained above, or at least it does in an almanac in my library. The International Longshoremen's and Warehousemen's Union does not. The Textile Workers Union of America, like many other unions and like Teachers College, doesn't bother with the apostrophe at all.

A public library will have various specialized reference works that can be accepted as authoritative, but some of these impose their own style on official names.

Possessives of compounds and phrases

The plurals of compounds quite frequently do not end in *s*: *brothers-in-law, courts-martial, commanders in chief*. Conversely, the singulars of some compounds end in plural forms: *master of ceremonies, dean of men*. When such compounds are made possessive, Rule 2-29 is applied to the form, not the singular or plural meaning: *I haven't met my brothers-in-law's wives; I didn't want to shake the master of ceremonies' hand.* Compounds that are open (that is, not hyphenated or solid) may look odd this way: *The commanders in chief's quarrel doomed the operation from the start.* Compounds in which the first word is a possessive may also look odd even when they are singular: *the bull's-eye's center,* the monk's cloth's nap. Compounds that are solid (that is, clearly composed of two words but spelled as one word) may be quite odd in the possessive plural: *The passersby's accounts disagreed.* There is always the alternative of using an *of* construction instead of the possessive case or avoiding the possessive completely: *The accounts of the passersby disagreed; The passersby gave conflicting accounts.*

Phrases such as *the grandees of Spain* and *the man from the colonies* are noun phrases—they are treated grammatically as if they were a single noun. Just as with the compounds discussed above, the possessive is formed according to the form of the last word, not according to the singular or plural meaning: *the grandees of Spain's displeasure, the man from the colonies' wives.* These phrases are not well-known, easily absorbed compounds of the sort discussed in the preceding paragraph; they are just put together for the requirements of the sentence. Consequently it may be particularly desirable to sidestep the troublesome possessive case and use an *of* construction.

179

Compounds and phrases that contain possessives give trouble when they are made plural. Should it be *sheriff's offices* or *sheriffs' offices*? There is disagreement on the point. I hold strongly with *sheriff's offices*. The singular, *sheriff's office*, is a compound just as much as *bull's-eye* is, and it should be made plural as a unit, not part by part. *Sheriff's offices* can be misunderstood—it can mean two or more offices of a single sheriff—but *sheriffs' offices* is shapeless; it obscures the fact that a sheriff's office is a generic thing and has some of the absurdity of *Adams' apples*. The same holds for many other phrases that denote generic things: *treasurer's reports, loser's games, actor's actors*.

She is the man who was knighted yesterday's wife is a poor use of the possessive; possessives should not be formed with word groups that contain dependent clauses and other complications, except possibly if the word group is very well known—*The boy who cried wolf's problem was credibility*—or, of course, for humorous effect.

Piled-up possessives

That's my brother's wife's sister's daughter's cat's leash is correctly punctuated, but such an accumulation of possessives should be avoided except to amuse. *That's the cat of my brother's wife's leash* is correctly punctuated, but it would take the reader some time to figure out that *the cat of my brother's wife* is all one noun phrase that has been made possessive.

Possessives combined with *of*

The son of the pharaoh's daughter is the daughter of the pharaoh's son. At first glance this may appear to be a comment on incest and hermaphroditism in some pharaonic line, but there are several ways of stating two other possible meanings that are less garish—they are dull, in fact—and unambiguous. They all require using either only the possessive case or only *of* constructions on each side of the "equation" signaled by *is*.

Keep the riddle in mind when combining possessives and *of* constructions; the combination may make several perfect senses.

2-30   Don't overuse contractions; when you do use a contraction, put the apostrophe in the proper place.

Contractions such as *don't* for *do not* are natural and convenient in speech. They are also natural in writing—in fact, they come too easily, for when they occur frequently they give the written work more informality than may be intended. It is important to read over any written work, except the most casual letter or note, to check for excessive use of contractions.

The contractions *don't, won't, wouldn't, aren't,* and others based on the combination of a verb with *not* are often incorrectly spelled *do'nt, would'nt,* and so on.

The contraction *it's,* meaning *it is,* is sometimes misspelled *its,* which is the possessive of the pronoun *it.* The opposite mistake—using *it's* for the possessive—is more common.

The contraction *who's,* meaning either *who is* or *who has,* is often misspelled *whose,* which is the possessive of the pronoun *who.*

The contractions *should've* (meaning *should have*), *I'd've* (meaning *I would have*), and others formed by contracting *have* to *'ve* are often misspelled *should of, I'd of,* and so on. Usually the mistake is from ignorance; the writer does not know the correct form and is misled by the similarity in sound of *of* and *'ve.* Some writers use *of* for *'ve* deliberately to add flavor; *should of* and *I'd of* have a drawled look that the more clipped *should've* and *I'd've* lack. Ring Lardner and John O'Hara often used *of* for *'ve,* and it is unlikely that either did it from ignorance. But I have noticed the usage outside dialogue or stylized narrative in O'Hara's writing—perhaps he was a bit hazy on the point.

Contractions to indicate nonstandard speech

I'se goin' to town fer feed; won' be back till mornin'. Anything is possible in dialogue, and almost anything is permissible. Note that *won'* drops the *t* of *won't,* so the apostrophe is doing double duty. Note also that the apostrophe, unlike the single closing quotation mark, goes inside the period.

Some novelists feel that if they have a character drop his *g*'s, that character has to drop the *g* every time he or she uses a word ending in *ing.* Dialogue so punctuated can be very tire-

181

some. Just an occasional dropped *g* in the right place, and the avoidance of any glaring inconsistency such as the same word two ways in the same sentence, will achieve the effect and spare both writer and reader.

Certain contractions are puzzling. Writers of westerns are fond of *th'* for *the*, as in *Gimme th' gun, Luke—you ain't goin' outta th' house.* The contraction *th'* may indicate that the speaker did not stretch out *the* to *thee*, as might an Anglican preacher searching for a felicitous noun, but the reader does not need to have this pointed out. (The same writers like to use *bin* or *ben* for *been*, even though almost all Americans, not just cowpokes, pronounce it *bin* or *ben* rather than *bean*.) Since contractions can be annoying anyway, there is certainly no point in using them when they are meaningless. One might argue that they aren't entirely meaningless when they are characteristic of a genre and the reader expects them.

Some novelists drop the apostrophes for contractions, perhaps hoping to make them less annoying: *"We allus goin, goin, never get noplace, like a lil mouse wit iz tail in de cat's mouf."* Sometimes it works, sometimes it doesn't. Usually the apostrophe is still used for possessives, as for *cat's* in the example.

One could do worse than study Mark Twain's *Huckleberry Finn.* Contractions and other devices to show substandard speech are very heavy in Jim's dialogue, quite heavy in Huck's, and rare or absent in some other characters' and in the narrative. Since the whole story is told in the first person by Huck, another writer might have put it entirely in Huck's diction, in the belief that a first-person novel's diction has to be as authentic as a transcript. Twain must have thought a great deal about his contractions and substandard diction; he wanted to communicate the flavor of the characters' speech faithfully, but he didn't want to annoy the reader. Modern writers don't have to follow Twain's pattern slavishly—Twain left in more nonstandard diction than most schoolchildren and some adults can read easily, and modern readers are less amused than Twain's contemporaries were by humorous dialect—but they should think about the matter just as Twain did.

HYPHEN

Most marks of punctuation serve in some way to separate words from one another (comma, semicolon, colon, dash, parenthesis) or sentences from one another (period, exclamation

point, question mark). The hyphen is the only mark of punctuation that has the specific function of joining words together,
though the diagonal may have a somewhat similar function
(see Rule 2-38). Words so joined are called compound words.
However, not all compound words contain hyphens; *high
school* and *schoolteacher* are compound words. The problem
with hyphens—and it can be quite a problem—is determining
when they are needed in compound words.

Some compound words are formed from a single base word
and a prefix or suffix that is not a word in itself. Very often such
compounds are written as one solid word, but some prefixes
and suffixes require a hyphen, some combinations of base word
and prefix or suffix require a hyphen to prevent an undesirable
sequence of letters (for example, *wall-less* requires a hyphen to
prevent three *l*'s in a row), some words are hyphenated to
prevent them from being identical with other words of quite
different meaning, and some words are hyphenated simply
because dictionaries, reflecting standard usage, list them that
way. Rules 2-31 to 2-33 concern compound words formed with
prefixes and suffixes.

Many compound nouns are formed from two or more base
words. Some are spelled as separate words, like *high school*,
some are spelled as a solid word, like *schoolteacher*, and some
are hyphenated, like *money-maker*, *city-state*, and *place-name*.
These examples are all so-called permanent compounds—they
are common enough to be found in most dictionaries, and their
form is permanent rather than dependent on how they are used
in a sentence, though when a noun compound that is normally
spelled as two separate words is used as an adjective it very
often does acquire a hyphen. The general principles governing
permanent compound nouns are discussed in Rule 2-34, but
the only way to be sure about a given compound is to check the
dictionary—and dictionaries vary on the spelling of some compounds, so it's best to stick to a single well-known dictionary
in its most recent edition. *Webster's Third New International
Dictionary* and the desk-size *Webster's Ninth New Collegiate
Dictionary* (both published by Merriam-Webster) are almost
universally used in book publishing; *Webster's New World
Dictionary* (from a different publisher despite the common use
of Noah Webster's name) is used by most newspapers. Even
those who routinely follow the practice of a given dictionary
may be wise to ignore the dictionary sometimes, as I advise in
Rule 2-34.

Many compounds, unlike those discussed above, cannot be
found in dictionaries. These are the difficult ones. They are so-

called temporary compounds—words that normally stand alone but are compounded when they play certain roles within a sentence, usually an adjectival role. There are countless thousands of possible temporary compounds, and therefore one must understand the principles of hyphenation to know when to hyphenate them.

Rules 2-35 and 2-36 explain when to hyphenate temporary adjectival compounds, and Rule 2-37 explains temporary compounds with numbers, some adjectival and some not. The rules recommend a rather rigorous use of hyphens that requires an understanding of grammar and particularly of the parts of speech and their functions. The tendency in American writing has been away from such rigorous use—I think largely because only in the last decade or so have schools returned to systematic teaching of the principles of grammar. Many teachers themselves were in school when grammar was neglected, and they are understandably uncertain about use of the hyphen and glad to tell their students—as current textbooks may allow them to—that hyphenation of temporary compounds is often a matter of nothing but individual taste. But the hyphen is as valuable an asset to English punctuation as it ever was; although not all of us know how to use it properly, we all still know how to read it. It still gives its signals, and we read properly hyphenated text much more easily than sparsely and inconsistently hyphenated text. Fortunately there is still plenty of properly hyphenated text around, because most book publishers hold to older standards and employ editors and copy editors who can apply them, even though current editions of the handbooks most used by publishers have lost some of their former rigor on the subject.

There have always been and will always be some difficulties in the use of the hyphen and some disagreements about its uses. Nevertheless, it can be used well or poorly. I advise making the effort to learn to use it well.

2-31 Don't hyphenate most compounds formed with the prefixes listed below; connect them solidly to the base word.

The list here includes some items that themselves can function as base words, but in compounds they can be considered prefixes.

ante	hypo	post
anti	in	pre
bi	infra	pseudo
by	inter	re
circum	intra	semi
co	macro	sub
counter	mal	super
de	micro	supra
dis	mid	trans
down	multi	tri
electro	non	ultra
extra	on	un
fore	out	under
hydro	over	uni
hyper	pan	up

Antedate, antiwar, bicameral, byplay, circumnavigate, coauthor, counterattack, deactivate, disinterest, downslope, electrolysis—a glance at the dictionary will confirm that these prefixes almost always combine with base words to form solid words, not hyphenated ones.

Exceptions

Alas, an exception can be found for every prefix on the list.

Compounds with prefixes that end in a vowel are often hyphenated to separate vowels that are pronounced separately: *anti-art, co-opt, de-emphasize,* and so on. But this exception has exceptions: Merriam-Webster dictionaries list *cooperate,* for example, though some other dictionaries (including older editions of Merriam-Webster dictionaries) use the hyphen, and some list *coöperate,* with a diaeresis over the second *o* to clarify the pronunciation, as an alternative. Although the more common a word is the more likely it is to lose the hyphen, some relatively uncommon words, such as *antiaircraft*, have lost it. When using any of these prefixes to form an unfamiliar compound not found in the dictionary, follow the principle of separating vowels that are pronounced separately. Certain vowel combinations, such as doubled vowels, are particularly likely to require the hyphen. For example, except in highly technical material containing rare compounds, one would never see words with a doubled *i*; a solid compound such as *antiinflationary* would be very difficult to read.

Some words with prefixes are hyphenated to prevent them from being identical with other words of different meaning: *I'll re-cover the sofa when I recover from the flu; The reform politicians re-formed behind their new leader; The recreation area of the park had to be re-created after the hurricane.* One has to be quite alert sometimes. Does *He's going to release the apartment* mean he's going to let it go or lease it again? If the latter is the case, it should be *re-lease.* But some words are just allowed to be identical: *I'm relaying the message that the workmen are relaying the tiles.* One must consult the dictionary.

When any of the prefixes on the list is combined with a capitalized word—that is, a proper noun or a word formed from a proper noun—the hyphen is standard: *anti-American, pre-Christian, sub-Saharan.* But sometimes the capitalized word is lowercased in such compounds; almost all modern dictionaries list *transatlantic* and *unchristian*, for example. Again, one must consult the dictionary. Note that sometimes a prefix is joined to a proper noun of two or more words, as in *post-World War II inflation.* Such compounds are difficult to read, because the hyphen draws the first word of the proper noun away from the rest of it, and they should be avoided if possible. In printing, readability is slightly improved in such situations by use of an en dash, which is longer than a hyphen but shorter than an ordinary dash, instead of a hyphen: *post–World War II inflation.*

Prefixes on the list also take hyphens when the word they are combined with is already a hyphenated compound and the prefix applies to the whole compound: *interest-bearing account, non-interest-bearing account.* (There are exceptions; Merriam-Webster lists *unself-conscious* in its desk dictionary and *unselfconscious* in its unabridged dictionary.) Note that when the prefix applies only to the first word of the compound, it can combine in the usual solid fashion. For example, in the phrase *hyperventilation-control techniques*, the prefix does not apply to the whole compound but only to *ventilation*, so there is no need to dismember *hyperventilation*.

The British routinely use hyphens with many of the prefixes in the list, though not with those that are most common in English word formation, such as *re* and *un*. This is one of the basic differences between British and American spelling; Americans should not make this routine use of hyphens any more than they should use spellings such as *labour* and *baptise*. However, many Americans do hyphenate compounds they consider unusual or difficult to read when spelled as solid words, even some that are solid in dictionaries, such as *prewar* and *postwar*. Such hyphenation is not really an error, but it does encourage inconsistency, since it is unlikely that one's judgment on which compounds benefit from hyphenation will be the same throughout a piece of writing of more than a few pages.

2-32   Hyphenate almost all compounds that begin with *all*, *self*, and *ex* when it means *former*, most that begin with *vice*, *wide*, and *half*, and all that begin with the kinship term *great*.

This rule is quite reliable for the first three prefixes it lists: *all-important, self-confident, ex-wife*. Still there are exceptions: *sound the all clear, selfsame*. More often than not it holds for the next three: *vice-chancellor, wide-ranging, half-truth*. Permanent compounds like these must be checked in the dictionary; the more common they are, the more likely it is that they do not conform. Those that are not in the dictionary can be hyphenated.

The current Merriam-Webster desk dictionary lists *vice president*, though the somewhat older Merriam-Webster unabridged lists *vice-president*; perhaps the editors of the desk dictionary decided their spelling should reflect the almost invariable *Vice President of the United States* favored by newspapers and other periodicals. *Viceroy* and *viceregal* have long been solid words.

Widespread is one word, though *wide-ranging* is hyphenated. *Widemouthed* is one word, though *wide-bodied* is hyphenated.

Compounds formed with *half* are especially unpredictable: *half-dollar* but *half crown; half title* but *halftone.* Many are listed in most dictionaries; those that are not, such as *half-smile,* can be hyphenated, except that in some cases *half* is an adverb—*The fault is half mine; He was half dead*—and other conventions apply (see Rule 2-35). Also, when *half* is a kinship term it does not take a hyphen: *half brother.*

The word *great* usually forms open compounds, such as *great ape* and *great circle,* and sometimes combines solidly, as in *greatcoat* and *greathearted.* But as a kinship term it is always hyphenated: *great-aunt, great-grandfather; Old North French is one of the English language's great-ancestors.*

2-33   Don't hyphenate most compounds ending in *down, fold, less, like, over, wide,* and *wise;* connect them solidly to the base word. Do hyphenate most compounds ending in *designate, elect,* and *free.*

Shakedown, manyfold, conscienceless, workmanlike, push-over, countrywide, and *crosswise* are typical examples of compounds with suffixes that connect solidly. Hyphens are used to avoid undesirable combinations of letters, as in *once-over,* or impossible combinations, as in *thrill-less* and *bell-like.* They are also used when the base word is a proper noun, as in *France-wide* and *Eisenhower-like,* and when the compound is multiple, as in *income-tax-like levy* and *twenty-two-fold increase* (for the use of suffixes with numbers, see Rule 2-37). They can be used in any unfamiliar compound that the writer believes will be difficult to read as a solid word—for example, in this book I have used *period-like* to describe the points used in abbreviations and in ellipsis.

Chairman-designate and *president-elect* are standard. When the suffixes are combined with a two-word compound, as in *county clerk-elect,* the compound may be difficult to read, but often it cannot be conveniently avoided. It would seem helpful to insert another hyphen—*county-clerk-elect*—but this is not done. In printing, an en dash, which is longer than a hyphen but shorter than a regular dash, is often used in such situations to improve readability: *county clerk–elect.*

Duty-free is standard. One occasionally sees solid compounds such as *sugarfree* in advertising copy, but they are not supported by the dictionary.

> **2-34**   Don't hyphenate most compound nouns that are formed of noun + noun, gerund + noun, or adjective + noun. Do hyphenate compounds of nouns of equal value; most compound nouns that are formed of verb root + adverb; some compound nouns that are formed of gerund + adverb; some compound nouns that end in *er* or *ing*; and certain compound nouns that are formed of three or more words.

It is completely standard in English for a noun to be modified by another noun, by a gerund (which is really a special type of noun), or by an adjective. In compounds such as *dog dish*, *living room*, and *electric motor*, a hyphen would be entirely superfluous, because no signal is required to indicate that in each compound the first word modifies the second. The relationship is fundamental to the language, and the rule is that such compounds are open—that is, spelled as separate words.

Nevertheless, the rule holds only for most compound nouns formed in these standard ways. Some such compounds are solid, and some are hyphenated, as explained below. Compound nouns formed in other ways are discussed later in the rule.

Solid compound nouns

A great many two-noun compounds have solidified in English. Merriam-Webster's desk-size dictionary lists *airboat, airbrush, airburst, aircraft, airdrop, airflow,* and other solid compounds that combine the noun *air* with another noun. But it also lists *air base, air brake, air gun, air lock,* and other open compounds that would seem to be just as good candidates for solidification.

The same has happened with adjective + noun compounds, so that now the same dictionary lists *hardball*, *hardhead*, and *hardwood* but also *hard core*, *hard hat*, and *hard sell*.

There is no pattern in the solidification of noun + noun and adjective + noun compounds. We must use the dictionary— perhaps less and less often over the years, because our minds are capable of storing many hundreds of such words, but new ones to look up will always come along. Of course, not all dictionaries agree with Merriam-Webster, and the present edition does not agree with previous ones, since it reflects changes in usage. When the third edition of Merriam-Webster's unabridged dictionary appeared in the early 1960s, it was a sad day for me; I had spent my first years in publishing absorbing the second edition and acquiring a knowledge of Merriam-Webster's forms that it was very difficult to update (see **usage** in the Glossary/Index).

Since compound nouns do tend to become hyphenated or solid over time and at any time can be listed differently in different dictionaries, only editors and the few professional writers who are sticklers for detail are likely to consider it important to follow the authority of a particular dictionary, and even they will flout the dictionary occasionally. Nevertheless, I advise taking some care with compound nouns and at least treating a given compound consistently; those who never bother looking words up are likely to write *hardhat* on one page and *hard hat* on the next, a kind of inconsistency that readers will perceive, consciously or not, as sloppy.

Solid compound nouns that must be separated in context

Schoolboy is a noun + noun compound found in almost all dictionaries as one word. *A private schoolboy* is, or seems to be, a shy boy who goes to an unspecified type of school. We could make it *a private school boy*, separating *school* from the compound, or, better, *a private-school boy*, forming a new hyphenated adjectival compound (see Rule 2-36) and making the meaning entirely clear. Similar examples are *aircraft, heavier-than-air craft; taxpayer, excise-tax payer.*

Professional and businessmen requires separation without recompounding: *professional and business men*. It could also be *professional men and businessmen* or *professionals and businessmen*.

Hyphenated compound nouns

A good many compound nouns in which the first word is a possessive are hyphenated: *bull's-eye, crow's-feet, adder's-tongue*. Often, like the examples, they are figurative formations or botanical names, but we can't make too much of that generalization; *crow's nest* and *bachelor's button* are not hyphenated. Such compounds must be checked in the dictionary.

Figurative compounds used as epithets, such as *bright-eyes*, are usually hyphenated and may solidify into one word, as *dogface* has.

Compounds in which a modifier follows rather than precedes a noun are often hyphenated: *court-martial, governor-general*. (Note that *major general* and similar compounds in which *general* is a noun are not hyphenated.) The hyphenation is quite helpful, since noun + modifier compounds are not standard in English.

As is ever the case in English spelling and compounding, general principles don't cover everything we find in the dictionary; some noun compounds are hyphenated for no apparent reason, among them *stepping-stone* and *place-name*. Such compounds are likely to be given differently in different dictionaries.

Compounds of nouns of equal value

In compounds such as *city-state, actor-director,* and *secretary-treasurer*, neither word is modifying or acting on the other in a standard way. In such a compound the nouns contribute their meanings to the compound equally; the compound is the sum of their meanings, and the hyphen essentially represents the word *and*. The commonest such hyphenated compounds are in the dictionary, and a writer can apply the same principle to invented compounds, such as *poet-thief*. Note that the apparently similar *gentleman thief* does not have the same claim to the hyphen; *gentleman* is functioning as an adjective, modifying *thief*, and the basic rule for such compounds is to leave them open.

Sometimes the diagonal is used instead of the hyphen: *secretary/treasurer*. The diagonal may give a slightly clearer signal that the nouns are equal in significance, because the hyphen, a joining mark, so often signals that one element of a compound modifies or otherwise acts on the other, whereas the diagonal has a separating effect. The diagonal should be avoided if there are convenient alternatives (see Rule 2-38). It is often used when one element of a compound is a phrase rather than a single word: *treasurer/director of sales*. The hyphen would make it less apparent that the entire phrase *director of sales* is being combined with *treasurer*, not just *director*. In printing, an en dash, longer than a hyphen but shorter than an ordinary dash, is often used to help the reader perceive the compound correctly: *treasurer–director of sales*. Since in such compounds the diagonal, hyphen, or en dash represents the word *and*, one might consider just using the word: *treasurer and director of sales*. This is probably the least likely to be misread of all the possibilities.

Compound nouns formed of verb root + adverb

Break-in, rip-off, and *put-on* are standard. Some such compounds of verb root + adverb have solidified—*breakup*, for example—but they should never be open.

Do not forget that these compounds are nouns. The verbs *break in, rip off, put on*, and *break up*, which are of a type sometimes called phrasal verbs because they combine a base verb with an adverb to form a phrase, are not hyphenated. (Note that *in, off, on, up*, and similar words, such as *out* and *through*, are adverbs when they combine with verbs, not prepositions. *Business fell off* uses *off* as an adverb, changing the meaning of the verb *fell; He fell off the building* uses *off* as a preposition, which, like all prepositions, has an object, *the building*.) It is a serious error to hyphenate phrasal verbs, as in *We built-in the bunks*, but when the same words form an adjective or noun, they should be hyphenated: *Notice the built-in bunks; The bunks are built-ins*. If a phrasal verb is judged to be capable of misreading—for example, *She painted in the shed* might mean either that the artist's studio was in the shed or that she added the shed to the painting—the adverb can be repositioned: *She painted the shed in*.

Compound nouns formed of gerund + adverb

Gerunds are of two types. One type has all the properties of nouns; it is modified by adjectives and cannot have a direct object. The other type retains some of the properties of verbs; it is modified by adverbs and can sometimes have a direct object. *The careful building of bunks was his craft* contains a gerund of the first type; *Carefully building bunks was his craft* contains a gerund of the second type.

Compound nouns formed of gerund + adverb should not be hyphenated if the gerund is of the second type: *Carefully building in bunks was his craft.* However, they can be hyphenated when the gerund is of the first type: *The careful building-in of bunks was his craft.* Usually hyphenation is helpful; note that one can "hear" a hyphen in the second example but not in the first. When the gerund is not modified and has no object and thus could be of either type, as in *Building in was his craft,* hyphenation is optional. A plural gerund is of the first type—it is entirely a noun—and benefits from hyphenation in such a compound: *His speech was full of trailings-off.*

Some common gerund + adverb compound nouns are found hyphenated in dictionaries, such as *summing-up.* Even these should not be hyphenated when the gerund is of the second type: *Carefully summing up arguments was not his forte.*

Compound nouns ending in *er* or *ing*

Mischief-maker, money-maker, and *moneymaking* are so listed in the Merriam-Webster unabridged dictionary. They are members of a special class of compound nouns in which the second word is based on a verb and the first word is the object of the verb's action. Such compound nouns may have a very strong tendency to become solid or hyphenated, and many of them are found either solid or hyphenated in the dictionary. We can "hear" the tendency—we pronounce such compounds as one word, with a strong stress on the first element and no pause before the unstressed second element.

Not all compounds so formed have the tendency to solidify, however: *homeowner, landowner,* and *shipowner,* but *dog owner.* The last compound follows the basic rule and is open, and we can "hear" the openness—*dog owner* is likely to be pronounced as two separate words.

A common practice with compound nouns that are not in the dictionary is to follow the basic rule and leave them as two separate words. This practice can cause annoying inconsistencies with similar compounds. For example, if one uses the Merriam-Webster unabridged dictionary, one may be forced to write *Childbearing may cause discomfort for many hours* and a bit later *Child rearing may cause discomfort for many years,* because the compound *child rearing* does not occur in that dictionary. Not even an unabridged dictionary can include every compound that has a claim to solidification or hyphenation.

It is a misuse of the dictionary to assume that by not listing a compound it silently prescribes not hyphenating it. I recommend making exceptions to one's usual authority when such annoying inconsistencies occur. One of the functions of editors is to make sensible exceptions to standard rules and authorities to suit the material they are editing. In a book that used *childbearing* and *child rearing* frequently, I would probably either hyphenate both or make both solid words. I also recommend hyphenating any compound nouns of this *er* and *ing* type that aren't in the dictionary but seem to want to solidify. The Merriam-Webster desk-size dictionary lists *policy-making* and *policymaker*. If *policy-making*, why not *decision-making*? I would not advise *decisionmaker*, but why not at least *decision-maker*? Many professional writers hyphenate such compounds without thinking about it; they may not follow conscious rules for forming compounds, but they have a good sense of the signal a hyphen gives and a good ear, and they generally use the hyphen appropriately.

Multiword compound nouns

Fly-by-night, good-for-nothing, hand-me-down, know-it-all, and *stick-in-the-mud* are fanciful terms, almost figures of speech, as multiword compound nouns often are. They are oddly formed—they are compound nouns, but in four of them the principal word is a verb and in the fifth it is an adjective—and because of their formation they would be puzzling without the hyphens. The hyphens are clearly "heard"—all the compounds are pronounced quickly, with a single stress and no pauses between the elements. Many such compounds are shown hyphenated in the dictionary, and any that are not can be hyphenated.

Compound nouns with *in-law* are always hyphenated: *daughter-in-law*. This convention reflects the way such compounds are spoken. Identically formed phrases such as *daughter by blood* and *daughter in fact* would not be hyphenated.

Commander in chief and *editor in chief* are not hyphenated in Merriam-Webster dictionaries, though they are in some others. Since they can be understood as ordinary nouns followed by a modifying phrase, there is no reason to hyphenate them or similar compounds. Note that they are pronounced with stresses on both the first and the last word and with at least slight pauses between the elements. In general, if a multi-word noun compound does not benefit from the signals hyphens give, it should not have hyphens. However, those who want some authority beyond their own ears must check the dictionary; *man-of-war, lady-in-waiting,* and some other compounds are commonly hyphenated in dictionaries.

Unskilled writers sometimes make hyphenated compounds of phrases that are not true compounds at all: *This is the view-from-the-top; Let's consider the man-in-the-street.* Such phrases may be clichés, but they are not compounds and should not be hyphenated. The error may result from mixed uses of the phrase; the writer sees it properly hyphenated as an adjective, as in *Let's consider the man-in-the-street aspect,* and, not entirely clear on the differences between nouns and adjectives anyway, concludes that it should always be hyphenated.

Noun compounds in British English

British and American hyphenation practices differ considerably, and the differences are particularly great with noun compounds. The British tend to hyphenate noun + gerund and gerund + noun compounds: *dog-dish, living-room.* They are usually careful to distinguish between gerunds and participles in compounds, hyphenating with gerunds but not with participles: *sitting-room,* but *sitting duck.* The distinction reflects the usual difference in pronunciation—both we and the British run together *sitting room* and pronounce *sitting duck* as two words—but only the British routinely signal the distinction with a hyphen.

Both compound nouns that have solidified and those that remain open in American dictionaries are likely to be hyphenated by the British, though British dictionaries are no more consistent than American. The *Concise Oxford Dictionary* lists a number of noun compounds with *air,* the first few of which are *air-balloon, air-bed, air-bladder, air-brake, air-brick, air-chamber, aircraft, air crew, air-cushion,* and *airdrome.* None of these is hyphenated in current American dictionaries.

British publishers seem to leave hyphenation and all other punctuation up to authors more than American publishers do; punctuation in books published in Britain varies widely. Consequently, generalizations about British preferences must be quite tenuous. It does seem safe to say that British and American readers get the same basic signal from the hyphen, even though they expect to find it in different types of compound.

2-35   Don't ordinarily hyphenate adjectival combinations of adverb + adjective or adverb + participle unless the adverb does not end in *ly* and can be misread as an adjective.

Since the function of adverbs is to modify adjectives and verbs, and since participles are merely forms of verbs that can act as adjectives, the combination of adverb + adjective or adverb + participle is just a simple case of one word modifying another, and ordinarily no hyphen is needed to show the relationship.

An appropriately-red bridal gown and *a completely-confused groom* are errors in American English; there should be no hyphens. (The British often do hyphenate such compounds, however.) Some writers are misled by three-part compounds, such as *a badly run-down neighborhood*, and insert a superfluous hyphen after the adverb: *a badly-run-down neighborhood*. In the example there should be no hyphen between *badly* and *run-down* (which is correctly hyphenated as a participle + adverb adjectival combination, a type discussed in Rule 2-36). Such modified compounds are discussed in detail later in this rule.

Note that a *scholarly-looking person* is not an error. *Scholarly*, *leisurely*, and a few other adjectives end in *ly*, which is the standard ending for adverbs, but they are still adjectives, and the combination of adjective + participle, as in *scholarly-looking*, should be hyphenated, as explained in Rule 2-36.

Adverbs that do not end in *ly* and can be mistaken for adjectives

An ill-clothed baby is not an error, even though *ill* is an adverb and the combination is adverb + participle. The reason for the hyphen is that *ill* can be misread as an adjective, meaning *sick* and directly modifying *baby* rather than the participle *clothed*. The hyphen links *ill* to *clothed*.

It is rare that the omission of such a linking hyphen causes real ambiguity. Even so, we naturally avert confusion in speech—we almost invariably run together such combinations as *ill-clothed* when they precede the word they modify and often when they follow the word as well, but we are likely to pronounce combinations with *ly* adverbs, such as *badly clothed*, as two distinct words. We should do the same in writing, running together certain combinations with a hyphen. Sometimes the ear is the best judge of when a hyphen is desirable, but there are some general principles and also some common conventions with specific words used in compounds.

There are many adverbs that do not end in *ly* and can also be adjectives, among them *half, well, better, best, fast, slow, little,* and *long.* The eight listed and some others should routinely be followed by a hyphen when they are used in adverb + participle compounds that come before the modified word: *half-asleep audience, well-dressed parent, better-clothed baby, best-written book, fast-moving traffic, slow-moving van, little-used car, long-awaited speech.*

Not all of these compounds need hyphens when they follow the modified word, but some do: *The parent was well dressed, The baby was better clothed, The car was little used,* and *The speech was long awaited;* but *The audience was half-asleep, The traffic was fast-moving, The van was slow-moving,* and probably *The book was best-written,* though the last example is an odd one that would be unlikely to occur. One can try to derive principles for dropping or retaining the hyphen when such compounds follow the modified word—for example, *slow* seems to require the hyphen in any compound that comes to mind, and perhaps compounds with present participles are more likely to require the hyphen than those with past participles—but usage varies so much on this fine point of punctuation that the ear is often the best judge.

Half is particularly variable. In one of the examples in the preceding paragraph, *The audience was half-asleep,* the hyphen seems desirable, perhaps because without the hyphen one might think the sentence meant that half those in the audience were awake and half were asleep. But often it does not, at least to my ear: *The man was half dead, The door was half open, The meal was half finished.* It is also tricky when it is used to modify verbs, usually requiring a hyphen before transitive verbs but not before intransitive verbs: *He half-turned the knob,* but *He half turned and looked out the window.*

Although most compounds with *well* do not require hyphens when they follow the modified word, many such compounds are so common that they occur in dictionaries as hyphenated compounds. They can therefore be considered permanently hyphenated compounds: *The groom was well-bred and the bride was well-heeled; she was also well-rounded, so the wedding was well-timed.* The compounds in the example are all supported by listings in the Merriam-Webster desk-size dictionary, but if a *well* compound not in the dictionary is added to the series—perhaps *but not well attended*—it also should be hyphenated or else all the other hyphens should be omitted, to avoid an inconsistency that would puzzle the reader.

I advise retaining the hyphen whenever the ear strongly suggests it. It is not wrong, though it may be counter to the current trend against using hyphens, to use hyphens in all of the preceding examples. The worst one could say of *The parent was well-dressed, The baby was better-clothed, The car was little-used*, and *The speech was long-awaited* is that the hyphens are an unneeded signal; the signal is still a valid one and it does not trouble the reader.

Some words that can be either adverbs or adjectives are much more common as adjectives. When such a word is used as an adverb in a compound, it is likely to be perceived as an adjective whether or not the compound follows the modified word, and the argument in favor of retaining the hyphen becomes very strong. *Some executives are hard-driving because their neuroses are deep-seated* must have the hyphens, in my opinion, though some major modern authorities would prescribe dropping them. The hyphens are very clearly "heard," and dropping them contradicts the fact that *hard-driving* and *deep-seated* are very closely bound compounds. (*Deep-seated* is so listed in Merriam-Webster dictionaries and could retain the hyphen on that ground, but *hard-driving* is not.) *Hard* and *deep* are genuine adverbs in the example, as they are in *He played hard and swam deep*, but the words are far more common as adjectives, and when they stand alone in a compound they are likely to be perceived as adjectives rather than part of the compound. To honor the ear and to keep the reader's eye from momentarily misreading the adverbs as adjectives, the hyphens are highly desirable.

More, most, and *least* can be either adverbs or adjectives. However, one rarely sees them hyphenated when they are combined with adjectives or participles: *a more comprehensive report, a most loving parent, the least forgivable sin.* I advise going with the crowd and not using hyphens with these words when misreading is impossible or highly unlikely; hyphens occur so rarely with them in published material of all kinds that when one does occur it surprises the eye and is an undesirable distraction. One must be alert to catch the ambiguities that do occur when such compounds precede the modified word. *We need more comprehensive reports* is truly ambiguous; it could mean either that we need more reports that are comprehensive or that we need reports that are more comprehensive. *We need more-comprehensive reports* would make the second meaning unmistakable, but the hyphen is not the happiest solution, because it looks odd with *more* compounds even when its signal is essential. The first meaning could be made unmistakable only by rephrasing; hyphens are a great help in clarifying English syntax, but they can't always do the job. Combinations that are not truly ambiguous but can momentarily mislead, such as *most prized awards*, must be considered for hyphenation individually; the context they are found in may make misreading more or less likely, and the decision should be made accordingly. I wish these adverbs did customarily take the hyphen, as do *well*, *little*, and others already discussed, but they do not.

Much can be either an adverb or an adjective. It commonly combines with either a participle or a comparative adjective, and though it is rarely ambiguous in either combination, with a participle it is usually hyphenated when the compound precedes the modified word and sometimes hyphenated even when the compound follows: *a much-loved baby*; *The baby was much-loved*. It should not be hyphenated with a comparative: *a much healthier baby*.

Adverbs that do not end in *ly* but cannot be mistaken for adjectives

Too, *very*, *almost*, *always*, *seldom*, *not*, and some other common adverbs do not end in *ly*, but they cannot be adjectives either. They do not normally require hyphens when used in compounds: *too loving parent*, *very comprehensive report*, *almost forgivable sin*, *always polite manner*, *seldom simple rules*, *not unwelcome guest*. They can be used in multiple compounds, still without hyphens: *too seldom loving parent*, *almost always very comprehensive reports*, and so on. They do require hyphens in unusual compounds, such as *too-many-cooks situation*, in which the noun phrase *too many cooks* is used as an adjective.

Ever and *never* are special cases. They do not end in *ly* and they cannot be adjectives, but they usually should be hyphenated in compounds before the modified word: *ever-polite manner, ever-loving parent; never-simple rules, never-comprehensive reports.* Often they should be hyphenated in compounds after the modified word as well, depending on whether they can be read as modifying the verb in the sentence. Thus *His mother was ever-loving* needs the hyphen, because in the common compound *ever-loving* the adverb *ever* clings to the participle; *His mother was never loving* should not have a hyphen, because *never* more naturally modifies the verb *was*. Note, however, that sometimes *ever* is used when *always* might be expected, and then the hyphen should not be used: *His mother, though ever loving, never allowed him to drive her motorcycle.* The ear is generally a good judge of whether to hyphenate such compounds; if they are run together, they should be hyphenated. Some compounds with *ever* have solidified into single words: *everblooming, everlasting.* See also the discussion just below for *ever* and *never* in more complicated combinations.

Adjectival compounds preceded by adverbs

When an adverb, such as *very*, modifies a normally hyphenated adjectival compound, such as *well-grounded*, the hyphen sometimes is dropped: *a very well grounded argument.* The hyphen is dropped in the compound if the preceding modifying adverb can naturally be understood as modifying the first element of the compound rather than the whole compound. In *a very odd-looking argument*, the adverb *very* must be understood as modifying the whole compound *odd-looking*, not just the word *odd*, so the hyphen is retained. Some handbooks with briefer discussions of hyphens than mine prescribe the omission of hyphens in all such compounds; this prescription produces *very odd looking phrases* that make the reader work to grasp their meaning.

Other adverbs as well as *very* can have the same effect on compounds they modify: *a too well grounded argument, a surprisingly well grounded argument*, and so on. It is not always easy to decide whether the adverb modifies the first element of the following compound or the whole compound. In *a certainly well-grounded argument*, the adverb *certainly* quite clearly modifies the whole compound and the hyphen should be left in. Furthermore, *too well* and *surprisingly well* are standard independent combinations, but *certainly well* is not, and the reader should not be encouraged to read it as one. When the issue is less clear, it is usually because neither meaning nor readability is much affected by deciding it one way or the other. My own preference in doubtful cases is to keep the hyphen.

Ever and *never* are again special cases. Though they usually are hyphenated in compounds, as explained above, when they precede adjectival compounds they lose the hyphen: *ever-loving spouse,* but *ever more loving union; never-final argument,* but *never entirely final argument.* They are unlikely to modify only the first element of the following compound, so they do not affect its hyphenation: *never well-grounded arguments.*

Some writers add hyphens to multiword compounds instead of dropping them: *very-well-grounded argument, never-entirely-final argument,* and so on. The hyphens perform their legitimate function, binding words together, but they are excessive, distracting, and contrary to convention. Though they demonstrate an understanding of their effect, they also demonstrate unfamiliarity with convention; they are the mark of an unpracticed writer. A hyphen following an *ly* adverb, as occurs in *never-entirely-final argument,* is particularly objectionable, and *never-entirely final* would be even worse. Of course, hyphenation is required in fanciful compounds formed of phrases and clauses: *She was quick to notice the never-entirely-final loophole; He made his usual these-decisions-are-never-entirely-final disclaimer.* Compounds formed of phrases sometimes are exceedingly clumsy and quite pointless, twisting English syntax for no purpose except to achieve brevity, as in *increasingly difficult-to-obtain permission.* In the example, the hyphens improve comprehensibility somewhat, but they can't much reduce the clumsiness. Such compounds should be avoided by rephrasing, unless they are justifiable in context to avoid some greater awkwardness.

2-36 Hyphenate most adjectival compounds not covered in Rule 2-35 when they occur before the word they modify and some of them when they occur after.

Rule 2-35 covers the most common adjectival compounds, those formed of adverb + adjective or adverb + participle and generally not hyphenated, though the rule discusses a great many exceptions. There are many other ways of forming adjectival compounds, and although most compounds formed in such ways are hyphenated, some are not.

The discussion in this rule covers all the usual ways of forming adjectival compounds that Rule 2-35 does not cover. It is consequently very long. Those who are uncertain about hyphenating a particular compound should first determine what parts of speech the compound is formed from and then find the appropriate section below. Late in the discussion there are sections on adjectival compounds with capitalized words, adjectival compounds with *and* or *or* in them, suspended adjectival compounds, and foreign phrases used as adjectival compounds.

Adjective + participle and noun + participle adjectival compounds

A high-powered executive may be soft-shelled. An adjective + participle adjectival compound should be hyphenated whether it occurs before or after the word it modifies. The adjective may be comparative or superlative: *The highest-powered executives are always softer-shelled than they look.* Note that *powered* and *shelled* are somewhat unusual participles; they are really nouns, not verbs, with *ed* added to permit them to function as participles do. That is why the compounds are formed with *high* and *soft*, which can be either adjectives or adverbs, rather than with the adverbs *highly* and *softly*—the compounds are based on the phrases *high power* and *soft shell*, which are nouns modified by adjectives. Other such compounds include *able-bodied* and *blue-eyed*. Some adjective + participle compounds are formed with genuine participles—*dark-painted house, sleepy-seeming man*—but usually the participle is artificial, based on a noun rather than a verb.

Is that heart-stopping freckle-faced girl the tot, mischief-loving and dimple-cheeked, who used to live next door? Noun + participle adjectival compounds should be hyphenated, both before and after the words they modify. Again, some of the participles are artificial; *cheek* and *face* can be verbs, but their meanings as verbs are not intended here—the compounds are formed on the nouns *cheek* and *face*.

Some handbooks advise not hyphenating adjective + participle and noun + participle adjectival compounds unless there is a real possibility of confusion; some say specifically not to hyphenate them when they occur after the modified word, since confusion is unlikely then. I advise using the hyphen in all cases. It helps show the relationship of words within the sentence and in no way discommodes the reader; it is a service to the reader. It is clearly "heard" in such compounds—when they are spoken they are run together. In addition, routine use of the hyphen makes it unnecessary to study every such compound for possible misreadings.

Many adjective + participle and noun + participle adjectival compounds have become one word: *kindhearted, towheaded*. They have gone the same route toward solidification as many compound nouns (see Rule 2-34). It is not wrong to hyphenate such compounds—one dictionary or another, especially an older dictionary, will list them with hyphens. Those who want to follow the practice of a specific dictionary must look them up, because they solidify unpredictably. The Merriam-Webster dictionaries, for example, list *lighthearted* but *light-headed*.

Do not confuse adjectival compounds such as *heart-stopping* and *mischief-loving*, which have participles as the second element, with compound nouns such as occur in *Heart stopping during operations is an example of modern medical miracle working*, which have gerunds as the second element. Adjective + gerund and noun + gerund compounds sometimes do not require hyphens even when they are used as adjectives; they are discussed later in this rule.

Participle + adjective, participle + adverb, noun + adjective, and adjective + adjective adjectival compounds

Burning-hot soup is a participle + adjective combination. The hyphen is usually optional if the compound follows the modified word: *The soup was burning-hot* or *The soup was burning hot*. The hyphen can be "heard" to some degree, and I generally use it. (The hyphen in *The cook was growing-angry* is, of course, an error; here *growing* is not an adjectival participle but part of a linking verb.)

Stirred-up soup is a participle + adverb combination. *The soup was stirred up* may require no hyphen, because *stirred up* may not be an adjectival compound; it may be part of a passive verb followed by an adverb, as in *The soup was stirred up by the cook*. When such a compound must be read as adjectival, I advise hyphenating it: *The soup was hot and stirred-up*. Similarly, *As the meeting proceeded, the agenda sheet was marked up* should not have the hyphen, because *marked* is part of a passive verb form, but *I noticed, that the agenda sheet was marked-up* benefits from the hyphen, because here *marked* is part of an adjectival compound. Note that *The cook stirred-up the soup* and *We marked-up the agenda sheet* are serious errors. *Stirred* and *marked* are not adjectival participles here but are active verbs in the past tense. *Please stir-up the soup* is the same error with the verb in the present tense; *The soup was stirred-up by the cook* is the same error with the verb in the passive voice.

Ice-cold soup is a noun + adjective combination. *The soup was ice cold* is permissible, and prescribed by some handbooks, but I advise retaining the hyphen when the noun + adjective compound follows the word it modifies. The hyphen is clearly "heard"—the compound is run together—in such compounds: *She was razor-sharp; He was girl-crazy.* Color descriptions are often noun + adjective compounds: *navy-blue soup; The soup was navy-blue.* Note that when such compounds are not adjectival, they are not hyphenated: *Navy blue is an inedible color.* Noun + noun color compounds such as *blue-green* are hyphenated, however; see the discussion of compounds of nouns of equal value in Rule 2-34.

Dark-blue soup is an adjective + adjective combination. Such combinations typically involve color, sometimes more than one color: *bluish-green soup.* I advise hyphenating these compounds before the modified word but not after; in *The soup was dark blue* and *The soup was bluish green*, the compounds would probably be spoken as two words rather than run togther, and there is no point in contradicting this natural tendency with a hyphen. Many handbooks advise never hyphenating compounds involving color, and I usually leave them unhyphenated if I find them that way in a manuscript I am editing. However, the hyphen is "heard" when such compounds precede the modified word, and misreading is possible when it is omitted: *You take the light brown suitcase—it must weigh a ton.* The reader's confusion may be fleeting and trivial, but that is no reason not to prevent it.

Adjective + noun and noun + noun adjectival compounds

Compounds of adjective + noun and noun + noun are not normally hyphenated (see Rule 2-34), but when they are used to modify another noun—that is, when they become adjectival—they usually should be hyphenated.

A *hard-science teacher* means a teacher of one of the hard sciences, such as physics. A *hard science teacher* means, or is apt to be understood to mean, a science teacher who is hard on students. If *hard* is to modify *science* rather than *teacher*, we need the hyphen; if we don't use it, we can't avoid ambiguity without rephrasing. As a child I came across the phrase *lost wax process* in a Baedeker guidebook; a pity, I thought, that metalworkers of old did not record their techniques and that the wax process was forever lost to us.

A *problem discussion group* could mean a group that discusses problems or a discussion group that is itself a problem, as many are. Probably, of course, it means *a problem-discussion group*, but the hyphen is needed to make this meaning unmistakable.

A *sheriff's office employee* probably wouldn't be misunderstood—it means an employee of a sheriff's office, not an office employee owned by a sheriff. Nevertheless, the possessive *sheriff's* functions as an adjective in the compound noun *sheriff's office*, and when the compound noun itself is used as an adjective, the hyphen is helpful: *a sheriff's-office employee.*

A few decades ago it was the rule in book publishing, and for the most part elsewhere, to hyphenate virtually all adjective + noun and noun + noun adjectival compounds. Some very common compounds, such as *high school*, were excepted, and editors customarily made temporary exceptions to suit whatever material they were editing so as to avoid apparent inconsistencies with compounds used frequently both as nouns and as adjectives. Thus whereas *science-fiction writer* would normally be hyphenated, in a work that used the compound constantly it would not be: *Science fiction has changed since the days of early science fiction writers Jules Verne and H. G. Wells.*

Nowadays it is common to hyphenate such compounds only when confusion is considered a real hazard, which is not very often—with a little work the reader can usually figure out the meaning. Many book publishers, however, prefer to save readers trouble and have resisted the trend toward dispensing with the services of the hyphen. Even the most familiar compounds can be ambiguous, and the writer, who knows the intended meaning, often will not notice the ambiguity; only the reader will. A *public school meeting* could be either a school meeting that is public or a meeting about public schools, and in a carelessly written newspaper account the ambiguity might be real, not just momentary. Even when ambiguity is not a problem, the hyphen is "heard" in adjective + noun and noun + noun adjectival compounds, so it might as well appear.

I recommend holding to the older standard, though I do omit the hyphen in compounds that are used frequently and unambiguously in a particular work. In addition, the number of common compounds that rarely or never need the hyphen has grown; I would not now normally hyphenate adjectival uses of *income tax, public relations, real estate,* and many other compounds. When I edit a book, I keep a list of compounds that I have decided not to hyphenate in that book, and such a list may contain several dozen items. For example, in a book on money management I might list compounds such as *financial services industry* and *bond investment program.* For me and most other book editors, the rule is still to hyphenate such compounds—we simply make more exceptions to the rule. A few publications, notably *The New Yorker,* hold very rigidly to the older standard and make virtually no exceptions.

One advantage of the older standard is that it helps counter the noun plague—the tendency of noun compounds to clump together in almost virulent fashion, as in *It was decided to postpone the hard science replacement teacher shortage problem discussion.* We could hyphenate the six-part modifier—in fact, we could hyphenate it in more than one way, and the effort of deciding which way is best might make us realize that we have written a very poor sentence and should rethink and rewrite it. Many fields of study or interest—education is, unfortunately, an easy target—have vocabularies that abound in compounds that are not customariy hyphenated in their literature. Thus *slow student techniques* and *teacher training requirements,* though at least the first might be ambiguous to someone not in the field of education, would not be apt to be hyphenated within the field. Then one compound is used to modify the other: *Slow student techniques teacher training requirements should not be relaxed this year.* This clumping of modifiers is perhaps more responsible than any other single fault of diction for the difficulty laymen have with works in education, sociology, politics, philosophy, psychology, and other wordy fields. See also the discussion of abstract diction in Rule 4-11.

There are some categorical exceptions to the rule. In the life sciences and in most general writing in natural history, phrases of two or more words that denote specific animals or plants are not normally hyphenated when used as adjectives: *Douglas fir forest, great horned owl scat.* (Many such phrases, however, have hyphens even as nouns, such as *adder's-tongue,* and these, of course, retain their hyphens when they are used as adjectives.) Chemical compounds do not usually have hyphens— *sodium sulfide solution*—but an incidental adjectival use of such a term in a work for laymen can follow the general rule.

Note that when an adjective + noun or noun + noun adjectival compound that normally needs no hyphen has added to it another element that does require a hyphen, hyphens must be used throughout the compound: *public works program, public-works-related program; sodium sulfide solution, sodium-sulfate-contaminated solution.* In these examples the addition changes the nature of the compounds; it makes them noun + participle adjectival compounds, with the noun elements compounds themselves.

When an adjective + noun or noun + noun adjectival compound that normally needs no hyphen has added to it another element that also normally needs no hyphen, the complete compound may or may not require hyphenation to clarify it. Thus if *junk bond market* and *bond market specialists* are accepted as requiring no hyphenation, *junk bond market specialists* can be accepted too, making it unnecessary to decide between the two valid ways of hyphenating it, *junk-bond market specialists* and *junk-bond-market specialists* (the second way is preferable). But even if *foreign bond market* is accepted as requiring no hyphenation, *foreign bond market investors* requires hyphenation—either *foreign-bond-market investors* or *foreign bond-market investors*—to make it clear whether *foreign* is part of the compound or modifies *investors* directly.

See also Rule 2-37 for information on adjectival phrases such as those in *a ten-year-old girl* and *The girl was ten years old.*

Adjective + gerund and noun + gerund adjectival compounds

A gerund looks like a present participle—it is based on a verb and ends in *ing.* However, whereas participles are used as adjectives, as in *a thinking man,* gerunds are used as nouns, as in *His thinking was faulty.* Since gerunds function as nouns, adjective + gerund and noun + gerund adjectival compounds are hyphenated or not according to the same principles as adjective + noun and noun + noun adjectival compounds, discussed just above.

Compounds in which gerunds are the second element look exactly like compounds in which present participles are the second element, but different principles of hyphenation apply. In *The home-building industry is in a slump*, the adjectival compound is formed with a gerund; in *Home-building couples are notoriously prone to divorce*, it is formed with a participle. In the first example, the compound is basically a compound noun, as in *Home building is an industry*, that has been used as an adjective and therefore hyphenated; in a book that used the compound often as both a noun and an adjective, it would be appropriate to omit the hyphen, or the compound could even be added to one's private list of those that can routinely do without a hyphen. In the second example, the compound is only an adjective and should always be hyphenated (see the discussion early in this rule of adjective + participle and noun + participle adjectival compounds).

In *rapid-reading techniques*, the adjectival compound is formed with a gerund, and the hyphen could be omitted in a book or article that used the adjective + gerund compound noun *rapid reading* frequently.

Often the *ing* word in an adjectival compound can be considered either a participle or a gerund, and a missing hyphen does not trouble the reader. Sometimes the *ing* word must be perceived as a participle, and then a missing hyphen is troublesome. Thus *Bond buying activities are slow* is not troublesome—*buying* is easily perceived as a gerund—but *Bond buying investors are scarce* is troublesome; a hyphen is needed. If both compounds must be used frequently, it might be wise to hyphenate adjectival uses of the gerund compound too, to avoid what the reader is likely to consider an inconsistency. (Such gerund compounds sometimes are hyphenated or solid even as nouns, as explained in the discussion of compound nouns ending in *er* and *ing* in Rule 2-34, but the compound noun *bond buying* seems better as two words.)

Adjectival compounds that are prepositional phrases or are formed with participle + adverbial preposition or participle + prepositional phrase

An off-the-wall report modifies *report* with the prepositional phrase *off the wall*. *An in-the-bag situation* modifies *situation* with the prepositional phrase *in the bag*. Hyphens are necessary when prepositional phrases are used as adjectives and precede the word they modify. The word order is not the standard English word order, and the hyphens clarify it.

Some prepositional phrases, including *off-the-wall*, have become permanent compounds and are hyphenated even after the word they modify: *The report was off-the-wall.* Dictionaries list many of them—*off-the-shelf*, *off-the-cuff*, and so on. They are not, of course, hyphenated when they are used as ordinary prepositional phrases rather than adjectives: *Please wipe that handwriting off the wall.* Prepositional phrases that have not become permanent compounds are not hyphenated when they occur after the modified word, and omitting hyphens in a permanent-compound prepositional phrase is not really an error, since dictionaries differ in what they consider permanent compounds worth listing. If the compound would be pronounced almost as one word rather than as separate words, it has a claim to being considered a permanent compound. Those who don't trust their ears can use a specific dictionary as an arbitrary authority, as many professional editors do.

The out-of-order motion came from the floor and *The from-the-floor motion was out of order* illustrate the difference between a prepositional phrase used as an adjective before the modified word, one used as a standard adverbial modifier, and one used as an adjective after the modified word. In the first sentence, *from the floor* modifies the verb *came.* In the second sentence, *out of order* is an adjectival prepositional phrase linked to the noun *motion* by the verb *was.* These phrases are not hyphenated. But when the phrases act as adjectives preceding the modified noun, *motion*, they are hyphenated.

A worked-out problem modifies *problem* with a participle that has its own adverbial modifier, *out.* Note that *out, in, under, by, from*, and other words that are usually thought of as prepositions (and are prepositions when they have an object, as in *out the window*) are not prepositions but adverbs when they directly modify the meaning of a verb and do not have an object of their own. Thus *a worked-out problem* really has a participle + adverb adjectival compound, a type covered earlier in this discussion. I will sound an alarm already sounded in that earlier mention of the type: *We worked-out the problem* is a serious error; *worked* here is not the past participle but the past tense of *work*, and the hyphen is as glaringly wrong as it is in *We worked-carefully on the problem.* A verb and an adverb modifying it should not be hyphenated.

209

A bounced-off-the-wall preliminary report modifies *preliminary report* with the participle + prepositional phrase *bounced off the wall.* As explained above, the prepositional phrase *off the wall* is hyphenated when it is used as an adjective before the modified word. When a participle is added to the compound, the whole compound is hyphenated. The hyphens usually disappear when such a phrase follows the modified word, because the participle can be perceived as part of a passive verb: *The preliminary report was bounced off the wall.* Rarely, such compounds must be perceived as adjectival when they follow the modified word and should then be hyphenated: *Proposals, both bounced-off-the-wall and thoroughly thought-out, overwhelmed the committee.*

Adjectival compounds with capitalized words

A French Canadian canoe means a canoe from French Canada. *A Spanish American revolution* means a revolution in Spanish America. But *the Spanish-American War* means a war between Spain and America, not a war in Spanish America; it requires the hyphen.

Compounds of national origin are always hyphenated when used as adjectives: *an Italian-American family.* There is some disagreement on whether they should be hyphenated when used as nouns. I advise hyphenating them: *She is an Italian-American.* Until fairly recently they were always hyphenated, as is reflected in the common phrase *hyphenated American.*

Someone who was born in Madrid and emigrated to New York is a Spanish-American, having combined two nationalities. But a native inhabitant of Cuba is a Spanish American living in one of the countries of Spanish America. (A Cuban now living in Miami might be considered a Spanish American–American, but fortunately the term *Cuban-American* is available.)

Except for compounds of national origin, proper nouns—that is, capitalized ones—and adjectives formed from them normally do not require hyphens when they are used in adjectival compounds, because their capitalization makes it evident that they are a unit: *Department of Defense spokesman, Wall Street firm, North Atlantic Treaty Organization general meeting.*

This dropping of hyphens sometimes carries over to book and article titles and similar capitalized phrases, where it is not justifiable; an article title such as "Factors Relating to the Eighteenth Century Drop Off of Currency Control Regulations in Long Occupied Countries" is almost unreadable. The capitalization, which exists only because it is conventional to capitalize main words in titles and not because there are any proper nouns, does not help to untangle the relationship of the words to one another. The title should be "Factors Relating to the Eighteenth-Century Drop-off of Currency-Control Regulations in Long-Occupied Countries."

Adjectival compounds containing *and* or *or*

The black-and-white awning was made of black and white strips of canvas. The compound *black-and-white* modifies *awning* as a unit, but the two later adjectives *black* and *white* modify *strips* separately, since each strip is either black or white, not both—the adjectives do not form a compound, and they should not be hyphenated. Somewhat similarly, *a do-or-die attitude* requires the hyphens for the adjectival phrase, but in *He resolved to do or die* the phrase is not adjectival and should have no hyphens.

The red-white-and-blue flag looks somewhat odd, because in a series of three or more words with *and* before the last word we expect at least one comma if not more (see Rule 2-6). However, it is permissible. I consider it preferable to *the red, white, and blue flag,* which is also permissible. In such adjectival compounds, either the hyphen or the comma must be slighted, and sometimes it may be better to skip the hyphen. For example, *a tall steel-and-concrete building* is fine, but *a tall steel-concrete-and-glass building* is probably more readable with commas: *a tall steel, concrete, and glass building.* Troublesome compounds can, of course, usually be avoided: *a tall building of steel, concrete, and glass.*

Suspended adjectival compounds

The century saw many large- and small-scale wars. The adjective *large* is part of a suspended compound; it has a hyphen after it to indicate that the rest of the compound is to come, and a space after the hyphen to keep *large* from linking with *and.* There are really two compounds—two first elements share a second element, *scale.* Suspended compounds can be useful to avoid tedious repetition of a word, but they can be tedious themselves: *The article attacks the myth of the kitchen-, church-, and children-oriented woman and the fame-, achievement-, and money-oriented man* is correctly

211

punctuated and gets a lot into a few words but is somewhat annoying to read.

Adjectival compounds with multiple first elements do not always require such suspension. A conjunction of nouns such as *kitchen and church* can combine as a unit with the second element to form a single compound. *A kitchen-and-church-oriented woman* is smoother than *A kitchen- and church-oriented woman,* and *a kitchen-and-church-and-children-oriented woman* is correctly punctuated, if far from smooth. However, *large- and small-scale wars* requires suspension; *large* and *small* have to combine separately with *scale,* since they have opposite meanings.

Solid compounds can be suspended, as in *pre- and postdepression buying surges,* which avoids repeating the long word *depression.* The privilege can be abused; *pre- and postwar buying surges* would be better off with the short word *war* repeated.

Suspended compounds are most common and most useful in phrases that include numbers, which are discussed in Rule 2-37.

Foreign phrases as adjectival compounds

It has to be a something-for-something deal requires hyphens for the modifying phrase, but *It has to be a quid pro quo deal* should have no hyphens. This holds true whether or not the writer chooses to italicize *quid pro quo* (see Rule 3-23). By convention, the foreignness of the phrase is assumed to be enough to set it off as a unit. It isn't always enough; sometimes foreign phrases can be momentarily misread. *I don't believe in absentia voting is permitted* is confusing, because *believe in* is a natural combination. Here the confusion could be eliminated by inserting *that* after *believe.*

2-37   Use hyphens properly with phrases containing numbers.

Phrases containing numbers follow a few special hyphenation conventions, and though the preceding rules generally apply to them too, there are differences. Some are obvious. For example, the prefixes and suffixes discussed in Rules 2-31 and 2-33 that normally combine solidly must, of course, be hyphenated when they combine with figures: *pre-1960, the 8-fold way.*

See also Rules 3-1 to 3-7 for more information on numbers.

Exceptions from standard rules

Five hundred men modifies *men* with the adjective + noun compound *five hundred,* and normally such a compound would be hyphenated. But unless the number compound is complicated by another word or phrase, as in later examples, spelled-out numbers do not follow standard hyphenation rules when they modify a noun, no matter how many words it takes to spell them out: *five hundred and thirty-six men.*

Ten-dollar loss and *two-hundred-million-dollar loss* follow standard rules; the spelled-out numbers are like any other words used in compounds. When figures are used, one often sees a hyphen where there is no justification for it: *$10-loss.* This is as incorrect as *ten-dollar-loss.* But there is one exception to the standard rules. When a large round sum of money preceded by the dollar sign (or a foreign sign or abbreviation such as £ or DM) is partly in figures and partly spelled out (see Rule 3-1), as in *$200 million,* it conventionally does not get a hyphen as an adjective: *$200 million loss.* One does see the hyphen occasionally, and though it can't be called wrong, since it is there if the number is entirely spelled out, it is troublesome; perhaps the eye is somehow aware that there are invisible hyphens with the adjectival elements represented by *$200* and wants all the hyphens in the compound to be invisible. Hyphens are used, and required by the eye, if such a compound is combined with another word or phrase that needs hyphenation: *$200-million-plus loss, $200-million-per-quarter loss.*

Similarly, adjectival compounds of figures + *percent* are conventionally not hyphenated unless they are part of larger compounds: *23 percent increase, 23-percent-a-year increase.* This holds even when there is no invisible hyphen in the figure and my speculation about the consistency-loving eye breaks down, as in *10 percent increase.*

Other adjectival compounds of figures and a word should follow the standard rules for hyphenation: *30-minute wait, 16-inch gun, 125-acre farm, and so on.*

Spelled-out fractions

Fractions should always be hyphenated when they are adjectives or adverbs, as in *They got a one-third share* and *The money is three-quarters gone.* Opinions differ on whether they should be hyphenated when they are nouns, as in *They got one-third of the money.* By standard rules of hyphenation, there is no reason to hyphenate them; they are merely noun compounds formed of adjective + noun. However, the hyphen is "heard"—we do not pronounce the elements of such compounds as distinct words but slur them together—and omission of the hyphen could conceivably mislead: *I used to save all my change in a bucket, but I've spent three quarters of it.* I prefer to hyphenate fractions routinely. One can think of the hyphen as representing the division bar in a fraction in figures.

The horse rounded the track five and three-quarters times. Adjectival compounds of a whole number and a fraction are not hyphenated throughout unless they are complicated by another word, as in *The horse fell at the one-and-one-quarter-mile mark.*

Ranges of numbers

The hyphen can be used to indicate a range of numbers, as in *The children were 12-14 years old.* However, this is really a kind of shorthand for *12 to 14 years old* or *twelve to fourteen years old;* it is not really acceptable in general writing that is intended to have some polish. Note also that if the first part of a phrase pair such as *from . . . to* or *between . . . and* is given, it is wrong to use the hyphen as a substitute for the second part of the pair: *They were from 12-14 years old* and *They were between 12-14 years old* are errors.

Similarly, *the years 1941-1945* is permissible but is inferior to *the years 1941 to 1945,* and *the years from 1941-1945* is incorrect. The excessively compact *in 1941-1945* and *in 1941-45* are so frequently seen that they must be accepted as permissible in prose in which grace is at best a secondary consideration. Such compounds are not usually objectionable when they denote a season rather than a spread of years, as in *Skiing conditions were poor in 1987-88,* and when they are adjectival, as in *the 1929-1939 depression* and *the 21-30 age group,* but the writer might consider whether there is any real virtue in using compact forms in whatever writing task is at hand.

In printing, the en dash, which is slightly longer than a hyphen but shorter than an ordinary dash, is frequently used instead of the hyphen for ranges of numbers.

See also Rule 3-7, which repeats some of the information here but also discusses some other considerations that affect ranges of numbers.

Adjectival phrases with numbers

A ten-year-old girl; a ten-year-old; The girl was ten years old. In the first example, *ten-year-old* is an adjectival compound preceding the word it modifies, and it is hyphenated throughout. Failure to hyphenate the compound throughout is a frequent error: *a ten-year old girl*, as if *ten-year* and *old* modified the noun separately, as the modifiers do in *a ten-year variable mortgage.*

In the second example, *a ten-year-old*, the hyphenated words are still an adjectival compound, but the phrase that the compound is part of is elliptical—the modified noun, which could be *boy* or *horse* or some other word, is omitted and left to the reader to supply. The compound means *ten-year-old [something]* and functions as a noun—it can have its own modifiers, it can be made possessive, it can be the subject or object of a verb: *The pretty ten-year-old pulled the eight-year-old's hair and hit the six-year-old.* The hyphens must be there; we cannot have *the ten year old pulling the eight year old's hair.*

In the third example, *The girl was ten years old*, the phrase *ten years old* is still an adjective, linked to *girl* by the verb *was*, but the hyphens have been dropped and *year* has become plural, as in the simple adjective + noun phrase *ten years.* The same happens in number compounds that do not involve ages: *a ten-minute-long speech*, but *The speech was ten minutes long; an eleven-man-strong squad*, but *The squad was eleven men strong.*

Often phrases that are not adjectival are mistakenly hyphenated as if they were: *a bill for five-dollars, a philosopher of the eighteenth-century* (or *18th-century;* mistakes with *century* are especially common in newspapers, which typically use figures for most numbers). In the examples, the hyphenated pairs are merely modified nouns—*five dollars, eighteenth century*—and the hyphens must come out. The error *$10-loss* has been mentioned above; *$10* represents the hyphenated compound *ten-dollar*, but *loss* is not part of the compound, it is the word the compound modifies, and there should be no hyphen.

215

Suspended compounds with numbers

I bought ten- and *twenty-year bonds.* Suspended adjectival compounds are discussed at the end of Rule 2-36, and numbers follow the same principles as other words in such compounds, but they are especially frequent and convenient with numbers and can be quite complicated without being objectionable. For example, *The ordinance affects one-, two-, and five-acre lots* and *We need 2-, 4-, 6-, 8-, and 10-inch lumber* avoid tedious repetitions of *acre* and *inch.* Still, in prose that does not require the convenience of suspended compounds, it is usually better not to suspend them; *The market in six-, ten-, and twenty-year bonds is slow* might be better with *year* supplied for each compound.

Note that *I bought ten- to twenty-year bonds* is wrong, because the compound is meant to indicate a range of bond maturities, not two separate bond categories, and it should be unified rather than suspended: *I bought ten-to-twenty-year bonds.*

Time of day

It was twelve-thirty; It was twelve thirty-five. When a time is rounded to the nearest ten-minute interval, a hyphen joins the hour and minute designations. When the time is not so rounded and the minute designation is over twenty and thus has a hyphen itself, the hyphen between the hour designation and the minute designation is conventionally dropped, though it is not wrong to keep it; *It was twelve-thirty-five* is acceptable too. Hyphens must be used throughout the compound when it is adjectival: *I had a twelve-forty-five appointment.*

It was four o'clock; I had a four-o'clock appointment. Adjectival compounds with *o'clock* are hyphenated. Sometimes the noun the adjectival compound modifies is omitted, but the hyphen should still be there: *I attended most of my classes faithfully, but occasionally slept through my eight-o'clock.*

DIAGONAL

The diagonal, though not quite a standard mark of punctuation, is sometimes useful to supplement the standard marks, and it has a few uses in special contexts. Other names for it are virgule, solidus, slant, and slash.

2-38   Use the diagonal only when it has clear advantages over alternatives; consider rephrasing to avoid using it.

Probably the most common use of the diagonal in general writing is in the word *and/or*—if it really is a word rather than just a convenient device to save writers trouble and suggest that they have gone to the trouble of considering every possibility. Generally the diagonal has something of the effect of the word *and* or the word *or*, and since neither *and and or* nor *and or or* is acceptable, we have *and/or*. Often when *and/or* is used, it can be replaced by *and* or by *or* or by a rephrasing that takes only a few more words—*this or that or both* rather than *this and/or that*. *And/or* can be effectively used, but too often it merely camouflages muddy thinking.

Sometimes the diagonal replaces the hyphen in compound nouns, and because it does not just join words but suggests that they have equal value, its effect is slightly different from that of the hyphen. It has a definite advantage over the hyphen in some compound nouns in which one or both elements of the compound are already compounds: *treasurer/director of sales, senior vice president/director of sales.* However, it usually has no advantage over the word *and* in such compounds.

As a mark of punctuation, the diagonal is not as firmly established in the language as the hyphen. There is something nonliterary about it; it seems more appropriate to summaries, notes, technical material, and other such forms of writing than to formal prose. I have used the diagonal myself in titling the last section of this book, the Glossary/Index, to suggest that the section can be used either independently as a glossary or as an index to the rest of the book or as both at once; it is not either just a glossary with some features of an index or just an index with some features of a glossary, but both a glossary and an index. However, I am not confident that the diagonal really communicates this message to many readers, and I have misgivings about my use of it. I advise not using the diagonal when the hyphen will do.

The diagonal can also indicate *per* or *divided by*, as in *50 miles/hour* and *price/earnings ratio.* Uses such as the first example would be appropriate only in compact technical prose. *Price/earnings ratio* is common in general writing on financial subjects, but the phrase is also commonly hyphenated.

The diagonal has some special uses that go beyond punctuation. For example, it is used to indicate line breaks in poetry that is run in with prose: *The bat that flits at close of eve / Has left the brain that won't believe.*

3

HOW TO STYLE WRITTEN ENGLISH: MISCELLANEOUS MECHANICS

◆

By using *style* as an infinitive rather than as a noun in the title of Chapter 3, I hope to make it clear at once that in this chapter the word does not have its usual broad meaning—the way writers and speakers combine diction and manner to express themselves.

To professional writers and to editors, the noun *style* means how such elements as numbers are treated (that is, whether in figures or spelled out) and how mechanics of English such as capitalization and italics are used in a specific piece of writing or when writing for a specific publication. The word can be used as a verb, as in *The editor styled the manuscript*, or as an adjective, as in *The manuscript contained style inconsistencies*. Sometimes the term includes matters covered in Chapter 2, such as whether a comma is used before a conjunction in a series of three or more items (see Rule 2-6).

Style is basically a matter of consistency. Poor style can make writing that is otherwise acceptable look shabby and amateurish:

The Company's[1] performance was judged relative to that of its major competitors, the Fulsome company, Flabbergast Inc., and Farfetch Company International Incorporated.[2] Our chairman of the board, Mister Shaw,[3] obtained figures for these companies with the help of a private Cybernetics[4] consultant who asked to remain unnamed in this Report.[5] Our Secretary-Treasurer,[6] Mr. Sleet, with the help of his Mother,[7] Mrs. Vedanta Sleet,[8] well-known as a Necromancer,[9] adjusted the raw data by means of a formula too complicated to explain in this stockholders' report. The results, shown in table three and Chart 2,[10] can be quickly summarized. Over the past twelve months (figures for the past 3 months are estimates) the company increased its gross net by eight and a half percent, while corresponding figures for Fulsome, Flabbergast, and Farfetch range from 2-6%.[11]

Good style is usually unnoticed by the reader, which is as it should be—it is only when style is inconsistent, unusual, or convention-flouting that it is noticed. Good style makes writing easy to absorb; it doesn't call attention to itself but unobtrusively serves the interests of the writer's meaning and the reader's comprehension.

[1] It is common for *company* to be capitalized when a company refers to itself in a publication such as a stockholders' report, though the capitalization is undesirable in most other contexts (see Rules 3-12 and 3-13). However, if it is capitalized here, it should be capitalized in the last sentence in the passage as well.

[2] The treatment of the three named companies is inconsistent, ranging from informal to abbreviated to formal.

[3] *Mister* should almost always be abbreviated unless it stands alone as a form of address, and in any case it is abbreviated in the next sentence, so the style is inconsistent.

[4] Capitalizing *cybernetics*, a field of science and technology, would be correct only if it meant a specific department of a school or unit of an organization's staff (see Rule 3-12).

[5] The word *report*, like *company*, could be capitalized when a report refers to itself, but if it is, *stockholder's report* in the next sentence should certainly be capitalized too.

[6] In a company's report, the title *Secretary-Treasurer* can be capitalized, though it usually shouldn't be elsewhere (see Rule 3-14). But if it is, surely the superior title *chairman of the board* in the preceding sentence should be capitalized.

[7] Kinship titles such as *mother* are often capitalized in direct address, but shouldn't be capitalized in this context (see Rule 3-16).

[8] *Mrs. Vedanta Sleet* would have been considered unacceptable a generation ago—*Mrs.* should be used only with the husband's given name, not with the

Style is less a matter of right and wrong than a matter of good judgment and poor judgment. A styling may be poor because it is needlessly clumsy, such as spelling out a year (*nineteen hundred and eighty-two*), or because it is inappropriate for a given kind of writing, such as using figures for all numbers in a novel full of dialogue (*"I want to be number 1," he said*). Books on etiquette and manuals for secretaries prescribe quite different styles for correspondence, since social and business correspondence are different. Large newspapers have their own stylebooks (smaller newspapers are apt to use *The Associated Press Stylebook and Libel Manual*). Most book publishers use *A Manual of Style* (University of Chicago Press) or *Words into Type* (Prentice-Hall), and some have supplementary stylesheets of their own. Most magazines have a so-called house style so that stories or articles by different writers in the same issue will not have conspicuously different styles. Technical journals have quite elaborate style manuals that may be accepted as the preferred style not just for a given journal but for all writing within a given technical field.

The rules given in this chapter are intended to assist those writing on general subjects. Not all of these rules are in complete agreement with any other guide; they do reflect the prescriptions of a number of guides as well as my own experience in styling many hundreds of books. They do not cover all the style problems a writer may encounter—only the most common ones—but they do show what considerations are brought to bear when making style decisions, and thus they can serve as a model for decisions that writers with unusual style problems have to make for themselves. They are full of qualifications and exceptions, because I have tried to foresee the problems writers inevitably encounter when they try to follow generalized rules in specific situations. Those who use this chapter as a guide and find rules in it they don't like may be right to break them—as long as they keep to a consistent style of their own and as long as their judgment is good.

wife's—but this usage is now quite common, especially for divorced women who have retained their married surnames. Nevertheless, the usage still seems inelegant to many. Just *Vedanta Sleet* would be preferable here—if she is well known it is probably as Vedanta Sleet, not Mrs. Vedanta Sleet.

[9] *Necromancer* should not be capitalized (see Rule 3-12).

[10] Charts and tables should be referred to in some consistent way, such as *Table 3 and Chart 2*.

[11] There are several inconsistencies in treatment of numbers in this sentence (see Rule 3-1, especially the exceptions, and Rule 3-7), and the writer should decide between *percent* and %.

NUMBERS

Numbers are very commonly mishandled. Numbers style can vary a great deal, but except in special circumstances it should not vary within a given written work, whether the work is a single sentence, a paragraph, an article, a book, or a multi-volume encyclopedia.

3-1. **When numbers occur infrequently, spell out numbers from 1 to 100 and round numbers beyond 100, except for certain exceptions noted below.**

This is the basic rule for general writing. Editors of newspapers and many magazines and journals are more likely to spell out numbers only from 1 to 9 and use figures for all the rest, both to save space and because in a publication that includes a variety of items it is better to force figures on items that don't contain many numbers than to force spelled-out numbers on items that do contain many. Writers in any field that relies heavily on numerical information may use figures for all such enumerations, even between 1 and 9.

A round number can be considered one that can be spelled out in no more than two words: *two hundred; fifty million;* but *110,* since spelling out *110* would require several words: *one hundred and ten.* One has to decide whether to consider hyphenated numbers one word or two—*2,500* or *twenty-five hundred*—and the decision will depend on which style is less conspicuous.

Very large numbers are often expressed with a combination of figures and a spelled-out word: *20 million people; $168 billion.* Decimals can be used: *2.5 billion; $3.2 billion.* This style is convenient, compact, and easy to read.

Exceptions

Year dates, days of the month, page numbers, street address numbers and sometimes the numbers of streets themselves, route numbers, percentages, and similar familiar uses of numbers are customarily exceptions to the rule. In dialogue, numbers are usually spelled out for some of these uses too; the writer has to decide which to spell out and which to leave as figures. For example, *John said, "It was in June 1990—the twentieth or twenty-first, I think"* uses figures for the year but spells out the days of the month, which is a reasonable compromise.

A written work may include precise and frequent enumerations for some categories of things but only occasional enumerations of other categories of things. For example, an article on building birdhouses would probably contain precise numbers for measurements in inches of birdhouse designs, less precise numbers for some other units of measurement, and various miscellaneous numbers. The writer may decide to use figures for all units of physical measurement: *When we inspected the martin house thirty days later—from about 20 feet away through binoculars—we estimated a population of ninety-eight birds, all in a volume of 1 ½ cubic feet (12 inches wide, 12 inches long, and 18 inches high). A farmer 4 miles away complained that the martins had deserted their former nests on his 80 acres of scrub woodland.* Or the writer may not like having to use figures for imprecise and incidental enumerations such as *about 20 feet, 4 miles*, and *80 acres*, and so may decide to use figures only for birdhouse dimensions and otherwise follow Rule 3-1.

When numbers both below 100 and above 100 are used close together to enumerate the same things or very similar things, the numbers are apt to be comprehended more easily if they are either all in figures or all spelled out: *There were 70 women and 108 men at the meeting.* Usually it is better to make all the numbers figures rather than spell them all out. This principle applies always within the same sentence, usually within the same paragraph, and often within a passage of several paragraphs dealing with the same subject. However, the principle should not be followed blindly: *We have 3 children—1 boy and 2 girls—which would seem laughable to my great-grandmother, who had 13 children who survived to adulthood and a total of 134 great-grandchildren when she died* lets *134 great-grandchildren* force all the other numbers to be figures, which is poor judgment. It would be better either to spell out *134* or to let it remain a figure but spell out all the other numbers; the inconsistency is the lesser annoyance.

With Rule 3-1 as a basis, the writer can make a list of exceptions that will tailor numbers style to what he or she is writing. A writer should try to avoid too complex a style; the simpler the style, the easier it will be to follow and the less obvious it will be to the reader. It is better to have a simple style and violate it for occasional exceptional reasons than to have a complex style that allows for all special circumstances but puzzles the reader throughout.

3-2   Spell out numbers that begin a sentence, except for years.

One hundred and twelve people attended this year, compared with 128 last year and 142 the year before. This does violate the principle of treating similar enumerations the same way (see exceptions to Rule 3-1), but the spelled-out number beginning the sentence should not be allowed to force every following number to be spelled out. Usually it is easy to avoid the problem by recasting: *This year, 112 people attended . . .*

1980 was the last year of his term. Figures denoting years can begin a sentence. Even *'80 was a good year for Chardonnay* is permissible, though it would be better not to abbreviate the year.

The conclusion was obvious: 121 members of the state legislature were foul-mouthed begins a sentence, or at least an independent clause following a colon, with a figure, but the colon permits it; the figure does not annoy the eye the way it would if it began a truly independent sentence.

3-3   Use figures for numbers accompanied by abbreviations.

Abbreviations used with numbers usually are for units of measurement: *lb., in., mm, mph, hrs., rpm,* and so on. Writing that contains such abbreviations is very likely to make heavy use of numbers anyway, and thus to require some special style rules in addition to Rule 3-1; perhaps the rule can be a simple one, such as to use figures for all units of measurement, or perhaps it has to be more complicated.

Exception

Occasionally an abbreviation is spoken—that is, used in dialogue. However, usually it is better to avoid figures in dialogue

(Rule 3-4). Therefore, when an abbreviation is spoken, Rule 3-3 is not followed: *"It begins to knock at about four thousand rpm,"* he said; *"Give her ten cc's now and ten more in an hour,"* the doctor said.

3-4   Spell out numbers in dialogue unless they are excessively awkward.

"You owe me one hundred and fifty-five dollars," he said is preferable to *"You owe me $155,"* he said. Numbers, and also the dollar sign and percent sign, somehow do not look right in dialogue, although we do accept them in quotations in newspaper accounts; newspapers do not follow Rule 3-4.

"The materials were $122.36, the labor comes to $88.50 plus $43 for overtime, and payoffs were $1,250 to the city and $10 for the doorman, giving us a grand total of $1,413.86," he said would be very tedious if all the sums were spelled out. They could be spelled out if the writer wants to stretch them out for effect, but they are easier to absorb as figures, and most readers would be much less put off by the figures than they would be by *one hundred and twenty-two dollars and thirty-six cents.* Thus Rule 3-4 permits figures when spelled-out numbers are unacceptably awkward.

Exception

The only general exception is years—they are always in figures in dialogue unless the writer wants them said in an unusual way: *"It was in nineteen-ought-six,"* he said, *"and long before anyone foresaw the ruckus that came in nineteen and fourteen."* Depending on the requirements of what they are writing, writers can decide to make any other exceptions they choose. *"We're expecting the probe to be closest to Titan at exactly 2236 hours"* and *"Don't use this stimulant if the temperature is below 96.5 or above 101.5"* could both spell out the numbers without excessive awkwardness, but if military time occurs constantly in the context of the first example and body temperature occurs constantly in that of the second, a writer may justifiably decide to use figures.

3-5   Spell out times of day with *o'clock* and phrases such as *in the morning;* in general, use figures with A.M., P.M., and M.

The meeting was held at eight o'clock; The meeting was held at 8:00 A.M.; The meeting was concluded at 12:00 M. sharp. Some stylebooks recommend *8 A.M.* for on-the-hour times; either is permissible, but *8:00 A.M.* is preferable if there are nearby times that are not on the hour: *The meeting was scheduled for 8:00 A.M. but didn't get started till nearly 8:30.* Since one may not be able to tell in advance whether times on the hour and not on the hour will be close together, one might as well always make it *8:00* and be assured of consistency throughout in this respect.

"*Be here at eight A.M. sharp,*" *he said* is all right; see the exception to Rule 3-3.

In printing, small capitals rather than full capitals are generally used for A.M. and P.M. They can also be lowercased, since the words they stand for, *ante meridiem* and *post meridiem*, are not capitalized, and this style is becoming more common. However, M., meaning noon, would be likely to puzzle readers if lowercased. *The meeting ran from 8:00 a.m. to 12:00 noon* avoids the problem.

When neither *o'clock* nor A.M. or P.M. occurs with the time

Most books, stories, articles, and other written works have a natural leaning toward either figures or spelled-out numbers for specific uses, such as for time of day. The direction of the leaning isn't always determined by the type of writing—a disaster novel that employs minute-by-minute fictitious reportage to heighten dramatic effect will probably require figures for times of day, and a scientific treatise in which time of day is mentioned only incidentally—the time when the guinea pigs were customarily fed, the times the dedicated researchers arrived in the morning and went home at night—may be better off with spelled-out numbers for times of day: *On the morning of the critical experiment, Dr. Smith arrived at seven-thirty and had scalpel in hand by seven thirty-five.* (Note the use of the hyphens; *seven-thirty-five* is also acceptable but is slightly harder for the reader to make immediate sense of. See Rule 2-37.)

If *A.M.* and *P.M.* occur frequently with times in a given work, the writer might as well use figures for all times and make sure *o'clock* and *in the morning* and similar phrases don't occur directly following a time of day; times should still ordinarily be spelled in any dialogue, however. If *A.M.* and *P.M.* occur infrequently or not at all and there are frequent times in dialogue, the writer may choose to spell out times without *A.M.* or *P.M.* and perhaps even to eliminate these abbreviations in favor of phrases such as *in the morning* and *in the evening*, so all the times of day can be spelled out.

3-6   Don't normally use the apostrophe to form the plural of a number in figures.

The 1890's is an unnecessary use of the apostrophe; the plural number is just as clear without it: *the 1890s*. The apostrophe with the plural is necessary in a few situations—for example, to form the plural of lowercase letters, as in *p's and q's*—but not to form the plural of numbers.

Plurals of numbers usually can follow Rule 3-2—that is, numbers to 100 and round numbers beyond 100 can be spelled out: *He was in his fifties; He started counting heads but gave up somewhere in the two hundreds.* Sometimes plurals of numbers have to be spelled out, even in work that uses figures whenever possible: *One bacillus dividing under optimum conditions can number in the thousands in a matter of hours.* We cannot write *in the 1,000s*, which would be read *in the one thousands*.

3-7   In an inclusive range of numbers, don't use the hyphen when the word *to* or *and* is called for, and adopt a style to handle the second element consistently.

The range was from 2-6% is poor style; it should be *from 2 to 6 percent* or *from 2% to 6%*, depending on whether the writer has chosen to spell the word *percent* or use the symbol. Since the symbol is so short, if it is used there is no reason to drop it after the first number; it makes the range a little clearer. The *to* is required to go with *from. The range was 2-6%*, dropping the *from*, is all right, especially in writing in which many percentages occur and the reader must be expected to understand compact ways of giving them.

Inclusive dates within the same century can be in the form *1922-1925* or *1922-25;* they should be treated consistently. Page numbers can be in the form *122-125* or *122-25;* some publications use the shortest possible form, *122-5,* except in the teens—*114-17*—because it would be peculiar to say *114-7.* Again, *from 1922-25* and *from pages 122-25* are wrong. When *from* does not introduce the inclusive numbers, the hyphen is correct: *He was headmaster, 1922-25.* Inclusive dates are frequently seen with *in: He was headmaster in 1922-25.* This seems to be accepted by most publications, but in principle is not correct; *in* should be used only for a specific single year, single decade, single century, and so on. *He was headmaster in 1922-23* is correct, however, since the reference is to a single school year. Similarly, *Snowfall was heavy in 1922-23* is correct.

In printing, the en dash, which is longer than the hyphen but shorter than the regular dash, is often used instead of the hyphen in ranges of numbers: *1922–23.*

DATES

Dates are simple, straightforward items of information, but enough different ways of expressing them exist to make inconsistent or inappropriate style very common.

3-8   When a date includes month, day, and year, use commas to set off the year; when it includes just the month and year, don't use commas.

The September 15 payment is due; The September 15, 1990, payment is due. When the year is given, it is treated as a parenthetical element (see Rule 2-1) and enclosed in commas. *The September 15, 1990 payment is due* is a common error.

The September 1990 payment is due does not require the parenthetical commas, because *1990* has more of a defining, restrictive function when only month and year are given than it does when all three elements are given. Nevertheless, it is permissible to make it *The September, 1990, payment is due,* and many publications do use this style. I advise dropping the commas just because they are unnecessary, and a sound general principle of punctuation is to avoid using it unnecessarily.

When the order of the three date elements follows the British and Continental practice—*15 September 1990*—there are no commas.

3-9 In general, use cardinal numbers for days of the month (*June 3*), not ordinal numbers (*June 3rd, June third*), except in dialogue.

We are much more likely to use ordinal numbers for days of the month in speech—*"We're going to Florida on December twenty-third," she said*—though occasionally we do use cardinal numbers. In writing that is not dialogue, however, the convention is to use cardinal numbers, except in wedding invitations and similar special material. *The school will open for registration on September 10th, 1990* has an amateurish look.

Exceptions

Certain holidays are customarily expressed with ordinal numbers, which are spelled out and capitalized: *July Fourth; the Fourth of July.*

When the month does not occur in the expression of a date, an ordinal number must be used: *He was hired as a clerk on May 17, and on the 24th he was appointed to the board of directors.*

ABBREVIATIONS

Abbreviations, like other matters of style, should be handled consistently. If a somewhat unfamiliar abbreviation occurs throughout a passage, it is often a good idea to spell the term out the first time it is used, with the abbreviation following in parentheses, and then use the abbreviation thereafter: *The silicon chip measured a mere 4 square millimeters (mm²), later reduced to 2.5 mm².*

Most dictionaries give proper forms for abbreviations. Everyone knows the most common ones—*Mr., Dr., oz.*—but not everyone knows that the abbreviation for *kilohertz* is *kH* and that for *megacycle* is *Mc;* we have to look them up. The United States may be in for a period of some confusion about abbreviations as the metric system takes over—or perhaps *if* it takes over; it has made little progress in recent years.

3-10 Don't use points with most abbreviations made up entirely of initials; do use points with most other abbreviations.

It is cumbersome and unnecessary to use points in such abbreviations as *CIA* (name of an agency), *UAE* (name of a country), *ILGWU* (name of a union), *UNESCO* (name of an international organization—and pronounced as a word), *NW* (name of a compass point—and written out as a single word, *northwest*, except in Britain and sometimes in Canada), and so on. Points should be avoided even with the initials of people, unless part of the name is spelled out: *JFK, J. F. Kennedy; Old GS was at the party, and Bill C. was there but Bill M. wasn't.*

There are a few initial-type abbreviations that do require points. *U.S.* always has points, perhaps to avoid momentary confusion with the word *us,* but *USA* rarely does. *U.K.* (United Kingdom) usually has points, perhaps to avoid the infelicitous result of trying to pronounce the abbreviation as a word. The abbreviations of academic and professional degrees—*B.A., D.D.S.*—usually have points; some of them, of course, are not made up entirely of initials: *Ph.D., Litt.D.* A few degree abbreviations are used informally to refer to people, usually without points: *He is a CPA; MBAs are taking over the publishing industry.* Initial-type abbreviations of state names have points—*N.Y., R.I.*—but not when they are used with ZIP codes: *NY 10036.* The ZIP code style was established by the U.S. Postal Service.

Other abbreviations almost always have points. *Saint* is abbreviated *St.; Mister* is abbreviated *Mr.; Lieutenant Commander* is abbreviated *Lt. Comdr.* Exceptions are mainly very common abbreviations for units of measure. The preferred forms are still *lb.*, *oz.*, *ft.*, and so on, but *lb*, *oz*, and *ft* are commonly seen and are accepted—unlike *in* for *inch* or *gal* for *gallon*, which can too easily be misunderstood. Points are not used with metric abbreviations: *cc*, *mm*, *kg*, and so on.

Enough exceptions to Rule 3-10 exist to make a dictionary essential in doubtful cases, but the general principle of the rule should be sufficient for abbreviations not found in the dictionary.

3-11   If a comma occurs between a proper noun and an abbreviation, and the sentence continues, use a comma after the abbreviation as well.

Oliver Wendell Holmes, Sr. was a medical man is a punctuation error, because *Sr.* has to be handled as a parenthetical element (see Rule 2-1) and enclosed by commas. Similarly, *John Smith, Ph.D., LL.D. gave the address* is an error; there should be a comma after *LL.D.* This is one of the few times a period and a comma can occur together—though actually the little round mark is not a period at all, it is a point. It may look like a period, just as points of ellipsis look like three periods in a row, and a typesetter as well as the rest of us might call it one. But in the strictest sense, a period is a full stop—the mark to show the end of a declarative sentence.

The parenthetical commas are somewhat cumbersome, and they are rarely heard in speech. In some contexts, both commas can be omitted: *Holmes Sr. was a doctor, and Holmes Jr. was a jurist* is acceptable, though it might be better to spell out *Sr.* and *Jr.* in such a case. The commas cause special problems with *Jr.* and *Sr.* when the name is being used as a possessive: *Oliver Wendell Holmes, Jr.'s, father* is correct but not completely satisfactory. Some publications quite sensibly avoid such problems by not setting off *Jr.* and *Sr.* with commas in any circumstances. See Rule 2-29 for more discussion of the matter.

The comma may not occur between the proper noun and the abbreviation: *the Macmillan Co.; Dynamic Learning Corp.* When the abbreviation is *Inc.* or *Ltd.*, the practice of the company itself should be followed; *National Notions Inc.* may have no comma in its official letterhead name, but *Regional Regi-*

mens, Inc. may have the comma and thus require one after *Inc.* as well. (It does not have the second comma in the preceding sentence because I have italicized it to indicate that it is an example rather than a normal part of the structure of my sentence. Similarly, *"The Noble Gerbil, Man's Most Prolific Friend" was the winning essay* does not have a comma following the appositive because the words in quotation marks are a title, and the comma the title contains is not part of the sentence structure.)

GENERIC TERMS

Most of the rest of the rules in this chapter require, in one way or another, an understanding of what a generic term is and how it should be styled—capitalized or lowercased, in italic or roman type, and so on—when it occurs with or is substituting for a term that is not generic.

3-12 Learn to distinguish generic terms from proper nouns and adjectives formed from them.

A generic term is merely one that is not the name of a specific thing and not a trademarked name but instead the name of a general class of things. Thus *river* is a generic term, appropriate to refer to any river in the world. But *Mississippi River* is not a generic term; the term *river* has become part of a specific geographical designation and thus part of a proper noun phrase, and so it is capitalized.

Specific terms often become generic terms in time. Thus *sherry* is lowercased in most dictionaries, but in previous centuries was usually capitalized, presumably because it had not been forgotten that the term is a corrupted pronunciation of *Jerez*, the Spanish city the wine came from. One often sees *Burgundy* and *Bordeaux*, wines named for the regions in France that produce them, lowercased, especially in reference to wines of the same general type that are produced elsewhere; and *burgundy* meaning a color is almost always lowercased. There are many other examples. The word *utopia* is lowercased in most dictionaries even though it comes from Sir Thomas More's sixteenth-century book *Utopia*, about an imaginary country of that name. The word *Olympian*, used in reference either to the Olympic Games or to the ancient Roman gods, is capitalized, but *olympiad*, meaning the four-year interval between Olympic Games, is not. One needs a dictionary as well as common sense to determine whether a capitalized specific term has become a lowercased generic one.

Trademarked terms sometimes become generic terms—usually to the distress of those who own the trademark—and they can be special problems for the writer, because only the most common trademarks are found in dictionaries. The term *kleenex* is often used for any face tissue, though the manufacturers of Kleenex retain the trademark and attempt to protect it. The manufacturers of Coca-Cola used to send book, newspaper, and magazine publishers letters of complaint whenever they found the registered trademark *Coke* lowercased. Many terms, such as *mimeograph* and *mason jar*, were once trademarks but have established themselves solidly as generic terms. Many others seem to be on their way; it is a surprise to most people to discover that they are actually trademarks: *Styrofoam, Formica, Lucite, Lexan, Plexiglas*, just to stick to the plastics industry. Some terms are generic sometimes and trademarks sometimes; a *jeep* is a military vehicle of the GP (general-purpose) type first used in World War II, and a *Jeep* is a somewhat similar nonmilitary vehicle sold under that trademark, as in *Jeep station wagon.*

The *Trade Names Directory* (Gale Research Inc.), available in many libraries, is a useful listing when it is important to style a term correctly. The United States Trademark Association, 6 East 45th Street, New York, NY 10017, will send anyone who asks for it a checklist of hundreds of trademarks. Common sense may be more important than correctness in some cases, however. It always bothers me to see *Ping-Pong* and *Jell-O* in figurative contexts such as *The Ping-Pong of international diplomacy reduced the ambassador to Jell-O*—but the words are trademarks. When I find a figuratively used trademark lowercased in a book I am editing, I am apt to pretend I don't know it should be capitalized, though I can't conscientiously recommend this course.

Actually, common sense should be brought to bear on most styling decisions. Sometimes editors seem to violate common sense for no reason other than to demonstrate awareness of some trivial and largely irrelevant fact. For example, some editors change the commonsensical styling *Korean War* to *Korean war*, on the ground that the event was a United Nations police action, not a formerly declared war, and perhaps in the belief that an occasional mysterious correction will inspire awe in those not trained in their esoteric lore. Editors should not violate common sense—after all, communication *is* common sense.

TITLES OF OFFICIALS AND NAMES OF THEIR OFFICES

Capitalization style for titles and offices varies somewhat from publisher to publisher and from stylebook to stylebook, and modifications of a given style must often be made for specific works. However, the following rules are a sound general style, and I have included instances of desirable modifications of the basic rules.

3-13 Capitalize formal titles of most specific offices and organizations, but in some cases distinguish between federal and state bodies, major and subordinate bodies, and so on.

Names of governmental and judicial bodies such as *Senate, House, Finance Committee, State Department, Supreme Court, Fourth Circuit Court of Appeals,* and *Juvenile Court* are usually capitalized when they refer to specific bodies. However, many such terms can be generic terms as well: *The country's legislature has no senate in the usual sense; The circuit-court system was changed considerably in 1912.*

Most of the states have governmental bodies with names identical to those of the corresponding federal bodies—the states have senates, houses of representatives, supreme courts, and so on. In a book dealing entirely with politics and history within a state, it would probably be appropriate to capitalize the names of state bodies. However, in a work dealing with regional or national politics and history, and also in works on general topics that make occasional mention of federal or state governmental bodies, it may be better to capitalize only the names of specific federal bodies: *The Arizona supreme court's decision was challenged unsuccessfully in the federal courts of appeal but was eventually reversed by the Supreme Court.*

Similarly, *Chamber of Commerce* should normally be capitalized to refer to the organization in a specific town, but in a work on the activities and functions of chambers of commerce throughout the country, it might be better to capitalize the term only when it refers to the central organization—the Chamber of Commerce of the United States, to which all local chambers of commerce belong—and to lowercase it elsewhere: *the Buffalo chamber of commerce.*

Some phrases are so strongly generic that they should not be capitalized standing alone even if they are the formal name or part of the formal name of a specific office, organization, or government body: *police department, criminal court, post office, customhouse.* However, some such terms may be capitalized when they refer to a specific building: *The town hall was an important institution in Brattleboro,* but *His office is in the Town Hall; He is a judge in the criminal court,* but *I'll meet you on the steps of the Criminal Court.*

Ordinarily when the proper name of an organization is cut back to nothing but a generic term, it is lowercased: *the Department of Defense; the department.* There are a few common exceptions: *the House of Representatives; the House.* Often *the Court* is capitalized when it means the U.S. Supreme Court. It is also often capitalized to mean the judge who is presiding in a given court: *If the Court pleases* means if the judge pleases, not if the courtroom or the court as a judicial institution pleases.

In the past decade or so, following a trend toward lowercasing, many newspapers and magazines have begun lowercasing some generic terms even when they are used with proper nouns or adjectives formed from proper nouns: *Democratic party, Republican national convention.* I prefer to consider such phrases unified proper nouns and to capitalize all the elements. However, the lowercasing is preferable to excessive and meaningless capitalizing, which begins to make English look like German: *We went to the Museum and then through the Park to the Conservatory; We stopped at the Bank on the way to the Beach.*

| 3-14   Don't capitalize titles of most officials unless the title occurs directly before a name, and sometimes not even then.

Titles such as *president, prime minister, king, senator, judge, governor, mayor, general, pope, archbishop, chairman,* and *professor* are all capitalized when they occur before a name— *President Bush, Professor Waggoner,* and so on—but are all also generic terms, and there is no need to capitalize them when they stand alone.

Other titles are really not titles but simply descriptive terms: *clinical psychologist, head nurse, foreman, author.* The magazine *Time* adopted the eccentric style decades ago of capitalizing such terms—*Clinical Psychologist John Smith*— and the magazine has been around so long that the style now looks right to many people, but it's not. (*Time* was deliberately flouting convention to achieve a snappy, important look.) It should be *the clinical psychologist John Smith;* the word *the* can be dropped, though this tends to make sentences seem hurried and telegraphic.

Note that *Doctor of Laws, Knight of the Garter,* and similar phrases are not titles in the sense discussed in this rule; academic distinctions and noble orders should be capitalized.

Titles used in address

Phrases such as *Mr. President* and *Madam Chairman* (or *Chairwoman* or *Chairperson*) are always capitalized, but there is no need to capitalize titles without *Mr., Madam,* or similar introductory polite forms. However, see modification 4 below. Forms of address are discussed at greater length in Rule 3-15.

Modifications of Rule 3-14

There are many possible modifications of the basic lowercase style of Rule 3-14. Here are a few.

1. Capitalize titles of high national officials and their foreign equivalents; lowercase lesser officials. This is a common and sensible modification made by a great many writers and imposed by many editors, and it is quite easy to apply. *The President approached U.S. Steel through its president* is an apparent inconsistency, but readers are so used to the principle

behind it that they do not notice it and are probably unconsciously aided by it. One does have to decide just where to draw the line—for example, titles of cabinet-rank officials and directors of executive departments and agencies, members of the House and Senate, and Supreme Court justices might be capitalized, but not titles of those below them in the federal hierarchy. Also, applying this style may result in anomalous indications of comparative importance: *The Congressman from Utah met with the governor of New York.*

2. Capitalize titles that are used throughout a work as a substitute for a person's name. This modification makes sense when a real person or fictitious character is referred to frequently as *the Judge* or *the Major* or *the Senator.* The titles become more nicknames than actual titles. The style runs into trouble when the Judge runs into another judge, the Major calls on a general, and the Senator gets a call from the president. Sometimes these problems can be avoided by using modification 3, below; sometimes it's better to hold to the basic rule and not capitalize any titles.

3. Capitalize all titles when they refer to specific people. Thus a sentence could be styled *Major Smith found the usual collection of colonels and generals between him and the bar, and an admiral kept sloshing his drink on the Major's freshly pressed sleeve.* Again, it seems anomalous to capitalize the lesser rank and lowercase the others. Also, one has to decide just when a character or real person has been sufficiently identified to deserve the capital. This is a difficult modification to apply successfully.

4. Capitalize all titles used in direct address. This is a common modification and often works well. Since a word used in direct address has a special significance within a sentence, the reader generally will not notice that the same term is sometimes capitalized and sometimes lowercased: *"Tell me, Major,"* said the tipsy admiral as the major pointedly wrung out his cuff, *"who told you you could play in this sandbox?"* However, there is no necessity for this capitalization, any more than there is for capitalizing *buddy, sir, young lady,* or any other term used in address as a substitute for a person's name; it should not be accepted as a convention appropriate to every written work.

5. Capitalize titles when they are used with the capitalized name of a political division, the name of a governmental body, or a similar term that completes the meaning of the title. This is often a sensible modification and is usually easy to apply:

the king, the King of England; the senator, the Senator from Maine; the chief justice, the Chief Justice of the Supreme Court; the director, the Director of Central Intelligence; the archbishop, the Archbishop of York; the ambassador, the Ambassador to the Court of St. James's. The completely lowercase style of Rule 3-14 may seem too extreme for a work in which titles are frequent and important, and then this modification is useful. Also, a work full of such titles as *the earl of Darlington,* used essentially as substitutes for names as in modification 2 above, may be better styled by modification 5: *the Earl of Darlington; the earl.*

6. Capitalize titles that would otherwise be ambiguous. This is a sensible modification on the face of it—it is always sensible to avoid ambiguity. Thus *Foley, the speaker of the House* could be unclear, especially to a young reader; even if *senator* and *president* are not capitalized, *Speaker of the House* often should be, and stylebooks that prescribe equivalents of Rule 3-14 often make this title an exception. Similarly, *General of the Army,* a specific rank above four-star general, would often be ambiguous if lowercased.

7. Capitalize all titles. This is going all the way to the opposite extreme and can result in a great many capitals. However, it may be a sensible style in a work for young readers or any others who can be assumed to be unfamiliar with the titles mentioned; the capitals help the reader absorb the titles and learn them.

FORMS OF ADDRESS

Many forms of address are not titles in the sense that the terms discussed in Rule 3-14 are. The tendency is to capitalize too many of them or to capitalize them inconsistently.

3-15   Don't capitalize *doctor, madam* or *madame, sir, my lord,* and similar forms of address unless they occur directly before a name.

There is no reason to capitalize terms denoting professions or terms of polite respect when they occur alone as forms of address. When they are used to preface given names or surnames, they are considered part of the name and are capitalized: *Doctor Smith* (or usually *Dr. Smith*); *Madame Bovary*; *Sir Walter*; *Lord Castlereagh* or *My Lord Castlereagh* (*my lord Castlereagh* is also acceptable).

The same rule applies when the form of address is in a foreign language: *monsieur* or *m'sieu*, *signore*, *señor*, *effendi*, *tovarich*, and similar foreign words do not require capitalization. The German *mein Herr* is an exception; *Herr* is always capitalized, because all nouns are capitalized in German. Note that none of these quite common foreign terms require italics (underlines on the typewriter) if they are used within an English sentence; they are italicized here only because they are used as examples.

Exceptions

Some major stylebooks that advise lowercasing *my lord* and *his lordship* nevertheless capitalize *your honor, your grace, your highness, your eminence, your excellency,* and their third-person equivalents *his honor, his grace,* and so on. I pass this exception along, but I do not understand it and usually do not make it. These terms of respect are not different in principle from *sir, ma'am,* and other polite forms, and certainly not different from *my lord* and *my lady* (which are the correct forms for addressing marquesses, earls, viscounts, and barons and their wives; *your grace* is used for dukes and their wives and for Roman Catholic archbishops).

A form of address that is used frequently throughout a work as a substitute for a person's name may be better off capitalized as a kind of nickname (see Rule 3-14, modification 2): *It was now six in the evening, and Madame was well into the sherry.* Similarly, shortened versions of forms of address such as *Doc* and *Rev* can be considered nicknames and capitalized.

3-16 Capitalize *mother, grandma,* and other kinship terms for preceding generations when they are used in direct address, but don't capitalize *brother, son,* and other terms for the same or succeeding generations.

239

When his mother and his son appeared, he greeted them, "Look, Mother, I've bought a new motorcycle—hop on the back, son." The first time *mother* occurs in the example, it is as an ordinary generic noun; the second time it occurs it functions as a name and is treated as one. *Mama, Mommy, Maw,* and similar terms follow the same rule: *"Where's your mommy?" "There's Mommy."* The word *son,* however, is not capitalized, because it is no more a proper name than *buddy* or *miss.* A person would normally address a brother or sister, a son or daughter, or a nephew or niece by his or her given name; the use of the kinship term as an alternative to the name does not make it a name in the same way *Mother* is.

Uncle and *aunt* are often lowercased in address when they stand alone, though they are capitalized just about as often. Since they usually occur with a given name—*Uncle John, Aunt Mary*—they are not quite as much names as *Mother* is.

Some stylebooks, including the University of Chicago Press's *A Manual of Style,* prescribe lowercasing all kinship terms except directly before a name, as in *Uncle Ed;* many others are in essential agreement with Rule 3-16.

When kinship terms occur with names

Rule 3-16 can be applied when kinship terms are used with names as well as when they are used alone: *Mother Hubbard, Grandma Moses,* and *Uncle Charley;* but *brother Bill, sister Mary,* and—though such a phrase would be rare—*nephew John.* However, *Cousin Pete* is better than *cousin Pete* if the combination is treated as a nickname: *Come here, Cousin Pete, and meet my cousin Jane.*

Kinship terms for priests, nuns, and friars and others who are not kin

In such forms as *Father William* or *Father Smith, Brother John,* and *Sister Elizabeth,* used either to address or to refer to a priest or member of a religious order, the kinship term is capitalized. When the terms are used without a given name or surname, usage varies. I prefer to lowercase the terms when they stand alone; they are then basically terms of respect, like *sir,* not substitutes for names.

Look out, dad—make way for the younger generation and *Excuse me, mother—I didn't mean to step on your goiter* contain kinship terms used rudely or politely to address older people who are not kin; I advise lowercasing them.

PLACE-NAMES

The correct forms for geographical features and political divisions are listed in atlases and gazetteers, and the most common ones are in most dictionaries, either in an appendix or with the general vocabulary. Style problems may occur when these terms are made adjectives and when generic terms that are normally used with them are used alone or are used in the plural.

3-17 Capitalize names of specific political divisions and subdivisions and the names of geographical regions and features; in most cases, also capitalize adjectives derived from such names.

The names of countries, states, provinces, counties, cities, towns, and villages are obviously capitalized, though sometimes a decision has to be made about generic terms that may occur with such names. *New York City* is an official name and *Kansas City* is the only name; there is no question that *city* is capitalized in these examples. But *Washington state* and *Washington State* both occur, to distinguish the state from the District of Columbia; and *New York state* and *New York State* both occur, to distinguish the state from the city. A workable rule with *state* is to capitalize it when it follows the proper noun but not when it precedes: *Washington State,* but *the state of Washington.* Canadian provinces, however, have the official form *Province of Quebec, Province of Ontario,* and so on.

The names of continents, oceans, rivers, lakes, islands and island groups, mountains, canyons, and similar geographical features are also capitalized, but again there may be some style problems when there are accompanying generic terms.

Adjectives derived from place-names are capitalized when the place is still an important part of the meaning: *Roman history, French literature, Brussels lace.* Many lose the capital when the place is no longer a significant part of the meaning: *roman type, french fries, brussels sprouts.* Sometimes even the

241

original nouns lose the capital: *morocco* (leather); *plaster of paris; china.* Check the dictionary when in doubt. If following the dictionary causes troubling inconsistencies, as in *The French windows were fitted with venetian blinds* or *He threw the french fries out the French window,* one can ignore it and establish one's own style for specific words in a specific work.

Generic terms used alone

Except for a few terms, such as *the States* for the United States, *the Union* for the United States, *the Dominion* for Canada, and, when the term is clear in context, *the Channel* for the English Channel, generic words used without proper names for political divisions and geographical features are lowercased. Some capitalized terms, such as *the Coast* for the West Coast, are somewhat slangy and, though common, may not be understood by everyone; they are certainly appropriate in novels, especially in dialogue, but may not be appropriate and usually will not be preferable to standard terms in nonfiction.

Here are some examples of complete terms and generic words used alone: *the Fifth Precinct, the precinct; the Twenty-first Congressional District, the congressional district; the Massachusetts Bay Colony, the colony; the Roman Empire, the empire; the Somali Democratic Republic, the republic.* Sometimes exceptions are made in special circumstances. For example, in a historical study *the Federal Republic* might well be used to underline the distinction between the Federal Republic of Germany (West Germany) and the German Democratic Republic (East Germany); otherwise the writer might feel it necessary to repeat the entire name each time it is used, since the names of the two Germanys are similar.

Occasionally a writer will capitalize a generic term to give it special significance. Thus *the Mountain* may be appropriate if a particular mountain looms large in a novel or in a work of popular nonfiction.

Generic terms in the plural with two or more proper names

Kings County capitalizes the generic word *county,* but *Kings and Queens counties* lowercases its plural. Similarly, *the White River* capitalizes the generic term, but *the White and Connecticut rivers* lowercase it. A plural generic term following two or more proper names is lowercased. One would not lowercase the generic term in *Rocky Mountains*, since the plural word is part of a single geographical term, but it should be lowercased in *the Catskill and Adirondack mountains*, even though *Mountains* is the proper term when either the Catskills or the Adirondacks are mentioned separately.

When the generic term precedes two or more proper names, it is usually capitalized—*Lakes Erie and Superior; the Rivers Styx and Lethe*—but sometimes lowercased; either is acceptable.

Geographical regions: some complications

Terms for regions within the United States are usually capitalized: *the East, the West, the East Coast, the Far West, the Southwest, the Midwest.* Stylebooks are divided on whether to capitalize the corresponding adjectives—*Eastern, Midwestern,* and so on—and related nouns such as *Easterner.* I prefer to capitalize them, because if they are lowercased, an occasional ambiguity will inevitably occur.

Similar terms for larger regions, such as hemispheres, are also usually capitalized: *the East* (that is, the Orient), *the Middle East, the Continent* (Europe). Again, there is disagreement over capitalizing the corresponding adjectives; I capitalize them.

Generic words used with names of geographical entities may or may not be considered part of the name and thus may or may not be capitalized—a dictionary, almanac, atlas, or gazetteer may be needed. *The Indian peninsula* uses an adjective derived from the name of a political division, India, to identify an enormous geographical feature that is not normally thought of as a peninsula, and the generic word is lowercased. *The Arabian Peninsula* uses an adjective derived from a historical political division that is frequently thought of as a geographical feature—a peninsula—and contains several modern nations. Sometimes one can think of a possible reason for the distinction, sometimes one cannot; it's easier just to adopt some standard gazetteer, atlas, or other reference as an authority.

Terms such as *Atlantic Coast* and *West Coast* are capitalized only if they refer to regions on land, not if they refer to offshore waters or the actual junction of land and water: *The Atlantic Coast is heavily populated; The Atlantic coast of the United States is heavily fished.* The word *seaboard* refers only to the land along a coastline, not to the water; it is usually capitalized with *Atlantic* and *Pacific* but lowercased with other terms, as in *Florida's Caribbean seaboard.*

3-18 Never capitalize *east, west,* and similar terms when they indicate a direction rather than a region or location, and don't invariably capitalize them even when they do indicate a region or location.

He traveled nine miles East is a very common error. Here the word *east* is merely a compass point or direction; there is no reason to capitalize it. *He left the East in 1849 and followed the Gold Rush west, but found the West a disappointment and headed east again* is correct, and though the apparent inconsistency in capitalization may seem glaring when attention is called to it, it would go unnoticed by most readers, who are accustomed to the distinction between region and direction.

Capitalizing terms such as *the North,* meaning the Northeast and part of the Midwest of the United States during the Civil War, a somewhat larger area of the United States today, or the North of England, depending on the context, is helpful. However, such capitalization is not helpful if a convention for capitalizing the term has not been well established. *In southern Nebraska the growing season is longer than in the North* is apt to distract readers, who, even though they may understand what is meant, can't help but think of irrelevant contexts in which they might expect the capitalized word—the Yukon, the U.S. Northeast, or whatever. When writing about a region unfamiliar to most readers, a writer can establish capitalization conventions that are appropriate to the region, but must do so carefully, making sure the reader can follow and is given immediate significant information to associate with the capitalized terms: *The region from the capital to the coast—the North—has been called the country's breadbasket. The South is almost entirely nonarable, though it is well populated.*

TITLES OF PUBLICATIONS AND WORKS OF LITERATURE, WORKS OF ART, MUSICAL COMPOSITIONS, AND OTHER WORKS

Style conventions governing the use of capitals, quotation marks, and italics (underlines on the typewriter) for the kinds of titles discussed in this section are basically quite simple, though complexities can occur. The rules given here are well established, but they are not universally observed; many publications have variant styles, and many fields of scholarship and research, particularly in the sciences and social sciences, have detailed styles of their own. A publishing house or publication will usually routinely impose its own style variants on work it publishes. A writer in a field with its own style will need a specialized stylebook.

This book does not cover title citations in footnotes and bibliographies. There are some general rules that could be given because they apply within a great many fields, but a number of fields have their own styles, and a writer within any specific field must become familiar with the style preferred in that field.

3-19 Use italics for the names of newspapers and periodicals.

A very simple rule—and as long as writers confine themselves to mentioning newspapers such as *Women's Wear Daily* and magazines such as *Outdoor Life*, they will have no problems. But should it be *The New York Times*, the *New York Times*, or the New York *Times*? Should it be *The Kiwanis Magazine* or the *Kiwanis Magazine*?

Some writers find some more or less official guide to use when deciding how much of a periodical name to italicize and whether or not to capitalize *the*. A common guide is the *Gale Directory of Publications* (Gale Research Inc.), which is available in most libraries. I know one book editor who, over many years, has stuffed a file with front-page logos and mastheads clipped from newspapers all over the country so that he can be certain what a newspaper's own preference is. I think this is going too far, and those who use authorities such as the *Gale Directory of Publications* or personal files are forced into such annoying inconsistencies as the *Chattanooga Times* in one sentence and *The Cleveland Daily Banner* in the next.

It is easier and better to adopt simple general principles, perhaps making exceptions to them in difficult cases. The principles below are supported by the stylebook most used in book publishing, the University of Chicago Press's *A Manual of Style*, but not by some other major stylebooks.

Newspapers

Do not consider *the* part of a newspaper's name, but do consider a city, town, or village part of the name:

the *New York Times*
the *Shelter Island Reporter*

Those who prefer not to consider city, town, or village part of the name must still consider other place-names part of the name:

the *Arizona Star*
the *Wall Street Journal*

Those who prefer to consider *the* part of the name must still consider it not part of the name when the newspaper's name is used as an adjective and *the* goes with the following word, or else the newspaper's name has to be made a possessive:

the *New York Times* account
The New York Times's account

Periodicals

Do not usually consider *the* part of a periodical's name:

the *American Historical Review*
the *Kiwanis Magazine*
the *Hillside Journal of Clinical Psychiatry*
the *New York Times Magazine*

However, the word *the* in the names of some periodicals is, or at least once was, an essential part of the meaning of the name. In some cases the original significance of *the* is retained strongly, in others only weakly, and one has to use one's own judgment to decide whether the word should be considered part of the name. The following are examples of my own judgment:

the *Living Church*
the *Commercial Fish Farmer*
The Nation
The American West

The last two do not seem right to me unless *the* is part of the title, but I cannot explain exactly why. They are not the same: I would say or write "I read an article in *American West* the other day" but not "I read an article in *Nation* the other day." Yet if *the* precedes the title *American West*, I would capitalize and italicize it as part of the title.

It may be a publication's own preference to capitalize and italicize *the* as part of its name—for example, *The New Yorker* is the magazine's own style—and a writer can choose to follow such preferences when aware of them. However, the more exceptions one makes to the general rule of not considering *the* part of the name, the less one can be said to have a style at all. In a work that mentions publications frequently, exceptions should be held to a minimum.

The alternative of reversing the rule and always considering *the* part of the name may seem attractive, but I advise against it. Convention in both book and periodical publishing strongly supports the rule, and consequently material that flouts the rule seems amateurish and not quite ready for print.

3-20   Use italics for the titles of books; independently published poems; plays and movies; musical compositions except single songs or short instrumental pieces and those known by generic titles; and paintings, sculptures, and similar works of art.

Many newspapers and periodicals use quotation marks for the titles listed in the rule, but many others follow the rule, and virtually all book publishers do.

Books

A Tale of Two Cities and *The Way of All Flesh* are typical examples. *A*, *the*, and any other word that is in the title is considered part of the title and is accordingly italicized, and capitalized if it begins the title or is a major word (see Rule 3-22). Well-known reference books are frequently an exception: the *Oxford English Dictionary*, the *Encyclopaedia Britannica*, the *Columbia-Lippincott Gazetteer of the World*.

Titles do not always have to be given in full, of course, and an initial *A* or *The* can be omitted if it does not suit the structure of a sentence, as is frequent when a title is used as a modifier:

He was an *Old Curiosity Shop* character.
The piece had a *Magic Flute* good humor.

When a book is part of a series, its own title is treated like any other. The series title may or may not be treated like a book title, depending on the type of series and the conventions within the field in which the writer is writing. Donald R. Dudley's *The Romans: 850 B.C.–A.D. 337* is part of the series The History of Human Society, edited by J. H. Plumb. Peter Gay's *The Enlightenment: An Interpretation* is a multivolume series that includes the book *The Science of Freedom*. Here we can draw the obvious distinction that in the first case the book is part of a series of books by various authors, and in the second case the series is the work of a single author—all the books in it make up a single work. However, the romances of Sir Walter Scott are usually collectively called the Waverley Novels, or sometimes the Waverley novels, even though they are all his work. (Sometimes they are called the *Waverley* novels, a reasonable enough style, since the first novel in the series was titled *Waverley*.) Perhaps we could make the distinction that in this case the collective term was not Scott's but was imposed by literary historians.

If a book title includes another book title, the included title is enclosed in quotation marks: *A Commentary on Kant's "Critique of Judgment."*

Poems

Milton's *Paradise Lost* is a long book; the title is italicized. T. S. Eliot's *The Waste Land* is much shorter—434 lines—but was independently published, so again the title is italicized. Whitman's "Song of Myself" is more than twice as long as *The Waste Land*, but it is part of the large collection *Leaves of Grass*; it was not published independently, so the title is not italicized but instead is in roman type and within quotation marks (see Rule 3-21). In works mentioning a great many titles, all poem titles are sometimes put in italics for consistency and to avoid troubling the reader with a distinction based on mere publishing history, which may be irrelevant. Nevertheless, the best style is to use italics only for independently published poems.

Plays and movies

Titles of plays, even short one-act plays, and of movies are italicized: *Oedipus Rex* (or, depending on the edition or production, *Oedipus Tyrannus* or *Oedipus the King*); *Star Wars*. When a play is part of a series, the series may or may not be italicized too, like a series of books. There are two other plays in Sophocles' *Oedipus* series—or Oedipus Trilogy or *Oedipus trilogy*, whatever style one chooses. The miracle plays of late-medieval England are grouped in cycles—the Wakefield Plays, the Chester Plays—the names of which are usually not italicized, but sometimes they are.

Television and radio programs

Style for television and radio programs varies considerably from publication to publication. I advise italicizing the name of a regular feature or a series: *Wall Street Week*; *Tales from the Crypt*. When an episode in a series has a title of its own, I advise not italicizing it but setting it off with quotation marks.

Musical compositions

Titles of musical compositions are more complicated than other titles, because sometimes they are entirely made up of generic terms, which are not italicized; sometimes they are real titles, like book titles, and are italicized; and sometimes they are mixtures. Also, short compositions are handled differently from longer ones (see Rule 3-21 for short compositions).

Here are examples of long compositions with titles that are entirely generic terms:

Beethoven's Symphony No. 9 (or Beethoven's Ninth Symphony)
Haydn's Concerto in E flat for Two Horns and Orchestra
Bach's Mass in B Minor (or Bach's B-Minor Mass)
Bach's Passacaglia and Fugue in C Minor for Organ
Copland's Duo for Flute and Piano

Here are examples of long compositions with titles that contain no generic terms:

Mozart's *Magic Flute*
Rossini's *The Barber of Seville*
Handel's *Messiah*
Gershwin's *Porgy and Bess*
Bernstein's *Trouble in Tahiti*

Some compositions are well known by both a generic name and a specific title, such as Schubert's String Quartet in D Minor, which has the specific title *Death and the Maiden*.
Here are examples of mixtures:

Beethoven's *Pathétique* Sonata (or Sonata No. 8 in C Minor)
Haydn's *London* Symphony (or Symphony No. 104 in D Major)
Rossini's *William Tell* Overture
Chopin's Variations on a Theme from *La Cenerentola*

When a generic term is a true part of a specific title rather than merely descriptive, the whole title is italicized:

Liszt's *Hungarian Rhapsodies*
Mussorgsky's *Songs and Dances of Death*
Britten's *Gemini Variations*

It is apparent from all the above that one must often know something about a musical piece to style it properly. It is permissible to adopt some much simpler style, such as italicizing all titles of longer compositions whether they include generic words or not. However, the best style is that shown here.
When problems come up, general encyclopedias and encyclopedias of music are helpful, but their styles often vary. One very handy guide is the *Schwann Record and Tape Guide*, which is issued monthly; for purposes of checking titles an old

issue will do as well as a new one. It is surprisingly scholarly and complete. It does have typographical conventions that must be interpreted. Major keys are indicated by capital letters, minor keys by lowercase letters. A strange symbol like a long, thin comma indicates a flat key, a regular sharp sign a sharp key, and the absence of a symbol a natural key. No italics are used; specific titles of compositions both long and short are enclosed in quotation marks if they occur with a generic title and are not distinguished in any way if they occur alone, so one must decide some things for oneself.

Paintings, sculptures, and other works of art

There are few problems with these titles:

Gainsborough's *Blue Boy*
Rodin's *The Thinker*
Duchamp's *Fountain*

Some works of art, especially drawings and etchings, are grouped in a series, in which case both the title of the series and the title of the individual item in it are italicized. Thus Hogarth's *The Innocent Country Girl* is the first plate of his six-plate series *The Harlot's Progress*.

Titles ending in marks of punctuation

Titles such as *Annie Get Your Gun!* and *Whither Goest Thou?* contain marks of punctuation that are part of the title. If they occur in a series, they cause a problem, since ordinarily the comma shouldn't occur with the exclamation point or question mark. When the series is of titles that are italicized or underlined, as are those discussed in this rule, I advise bending the rule and using the comma:

Annie Get Your Gun!, *Whither Goest Thou?*, and *Outrageous!*, the last rather tattered, were the only works in the piano bench.

However, I have misgivings about using the comma when the titles are in quotation marks; see Rule 3-21.

251

Titles used as possessives

The apostrophe and *s* following an italicized title are roman:

The Thinker's pose occurred to Rodin only after a lot of pondering.

> **3-21   Use roman type, enclosed in quotation marks, for titles of parts of books; poems unless independently published; short stories, essays, and articles and features in periodicals; and individual songs and short instrumental compositions or parts of longer compositions.**

This rule causes few problems.

Parts of books

Leslie A. Fiedler's *Love and Death in the American Novel* is divided into parts and chapters. Part III is titled "Accommodation and Transcendence," and within that part Chapter 13 is titled "*The Scarlet Letter*: Woman as Faust." The titles of the part and the chapter are both in roman type and set off by quotation marks. (Note that *The Scarlet Letter* is nevertheless italicized as part of the title of Chapter 13, because it is the title of Hawthorne's novel.) However, parts of a book that are merely generic words, like *index* and *preface*, are usually lower-cased and are not enclosed in quotation marks.

Poems

Subdivisions of long poems are handled the same way as parts of books. For example, T. S. Eliot's *Four Quartets* contains four moderately long poems—"Burnt Norton," "East Coker," "The Dry Salvages," and "Little Gidding."

Any poem that has not been independently published, whether it is short or long, should be in roman type within quotation marks, not in italics. Thus in general, any short poem's title is apt to be in quotation marks, but longer ones may be tricky; Whitman's "Song of Myself" is long enough to be a book but in fact was only part of the collection *Leaves of Grass.*

Sometimes all poem titles in a work that gives a great many will be either in quotation marks or in italics to avoid troubling the reader with a technical distinction that may be irrelevant. Nevertheless, careful writers do make the distinction.

Short stories, essays, and articles and features in periodicals

Hemingway's story "My Old Man," Pedro Arrupe's article "Marxist Analysis by Christians," and William Safire's column "On Language" are examples. Names of some parts of a periodical, such as Directory of Advertisers, are not likely to be in quotation marks. The *New York Times*'s op-ed page is usually referred to with neither capitals nor quotation marks, as a mere descriptive term rather than a title; the newspaper itself calls it the Op-Ed page, and so named it because it is opposite the editorial page. Usually when a feature, column, or section is by a specific person, the quotation marks are used, but even this is not invariable; magazines may have a Publisher's Page, for example. However, titles of short stories and essays are always in quotation marks.

Songs and short compositions

"Greensleeves" and "A Hard Day's Night" are individual songs; their titles are in roman type and within quotation marks. Titles of short instrumental compositions such as "Fiddle-Faddle" are treated the same way.

Titles of cantatas and arias from operas are in roman type and within quotation marks, but in one other respect they are handled differently: They do not have normal title-style capitalization (see Rule 3-22) but capitalize only the first word, unless some of the words are normally capitalized anyway. These titles are actually just the first few words of the song or cantata. Bach's cantata "Ihr werdet weinen und heulen" and Puccini's aria "Che gelida manina" from *La Bohème* are examples. Sometimes English titles of well-known cantatas do follow normal title-style capitalization; Bach's "Jesu Joy of Man's Desiring" is usually so styled.

Titles ending in marks of punctuation

Titles such as "Whales Weep Not!" and "Why Should Not Old Men Be Mad?" that end with marks of punctuation cause problems when they are used in a series, because ordinarily the comma shouldn't occur with the exclamation point or question mark and shouldn't be outside a closing quotation mark. For italicized titles I advise using the comma anyway (see Rule 3-20), but I advise not using it for titles in quotation marks, because the combination of exclamation point or question mark, comma, and closing quotation mark is too awkward. The problem has no really good solution, but using the semicolon instead of the comma will at least get the quotation mark in the middle, making the clump less awkward:

> His favorite poems were Lawrence's "Whales Weep Not!"; Yeats's "Why Should Not Old Men Be Mad?"; and Graves's "Down, Wanton, Down!"

In a given series that presents this problem there is usually some alternative phrasing or punctuation or both, but it may create other problems, such as repetition of *and*:

> His favorite poems were "Whales Weep Not!" and "Why Should Not Old Men Be Mad?" and "Down, Wanton, Down!"

Some carefully styled publications, including *The New Yorker*, do use the comma; anyone to whom this seems the best solution is in respectable company. My own dislike of the clumped !," and ?," may be excessive.

Titles used as possessives

The apostrophe and *s* can follow the closing quotation mark of a title, as is logical:

> He knew all of "A Hard Day's Night" 's lyrics.

This is, however, a confusing combination of punctuation marks; it is apt to be perceived as a single and a double quotation mark. Whenever possible, the possessive case should be avoided and an *of* construction used instead.

3-22   Capitalize the main words in a title and the first and last word, but do not capitalize *a*, *the*, *to*, or prepositions and conjunctions of fewer than five letters when they occur in the middle of the title.

This rule applies to all capitalized titles discussed in Chapter 3, not just the kinds that are the subject of this section. I have chosen to put the rule here because errors are most frequently made with titles of literary and artistic works.

The Bridge Of San Luis Rey is such an error; *of* should not be capitalized, because it is a preposition. *The Rape Of The Lock* is worse; both the preposition *of* and the article *the* should be lowercased. *The Moon is Down* is an error; *is* is a short word, but it is an important one, a verb, not a mere preposition or conjunction, and it must be capitalized.

Travels With Charley is wrong; the preposition *with* should be lowercased. *Clock Without Hands*, however, is right; the preposition *without* has more than four letters. *They Came By Sea* is wrong; the preposition *by* should be lowercased. *The Parade Passed By and the Music Died* is not wrong, however—here *By* is an adverb modifying *Passed*, not a preposition. This is a tricky one that fools most people. Faulty capitalization in titles may result from insufficient understanding of the parts of speech; the writer who is not sure when a word that is often a preposition is actually an adverb is at a disadvantage.

Note that Rule 3-22 specifies that the last word of a title should be capitalized. Titles are unlikely to end in conjunctions (though titles such as *I Tried, But . . .* are possible), and when they end in a word that looks like a preposition, the word is almost always functioning as an adverb (though occasionally there are titles such as *Things I Believe In*) and thus should be capitalized anyway.

Listening with Both Ears is properly styled; here *Both* is an adjective. *A Life both Brutish and Short* is also properly styled, because here *both* is a conjunction—a special type called a correlative conjunction, used in partnership with *and*.

Sometimes it may make sense to bend the rule. For example, the word *as* can be a preposition, a conjunction, an adverb, or a pronoun. In the title *Not As Kind as Those Who Come as Friends*, the word is first an adverb, then a conjunction, then a preposition and is capitalized or lowercased accordingly—but in display type such as is used on book jackets and title pages, this variation is likely to be annoying, so either capitalizing or lowercasing all three instances would be defensible. Regardless of whether the rule has been bent on a title page or book jacket, it should not be bent when the title appears in ordinary text.

A colon in the middle of a title

The Corporation: A Theological Inquiry is correctly styled. A colon interrupts the title, and any word following it is capitalized just as if it began a new title, which in a sense it does. However, the colon is the only mark of punctuation—except for question marks and exclamation points, which may be used in some wordy titles—that is automatically followed by a capital. If a word follows a semicolon or dash, it also follows Rule 3-22: *The Corporation—a Theological Inquiry.*

Sometimes on the title page of a book there is no punctuation between title and subtitle; the distinction between them is made by typography or layout or both. A colon should be supplied when the title is referred to elsewhere.

FOREIGN WORDS

The basic style for foreign languages is very simple—isolated common words and phrases are treated as English words, and uncommon words and phrases and complete sentences are italicized. However, many writers do not realize that generic words and proper nouns should be treated differently; proper nouns should not be italicized.

3-23   Use italics for isolated foreign words if they are too uncommon to treat as English words, but not for foreign proper nouns and proper noun phrases except when special emphasis or clarity is needed.

Some dictionaries indicate which foreign expressions they consider it necessary to italicize, and some don't. Even writers who use a dictionary that does include this indication should not rely too much on it but should use their own judgment. For example, *laissez-faire* may be perfectly clear to the probable readers of some works but a mystery to the probable readers of others, and the latter will be happier if the mystery is acknowledged with italics.

Foreign proper nouns, including the usual nouns denoting persons and places and also noun phrases such as are formed when a title is used with a person's name, do not require italics. Annoying combinations can occur when such terms are italicized:

> *Ciao, Dottore* Einaudi's latest book . . .
> The *Bundesrepublik Deutschland*'s *Bild-Zeitung* announced . . .

Is *Ciao* the title of Dottore Einaudi's latest book, or is the sentence badly punctuated and is *Ciao, Dottore* the title of Einaudi's latest book? Is the *Bundesrepublik Deutschland*'s *Bild-Zeitung* the name of a newspaper, or is it the *Bild-Zeitung*, published in the Bundesrepublik Deutschland (West Germany)? Care in reading punctuation would help (if similar care was shown in writing) in the first example, and a fair store of general information or a knowledge of German (which does not use the apostrophe as it is used in the example) would help in the second, but the possibility of misunderstanding is there—as it often is when legitimate uses of italics, such as for book titles and newspaper names, are mixed with unnecessary uses.

Here are some proper uses of foreign proper nouns:

> Bibliothèque Nationale (French form Bibliothèque nationale)
> Palacio Nacional; the *palacio* (italics optional)
> Rue de la Paix (French form rue de la Paix)
> Oberstleutnant Braun; the *Oberstleutnant* (capitalized as a German noun)
> the *canaille* in the Jardin des Tuileries
> the duc de La Rochefoucauld (or Duc; see Rule 3-14, modification 5)

Note that I have given foreign forms as well as English ones in some cases. When a foreign proper noun is used in English, it is essentially a temporary English word, and I prefer to impose

English capitalization on it; otherwise *Bibliothèque nationale* and similar noun phrases may be unclear to readers not accustomed to foreign capitalization conventions. I do nevertheless capitalize German words when they are generic nouns and are italicized—the italics show that they are being presented as foreign words, and the capitalization conventions of the foreign language should be retained.

Whereas German employs more capital letters than English does, many languages employ fewer. For example, *Parisian* is capitalized in English as the derivative of a proper noun, but the French *parisien* and *parisienne* are lowercased—such derivatives are treated as generic words in French. They should therefore be lowercased and italicized when used with English even though their English equivalents are capitalized.

Foreign titles of books, paintings, and so on follow Rules 3-20 and 3-21. A title is essentially a proper noun, so it is not affected by being in a foreign language but is in italics or in roman enclosed by quotation marks just as an equivalent English title would be.

Plurals and possessives of foreign words

When a foreign word is italicized, it is common to add an *s* to make it plural whether or not the foreign language forms its plurals that way:

> The *chador* is no longer required, but at a recent reception I counted thirty *chadors.*

This creates a bastard word—neither English nor foreign. The University of Chicago Press's *Manual of Style* advises making the added *s* roman—*chadors*—but this distinction is almost invisible in printed type and looks odd in typewriter underlining, and it doesn't really make the plural legitimate but just shows that the writer is aware it is illegitimate. Purists would insist on using the foreign plural—whatever it is, in this case. Often the problem can be circumvented by avoiding plural use of the word or by deciding not to italicize the word in the first place. If a foreign word, even a most uncommon one, occurs so frequently in a written work that plural uses are unavoidable, it might as well be considered a temporary adoptee of English and not italicized except on its first mention, when it is defined.

Possessives are often formed in the English manner, too:

The *chador*'s folds concealed her form.

The Chicago *Manual of Style* practice—making the apostrophe and *s* roman—seems more acceptable here; because of the separation provided by the apostrophe, the distinction is more apparent in printed type and less awkward-looking in typewriter underlining. But the same objections can be made by purists—a foreign word has been given an English inflection.

I advise avoiding use of English plural and possessive inflections for italicized foreign words, but allowing an occasional exception to avoid awkward rephrasing. The lapse is a minor one.

4

BEYOND THE SENTENCE: DICTION AND COMPOSITION

◆

Diction and composition cannot be judged right or wrong in the same way that grammar and punctuation can, but they can be judged appropriate or inappropriate, effective or ineffective. People who have little trouble with grammar and punctuation may still be unsure of their diction and composition.

Diction includes grammar but goes beyond it; it is the choice of words and word relationships that we make whenever we express ourselves, either vocally or in writing, and it can be ineffective or inappropriate even when our grammar is faultless.

Composition is the combination of sentences into larger structures, from paragraphs to books; it is the context within which sentences operate, and it can be ineffective or inappropriate even when each individual sentence is well made.

Diction and composition together give a speech or written work its character. Listeners or readers will not be much aware of grammar or punctuation, unless faulty enough to make them wince, but they will be aware of diction and composition, for these communicate both the personality of the speaker or writer and the message—and they can be evaluated almost as we evaluate a person and his or her message: interesting or dull, intelligent or stupid, attractive or repellent.

Good diction and composition are hard to define. Generally we have been exposed to them if we have been effectively instructed, entertained, or persuaded by something we have read or heard—though the dramatic subject of a newspaper account, the luridness of an adventure novel, or the personal importance of a notification from the IRS may hold our attention even when diction and composition are poor. Also, the diction and composition of the best writers and speakers are not easy to analyze; such writers and speakers may break the rules that this chapter discusses, but their diction and composition are in service to an unusual overall talent for expression—expression that can be admired, and can even be learned from, but cannot be dissected without threatening its unique life.

Poor diction and composition, however, are fit subjects for analysis, and ineffective and inappropriate expression should be dissected—it's dead anyway, and maybe the postmortem will make it possible to give life to the next creation. This chapter, like those on grammar and punctuation, concentrates on common errors and suggests routine ways of avoiding them. Its final section, on revision, concerns catching errors that have not been avoided.

OCCASION AND INTENT

Communication is a triad: speaker or writer, listener or reader, and matter. The speaker or writer, with the qualifications discussed in Rule 4-1, can accept himself or herself as a relatively constant member of the triad. The listener or reader is not constant; each one, or each group, represents a different occasion—a conversation with a friendly or unfriendly subordinate or superior at work, a speech before a sober or drunk audience of ecclesiastics or teamsters, an article for an ignorant or knowledgeable readership of taxpayers or economic advisers. Nor is the matter constant; each time we speak or write we have a specific intent—to give or request information, to amuse or alarm, to persuade or dissuade.

We don't have to think consciously about each member of the triad every time we open our mouths or put pen to paper, though doing so more often might keep us out of trouble and make us better company. Such conscious thought does help when either the occasion or the intent is not a familiar one.

4-1   Remember who you are.

Each of us has many aspects—each of us represents a sex, an age, a marital category, an occupation, a type of background, and so on—but each of us is one person. Even a neurotic or psychotic person who is aware of having two or more distinctly different personalities is a single person, if an erratic one, and is so perceived by others. We can change ourselves, and time and circumstances change us, but at any given instant we are each what we are. Within limits, we can choose to accentuate some aspects of ourselves and conceal others, and this is no more dishonest than changing clothes between cleaning the chickenhouse and going to church, but we should not pretend to be what we are not or not to be what we are.

I do not mean this rule to be a homily on character, yet a prescription of honesty about oneself and with oneself is as close as I can come to a Golden Rule of expression—and specifically of diction, for it is usually ineffective or inappropriate diction that gives the pretentious speaker or writer away.

Pretending to be what we're not

We've all done it and will do it again. Once we did it transparently, as a look at the stories and essays we wrote in school would prove; we aped the suavity and acidity of writers we admired. A story about a preppie written by a preppie: *He arched an eyebrow, then tipped up her chin and kissed her expertly.* A college sophomore's essay on the metaphysical poets: *George Herbert, though occasionally capable of an amusing twist, fell far short of Donne's aesthetically satisfying complexity.*

We may still be embarrassingly transparent when we pretend more knowledge or authority than we have. The junior executive who writes *Let me assure you that such fluctuations are acceptable* in a report intended for his seniors may have forgotten who he is—a young man addressing older ones with considerably more experience with fluctuations and their acceptability—or may be trying to give the impression that he's one of them; in any case, his seniors are apt to be annoyed by his diction rather than reassured. The junior executive probably does know more than his seniors about some matters, and would be justified in writing authoritatively about them, but he should confine his larger judgments to *I believe I can demonstrate that such fluctuations are acceptable* or some similar unassertive diction.

Pretense comes in all forms and degrees, and it is often quite unconscious. Sometimes we get away with it; more often at least some of our listeners or readers catch us at it.

Pretending not to be what we are

No one likes being talked down to. The company president who in a newsletter to employees makes jokes about supposed romances between the *boys* who drive the trucks and the *girls* in the office, the headmaster who uses, and probably misuses, his students' slang, the clergyman who laces his instructions to the affianced with mild vulgarities—all are being falsely magnanimous, pretending not to be in the positions of authority that they hold.

We may sincerely want to put aside the trappings of office for a while and to be treated as an equal rather than a superior, and those who perceive our sincerity may oblige us. But in any context in which our authority, experience, or position is relevant, we shouldn't pretend we don't have it. Talking down, after all, is only a form of bullying.

I: the perpendicular pronoun

Sometimes it doesn't matter much who we are—we simply have the job of transmitting information, in an impersonal fashion, to a listener or reader, or we are writing an account in the third person. In such circumstances, *I* can be an intrusion and should be avoided.

Just avoiding the perpendicular pronoun may not be enough. Its shadow may be much in evidence if the speaker's or writer's diction is loaded—that is, if it includes words that indicate the speaker's or writer's opinions and reactions. *The senator slipped still another rider into the bill* suggests that the senator was being sneaky and had already added a sufficiency of riders—which are matters of opinion, not impersonal fact; an *I* must be casting a shadow, and shouldn't be if the context is an impersonal news report.

4-2   Remember who your listeners or readers are.

All spoken expression is intended for a specific audience. Much written expression is similarly intended for specific readers, though a given work of writing may find its own uniquely composed readership among the general public. Speakers whose diction is inappropriate to their audience, whether they are in church or in prison, will often be told so by their listeners' responses or behavior and may be able to adjust their diction accordingly. Writers have no such immediate feedback; they must start with a good idea of who their readers are, or their writing will be ineffective.

Usually, listeners or readers can be roughly characterized by terms such as the following:

friendly/unfriendly/neutral
well educated/average/poorly educated
knowledgeable/ignorant
concerned/unconcerned
alarmed/relaxed
young/old/mixed
male/female/mixed

Diction that is appropriate to listeners or readers who are friendly, poorly educated, knowledgeable about the topic, unconcerned, relaxed, young, and female—for example, the diction a shop steward might employ in a memorandum to cannery workers about the company picnic—would obviously be inappropriate in a brief to the Supreme Court.

Even a single slip of diction can be disastrous. An ugly example is the phrase *final solution*—the Nazi term for the attempted extermination of the Jews—used casually to mean any drastic measure; in spite of its import, the phrase has become common currency among many who are not anti-Semitic (and may be Jewish) and do not mean to offend but are simply insensitive. Offend the phrase does, and the listener or reader it offends may choose to be as unforgiving as the speaker or writer is insensitive. All of us are insensitive to some degree and to some things; all of us should try to be less so.

Inappropriate diction is usually, however, less dramatically off—it is too jocular or too serious for the occasion, it expects too much or too little of those addressed, or it is too colorful or too bland to appeal to a significant number of those addressed; no one may be offended, but few are entertained, informed, or persuaded. We cannot always achieve maximum effectiveness in what we say and write, but we can usually avoid complete ineffectiveness by considering who our listeners or readers are.

4-3   Remember what you intend to express.

Each of us lives with an interior monologue that obeys none of the rules in this book, let alone the rules in this chapter. The monologue may be in words—though not always, at least not always in recognizable words—but thoughts are often unfinished or oddly connected to other thoughts, and attention and point of view shift and evolve. Our stream of consciousness, though we are capable of concentrating it, is in its unconcentrated state as flighty as any animal's.

Thus spoken and written expression is in a sense unnatural. It takes an effort to achieve it—to focus the mind's monologue on a specific task and keep it from wandering. We may merely want to convey an emotion or attitude, such as pleasure, satisfaction, disappointment, grief; we may want to impart information; we may want to persuade. Whatever spoken or written expression we intend, the mind's monologue constantly expands, contradicts, digresses; it must be jerked back to the task by deliberate effort.

This effort is the process of composition. In conversation and casual public speaking, composition can be very loose and is sometimes modified on the spot as listeners react; often we digress, following an interior monologue, and have to remind ourselves of our intent: *Where was I? Oh yes, the gerbil situation.* In less casual public speaking and in writing, composition is less loose and sometimes has to be very tight indeed; a politician can ramble considerably in speaking for a bill on the Senate floor, but the bill itself must be carefully organized and unambiguously expressed or—perhaps—it will go back to committee.

A constant awareness of intent—a persistence in intent— will give some shape to almost any expression and make it more effective, even if all the other rules in this chapter are ignored.

ORGANIZATION

Sinclair Lewis wrote well-constructed novels, but before he hit his stride, he must have been familiar with the difficulties that afflict the beginner. In *Babbitt*, his hero sits down one evening to outline a paper he has been asked to deliver before a professional group. The result:

He had written seven pages, whereof the first page set forth:

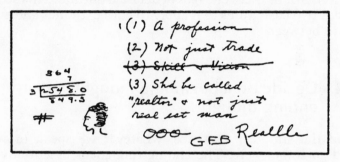

The other six pages were rather like the first.

After some days of similar fumbling, Babbitt does succeed: "One evening . . . Babbitt forgot about Style, Order, and the other mysteries, and scrawled off what he really thought about the real-estate business and about himself, and he found the paper written." He even delivers it well: "When he stood on the low platform before the convention, he trembled and saw only a purple haze. But he was in earnest, and when he had finished the formal paper he talked to them, his hands in his pockets, his spectacled face a flashing disk, like a plate set up on edge in the lamplight. They shouted 'That's the stuff!' and in the discussion afterward they referred with impressiveness to 'our friend and brother, Mr. George F. Babbitt.'"

There is much to be said for Babbitt's artless route—above all, that it was the only route open to him; the principles of organization and structure half-remembered from his school days were not enough. However, besides his sincerity, Babbitt had the advantage of a friendly audience of men just like himself, men who could be counted on to like him and his message. We are not always so lucky as Babbitt, and what we have to say or write is not always so close to our hearts that our sincerity alone can make it persuasive.

Sometimes organization is "organic" in the sense that Babbitt's speech presumably was, developing naturally in the actual course of composition and then continuing to grow beyond his written words, but more often at least some conscious thought has to be given to it. In fictional fact, Babbitt's apparently fruitless attempts at conventional outlining may have organized his thoughts more than he knew.

The organization of a speech or written work may be very simple or very complex; it may be reducible to a list of two or three items or may cover pages of detailed outline. This section includes two basic rules that apply to both extremes and everything in between.

4-4 Decide on a beginning thought and an ending thought.

Beyond the simplest sentence, whatever we speak or write should go somewhere. The ending thought is essentially our intent (see Rule 4-3)—the thought we want transmitted to the listener or reader. The beginning thought is the initial link in the chain of thoughts that gets us to the ending thought—and often it is the hardest link to forge.

A beginning thought may be simply a bald statement of intent: *As your new president I would like to explain some modifications I will impose on our electoral system.* This approach is adequate, and usually desirable, when the listener or reader can be assumed to be interested in the matter at hand from the start or, as in newspaper accounts, when the writer wants to expose the topic as concisely and quickly as possible so that readers can decide immediately whether they are interested.

Often, however, the writer or speaker must connect the first link not just to what follows but to what precedes. The connection may be very obvious in a spoken address—the speaker takes off in some way from a previous speaker's words or from the occasion itself. It is less obvious, but still there, at the beginning of any successful written work; the opening words connect somehow to the reader and his or her desires, whether those desires are for information or for entertainment. A novel may start by immediately gratifying the reader's appetite for blood: *As the furtive little woman who had jostled him disappeared into the crowd, Hamilton looked down incredulously at the machete sunk to the hilt in his breastbone.* What precedes these first words is the reader's appetite and the writer's ability to satisfy it, and the first words are the link. A book or article on a comparatively bloodless subject may begin by doing its best to link the subject with the reader by arousing interest: *John Gant is as obscure today as he was in life, but were it not for his courageous anatomical studies we would all be wearing gloves with no thumbs.*

The first link may be no more than a joining of the writer's perception and literary skill and the reader's willingness to appreciate them. Many novels begin with scene-setting paragraphs that please or intrigue readers and lead them into the story. An essayist may begin at a tangent to the subject, trying to inveigle readers with a few urbane paragraphs designed, more or less ingeniously, to introduce the true subject and the writer's cast of mind at the same time; this is a somewhat leisurely, old-fashioned approach to an essay, but does survive—the editors of *The New Yorker*, for example, seem to consider it essential for the magazine's longer articles.

Even if the beginning thought is at a tangent to or apparently unrelated to the ending thought, the speaker or writer should have the connection in mind and should be able to trace it for a listener or reader—the subject of the next rule.

4-5 Connect the beginning to the ending.

Just as the words in a sentence are related by the rules of grammar, the sentences in a paragraph and the paragraphs in a speech or written work are related by the principles of composition. One thought must follow another; each thought must be linked with the preceding one and with the following one.

A simple linear argument may merely trace cause and effect, connecting an opening assertion with a conclusion: *No one seems to have realized that the gun club is responsible for the tick infestation of recent years. The club imported pheasants for its fall shoots a few seasons ago, and soon found it necessary to trap out our local foxes to protect the birds. Our rabbit population has exploded, of course, in the absence of the foxes, and so has the population of the ticks they carry. We must restore the foxes and restrain the gun club.* Gunners, pheasants, foxes, rabbits, ticks, gunners.

A more complicated argument may require several chains of reasoning that eventually link together. Similarly, a narrative may require several story lines that eventually converge. To form the connection between beginning and ending, the speaker or writer needs two things: an outline, whether written or mental; and a sense of when digression is permissible and when it is not.

Outlines

Formal outlines—with main heads I, II, III, subheads A, B, C, subordinate subheads 1, 2, 3, and so on—are often essential, both for the writer and for the reader. Some material must be presented in a systematic, highly structured way. Textbooks are an obvious example; they are intended to organize a field of study, or some aspect of it, for the reader, and the formal outline is the necessary basis of organization.

Formal outlines can be useful even when they are not essential. A speaker or writer, even a practiced one, may not start with an outline—he may not be sure when he begins how he is going to arrive at his ending thought, and may find himself modifying his ending thought as he speaks or writes—but by the time he finishes, either something like a formal outline will have emerged or he will leave his listeners or readers up in the air and dissatisfied. Therefore he might as well start with one, and avoid the backtracking and filling in that will otherwise be necessary to cover his subject. An outline makes the actual composition much easier, because it keeps the speaker or writer focused on where he is, and aware of the links connecting where he is with where he has been and where he is going.

Some of us simply cannot start with an outline; we end up staring at a jumble of severed heads and insubordinate subheads. Outlining does take practice, as any kind of logical thinking does. It may be easier just to get some words down on paper, letting one thought lead to another without worrying about a final structure. Then it will be apparent, perhaps, what has been left out, what has been misplaced, what has been left hanging—in fact, then it will be apparent what the structure, which is to say the outline, should be. At this point, it may be quite easy to write out a good outline and do a second draft, picking up most of the words from the unorganized first draft.

I favor tight, formal organization for almost any composition, from an "informal" speech to a textbook, and therefore I recommend outlining a speech or written work early. However, especially for the beginning speaker or writer, tightness and formality are not ends in themselves; they are nothing but impediments if they prevent or constrict expression instead of merely organizing it. Those who are impeded by trying to write to an outline—or, indeed, by any of the advice in this chapter—should get some words down, words no one else yet has to hear or read, and then see if the words can be better arranged.

Digressions

The *Where was I?* syndrome has no place in formal speech or writing, but digression itself is often useful and desirable. A digression can illuminate a point or make it more vivid, or it can serve as a breather between one chunk of complex material and another, or it can—when used skillfully—heighten suspense in the middle of a dramatic passage. A digression that serves no purpose at all, of course, should be eliminated, and therefore we should ask ourselves a few questions before allowing ourselves a digression. Will it illuminate the topic? Will it provide a breather, and will listener or reader remember what we've been discussing? Have we actually created enough suspense to carry through a digression, or will listeners or readers just forget what it is we're making them wait for?

An odd feature of amateur public speaking and writing is the digressive ending. A speaker or writer reaches his ending thought—and continues, and continues. Perhaps he is trying to supply something that should have been an earlier part of his composition, and would have been if he had been more careful to link beginning and ending. Perhaps he is afraid of an abrupt conclusion and wants to ease away from it; he is uncomfortable with the role of authority he has temporarily assumed and hopes to reestablish his customary conversational manner. Whatever the reason, the ending should never be a digression— it will just puzzle listeners or readers and weaken the true ending thought.

TONE

This section is an expansion of the advice given in Rules 4-1 and 4-2; writers or speakers who remember who they are and whom they are addressing will probably avoid errors of tone. However, amateur writers or speakers are often nervous, or angry, or perplexed and troubled, and hence may make an unwise choice of tone; and practiced writers or speakers may have long ago assumed an accustomed tone that serves them poorly. The three rules in this section are intended for both.

4-6 Avoid haughtiness; avoid chumminess.

Army drill instructors, not ordinarily men of broad or deep intellect, are haughty because part of their function is to humble recruits and make them long for the status of trained soldier. Critics, not ordinarily people of much artistic, dramatic, or literary achievement themselves, may be haughty because they believe part of their function to be to force improvement, excoriate the shabby, and increase the sophistication of their readers. But few of us stand at such an elevation above those we speak to or write for.

As speakers or writers we can, and should, judge the capacities of our listeners or readers (Rule 4-2), but we should not talk down to them or sneer at them; we should treat them civilly. In addressing them we assume the responsibility of entertaining them, informing them, persuading them, perhaps even rebuking them—but not the privilege of insulting them or sneering at their attention, which we have presumably solicited.

Few of us think we are overendowed with self-esteem, and thus few of us think we are apt to be haughty. But haughtiness is just as apt to result from a defensive, combative attitude as from excessive self-esteem—and a beginning speaker or writer is quite likely to feel defensive, and to defend himself or herself with haughtiness. Listeners or readers, not aware of the quivering creature behind the Oz of haughty words, respond defensively themselves.

Chumminess, though not as directly insulting to listener or reader as haughtiness, is still something of an insult. If we are chummy we may give the impression that we think we can win over those we address with a wink or a nudge in the ribs. As chumminess progresses to clowning and buffoonery, we may become insulting to ourselves as well as to our audience.

When we speak or write, we do assume a position of authority—granted us by those we address—and should assume some dignity along with it. A speech or written work may be friendly and may reveal the personality of the speaker or writer, but it can still be dignified.

4-7 Avoid excessive or false emotion.

Often we want both to make a statement and to express our feelings about it. If our feelings are strong—whether feelings of anger, humility, sorrow, or some other emotion—we are apt to overdo our expression and obscure the statement. Hyperbole in such expression can be effective and amusing, especially in speech, but it can also be offensive.

Often the stronger the expression of the emotion is, the weaker or more diffuse the result is. Consider the examples below—all of overwritten and rewritten correspondence.

Anger

> I have just received your infuriating letter informing me that my assessment has been increased because of the addition of a swimming pool to my property. This moronic missive confirms my fears that when my benighted fellow citizens voted you Democrats in they were tolling the death knell for the town. If I must be taxed—which I do not for an instant concede; I don't have any children in the schools and I was happier before the roads were paved— why does the assessment have to be left up to you nitwits?

This sorehead may eventually make his point, but all he has done so far is insult his addressee. A temperate version:

> I have just received your letter informing me that my assessment has been increased because of the addition of a swimming pool to my property. This increase is the result of a misunderstanding that would have been avoided if your assessor had been diligent enough to consult me or at least to inspect the so-called improvement. The body of water in my backyard is not a swimming pool but a collapsed septic tank.

The second version expresses indignation and makes a rebuke, but the rebuke is directed only at the probable culprit, not at all members of the town government, the writer's neighbors, the Democratic Party, and the principles of taxation. Its tone of justified annoyance would probably be more effective in getting the wrong righted than the first letter's rabid wrath.

273

Humility

I probably should not take up the time of anyone who has written such a magnificent book as *Poison Oak Simplified*, especially since I am in no way a botanist but merely the humble owner of an ancient and honorable shade tree now threatened by the dire vine, and I hope you will believe that I do so presume only because I have exhausted not only my own poor store of horticultural lore but also the problem-solving tips contained in your otherwise excellent book.

This mannered opening admittedly has more faults than merely its excessive and insincere humility—it squirms from cliché to cliché, constantly calling attention to the writer and to his satisfaction with his own words, and it ends with an unnecessary criticism of the *otherwise excellent* book. But false humility is apt to be accompanied by an overall fulsomeness of diction; the falsely humble are apt to be false in every way. A respectful but also self-respecting version:

I hope you can take the time to help me with a special problem that I haven't found covered in your excellent *Poison Oak Simplified.*

This straightforward approach is polite, establishes the writer's claim to the author's time (he has bought, or at least borrowed or stolen, the author's book and tried to use it), and avoids seeming to criticize the book (the problem is *special*; the book is without qualification *excellent*; the writer leaves it as a possibility that the information he needs may actually be in the book). The tone is appropriately humble—the writer is asking a better-informed person for advice—but it is not abject or fulsome.

Sorrow

John's passing has left us prostrate. I wish I could think of what to say to comfort you in what must be a comfortless time, with the prospect of dismal years ahead. Your grief must be unbearable, on top of the past months of sadness as John failed so pathetically—months that were hard for us all, for he was much in our thoughts even though we were unable to see him because of our busy schedule. Please let us know if we can help in any way.

Letters of condolence are difficult to write. They may be sincere, written with feelings of genuine sympathy, and yet have a tinge of insincerity—*prostrate* is too strong a word for the emotional condition of one who was too busy to call on the dying man in his last months, though a sincere writer might use it from fear that a milder word would belittle the importance of death. The writer's perception of the widow's situation may be accurate, but it is certainly no comfort to the widow to dwell on it so gloomily. A version that evinces less sorrow but more real concern for the feelings of the widow:

> We were saddened to hear of John's death. Nearly thirty years ago he became an important part of our lives—the cheerful and friendly man who attended our ills and always made a checkup or even an inoculation something of a treat for our children. He was our friend as well as our doctor, and we wish we had seen more of him after his retirement.
>
> I understand that you have had a houseful of guests. May I come over and help you clean up after them, or cook for any that remain? I'll call you later in the week.

I do not offer the second version as a model. A letter of condolence should not follow a pattern but should be governed by a conscientious and self-controlled estimate of what will comfort most and trouble least, and this estimate will vary greatly depending on circumstances and personalities. However, this version does exemplify some useful principles. Implicit in the letter is an assumption that the widow is strong enough to withstand her loss and that her life will go on; explicit in the first version is the assumption that the widow must be, even should be, miserable and without recourse. The second version does not overstate the writer's emotion or seem to ask for sympathy as well as offer it. It evokes thoughts of the dead man's prime, not of the sad immediate past or future, and explains why the writer's family had affection and respect for him. The ticklish topic of failure to call on the dying man, a failure that may genuinely trouble the writer, is not allowed to trouble the reader, though a regret is expressed, in an undefensive way, for failure to keep in touch. The offer of help is explicit and specific, to be followed by a phone call—if the writer is not actually willing to help, no help should be offered.

4-8   Avoid inconsistencies and improprieties of tone.

Variety is desirable for some aspects of diction, such as sentence structure (see Rule 4-11). It is not ordinarily desirable for tone; a speaker or writer should not slip back and forth from formal to informal, from precise to slangy, from assertive to beseeching, from indignant to jesting, from complacent to alarmed.

Admittedly, some good speakers and writers, those who are sure of their effects, can get away with abrupt changes in tone that make listeners prick their ears, readers widen their eyes. The speaker or writer who can satisfy the suddenly increased attention he or she has stimulated is justified in stimulating it. More often, inconsistency of tone is pointless and annoying: *The ponderous logographic system employed for so many centuries by the Mesopotamians was retained by some successor cultures but almost completely discarded by others—which is why there ain't no such animal as a vowel in early Semitic syllabaries, although later syllabaries do show tentative vowel indicators.* The jocular substandard diction in the middle of the scholarly sentence is distracting, not amusing.

Progression of tone

Progression of tone is not inconsistency of tone. Antony's speech over Caesar's body begins on a tone of sorrow, passes through irony, and ends with anger, and his listeners follow. A speaker or writer, like a moviemaker or playwright, can use deliberate changes of tone to lead people from mood to mood. Tone usually should be varied in this way in a speech or written work of considerable length. We should try to do it consciously, because if we try to sustain the same mood at the same pitch forever, our listeners or readers will tend to seek relief in random mood changes of their own, usually easing toward boredom; we might as well control and direct the natural volatility of those we address by intensifying or changing our tone to fit the course of our words.

Progression of tone does not come easily to beginners, but it is a device they should be aware of and may find themselves capable of using in some circumstances.

Comic relief, ridicule, and black humor

Comic relief is the injection, sometimes inadvertent, of humor in a spoken or written passage that is intensely serious or tragic in tone. It is a clear violation of Rule 4-8, but thoroughly justifiable when it serves a true function—purging for a moment feelings that have become clotted and need relief, so that listeners or readers can return clearheaded to the serious or tragic matter at hand. Inadvertent comic relief in a speech must be accepted; if we are startled by unexpected laughter we can only hope our audience will purge itself and return to us and the tone we have tried to establish, as it probably will if we keep our composure. Deliberate comic relief in either speech or writing is dangerous, because it is difficult to know when it is really needed and when it is merely incongruous, but it is splendid when it comes off.

Ridicule is the use of humor for a serious intent—to destroy someone or something. It is appropriate in conjunction with some tones, such as anger and assertion, but not others. Whether appropriate or not, it should be used sparingly; it is overused by many speakers and writers who are unsure of themselves and their message and consider offense the best defense.

Black humor, laughing at death and disaster, is more an attitude than a tone. Some consider it an inescapable attitude—the only rational response a sensitive intelligence can make to the horrors of a world of contradiction, disappointment, and pain. Others are repelled by it and consider it a kind of sniggering at serious matters, a cowardly refusal to be truly serious and thus to risk being the butt of someone else's black wit. Black humor is in itself inconsistent, being composed of contradictory emotions, but inconsistency is not its danger— rather it encourages too much consistency, a consistently irreverent, wry, uncommitted attitude that is habit-forming. As an occasional device, it has always had legitimate uses, either to heighten emotion or, like comic relief, to purge it. As an unvarying attitude, it is a vice. The addicted black humorist may think that once he has gotten his laugh or easy shudder he has polished off his subject, but many listeners or readers will be aware that he has merely failed to deal with it.

REVISION

Revision—derived from Latin *revidere*, "to look back," though the English word means actual changing rather than mere review—is a reconsideration of both the broadest and the tiniest elements of a draft. It may result in no more than a word or punctuation change here and there, or it may involve massive reworking and successive drafts that take far longer than the initial composition. Each of us has different habits of composition and different standards to meet, our own as well as those of the occasion, and consequently the process of revision differs, but "looking back" is always an essential part of it and should never be omitted. Don't overlook looking back. The rules in this section concern what to look for.

Most of the rules earlier in this book are intended to be fault-preventing, but the rules here are fault-finding. There is some danger in any fault-finding approach, because it can be endless. Faults can always be found; anyone who doubts it should read Robert Graves and Alan Hodge's *The Reader over Your Shoulder* (Vintage paperback), which pillories short passages by exemplary writers such as J. B. Priestley, G. B. Shaw, and T. S. Eliot. If the expression of these writers—who are no less admirable because of Graves and Hodge's criticism and are indeed admired by Graves and Hodge—can be picked away at, most of the rest of us cannot expect to grasp the perfection we should nevertheless reach for.

Revision can be excessive and destructive. It is all too easy to revise while in the wrong mood—the mood of despair and self-doubt that so commonly descends after making love, after giving birth, after creating anything. Composition, whether of notes for a short speech or of a long book, can be an intense experience, overloading the writer, and the more intense it is, the worse the hangover. Experienced writers are familiar with the depression that afflicts them at various stages of composition and especially toward the end, and they know enough to avoid revising their work while their mood is negative and hypercritical, or, if a deadline gives them no choice, to make allowances for their mood as best they can.

Revision can be pointless if done in the opposite mood, which is also common—a mood of elation and exultation, even of joy. If we revise in this mood we will probably do our work no damage—every word is magnificently right!—but will do it no good either; we are still too absorbed in it to see the flaws our readers will. If we get too excited by our rereading, we may well damage it, by adding new bright thoughts that it inspires, thoughts that readers will consider digressive and scattered. Revision can be almost as absorbing and intense an activity as composition, but it is a different kind of intensity—intellectual and cool-headed, even somewhat impersonal. Try to do it when you can achieve that mood. If you can't get in the mood, you really need an editor—a professional whose primary skill is revising the words of others.

Revision can be immobilizing to a writer, even a cool-headed one, who just will not stop. There is a point of diminishing returns even in the most carefully wrought work. Don't be obsessed with revision; go on to something else.

4-9   Check for logic and continuity.

This is essentially a check for continuity of thought—for missing links, bent links, or dangling links in the chain that connects the beginning thought and ending thought (Rules 4-4 and 4-5).

Missing links

We know what we mean; we know why one clause or sentence follows from another and leads to the next. The listener or reader doesn't know unless the connection is obvious or explicit. The connection may be obvious, as in *The forecast was for rain; they postponed the picnic.* It may be mysterious, as in *The forecast was for rain; they postponed waxing the floor—* the writer knows that waxing is more successful on dry days, but the reader may not, so the writer must make the connection explicit. Sometimes the missing link is as simple as a *but* or *therefore* that will show whether what follows is an opposing statement or a logical conclusion.

The speaker or writer usually knows more about the subject at hand than the listener or reader (see Rule 4-2). *In that winter at Valley Forge, the starving troops were reduced to gnawing at scraps of harness, and their commander, of course, was denied even that fare* would amuse those who know that Washington had dental problems and a succession of ivory and wooden dentures, but puzzle or mislead everyone else—some might think Washington's tastes were too dainty. Even a trivial

279

obscurity is annoying, and a major one may make some listeners or readers miss the entire point.

The listener's or reader's memory is shorter than the speaker's or writer's. Whodunit writers take advantage of this by dropping in clues that almost all readers will forget; the rest of us, especially if we are public speakers, should take notice of it, not advantage, and spare the reader or listener puzzlement. This often means repeating information and reinforcing connections. Excessive repetition can be tiresome, but when clarity is important, too much repetition is better than too little. Heavy repetition can be made a virtue; repetition of key words or key points is a standard device of diction and composition to fix them in the listener's or reader's mind.

Whole paragraphs of linking exposition may never have made it from our mind to the page, and we won't know it unless we consciously look for the connections our listener or reader needs. Or a paragraph may have made it, but too late in the composition; it should be moved to where it belongs. Or an objection to our line of reasoning that many listeners or readers might make may not have been brought up and dealt with. Now is the time to repair all these gaps in the chain of thought.

Bent links

Thoughts may be connected, but some of the connections may be faulty; that is, our logic may be flawed. *All men are mortal, and Socrates is a man; therefore Socrates is mortal* is sound deductive logic. Another syllogism—that is, a three-part argument consisting of a major premise, a minor premise, and a conclusion—may be flawed: *All men are two-legged, and chickens are two-legged; therefore men are chickens.* Or the syllogism may be sound within itself but have a flawed premise: *All two-legged beings are men, and chickens are two-legged; therefore chickens are men.* Or the phrasing of the premises may be ambiguous, permitting a false conclusion: *No cat has eight tails, and every cat has one tail more than no cat; therefore every cat has nine tails.*

There is no room here for any further discussion of logic itself. It is a topic of immense complexity, and an open-ended one—human minds will never come up with the last word on it. However, our logic should be as good as we can make it, unless, of course, our intention is to flummox listeners or readers rather than address them honestly. Therefore, in reviewing a draft for bent links, we must test each one with

suspicious questions. Does this sentence really follow necessarily from that one? Is this conclusion really the most reasonable one, or are there other equally reasonable conclusions?
Has some information that would make the conclusion seem
less reasonable been conveniently left out?

Logic that is based on false information, such as the premise
All two-legged beings are men, leads to false conclusions, and
thus an item of information can be a bent link too. We should
be sure of any facts, but particularly of those that are parts of
chains of reasoning rather than mere illustrations or window
dressing.

Dangling links

We may get so interested in a particular thought in a chain of
thoughts that we take off from it, beginning a new chain from
it. Then, collecting ourselves, we go back and hitch on to the
particular thought again and resume our original chain. This
can be a problem for the listener or reader, who is left dangling
at the end of the unfinished new chain, trying to see how it
connects to the resumption of the old chain.

Dangling links are digressions (see Rule 4-5). They are not
necessarily bad. Not every chain of thought has to stretch
straight and tense to its conclusion; especially in a speech,
there should be occasional times when the logical tension is
relaxed and the listener can catch up. However, we must make
it clear just when we are dropping a dangling link and where we
are hitching back to the main chain: *Gerbils are fascinating
little creatures, and I wish I had time to say more about them.
But to get back to the Greeks' use of bird entrails for divina-
tion . . .*

We may even find ourselves adding a dangling link or two in
the course of revision as new thoughts occur to us. Fine—but
too many dangling links and long chains of dangling links
begin to weigh down the main chain of thought. Part of revision is reconsidering the desirability of such digressions; they
may seem acceptable at the slow speed of composition but be
troublesome at normal speaking or reading speed.

4-10   Check for rambling.

Rambling is what we do when we're in no hurry and merely
want to enjoy the walk. Sometimes rambling is enjoyable in

speech and writing too—in friendly conversation, in personal letters, even in periodical features and columns by writers whose personalities are familiar to and enjoyed by their readers, and in books of the reflections of those with interesting minds. It is not enjoyable when the speaker or writer should be proceeding somewhere without unnecessary delay; for the listener or reader it's like walking a dog with infinite interest in everything within the radius of the leash.

A common symptom of rambling is very heavy use of coordinating conjunctions—*and, but, or.* Coordinating conjunctions are used to connect words, phrases, or clauses of equal grammatical value: *Dickens was a great novelist, and his best books are still read today, but his life was not a happy one, and he was only in his fifties when he died, or he might have given us still more books.* This rambling sentence covers a fair amount of ground, but doesn't chart a course or take it. The individual clauses—clauses of equal grammatical value—are plopped down one by one, like isolated links still waiting to be forged into a chain. Sentences such as this can go on endlessly, becoming more and more tiresome; a listener or reader will soon get impatient with such a dull ramble and give it up.

Rambling may result from a kind of fear of the brief silence imposed by a period or other strong mark of punctuation, as if the silence might give the listener or reader a chance to interrupt. Some conversationlists speak in endless rambling sentences; perhaps they all come from talkative households in which to end a sentence is to yield the floor. The public speaker and the writer do not have to fear this kind of interruption; they do not have to keep the words coming, using whatever floats to the surface of the stream of consciousness (see Rule 4-3).

One way to get out of the habit of rambling is to try to use stronger conjunctions, such as *although* and *because,* and conjunctive adverbs, such as *however* and *therefore.* These words indicate logical connections between clauses and sentences and form them into a chain. Simply eliminating *and* and *but* and putting in periods may help too, but the result may be a succession of short, babyish sentences that still rambles.

4-11   Check for monotony.

Monotony in speech is the drone that puts us all to sleep no matter how interesting the matter. An unvarying bellow has almost the same effect; it may keep us awake, but our minds go to sleep and we stop hearing the actual words. Avoiding monotony in speech is achieved by variations in delivery—in pitch, volume, pace, and so on—much more than by variations in diction, and is thus a subject outside the scope of this book. Occasionally diction that would be monotonous in written work is not monotonous, or does not have to be, when the same words are spoken; emphasis and variation in vocal inflection can even make a virtue of such diction.

Monotony in writing, despite the derivation of the word from Greek *monotonos*, "having one tone," is not prevented by alternating formal and informal tones, cool and friendly tones, and so on; such alternation is usually a mistake (see Rule 4-8). Nor is it prevented by so-called elegant variation, which is discussed at the end of this rule. It is prevented by varying sentence structure and by avoiding excessive use of either abstract or figurative diction.

Monotonous sentence structure

The basic types of sentence structure are discussed in Rule 2-1—the simple sentence, the compound sentence, and the complex sentence; sentences containing parenthetical or defining subordinate phrases and clauses; and sentences that begin with the main clause and those that begin with subordinate constructions. To these we can add two more types: short sentences and long ones. Above the level of first-grade readers, a written work should be composed of a variety of types.

I have had difficulty varying sentence structure in this book. Almost everything I write seems to require qualification or exception, and consequently many sentences begin with *but* or *however*. Sometimes a sentence containing a *but* clause is followed by a sentence beginning with *however*—every *but* has little *buts* upon it, or big *buts* about to devour it. I apologize to readers who have noted this failing.

I have also made heavy use of the semicolon and the dash, the first because it helps keep expression compact and implies a relationship between the clauses it connects that it would be tedious to write out, and the second because pairs of dashes are such a convenient way to slip almost anything in, including *but* and *however* constructions. The result is that many of my sentences are long and have a compound-complex construction that readers may find wearing. When preparing the second edition of the book I reduced these flaws somewhat, but they still exist.

I shrive myself here not to disarm critics, though I am not above that intent, but to dissociate my advice on variation of sentence structure from my practice in this book. My variation of sentence structure is not exemplary. I do consider my sentences to be workmanlike and to be a reasonable compromise between easy readin' and scholarly denseness, and they are the best I can do for this book; they will probably strike the rare cover-to-cover reader of such a book as monotonous.

A common monotony is a succession of compound sentences joined by *and* or *but*. *The morning passed slowly, and by noon Mary felt ill. She went to the school nurse, and the nurse told her to go home and get into bed. She woke the next day, and Dr. Smith was bending over her. "You have measles," he said shortly, and then his face disappeared, and she saw nothing but the pale ceiling.* With some adjustments, this passage could have a certain cadence that would help express the plodding feeling of illness, and the monotonous succession of compound sentences would be a justified monotony contributing to the effect. (If the words are read aloud, a good speaker could bring out their latent cadence without any revision.) But imagine the same structure going on and on—one might as well have the measles oneself.

A succession of short sentences is choppy; it jerks the reader from one subject-predicate combination to another. A succession of long sentences can be overwhelming, with the structure of one complicated sentence imposing itself, like the image of a bright light when we turn our eyes from it, on the different structure of the next. After a long, complicated sentence the reader wants a break.

A succession of sentences that begin with the subject of the main clause seems to hammer at the reader: *France had not yet fallen, and America had not entered the fray. Trench warfare and the Maginot Line had not yet proved to be antique. The policy in all quarters of the globe was to avert the eyes. Roosevelt was one of the few who had even privately made a commitment.* The hammerblows have a cadence, but it turns out to be a spurious one; *France, Trench warfare and the Maginot Line, The policy,* and *Roosevelt* are not closely enough related to support the cadence. Even a practiced speaker would probably have difficulty making the succession of similar constructions sound good; to do so he or she would have to downplay the similarity of construction and the cadence rather than exploit them.

A succession of sentences that begin with subordinate constructions is tiresome too. *At the end of the year, France had not yet fallen. Despite the advances in armament, the Maginot Line still seemed impregnable. In all quarters of the globe, the policy was to avert the eyes. Across the Atlantic, Roosevelt was one of the few who had made even a private commitment.* The passage, with the pauses required between the introductory constructions and the beginnings of the main clauses, seems to sway like a very slow pendulum. Sleep . . . sleep . . .

A succession of introductory participial constructions is especially boring. *Crossing the room, he sat down. Opening the file, he began to read aloud. Noticing that her attention was wandering, he raised his voice to a bellow.* Such use of participles is poor for other reasons as well; see Rule 1-16.

Any repetition of the same type of sentence can be monotonous. A skillful writer can sometimes use the repetition to achieve the emphasis of an orator, but usually such repetition is accidental and annoying.

Too much abstract diction

Abstract diction is almost a language by itself, and in certain types of writing is edging out English. It is characterized by heavy use of abstract nouns—that is, nouns that refer to concepts, to classes of objects or beings rather than to objects or beings themselves, and to other things that exist in the mind but not in the concrete world—and by heavy use of nouns as adjectives. Some call it the noun plague. Often the writer abstracts himself or herself as well, avoiding at all costs the use of the personal pronoun, so that instead of a straightforward *I believe* or *we doubt* everything *is believed* or *is doubted.* Here is an example of abstract diction:

The addition of subject chronological age consideration factors to raw measurements of ideation variety and complexity reveals a modality of progression rate consistency in both variables in the third decade, and measurement repetition over two or more temporal units, in this study one year, can provide sufficient ideation level data to serve as an index of progression rate expectation on an individual basis.

In English:

> Our study shows that from age twenty to age thirty, think-
> ing tends to increase steadily in both variety and complex-
> ity, and that if we test the same subject twice or more at
> yearly intervals we can predict the subject's rate of pro-
> gression.

To a social scientist, the first version is probably sufficiently
clear, and the second version, though much clearer to laymen,
may seem imprecise and even puzzling, because it does not use
the abstract vocabulary and sentence structure that social scientists are accustomed to. (The very brief summary that often
appears at the beginning of a scientific article is actually called
an abstract, and the preceding example is such an abstract.)
Abstract diction is legitimate in some sciences; it forces speakers and writers to keep themselves out of what should be
impersonal statements about objective reality, and it is meant
for those who are interested in the data, not in the expression,
and who in any case are used to the special diction of their
field.

Abstract diction has been taken up by the "science" of education. To a student, a parent, or a teacher, education is neither
impersonal nor objective, and one is tempted to accuse educa-
tionists who use abstract diction of being off in a pretentious
and self-important world of their own far from the classroom.
One might go further; anyone who uses abstract diction excessively in any type of speaking or writing may be hoping the
long words, passive constructions, and complicated sentences
will awe the listener or reader.

It is perfectly appropriate to have some abstract diction in a
speech or written work. *It is evident that in some circumstances justice may be served better in a biased court than in
an unbiased one* is an abstract conclusion that is fine if it
follows concrete examples, but if it follows a string of similarly
abstract statements, it is just playing with words; the actual
argument may be the same whether concrete or abstract, but
listeners or readers will find the abstract version monotonous,
and their attention will wander.

If in revising you find successions of abstract sentences, try
to replace most of them with concrete ones.

Too much figurative diction

Figures of speech can add variety to writing. They can, however, be distracting if misused and monotonous if overused. The most common figures are the simile, such as *Love is like a blooming flower*, in which love is said to be like a flower; and the metaphor, such as *The boldest flower in life's garden is love*, in which love is actually taken to be a flower and life to be a garden.

His campaign has been like a becalmed ship is a fair enough simile, and the writer might go on to sharpen the comparison, with campaign workers idly doodling just as sailors carve scrimshaw. However, continuing this simile could quickly become tiresome, as voter apathy is likened to failing winds, opponents to cruising sharks, and so on; it is monotonous to harp on the trivial comparisons that can be made between one thing and another.

In the last week he has trimmed the sails of his campaign is a fair enough metaphor, with some useful implications—the candidate is in control, and his campaign must be picking up speed. *He has left no stone unturned in trimming the sails of his campaign*, though not a mixed metaphor of the thigh-slapping sort gleefully collected by *The New Yorker*, begins to show the danger of trying to say everything figuratively rather than directly. Senseless and often ludicrous juxtapositions occur; turning stones has nothing to do with trimming sails. If the writer goes on jumping from one figure to the next, readers will give up following, because the tiresome succession of figures will bore them.

Figurative diction can also lead to errors of logic (Rule 4-9). A writer may liken a brain to a light bulb, and then note that a light bulb will last forever if it is never turned on, but the writer has not proved that we should avoid thinking. A subject that is abstract itself may be enlivened by the use of figures—this is the essential method of many poets—and a complicated subject, such as economics, may be elucidated by discussing it in terms of something simpler, such as a pie, but any figure that befuddles, distracts, or bores should be eliminated.

If you find too much simile and metaphor in your work when you revise, try to cut it down. You may both save yourself embarrassment and clarify your thoughts.

Elegant variation

That man took another individual's hat and *Mother wore a flowered hat, Father proceeded under a homburg, and my pate was graced by a beanie* take care not to repeat a word or a construction—they attempt to be "elegant" by demonstrating the speaker's or writer's ability to find a synonym or alternative construction. This is no way to achieve elegance; it is far better to repeat the straightforward word or construction than to vary it. The variation, though it does not violate rules of grammar, is a misuse of grammar; see Rule 1-5 on parallel constructions. *Mother wore a flowered hat, Father wore a homburg, and I wore a beanie* is fine, and far less boring than a succession of increasingly complicated variations.

This is not to say that words should never be varied. *Mother wore a hat that brought a smile to Father's worn face and somewhat lightened the wearing occasion* is a different sort of error of diction. The various forms of the verb *wear* should be varied, because they have different meanings: *Mother wore a hat that brought a smile to Father's tired face and somewhat lightened the tedious occasion.* Avoiding jarring repetitions of a word used in different senses is not elegant variation; these repetitions should be looked for in the course of revision and should be eliminated. Such repetition occurs very often—perhaps the mind fixates on a word and unconsciously begins to use it in several senses, and unhappy echoes such as that in *We passed a rubber-tired cart pulled by a tired donkey* result.

Elegant variation pure and simple, as in *The World Series, with the Yankees and Dodgers engaged for the eleventh time in an October duel, promises to be one of the most gripping of fall classics,* has won some place in sportswriting and sports announcing, in which a certain humorous resonance is thereby achieved. But the variation is often witless even then.

4-12   Check for clichés and awkward expressions.

Whether a given word or phrase is a cliché or is awkward is, of course, a matter of judgment. Judgment differs from one of us to another, but it is probably fair to say that the more experience we have in public speaking or writing, the harsher our judgment of our own words becomes and yet the less often we have to deal harshly with our own words, because we automatically discard tired and awkward expressions as we write.

The beginning speaker or writer is usually too easily satisfied by the first phrasings that come to mind and may even be delighted that familiar expressions such as *generous to a fault*, *view with alarm*, and *poor as a churchmouse* flow so neatly into place. They flow too neatly; they will bore the listener or reader.

Some expressions are clichés if addressed to one group but retain their original force if addressed to others. Telling a group of architecture students that a house should be a machine for living would be a mistake—the phrase is far too familiar to them already—but might be a new and interesting thought to a younger and less sophisticated group, such as students in a class in home economics.

The beginning speaker or writer is bound to be awkward. Fluency comes much easier to some than to others, and some never achieve it, perhaps because of a limited vocabulary, a lack of self-confidence, or a mind oriented toward the graphic or the mechanical rather than the verbal. Still, every conscientious effort made during the process of revision to find and reword awkward expressions will improve both the speech or written work itself and the speaker's or writer's overall command of language.

4-13   Check grammar, punctuation, and other mechanics.

Even though the mechanics of English may have been much on the writer's or speaker's mind from the beginning, and even though they may have been flawless in the first draft, they need checking once again. Revisions may have changed the grammar of a sentence or affected the way it should be punctuated, and a final look at this stage may uncover some surprising lapses.

In a written work of book length, one will almost always find inconsistencies of capitalization and other matters discussed in Chapter 3—even in published books that have been through many drafts and have been read by one or more editors and a proofreader. Periodicals and publishing houses do try to catch these details, along with errors of grammar and punctuation, but they are never perfect at it and are more and more frequently unable to do it well, either because they cannot spend the time or because their staff members are not adequately trained. It helps to keep a list of certain decisions that have been made along the way:

Use comma before *and* in a series
Spell out numbers to 100, except in the statistical section
Put titles of the Whitman poems in quotes—not italics
Capitalize *Farm*, for Brook Farm

Such decisions are for consistency, not for rightness, so it's easy to forget just what decisions have been made unless a list is kept.

4-14   Practice delivering a speech at proper speed, or read a written work at normal reading speed; seek a test listener or reader if someone conscientious is available.

This rule may seem not to need stating, since most of us will declaim or reread our work over and over again. But it should be done with the proper attitude; we should be pretending that we are someone else, hearing or seeing the words for the first time. It takes practice to displace ourselves this way and assume objectivity.

A test listener or reader can be invaluable, especially if the listener or reader is representative of the group the speech or written work is for, but it is hard to find a truly conscientious person to play this role. A relative or close friend will rarely be critical enough unless he or she has been trained in dispassionate evaluation. Many people will snatch idly at some phrase that is quite all right to start with and then harp on it, just to demonstrate acuity and a willingness to help. A poor listener or reader will not pay attention. A listener or reader who is monomaniacally interested in something else will argue that our carefully written history of the dog should concern itself more with the future of the cat.

Choose your test person carefully. For example, suppose you are preparing a paper to be read to a group of executives in your company. Perhaps you know one of the members of the group well enough to ask him or her to read your draft. The person you ask is likely to be flattered, and so you will almost certainly guarantee yourself one approving eventual auditor, but more important, you will almost certainly get knowledgeable and helpful advice. Even a quarrelsome or otherwise negative reaction will enable you to anticipate, and thus possibly to obviate, negative responses from the full group. There is, of course, some hazard in soliciting an important person's advice and then ignoring it.

Don't let one test, or even several, entirely overcome your own judgment of your work. You have put in a lot more time and thought than your test person; you may be right and he or she may be wrong. You will find out when your work reaches its intended audience or readership.

GLOSSARY / INDEX

◆

As well as serving as an index to the preceding four chapters and providing definitions of the terms used in them, the Glossary/Index includes entries on many controversial usages—that is, on individual words, phrases, and constructions that are used by some in ways that are considered misuses by others. A dictionary should be the first reference consulted on most questions involving words rather than sentences, but the best modern dictionaries are based on actual occurrences of words in literary and general language, not on opinion. Dictionaries do include occasional usage labels, such as "colloquial," "substandard," and "vulgar," and some of them comment on usage controversies, but they cannot say, as I sometimes do, that a word is used incorrectly more often than it is used correctly, because to a lexicographer a predominant use cannot be a misuse. I assume that readers of this book want to be warned away from usages that are likely to be condemned by a critical minority, even though some of these usages appear, and in some cases have appeared for centuries, in the best writing and are therefore accepted as standard by dictionaries and by serious scholars of usage. I comment accordingly, and I even air a few prejudices of my own.

a*, *an   *An* should be used only before a word that when spoken begins with a vowel sound. *An ear* and *an heir* are correct. *An utopia* and *an eulogy* should not have *an* because the nouns begin with the sound of a consonantal *y*, and *an hotel* and *an historian* do not need *an* because in American pronunciation the nouns generally begin with a sounded *h*. The British frequently say and write *an hotel* and *an historian*, but unlike most Americans, they generally do not pronounce the *h* in the nouns or they pronounce it only very faintly. Americans who follow the British practice may be suspected of pretension. Although the frequency of dropped-*h* pronunciations varies considerably from word to word—for example, though few Americans would say *an 'istory book*, a good many would say *an 'istorical occasion*—I recommend using *a* in writing whenever the case is doubtful: *a historical occasion*.

Initial-style abbreviations take *a* or *an* according to how they are pronounced: *an FDA report; a UNESCO report.*

abbreviations   with periods, Rule 3-10; with commas, Rule 3-11; *Jr., Sr.,* and similar abbreviations in possessive constructions, Rule 2-29

about   The word is sometimes redundant, and it has picked up some questionable applications.

They estimated the crowd to be about 25,000 indicates approximation with both *about* and the verb *estimated*. *They estimated the crowd to be about 25,000 to 30,000* provides a third indicator of approximation, the range of numbers. Often *about* isn't needed and should be dropped.

Vanity is what autobiographies are all about contains a peculiar use of *about* with *all* that appeared two or three decades ago and may be going out of fashion. Of course, autobiographies cannot be said to be about vanity in a literal sense; they are presumably about the lives of their authors. What is meant is not that such books are about vanity—that is, have vanity as their subject—but that vanity inspires or pervades them. Still, *about* does not always have to be used in its most literal sense, and *Vanity is what autobiographies are about* is inoffensive, as a mildly witty aphorism. It is the combination *all about* in such statements that bothers me. It seems offensively glib; the writer or speaker employs a correct but rather childish construction (*What's birth control all about, Daddy?*) in hopes its childishness will coax or bully readers into thinking that a complex subject is being ingeniously reduced to even-a-babe-can-grasp-it simplicity—really telling them what it's all about. I do not know if my dislike of *all about* is shared by many; I can say that I have generally found it in writing that I believe many would consider offensively glib overall.

I'm not about to pay him and *He's crazy if he thinks I'm about to pay him* contain another new and peculiar use of *about; about to* replaces the straightforward *going to* and intensifies the negative thought. This usage gives an ersatz toughness to the expression of those whose language lacks natural flavor; to me it often suggests not just determination but a kind of mean defiance. A vogue usage of this kind can be considered a cliché; it may have been effective as a colorful misuse when it was originated, but now it is tired. Note that *I was about to pay him when he suddenly started making threats* is a standard and inoffensive use of *about;* the phrase *about to pay* is equivalent to *on the verge of paying.*

absolute   Certain adverbs and adjectives that cannot logically be compared, such as *infinitely* and *unique,* are called absolute; see **comparative and superlative.**

absolute construction   a phrase that is not an independent clause but is nevertheless not grammatically dependent on any particular element in the rest of the sentence. *John having arrived, we began the meeting* contains the absolute construction *John having arrived* (which is not a dangling participle; see Rule 1-21). *It was, to be sure, a difficult meeting* contains the absolute construction *to be sure.* Interjections and words or phrases used in direct address are absolute constructions: *Oh my, I forgot my notes; I think, Mr. Chairman, that Mr. Smith is out of order.*

abstract diction   speech or writing that makes heavy use of abstract words—those that denote ideas, classifications, quantities, emotions, and other things that exist primarily in the mind rather than in the physical world. Abstract diction can be monotonous (see Rule 4-11), and it is sometimes difficult to follow, especially when chains of abstract nouns are used to form compound adjectives (see Rule 2-36).

active voice   See **voice.**

A.D.   means *anno domini,* "in the year of the Lord," and therefore, in strict usage, should precede the year, as in *Ti-*

berias was born in 42 B.C. and died in A.D. 37, and should be used only with a year, not with a century; *He died in the first century A.D.* does not make sense if the abbreviation is spelled out. Moreover, *in A.D. 37* can be criticized as redundant, because the Latin ablative *anno domini* includes the meaning of *in*; *He died A.D. 37* may sound a bit clipped but is impeccable. However, these are rather fussy points; the meaning of a word can change drastically, making its etymology irrelevant, and the meaning of this abbreviation has broadened. Any reader who sees *A.D.* after the year or after a century understands it to mean "after the birth of Christ" or some equivalent phrase. The "correct" placement may even look rather odd except in scholarly or other determinedly formal writing. I advise letting *A.D.* fall where it does naturally; for one thing, there is no short, convenient alternative to *first century A.D.*

A.D. and *B.C.* can be replaced by *C.E.* (meaning "current era," "common era," or "Christian era") and *B.C.E.* ("before the current era" and so on). The replacements are significant and desirable in some contexts, but needlessly puzzle readers in others.

In printing, *A.D.* and *B.C.* are sometimes in small capitals rather than full capitals, as, more frequently, are *A.M.* and *P.M.* I usually prescribe small capitals for *A.M.* but not for *A.D.* Some publishing houses and publications have a preference.

address   forms of address, Rules 3-14 to 3-16; punctuation with words used in direct address, Rule 2-10

adjective   one of the **parts of speech**; a word used to modify the meaning of a noun. Often an adjective is misused as an **adverb**; see Rule 1-22. When two or more adjectives are used to modify the same noun, problems may occur with punctuation and with the order of the adjectives; see Rule 1-20. For hyphenation of compound adjectives, see Rules 2-35 and 2-36.

Adjectival phrases and *adjectival clauses* are so called not because they contain adjectives—often they do not—but because they function as adjectives. *The man wearing the hat is married to the woman who is on his right* contains the adjectival phrase *wearing the hat*, modifying *man*, and the adjectival clause *who is on his right*, modifying *woman*. Since *man* and *woman* are nouns, the modifying phrase and modifying clause are considered adjectival. An adjectival clause is usually called a **relative clause**, because it includes a relative pronoun—*who* in the example—or an omitted but understood relative pronoun, as in *That's the woman he married*, in which the relative pronoun *whom* does not appear but is understood.

adverb   one of the **parts of speech**; a word used to modify a verb, an adjective, or another adverb. An adverb can also modify an entire sentence, as in *Regrettably, my opponent won.* Almost all words that end in *ly* are adverbs (*quickly, largely*), but some are not (*friendly* and *leisurely* are adjectives, though the latter is correct, if awkward, as an adverb too). Many common adverbs do not end in *ly* (*very, quite*), and some of these are adjectives as well as adverbs (*better, long*) and may require a hyphen joining them to the word they modify to prevent misreading; see Rule 2-35. Often a word that is usually a preposition becomes an adverb, as in *Used-car buyers like to trade up*, in which *up* modifies the verb *trade* rather than acting as a preposition.

Adverbs are often misused as adjectives, as in *I feel badly*; see Rule 1-22. They are also often used when adjectival forms might be better; see **first . . . second** vs. **firstly . . . secondly** and **more important** vs. **more importantly.**

Adverbial phrases and *adverbial clauses* are so called not because they contain adverbs—often they do not—but because they function as adverbs. *He swore when shaving and sang while he showered* contains the adverbial phrase *when shaving,* modifying *swore,* and the adverbial clause *while he showered,* modifying *sang.* Since *swore* and *sang* are verbs, and adverbs are the part of speech used to modify verbs, the modifying phrase and clause are considered adverbial.

A *conjunctive adverb* is one used to join clauses or to connect the thought of a sentence to the preceding sentence. In *They won the first two games; however, they lost the series,* the adverb *however* is conjunctive. In *However, they lost the next four games,* the adverb *However* connects the thought of the sentence to that of some preceding sentence and thus is conjunctive. It is also a sentence modifier.

aggravate   means *make heavier* or *make worse,* like the Latin verb it is derived from, but for over a century has also been used to mean *annoy.* The second meaning is now far more common than the first and is accepted as standard in modern dictionaries. In my experience, the few who use it in the first meaning never use it in the second, and the many who use it in the second meaning never use it in the first—I believe that for the most part the many are ignorant of the first meaning. The few are highly critical of the many on this point, so I advise never using the word to mean *annoy.* Well-educated people do so use it, but at least to my ear the usage seems a **malapropism,** which is probably what it was when it first appeared, and has the untutored ring of such rustic polysyllables as *discombobulate* for *upset.* In short, the usage lacks class, like many other well-established usages.

agreement   in grammar, the change in the form of a word caused by its relationship to another word. Some words change their form depending on their **person, number, gender,** and **case.** A subject and its verb should agree in person (Rule 1-10) and in number (Rule 1-11). A pronoun and its antecedent should agree in person, number, and gender (Rule 1-12), and when the pronoun is in apposition it should also agree in case (Rule 1-6). Disagreements such as in *Everyone was clapping their hands,* in which the singular word *Everyone* is assigned the singular verb *was* but the plural possessive pronoun *their,* are sharply criticized by many and should be avoided, though they are defended by some usage scholars; see Rule 1-12.

all   As a pronoun, *all* is often plural, as in *All were glad to see him go,* but is also often singular, as in *There used to be gold here, but all is gone now.* It is also singular in *All I saw in the forest was trees,* in which it means the totality of what I saw, not the trees. Often the verb is mistakenly made to agree with the **complement** rather than the subject; *All I saw in the forest were trees* is an error. It is the subject of a verb, not its complement, that determines the number; see Rule 1-11.

A good test of the plurality or singularity of *all* is to see if some plural noun or noun phrase can be understood to follow it. In the first example above, *the people* or some such phrase can be understood after *all,* so *all* is plural. In the second example, *the gold* or *of it* can be understood, but of course those phrases are singular, so *all* is singular. In the third example, there is no noun or noun phrase that can credibly follow *all,* unless we make a considerable effort to change the singular meaning of *all* by complicating the context: *I have many friends in the world, and some of them are not in the animal kingdom. All (the friends) I saw in the forest were trees.* The test has to be made with a little common sense, because not every sentence is so easily tested by it. One could argue, for example, that *All we found in the drawer were documents and old letters* is correct because it can be said to mean *All (the* objects) *we found in the drawer were documents and old letters*, but what it really means is that the totality of what we found *was* documents and old letters. When *all* does not stand for a plural noun or noun phrase but means a totality, it is singular.

all right* vs. *alright *Alright* is common in print but very widely criticized; I advise never using it.

all together* vs. *altogether *All together* means *in a group*, as in *We went in to dinner all together. Altogether* means *entirely*, as in *I skipped dinner altogether* and *Dinner was altogether dreadful.*

all* vs. *all of In a few constructions, such as *all of them, of* is necessary, but generally it is optional: *all of the money, all the money.* Usually omitting *of* improves a construction, making it tighter, but the small unstressed word may be desirable in the cadence of a specific sentence (see Rule 1-4). It is wise for a writer to have some reasonably consistent personal policy—an optional *of* in one sentence and the omission of an optional *of* a sentence or two later is the kind of inconsistency that, though trivial in itself, can make writing seem characterless—but usually there is no need to question what comes naturally.

almost Often *almost* is used oddly with a comparative adjective or adverb, as in *It's cold today, but it was almost colder yesterday* and *You drive almost worse than my mother.* The usage is common enough to be considered an idiom rather than an error, but its muddiness is annoying to some—does *almost colder* mean *just as cold* or *almost as cold*, or possibly *perhaps even colder*? I advise avoiding it.

A.M., P.M., M. See Rule 3-5.

ambiguity possession of more than one possible or likely meaning. Ambiguity can be deliberate and useful, as in poetry that is meant to be meaningful in more than one way, but it is usually accidental and confusing. It can have many causes. Frequently **ellipsis** results in ambiguity; see Rules 1-1 and 1-3. Another cause is a pronoun with more than one possible antecedent; see Rule 1-13. Modifiers, particularly adverbs, are sometimes ambiguous because they are positioned carelessly; see Rule 1-20.

ampersand   Except in casual notes, the ampersand, &, should be used only in names of firms: *Smith & Brown, Inc.* A comma should not be used before an ampersand: *Smith, Jones & Brown, Inc.*

and   It is not an error to begin a sentence with *And* or any other **conjunction;** see Rule 1-1.

and/or   a convenient and compact device—it isn't really a word or even a conventional compound—but a graceless one. It has a place in legal, commercial, and technical writing, in which precision and compactness are more important than grace, but even in such writing it is often unnecessarily used when *or* alone would carry the meaning. Elsewhere it should be avoided, even though avoiding it may require several additional words. See also Rule 2-38.

antecedent   the word or phrase that a **pronoun** represents. In *John, who is of royal blood, demeans himself by asking his servants to dine with him,* the pronouns *who, himself, his,* and *him* all have *John* as their antecedent. Indefinite pronouns such as *anyone* and *whoever* cannot have an antecedent—that is why they are indefinite. Interrogative pronouns such as *who?* and *what?* cannot have an antecedent—the person or thing that such a pronoun represents is unknown. Personal pronouns such as *he* and *them* do not need to have their antecedents in the same sentence, but there should be an unambiguous antecedent somewhere close by. Sometimes pronouns are used excessively and the reader must try to figure out which of two or more grammatically possible antecedents a pronoun represents; see Rule 1-13.

antithetical construction   a *not . . . but* construction, in which something is held to be untrue and something else is held to be true: *Her hair was not red but purple.* The construction can be signaled by *but not* or just by *not: Her hair was purple but not garish; Her hair was purple, not red.* In more complicated sentences, *not* or *but* is often wrongly positioned; see Rule 1-5. For punctuation of *not . . . but* constructions, see Rule 2-7.

any   can be either singular or plural as a pronoun: *Six candidates have come forward, but I don't think any of them is going to get the nomination; Six candidates have come forward, but I don't think any of them are nationally known.*

302

There are those who think *any* must always be singular and would therefore change *are* to *is* in the second example, but sometimes a singular verb would be absurd, as in *The stream is full of brown trout, but I don't think any is native.* I advise letting *any* be plural whenever the plural comes naturally.

any more vs. anymore   The one-word form *anymore* is now accepted as standard when it is an adverb modifying a verb in negative sentences and in questions: *He doesn't play golf anymore; Does he play golf anymore?* However, *anymore* cannot be used as an adjective, as in *There isn't anymore meat*, or as an adverb modifying an adjective or another adverb, as in *I couldn't come anymore quickly;* it should be *any more* in both examples.

The two-word form *any more* was formerly the only one considered correct, and those who want to continue to use it in all constructions can do so, though publishing houses generally accept or prefer the one-word form when it is correct. *Anymore* has apparently solidified in imitation of other *any* words such as *anyone, anything, anytime, anyway,* and *anywhere*, even though *anymore* is not the same kind of formation as these other words, a fact borne out by pronunciation; in *anymore,* the *more* gets the stress or there is no stress, but in all the other words, *any* gets the stress.

The one-word form has the advantage of occasionally preventing ambiguity. *He can't eat any more* can mean either that he's had all he can eat for the moment or that he's wasting away, whereas *He can't eat anymore* can have only the second meaning. The context, of course, usually would prevent such ambiguity anyway.

Any more and *anymore* are used in some regions of the country to modify a verb in positive sentences: *Last year was a bad one, but we're all right anymore.* The usage puzzles readers from other regions.

anyone, anybody   These are singular pronouns and should not be used as the antecedent of a pronoun such as *their*, as in *I don't want anybody to forget their manners.* The prohibition can be troublesome; see Rule 1-12.

anytime, sometime   As adverbs, these words are contractions of *at any time* and *at some time.* Whenever the full forms cannot be substituted for the contractions, they should not be contractions but two words: *Come anytime today, but I can't* *give you any time tomorrow; He said he'd come sometime soon, but the TV may take some time to fix, and we might have to leave it with him for some time.* Both *anytime* and *sometime* are occasionally used as adjectives: *Litchi nuts are an anytime snack; He's a sometime friend,* meaning an inconstant friend; *He's a sometime state senator,* meaning a former, or **onetime**, state senator.

apostrophe use of for the possessive case, Rule 2-29; use of for contractions and dropped letters, Rule 2-30; use of to form the plurals of figures and letters, Rule 3-6

apposition, appositive A word or phrase is in apposition to another word or phrase when it immediately follows the other word or phrase to identify or explain it. *Mr. Smith, our chairman, has resigned* contains the appositive *our chairman; Our chairman, Mr. Smith, has resigned* contains the appositive *Mr. Smith.* Words in apposition can be either **parenthetical** or **defining.** Usually if they are parenthetical they are set off with commas and if they are defining they are not set off, though there are exceptions; see Rule 2-1. Pronouns that are in apposition should agree in case with the words they are in apposition to; see Rule 1-6. An appositive is not the same as a **complement,** which does not just follow another word or phrase but is joined to it by a verb.

Sometimes an appositive precedes the phrase it is in apposition to: *A plainspoken man, Smith had alienated the rabble.*

article a classification including only the two words *the* and *a* (or *an*). *The* is called the definite article, *a* is called the indefinite article. Some grammarians consider the article one of the **parts of speech,** but most consider it an adjective, since it modifies nouns just as other adjectives do.

as a tricky word that sometimes is wrongly omitted (see *as well as . . . or better than*) but in the cases below is wrongly or unnecessarily included.

He is equally as wrong is redundant; it should be either *He is equally wrong* or *He is as wrong.* Of course, since *as* is not always an adverb meaning *equally,* there are times when *equally as* is correct. For example, *He is famous equally as a playwright and as a novelist* uses *as* as a preposition meaning *in the role of.* There are also times when the several meanings of *as* permit it to recur correctly but extremely awkwardly, as in *He is as famous as a playwright as as a novelist,* in which it is first an adverb, then a preposition, then a conjunction, then a preposition again.

They elected John as treasurer needs no *as; They elected John treasurer* is better. (See also **complement.**) However, the *as* in the example is not incorrect, and after some verbs the construction does require it: *They installed John as treasurer.*

As he said, a mirror should reverse up and down, not just right and left is a careless use of an *as* construction. The *As* that begins the sentence indicates that the writer agrees with the content of the sentence. If the writer does not agree or does not want to take a stand, it should be *He said that a mirror . . .* or *He said, "A mirror . . ."* to keep the writer's own opinion out of it. See Rule 2-23.

Consider our connections severed as from this date contains a superfluous *as;* the word has a function in some similar legal expressions but is usually merely pompous.

See also the discussions immediately following of *as* in some common constructions and as a substitute for *because* or *since.*

as . . . as   joins the elements in a comparison, as in *I play as well as he does* and *He doesn't play as much as I do.* The second *as* in each example introduces a clause, and in this construction it almost always does so, even though the clause may be elliptical. *I love money as much as she* and *I love money as much as her* therefore have different meanings; when the elliptical clauses are filled out, the sentences become *I love money as much as she does* and *I love money as much as I love her.* But in current usage, the second *as* is often taken not as a conjunction introducing an elliptical clause but as a preposition, as in *I am responsible as much as her,* in which the pronoun *her* is in the objective case as the object of a preposition rather than in the subjective case as the subject of an understood verb (*as much as she is*). Consequently, someone who says *I love money as much as her* may mean *I love money as much as she does.* The context would almost certainly make misunderstanding unlikely, and some grammarians accept *as* as a preposition in such comparisons. However, the usage seems untutored to my ear and, I believe, to many other ears; I see it much more often in mediocre writing than in good writing. I advise avoiding such use of *as* as a preposition. See the longer discussion of prepositional uses of **than.**

as . . . as vs. so . . . as   There used to be an arbitrary rule that *as . . . as* should be used in positive constructions and *so . . . as* in negative constructions: *You are as hidebound as she; You are not so hidebound as she.* The rule is now defunct; *as . . . as* is often used in negative constructions, and *so . . . as* can be used in an occasional positive construction, though only in sentences with a negative force, such as *I doubt if he is so hidebound as you.* I advise using *as* rather than *so* whenever it comes naturally, though I do sometimes find the formerly common distinction made in current writing that I admire.

as follows vs. as follow   Never use *as follow* to introduce a statement or list. *The people were divided into categories, as follows: men, women, and children* is correct. The word *people* is plural, *categories* is plural, and *men, women, and children* is plural both in its parts and as a whole, but none of these is the subject of *follows*. In fact, *as follows* and a very few other phrases (*as concerns, as regards*) are idioms in which the verb has no subject.

as for because or since   As, *because,* and *since* can all be used as subordinating conjunctions—that is, to introduce dependent clauses—but they are not interchangeable. A specific meaning of *as* is *at the same time as: As he went down the steps, he slipped.* A specific meaning of *since* is *after the time that: Since he slipped on the steps, we have slipped ourselves.* The specific, and only, meaning of *because* is *for the reason that: Because he broke his leg, we're being sued.* But both *as* and *since* are also often used to mean *for the reason that: As he went down the steps, the elevator man didn't see him; Since he slipped on the steps, he went away mad.* The result is that *as* and *since* can be ambiguous; they may carry their special meanings that relate to time, or they may mean *because.* It is too late, by centuries, to pummel *as* and *since* into strict definitions that do not overlap, but it is sensible to beware of the ambiguities they permit—which, in my experience, are quite often not resolved by the context—and perhaps to be especially suspicious of *as* for *because,* which many consider inelegant.

Since for *because* does not seem to offend, as long as there is no ambiguity: *Since it began to rain, I didn't go out* is unambiguous and unobjectionable. *Since it began to rain, I haven't gone out* may be ambiguous—I may have not gone out after it began to rain for reasons unrelated to the rain. When the dependent clause follows the main clause, a comma or its absence may make *since* unambiguous: *I haven't gone out, since it began to rain* uses *since* in the sense of *because; I haven't gone out since it began to rain* uses *since* in its time-indicating sense. *Since* in the sense of *because* does have a useful function; it is less emphatic than *because* and can give a dependent clause a parenthetical effect.

As for *because* does seem to offend even when there is no ambiguity; I cannot explain the prejudice against it, but I share it. I think those who use it are likely to overuse it, somewhat as **while** is overused, and perhaps it is just the repeated use that bothers me. I advise making very light use of it, if any; if *because* seems too emphatic, *since* should work. Sometimes it can be defended. *As he's suing us, I suppose we should postpone the wedding* uses *as* not to replace *because* but to replace, and perhaps deliberately weaken, *since;* the meaning is not *for the reason that* but *in view of the fact that,* which is a common meaning of *since.*

as if, as though　　These conjunctive phrases are interchangeable, though some grammarians have tried to make distinctions between them; to my ear and eye, one is as good as the other. They often introduce a clause that is in the **subjunctive mood,** as in *He acts as if he were better than we are,* but also often introduce a clause in the **indicative mood,** as in *He acts as though he is angry;* see the discussion at the end of Rule 1-14.

If a writer depends on these phrases too much, they begin to wear on the reader; see Rule 4-11 for a general discussion of monotony. Often the phrases can be eliminated, especially when the statement is indicative: *He acts angry.*

as well as　　Often when this phrase is a **conjunction** it leads to errors of agreement in number between subject and verb, as in *John as well as his parents were at the party,* in which the phrase *as well as his parents* is merely parenthetical; the true subject is *John* and the verb should be *was.* See the discussion at the end of Rule 1-11.

See also **both,** which is sometimes used redundantly with *as well as.*

as well as . . . or better than, as much as . . . or more than　　These pairs and similar adverbial pairs are often incorrectly shortened by omitting the second *as. He did as much or more than I did* should have *as* after *much* as well as before it. See Rule 1-2.

attraction   the tendency of the form of one word in a sentence to reflect the form of another even though there is no grammatical requirement that it do so. Sometimes such attraction is condoned or even preferred, as in *I thought she was single, but she's not,* in which the past tense of *thought* attracts the verb in the following noun clause to the past tense (see Rule 1-14). Sometimes such attraction is an error, as in *He is one of those men who likes to travel,* in which the singular *He, is,* and *one* attract the verb *like,* which should be plural—*those men who like*—to the singular (see Rule 1-11).

attribution   the addition of *he said, John asked, she wrote,* or some similar construction to a direct or indirect quotation to indicate the source. For punctuation with attributions, see Rule 2-11. Attributions such as *as he said* indicate that the writer agrees with the quotation, but many writers do not seem to realize this; see *as.*
Verbs such as *smile* and *frown* have been used for attributions for generations: *"You're a penny short," he frowned.* This practice permits writers to vary their verbs of attribution and to express very compactly the manner in which something is said, but it is absurd, from the strictest point of view, and many readers are annoyed by it. There are many verbs that are not objectionable in attributions but still connote manner, such as *agree, beg, complain, hint, insist, propose,* and *scold.* Even these should not be used just to vary the common *said* and *asked.* A writer may feel that there are too many repetitions of *said* and *asked,* but in fact these verbs of attribution are almost invisible to the reader, and their repetition is not annoying. Dialogue sometimes can, of course, run for quite a few exchanges without any attributions and still be clear to the reader, though the writer, who always knows who's talking, may sometimes overestimate the reader's ability to follow.
Colorful verbs such as *grunt* and *hiss* are acceptable when they are appropriate—*"Hunh!" he grunted; "Just taste this, my sweet," he hissed*—but *grunt* and *hiss* are ludicrous when the quotation could not actually be grunted or hissed: *"I suppose you consider this an adequate periphrasis," he grunted* (difficult to grunt); *"You will enjoy the cocktail," he hissed* (impossible to hiss).

attributive   An attributive modifier is one that comes just before, or occasionally just after, the modified noun or noun phrase. In *big baby* and *I prefer a baby burping to a baby bawling*, the adjective *big* and the adjectival participles *burping* and *bawling* are attributive. In *The baby is big*, the adjective *big* is not attributive; it is called a predicate adjective, since it is part of the predicate. When a string of modifiers precedes the modified word, all the modifiers are attributive: *big bald burping and bawling baby*.

The term is convenient to describe a noun that is functioning as an adjective. In *Nursery school is a baby heaven*, the words *Nursery* and *baby*, which usually are nouns, function as adjectives, but instead of calling them adjectives we can call them attributive nouns. Similarly, a possessive pronoun such as *her* in *her baby* functions as an adjective and can be called attributive.

auxiliary verb   a "helping" verb, used to form the compound tenses of another verb (see also **compound** and **tense**). *I am going* contains the auxiliary verb *am*; *I have gone* contains the auxiliary verb *have*. The most common auxiliary verbs are forms of *be* and *have*, but *do, can, may, might, must, ought, shall, will, should, could*, and others are also often auxiliary verbs, and some function only as auxiliary verbs. For example, *I shall* has no meaning unless it occurs with another verb or another verb is understood to be occurring with it.

Auxiliary verbs are often contracted: *I have, I've; I would* or *I had, I'd; I would have, I'd've*. The contraction *'ve* is sometimes mistakenly written *of*, because of the similarity in sound: *I'd of baked a cake*.

a while* vs. *awhile   *Awhile* is an adverb, with the same meaning as the adverbial prepositional phrase *for a while*: *Let's rest awhile; Let's rest for a while*. When *for a while* cannot be substituted for *awhile*, *awhile* should be *a while*: *Spend a while with me*. When *for* occurs, *awhile* should not follow; *Stay for awhile* should be *Stay for a while* or *Stay awhile*. The modifier *quite* is a complication. *She stayed for quite a while* is no problem, but one could argue in favor of either *She stayed quite a while* or *She stayed quite awhile*; I favor *quite a while* and also *a while longer*, though I think *quite awhile* and *awhile longer* may occur more frequently in print. *For awhile* too is by no means rare in print; most editors routinely change it, but it may be that very few readers aside from editors notice it.

barbarism   a usage or grammatical construction that is considered an ignorant misuse or a corruption of standard English. Many of the barbarisms of yesteryear are standard English, and good English, now. Coleridge attacked *talented* as a barbarism—if *talented*, he asked, why not *shillinged* and *tenpenced?* De Quincey attacked Coleridge for using *unreliable* and recommended *unrelyuponable.*

B.C.   See *A.D.*

because   can be ambiguous in negative sentences; see *not.* See also *due to* vs. *because of* and *reason is because.*

behalf of   A lawyer speaks *on behalf of* a client; that is, as the client's agent. A character witness gives evidence *in behalf of* a defendant; that is, for the benefit of the defendant. However, the distinction is no longer much observed and is sometimes difficult to draw. If the phrase must be used repeatedly, it is probably better to make a choice and stick to it for all uses, since readers are likely to perceive variation between *in* and *on* as inconsistency rather than distinction.

behaviors, a behavior   These usages are a great convenience in, appropriately, behaviorist psychology, which needs a word for a specific action or reaction of an organism and often needs to make it plural and use it in a special way in the singular: *Subject 47 salivated and vigorously moved its tail when the investigator unwrapped his lunch, behaviors that when simultaneous are suspected to indicate hunger and the anticipation of satisfying it, though so far it is a mystery why a behavior at the front of the animal and another behavior at the back of the animal should combine to signal the emptiness of an organ in the middle of the animal.* Such usages have made their way through popular self-help books and the jargon-happy literature of educators to the general language. They seem pretentious when the singular *behavior* without *a* will do: *Rusty drooled and wagged his tail—familiar behavior at lunchtime.*

beside vs. *besides*   *Beside* means *alongside,* as in *He parked his car beside mine. Besides* means *in addition to,* as in *There were ten cars besides mine in the lot,* and *except,* as in *There were no cars besides mine in the lot.* Both words have other meanings too, and sometimes their meanings are very close or even overlap. However, using *beside* to mean *in addition to* or *except*, as in *No one beside them was there*, is likely to draw criticism. The usage has something of the flavor of a **hyperurbanism**, perhaps committed because of awareness that *s* often marks a colloquialism such as *somewheres else* and *It's quite a ways*, though it is not new and not rare in general writing.

better　In constructions that combine *better* with *had*, such as *You had better go* and *He'd better go*, the verb *had* or its contraction, *'d*, should not be dropped; *You better go* is incorrect. The *had* or *'d* is the real verb; it is a subjunctive form, like *should* in *He should go*. The following verb, *go* in these examples, is merely an infinitive. *He better go* seems somehow to make a verb out of *better*, since the sentence needs a finite verb—it can't get by with just an infinitive. However, it might be argued that it leaves *better* alone and instead makes *go* no longer an infinitive but a third-person subjunctive, as it is in *I insist that he go*. *He better go* thus becomes quite an elegant use of the subjunctive; I like my analysis even though I don't like the usage. The dropped *had* is barely noticeable in speech, but is quite evident in writing, and also quite common. It may eventually be accepted even by the fastidious, since it is simpler or at least seems simpler than the correct construction; I have seen it in the dialogue of a well-educated poet in a *New Yorker* short story, which must mean something. But for now I strongly advise retaining *had*.

On the other hand, *It better* as a verbless sentence seems to have won a place in correct, if informal, speech: *"I sure hope the market improves." "It better."* In fact, *It had better* might seem excessively formal in such an exchange. Nevertheless, *It better not get worse* would be noticeably incorrect, and so would the verbless sentence *He better*.

between vs. among　*Between* indicates a relation to two items, as in *He stood between his parents* and *The city lies between the mountains and the plains*. *Among* indicates a relation to more than two items, as in *He stood among his relatives* and *The city lies among the mountains*. However, this basic distinction should not be thoughtlessly applied to every occurrence. For example, *between* is also often correct and sometimes is required when the relation concerns three or

311

more items. *No agreement was reached between him, his wife, and their therapist* requires *between* because it concerns agreement between each of the three persons and the other two. It may seem unlikely that anyone's ear would lead him or her to choose *among* in this example, but I have often seen it in similar sentences, I think because the writer knows the basic distinction between the words and thinks that distinction must be forced on every situation. Inexperienced editors often impose it on writers, too. The words are not simple, and their function is not always easily analyzed, but we don't always have to analyze it; when *among* seems odd and unnatural, *between* is almost certainly defensible.

When both words are natural, the choice may make no difference in meaning or may make a considerable difference. *There are few areas of total agreement between teachers of grammar and scholars of grammar* means that teachers generally don't agree with scholars—the relation is between only two things, though both things happen to be plural. *There are few areas of total agreement among teachers of grammar and scholars of grammar* means that teachers and scholars, lumped together as a single group, have many conflicting opinions, and presumably that members of either group alone have conflicting opinions. But note that of the second example we could say, and probably would naturally say, that *the relation is between many things.* We could think of various justifications for failing to make the basic distinction here—we are echoing *between only two things* earlier in the paragraph; we are thinking of a relation between each member of the combined group and all the others. Or we could change *between* to *among*, since it is not unnatural and there really is no significant difference in meaning; I have often made similar changes when editing bad writing, since routine application of even the flimsiest usage prejudices tends to improve such writing. Or we could not worry about it, which is what I recommend.

black humor   humor directed at matters generally considered to be sad, tragic, or solemn. See Rule 4-8.

both   Often *both* is redundant because it is used with words that include its meaning: *They both agreed to make up; Both are equally at fault; Both John as well as his wife want to try again.* The first example is inoffensive compared to the others, because *agreed* contains the idea of *both* somewhat subtly, but in writing it would be noticed and objected to by some. It is possible to be excessively afraid of redundancy; see Rule 1-4. The second example is a more glaring redundancy. The third example is a grammatical tangle; *Both* requires that the subject be plural, but *as well as* disqualifies *his wife* from having an effect on the number of the verb (see Rule 1-11) and leaves only the singular *John* as subject of the plural *want*. See also **as well as**.

brackets   Brackets can be used within parentheses, though this use should generally be avoided; see Rule 2-18 and the introductory discussion preceding it. Brackets are useful primarily within quotations; see Rule 2-19.

bring vs. *take*   These verbs can mean the same thing—*transport* or *escort*—but they usually have different points of view. *Bring* implies motion toward; *take* implies motion away from. The distinction is much the same as that between *come* and *go*, which are very rarely misused. Nor is *take* a problem. *Bring*, however, is often used when *take* is meant: *When you go to the Caribbean, don't bring winter clothes.* I do not think this error indicates that *take* and *bring* are actually confused. I think it results from some broadening of the meaning of *bring* to envelop *take*, perhaps a broadening that first occurred among immigrants and survived the education of their native children and grandchildren, though that is a guess based on my own experience of hearing the error. Since the point of view the verbs imply is not always particularly evident, as it much more often is in the case of *come* and *go*, it would be easy for someone learning English as an adult to ignore point of view and use one word in all *transport* and *escort* contexts.

   Sometimes the point of view is clear, and one verb is obviously better than the other: *If you take a book from the reference shelf, please bring it back by the end of the day; If you must bring uninvited guests to my party, I wish you would take them with you when you go.* Sometimes the choice of verb alone establishes the point of view: *He brought his child to the office* indicates that it is the arrival at the office that is in mind; *He took his child to the office* indicates that it is the departure for the office that is in mind. *When you go to the Caribbean, don't bring winter clothes* is a poor choice of verb because *go* indicates that departure is in mind and *bring* indicates that arrival is in mind; the points of view conflict. Either *come* in the first clause and *bring* in the second or *go* in the first clause and *take* in the second would indicate a single point of view.

Sometimes the point of view is not so clear and it becomes more difficult to explain why *bring* seems wrong. *Let's bring the dog* does not seem wrong—the point of view can be in a future "there" that includes the animal's presence. *Let's not bring the dog* does seem slightly wrong; the point of view is more likely in a present "here" where the decision about *taking* the dog is being made. *Don't forget to bring your report cards home for your parents to sign* seems quite wrong; the teacher must be thinking of the departure of the children and their report cards from the classroom, not of their arrivals at their homes. *Take* can be used in all these examples, and it is probably safe to use *take* whenever in doubt. I don't recall ever seeing *take* used where *bring* was required; everyone does seem to understand when it doesn't fit the point of view.

but As a **conjunction,** *but* is used to connect things that are opposed in some way but are equal grammatical elements. *He came to the party but didn't stay* has two predicates, *came to the party* and *didn't stay,* which have the same grammatical value and are connected by *but.* The word *but* can also be other parts of speech. In constructions such as *Everyone but him was invited,* it is a **preposition** (see Rule 1-9). In the rather old-fashioned *There was no one else there but had been invited,* it is a kind of negative **pronoun,** standing for *who . . . not* (*who had not been invited*). In *He is but a gatecrasher,* it is an **adverb,** with the meaning of *only* or *merely.*

But is sometimes used unnecessarily, as in *I do not doubt but that you will succeed.* Since *but* has a negative implication, this construction can be considered a **double negative.** The construction is found in the best writing, because the best writers do make use of it, but those of us whose writing is merely good should avoid it—observing such niceties couldn't but help our writing, to use a double-negative *but* that is intended and correct.

She did not bring but twenty dollars, in which *but* means *only,* is a double negative that is incorrect; *She brought but twenty dollars* is correct.

When *but* is followed by a comma, as in *But, we must do what is best,* it is usually being used in place of a stronger word or phrase, such as *however* or *on the other hand,* that is normally followed by a comma. Generally the stronger word or phrase should be used to start with, though the distinct pause forced by the unexpected comma actually makes *but* stronger still, which may be a deliberate and justifiable effect.

314

can* vs. *may   *Can* is used in reference to ability and physical possibility, *may* in reference to permission: *He can swim, so he won't drown; He may swim after he has finished his chores.* This distinction is no longer as rigidly imposed as it once was; *can* is often used for *may*, especially in negative constructions, perhaps because the contraction *mayn't* has never been popular: *You can't swim until you've finished your chores.* It is nevertheless still alive—a notice such as STUDENTS CANNOT USE THE FACULTY BAR would be disputed as a usage and disproved as a statement by those it bars—and should be observed in writing.

   Could has almost completely displaced *might* in reference to permission, except in Britain; to almost all Americans, *He asked if he might go swimming* is quaint, and *She told him he mightn't go swimming* is quainter. I advise accepting the displacement and using *could* and *couldn't* in both speech and writing, unless the writing is for some group that prefers or is likely to be impressed by British diction. Most people perceive Americans who use British diction as pretenders.

capitalization   after a colon, Rule 2-15; of directions or locations such as *east*, Rule 3-18; of forms of address, Rule 3-15; of kinship terms, Rule 3-16; of main words in titles, Rule 3-22; of offices and organizations, Rule 3-13; of officials' titles, Rule 3-14; of political and geographical terms, Rule 3-17; of *the* in titles of books and works of art, Rule 3-20; of *the* in titles of newspapers and periodicals, Rule 3-19.

case   a form of a noun or pronoun that indicates its function within a sentence. English has only three cases, the **subjective case,** the **objective case,** and the **possessive case,** and the subjective and objective are the same except for a few pronouns. See Rules 1-6 to 1-9.

   Some grammarians consider the case of a word to be not its form but its function in a specific sentence. This permits them to claim the existence of such phenomena as the "subjective *me*," as in *It's me.* Thinking of case as function rather than form is useful in scholarly study of language but is apt to cause confusion in discussions of recommended and condemned usages.

clause   a group of words that contains a subject and a predicate, like a **sentence,** but is only part of a sentence. An *independent clause* could stand alone as a complete sentence. *I* *don't want this hat; it is too small* contains two independent clauses. A *dependent clause* cannot stand alone; it usually includes some word or phrase that indicates its dependence on another clause or on some word or phrase in another clause. *I don't want this hat, which is too small* contains the dependent clause *which is too small;* the relative pronoun *which* indicates that the clause depends on something outside itself, in this example the word *hat.* Clauses sometimes have adjectival or adverbial functions and can play the role of nouns; see **adjective, adverb,** and **noun.**

cliché   a phrase or figure of speech that has become too familiar and no longer seems clever or forceful, such as *like a bat out of hell.* Phrases that are new and effective to one group of listeners or readers may be clichés to other groups; see Rule 4-12.

coinage   a word or phrase invented by a writer or speaker for the occasion. Everyone is entitled to play Adam occasionally, but some coinages are poor; they are clumsy or are pointlessly used in place of existing words. Others pass quickly into the language, either because they seem especially clever and appropriate or because they name something new to the world, like *software.* Still others are unlikely to become part of the language but are splendid in their one-time application. My seventeen-year-old son recently coined the word *ruffianic* to describe a tennis player—not because he did not know that *ruffianly* exists but because he thought *ruffianic* was more meaningful, which it was. I have not quizzed my son on the coinage, since quizzing a creator is apt to take the joy out of creation, but, having been present at the creation, I understood well enough; he meant to express not just the manner of a ruffian but the ethos of a ruffian, the intent to appear to be a ruffian, the pride a ruffian takes in his ruffianly mission, and in forming the word he perhaps had in mind some similarly formed word such as *messianic.* The coinage won't pass into the language— maybe not even into the language my son and I use between ourselves—but it demonstrates both the limitations of standard usage and the freedoms of English that is better than good.

collective noun   a singular noun that means or can mean something plural, such as *group.* Many collective nouns can take either a singular or a plural verb, depending on whether they are being thought of as singular or plural; see Rule 1-11.

Errors of agreement can occur with collective nouns, as when a collective noun is accompanied by a singular verb but then is referred to later in the sentence or passage by a plural pronoun; see Rule 1-12.

colon a mark of punctuation that introduces what follows or sometimes links what precedes to what follows. It should not be used to introduce words that fit naturally into the grammar of the sentence; see Rule 2-16. The word following a colon often begins with a capital if it begins a grammatically complete sentence, but sometimes it does not; see Rule 2-15. In general prose, a sentence should not contain more than one colon, though there are excellent writers, such as Faulkner, who sometimes use colons very freely.

colors Words denoting color, such as *blue*, are basically nouns, as in *Blue is a quieter color than red*, but are much more often adjectives, as in *He wore a blue tie with a red suit*. Both as nouns and as adjectives they are often modified by words such as *light, dark,* and *bright*, which are also adjectives; this may seem to be an exception to the usual pattern in English, since generally it is adverbs that modify adjectives, but in fact it is merely the result of using modified nouns (such as *light blue* in *The color he selected was light blue*) in adjectival situations such as *He wore a light-blue shirt*. I recommend hyphenating such compound adjectives: *light-blue shirt, bright-red suit*. Most writers, and also most editors, do not hyphenate them, but the hyphen is "heard"—that is, the words are run together rather than spoken separately—when such compounds are spoken, and occasionally when there is no hyphen the first adjective will be perceived as modifying not the color adjective but the noun beyond. Rules 2-31 to 2-37 explain the principles of hyphenation that I and many other editors follow; compound adjectives such as *light-blue* are discussed in Rule 2-36.

comma the most common mark of punctuation within sentences, used to separate a word, phrase, or clause from surrounding or abutting words. Its many uses and misuses are dealt with in Rules 2-2 to 2-11 and a few others: after *that, if, when,* and other subordinating conjunctions, Rule 2-8; before *and* or another conjunction in a series, Rule 2-6; before or after direct quotations, Rule 2-11; between a modifier and the word or phrase it modifies, Rule 2-5; between compound predicates,

317

Rule 2-3; between independent clauses, Rule 2-2; between subject and verb, verb and object, or preposition and object, Rule 2-4; in a series of adjectives, Rule 1-20; following a title that ends with a mark of punctuation, Rules 3-20 and 3-21; in a series when *and* is omitted, Rule 2-6; position of when used with a closing quotation mark, Rule 2-24; to indicate an understood word, Rule 2-9; to set off a negative element from a positive one, Rule 2-7; to set off names in direct address, Rule 2-10; to set off parenthetical elements but not defining elements, Rule 2-1. See also Rule 2-1 for a general discussion of sentence structure that includes many examples of comma use and Rules 2-12 to 2-14 for examples of commas that should be semicolons.

comma fault   use of a comma without a conjunction to connect two independent clauses, as in *They dropped in unexpectedly, we had to feed them.* Though ordinarily an error—either a conjunction should be added or a semicolon should replace the comma—such use of the comma is sometimes justified; see Rule 2-12. A sentence with a comma fault is sometimes called a run-on sentence.

comparative and superlative   the forms taken by adjectives and adverbs to indicate comparison or degree. Many adjectives and adverbs form the comparative by adding *er* and the superlative by adding *est* (*small, smaller, smallest; soon, sooner, soonest*), but some of the most common have special forms (*good, better, best*), and most of two syllables and almost all of three syllables or more are combined with *more* and *most* instead of changing form (*respectable, more respectable, most respectable*). Using both the *er* or *est* ending and *more* or *most*, as in *more smaller*, is a redundancy and, of course, an error, and forms such as *more well-paid* and *most well-paid*, though not true errors, are criticized; *better-paid* and *best-paid* are preferred. See *more, most.*

The superlative form is logically inappropriate when only two things are being compared. *John and Mary are both good players but Mary is best* is wrong; it should be *Mary is better.* However, few writers and probably almost no speakers entirely avoid the logical lapse, which is centuries old in the language, and there are common expressions that would suddenly become uncommon if logic were imposed on them, such as *best foot forward*, which is illogical in reference to bipeds. Nevertheless, everyone who has gone to grammar school seems to remember, if little else, the rule against the superlative for two, and many people would notice and criticize *Mary is best* in the example, where the logical lapse is quite apparent. Few people would notice it in *It's best to be tolerant*, though the only alternative is to be intolerant. It is worth making some effort to avoid illogical superlatives, but an illogical superlative is better than an unnatural comparative such as *better foot forward*.

Comparatives are sometimes used vaguely, as in *older people* and *better stores*. Such vague use has its critics and should be avoided whenever precision is preferable, but it is well established in many common phrases such as the two examples. Sometimes vagueness is appropriate.

Some modifiers cannot, in their strictest senses, logically have comparative or superlative forms but are often given them anyway. The most often mentioned is *unique;* it is a so-called absolute adjective, one that describes an absolute quality rather than a quality that can exist to a greater or lesser degree. *More unique, less unique,* and *most unique* are generally considered errors. *More nearly unique* is acceptable—something can approach an absolute quality to a greater or lesser degree—but shows the strain of avoiding the error; *more unusual* or some other phrase that avoids *unique* would be simpler and better.

Many other modifiers, such as *complete* and *perfect*, have as much right to be considered absolute as *unique* does, but uses of them with *more, less, most,* and *least* often escape the notice of those who shudder at every *more unique*. Still other modifiers may be made to run the absolutist gauntlet. For example, of two ripe apples, can one be *riper* than the other, or does it have to be rotten? If we don't allow degrees of perfection, why should we allow degrees of ripeness? I advise never using *more unique* and being cautious with comparatives and superlatives of other modifiers that have a good claim to being considered absolute, such as *complete* and *perfect*, but it is wrongheaded to go looking for words to add to the list of absolutes. Some words are absolute in their narrowest meaning but have broader meanings that are not absolute.

comparative elements   elements—that is, words, phrases, or clauses—that are joined by phrases such as *more than, less than,* and *as much as.* Usually elements so joined should be parallel in structure; see Rule 1-5.

complement   a word or phrase that is linked to another word or phrase by a verb to complete the meaning of the verb. *John is the treasurer* contains the subject complement *the treasurer*, completing the meaning of *is*. *They elected John treasurer* contains the object complement *treasurer*, completing the meaning of *elected*. Often a complement is an adjective: *The house is red* and *He painted the house red* both contain *red* as a complement. Sometimes the complement precedes the verb: *Even worse than his spelling is his grammar.*

Usually a complement should agree in case with the word it is linked to, but common expressions such as *It's me* are acceptable in all but the most formal writing; see Rule 1-6. A complement does not have to agree in number with the word it is linked to; *The main ingredient was onions* and *He made onions the main ingredient* are correct. However, this construction often leads to errors of agreement in number between subject and verb; see Rule 1-11. See also **linking verb.**

complex sentence   a sentence that includes at least one **dependent clause;** see Rule 2-1.

composition   the arrangement of words, sentences, and paragraphs in a speech or written work. Chapter 4 suggests several basic rules of composition.

compound   composed of two or more elements; as a noun, something so composed.

A *compound word* can be hyphenated (*city-state*), two or more separate words (*prime minister, commander in chief*), or one solid word (*racehorse*). So-called permanent compounds, such as the four examples above, must often be looked up in the dictionary, because there is no broad rule governing whether they are hyphenated, separate, or solid, though there are some general principles involved; see Rule 2-34. Temporary compound modifiers such as occur in *a bright-seeming child* and *a teacher-shortage problem* do follow rules for hyphenation; see Rule 2-36. Words such as *antiaircraft* and *conscienceless*, which are formed of a word and a standard prefix or suffix, are also usually called compound words. Many of them, but by no means all, are solid words; see Rules 2-31 to 2-33. All the rules on hyphenation in this book, Rules 2-31 to 2-37, are concerned with compound words.

A *compound verb* can be simply a compound word that happens to be a verb, such as *window-shop*, but usually the term means a verb in a compound tense, discussed below.

Sometimes the term is used to mean a compound predicate, also discussed below.

A *compound subject* or *compound object* is a subject or object consisting of two or more elements. *The man and the woman bought pretzels and beer* contains the compound subject *The man and the woman* and the compound object *pretzels and beer.* Compound subjects that are joined by *or* rather than *and* sometimes cause problems of agreement in person (Rule 1-10) and number (Rule 1-11).

A *compound predicate* is two or more predicates with the same subject. *They eat pretzels and drink beer* has two predicates, *eat pretzels* and *drink beer.*

A *compound tense* is one that is formed with an **auxiliary verb;** in *I have gone,* the words *have gone* form a compound tense of the verb *go.* Usually such a form is called a compound verb, as mentioned above; sometimes it is called a verb phrase.

A *compound sentence* is one that has two or more independent clauses. A *compound/complex sentence* is a compound sentence that also has at least one dependent clause. Both types of sentence are discussed in Rule 2-1.

comprise   means *include* or *embrace,* as in *The whole comprises the parts* and *The parts are comprised by* (or *in*) *the whole.* It is much more often used to mean *compose* or *constitute,* as in *The parts comprise the whole* and *The whole is comprised of its parts,* and this meaning is accepted by dictionaries, but I advise against it; the few who are aware of the first meaning look down on the many who use the word in the second meaning.

concrete diction   speech or writing that uses concrete words—that is, words denoting tangible or visible things or actions rather than ideas or emotions. *He wept* is more concrete than *He was sorrowful.* Concrete diction is usually clearer and often more forceful than **abstract diction,** which can be tiresome and monotonous when overdone; see Rule 4-11.

conditional clause   a dependent clause that indicates under what conditions some independent clause is, was, would have been, or will be true. Conditional clauses are very often introduced by the subordinating conjunction *if: If it's noon, he's late; If he arrived late, he missed me; If he had been here on time, I would have seen him; If he comes before noon, I will* *see him.* In a sentence with a conditional clause that states a condition known to be or strongly thought to be contrary to fact, such as *If I were rich, I would wear shabbier clothes* and *If he were rich, he wouldn't wear such fancy clothes,* the verbs are in the **subjunctive mood.** In the earlier example *If he had been here on time, I would have seen him,* the condition is contrary to fact and the verbs are subjunctive; see Rule 1-17 and the discussion preceding it. The subordinating conjunction *unless* and various conjunctive phrases such as *in the event that* and *provided that* also introduce conditional clauses.

conjunction   one of the **parts of speech;** a word or phrase that is used to conjoin, or connect, other words or phrases. The most common conjunction is *and.*

A *coordinating conjunction* is one that connects elements of equal grammatical value—that is, it is used when neither element is subordinate to the other. *Read it and weep* uses the coordinating conjunction *and* to connect the two imperative verbs. Other coordinating conjunctions are *or* and *but. For, yet,* and *so* are sometimes coordinating conjunctions but can be difficult to classify. A special type of coordinating conjunction is the *correlative conjunction,* which is found in pairs: *either . . . or, not only . . . but also.* Correlative conjunctions are sometimes misplaced in a sentence; see Rule 1-5.

A *subordinating conjunction* is one that joins a subordinate clause—that is, a **dependent clause**—to another clause. There are many subordinating conjunctions, including *after, although, as, because, if, since, than, until, when,* and *while.* Usually there should be no comma after a subordinating conjunction; see Rule 2-8.

A *conjunctive adverb* is an adverb such as *however, therefore, thus,* or *nevertheless* that is used to join a clause to the preceding clause, as in *I was invited; however, I did not go.* Unlike a subordinating conjunction, it can join independent clauses. It can also "join" a sentence to the preceding sentence—that is, the meanings of the sentences are connected even though they are punctuated as separate sentences: *I was invited. However, I did not go.* Usually a conjunctive adverb is followed by a comma; see the discussion of sentence modifiers in Rule 2-5 and the discussion of introductory constructions in Rule 2-1. It is usually preceded by a semicolon, unless, of course, it begins the sentence; see Rule 2-13.

Schoolchildren used to be told not to begin sentences with conjunctions, especially the coordinating conjunctions *and*

and *but* (see Rule 1-1) and the conjunctive adverb *however*, and some handbooks of usage preserve the rule. I advise not beginning too many sentences with conjunctions, since the effect can be wearing. My very heavy use of *but* and *however* to begin sentences in this book—everything I write seems to require immediate qualification—probably annoys some readers.

contraction   a shortened form of a word, such as *don't* for *do not*. Contractions are a prominent feature of speech. In writing they should usually be less frequent as the writing becomes more formal, and the apostrophe should be used with them properly; see Rule 2-30.

convince vs. persuade   *Convince* is a strong word; it suggests winning over completely, perhaps against some opposition. *Persuade* is not as strong; it implies talking into, perhaps against little or no opposition and perhaps without producing real conviction (a word based on *convince*). Although often it does not much matter which word is used, sometimes it does; *I convinced him that he should try the escargots* is a questionable use of the stronger word. Moreover, most people who use *convince* this way would make it *I convinced him to try the escargots*, which is a questionable choice of construction as well as a questionable choice of word.

Convince followed by an infinitive, as in *I convinced him to cancel the contract*, is common but will draw considerable criticism. *Convince* is correctly used with *that* and *of* constructions: *I convinced him that he should cancel the contract; I am convinced of his honesty.* When people are convinced, they are convinced *of* the truth of something or *that* something is true or *that* they should do something, not *to do* something. *Persuade* is the proper verb when an infinitive follows: *I persuaded him to cancel the contract.* When people are persuaded, they are persuaded *to do* or even *to believe* something, not *of* the truth of something or *that* something is true, and just about everyone seems to hold to this meaning for *persuade. Persuade* does occur with *of* and *that*, as in *I persuaded him that we were the better firm*, and this usage seems to be accepted, but in my experience it is rare. It is *convince* that has been encroaching on *persuade*, not the other way around. The liberal view of the matter would be to accept that *convince* sometimes means *persuade* and to accept the infinitive with *convince* when it does mean *persuade*, but I advise holding to the more restricted meaning of *convince* and not using it before an infinitive. Those who want to avoid criticism for their usage should not take too liberal a view of usage.

When neither an infinitive nor a *that* or *of* construction is involved, either *convince* or *persuade* can be used, whichever is more appropriate: *They made a fairly good case for the plan, and we were persuaded; They made an excellent case for the plan, and we were convinced.*

coordinate, coordinating   Two or more elements in a sentence are coordinate if they have the same grammatical value in the sentence. *I always wake up when the sun rises and the cock crows* contains the coordinate clauses *the sun rises* and *the cock crows*, both linked to the main clause, *I always wake up*, by *when*. A conjunction is coordinating if it connects coordinate elements; in the example, *and* is a coordinating conjunction.

copula   a verb that does not have an object but nevertheless connects its subject to the predicate; in *The river seems high*, the verb *seems* is a copula or copulative verb. *Copula* means *bond* in Latin; the word *couple* is derived from it. See **linking verb**, which is the term I use in this book.

correct, incorrect   When I use one of these words in this book, it means that the usage, construction, punctuation practice, or styling convention I am discussing has been approved or condemned by many of the other books I have consulted while writing my book and in thirty years of editing—that is, that I have considerable support for the approval or condemnation I make my own. When I have less support, I use some other word, such as the hedging *questionable* or the obviously opinionated *annoying*, or I make it clear that I am making a private judgment public. Since this book, like most other books on the subjects it covers, is intended to warn the reader away from uses of language that most users of the language would not condemn or even notice but that a critical minority would condemn, it labels incorrect some uses that lexicographers and other scholars of usage could prove well established.

correlative   Correlative elements are ones connected by certain words or phrases that are used in pairs, such as *either* and *or*, *neither* and *nor*, and *not only* and *but also*. See also **conjunction** and Rule 1-5.

could care less usually means *couldn't care less*; logically, *I could care less* means that I do care to some degree. When I first heard *I could care less*, in the 1950s, it was usually as an ironic elliptical question—*I could care less?*—that when filled out would be something like *Can you imagine that I could care less?* Now it is almost always a statement rather than a question, though I have heard it with the classic rising inflection quite recently (1990). Both it and the logically correct *I couldn't care less* are tiresome, and appearances even of the logically correct expression in prose that aspires to much dignity can be objectionable. For example, in *Nimitz made it clear he couldn't have cared less about the predicted hurricane*, it seems overly breezy.

couple* vs. *couple of *Couple* is a noun, not an adjective; therefore *There were a couple books on the table* should be *There were a couple of books on the table*. However, in informal usage *a couple* is often an adjective meaning *two*: *We saw a couple movies; Then we saw a couple more movies; There were a couple dozen people in the place.* One also hears, and in casual prose sees, *There were a couple of dozen people in the place*, which isn't quite the same; it seems to use *couple* as a noun, but then to treat *dozen people* as a compound noun or modified noun and say there were two of them. In fact, the whole phrase *a couple of dozen* has to be understood as an adjectival phrase equivalent to *two dozen*; analysis of its parts leads nowhere. Except in informal usage, *couple* should be a noun and should not be used with *more* or with *dozen, hundred*, or other number adjectives.

dangling construction a word or phrase, often a participle or participial phrase, that is intended to modify something that is either missing or misplaced in the sentence. The word or phrase thus dangles with nothing to modify or else grammatically modifies the wrong thing, as in *Born in Philadelphia, the serape seemed exotic garb to him*, in which *Born in Philadelphia* is intended to modify *him* but in a grammatical sense modifies the subject of the sentence, *the serape*. See Rule 2-21.

dash use and overuse of, Rule 2-17

data a plural, with the rather rare singular *datum*, but very often used as a singular, as in *This data is not current*. As a singular, *data* means a more or less coherent collection of bits of information; as a plural, it means the bits of information themselves. Its use as a singular is convenient but very much criticized; I advise using it only as a plural and not using it at all if it seems odd as a plural, as it does to me in *His data themselves were less startling than his conclusion* and *The study ignored these inconvenient data.* Usually some word substitution or recasting will be convenient: *This information is not current; His data startled his colleagues less than his conclusion; The story ignored such inconvenient data.*

dates   commas with month, day, and year, Rule 2-38; cardinal rather than ordinal numbers with day of month, Rule 3-9; whether to use words or figures for days of the month, Rule 3-1

defining construction   a construction used not just to modify but to identify a word or phrase. *The man in the hat is the winner* contains the defining prepositional phrase *in the hat; The man who is smiling is the winner* contains the defining relative clause *who is smiling.* Defining constructions are often called restrictive, because they restrict the meaning of the words they modify. Proper punctuation often depends on determining whether an element is a defining construction or a **parenthetical construction;** see Rule 2-1.

dependent clause   a clause that cannot stand alone as a sentence but depends on some other clause or some word or phrase in another clause; also called a subordinate clause. Dependent clauses can be either parenthetical or defining, and they are punctuated accordingly; see Rule 2-1. They can be either adjectival clauses (also called relative clauses), adverbial clauses, or noun clauses, depending on their function in a sentence; see **adjective, adverb,** and **noun.** A sentence **fragment** is apt to be a dependent clause incorrectly standing alone; see Rule 1-1.

deprecate vs. depreciate   These words and their derivatives, *self-deprecating, depreciatory,* and so on, have become quite confused. In its origins, *deprecate* is a very strong word—the Latin word it is derived from means *avert by prayer* or *pray against,* roughly equivalent to *curse.* It still is used to mean *deplore,* as in *The appeasement policy was widely deprecated,* but it has picked up weaker meanings that are now more common. In *He deprecated his opponent's appeal to minorities,* it means merely *disparaged* or *belittled.* And *deprecate* has become something that people can do to themselves. In *He deprecated his tousled appearance,* it has weakened further to mean something like *apologized for,* and in *He deprecated his appeal to minorities*—his own appeal, that is—it means *played down* or *was modest about.* Finally, *self-deprecating* has become a synonym for *modest* or *unassuming. His self-deprecating manner won him the affection as well as the respect of his colleagues* means that his colleagues liked him for his modesty, not for his calling down the vengeance of heaven on himself. This evolution of meanings has brought *deprecate* onto the same turf as *depreciate,* which in a financial sense means *devalue* and in a broader sense means *belittle.* If we hold *deprecate* to its older meaning, *deplore,* then *self-deprecating* is clearly not a good word when *self-belittling* is meant; *self-depreciating* is far better. Many handbooks of usage, including the first edition of this one, have taken this attitude; I went further and advised avoiding *deprecate* altogether as too much misunderstood to be useful and using *depreciate* only to mean *devalue.* Perhaps that advice was too cowardly. *Self-depreciating* may be "better," but I almost never find it in either print or manuscripts, and I don't remember ever hearing it; when I do see it, it may well be the result of the artificial support that writers on usage from the famous H. W. Fowler to me have given it—some writer or editor put it in instead of what came naturally, which these days is *self-deprecating.* Now I advise accepting *self-deprecating*—it is a useful word—and the various other relatively new meanings of *deprecate.* They may still draw occasional fire, but perhaps this book, despite its overall intent to protect the reader from criticism, should encourage an occasional boldness.

diagonal   a slanted line used in certain compounds, notably *and/or*; see Rule 2-38.

diction   choice of words and grammatical constructions. Chapter 4 discusses some basic aspects of diction; see especially Rules 4-11 and 4-12. Chapter 1 and many of the entries in this Glossary/Index are concerned with specific points of diction. The word *diction* is sometimes used to mean *enunciation* or *pronunciation*; generally those more precise words are preferable.

different from vs. different than, differently from vs. differently than   *Different from* is the standard American phrase, as in

My children are different from me; the British also use *different to*, which sounds very odd to Americans. *Different than,* as in *My children are different than me,* is quite common but much criticized, on the grounds that *than* should be used only with comparatives, as in *My children are younger than I,* and that it should not be used as a preposition but only as a conjunction. However, when a clause follows, *different than* is correct; *I am different than I was a decade ago* uses *than* properly as a conjunction, and the preposition *from* would be impossible, because a preposition cannot have a clause as its object unless it is a noun clause, as in *I am different from what I was a decade ago.* Similarly, *differently than* is correct when a clause follows: *I do it differently than I did it a decade ago.*

Some people, including some writers on usage, condemn any use whatever of *than* with *different* or *differently;* if *from* is impossible, they prescribe recasting the sentence to make it possible. Since in this case I do not advise heeding the criticism and avoiding the usage, as I so often do in this book, I explain here at some length why I consider the criticism invalid.

The argument that *than* should be used only with comparatives ignores the fact that it is correctly used with *other*: *There is no world other than this one. Other* is no more a comparative form than *different;* in fact, in a narrow sense, *other* might be considered an **absolute** adjective, one that cannot logically have a comparative form (see **comparative and superlative**). More to the point, *different* does have some of the properties of comparatives—certainly when we consider whether two things are the same or different, what we are doing is comparing them. *Different* is found in some of the same constructions as comparatives. For example, adverbial modifiers such as *far, any,* and *much* cannot be used with the positive form of an adjective but only with the comparative form; we cannot say *far young, any young,* and *much young,* only *far younger, any younger,* and *much younger.* We can say *far different, any different,* and *much different,* however. *Different* is, appropriately, different from ordinary comparatives, but I believe it is enough of a comparative to be used with *than.*

Different is often followed by something elliptical, as in *His behavior is different from yesterday.* (The sentence does not mean what it literally says, that *His behavior* and *yesterday* are different things, so it must be somehow elliptical.) It can be understood as elliptical for *His behavior is different from his behavior yesterday,* with a noun supplied to serve as the object of *from.* However, I believe that what we unconsciously add to such elliptical sentences to make them meaningful is more often not a noun or phrase but something with a verb in it—that is, a clause. Ellipsis very often involves verbs and verb forms, so we expect it to involve them. Sometimes we almost must add a clause; for example, we would fill out *I am different from a decade ago* not to *I am different from me a decade ago* but to *I am different from what I was a decade ago*. Similarly, I think we would tend to fill out *His behavior is different from yesterday* to *His behavior is different from what it was yesterday*, supplying a noun clause to serve as the object of *from*. If we accept that the ellipsis involves a clause and not just a word or phrase, then *His behavior is different than yesterday*, which is to my ear equally natural, can be justified as short for *His behavior is different than it was yesterday*, a slightly simpler way of filling in the sentence with a clause. Sometimes *different from* is quite unnatural, as in *His behavior is different from formerly*. One could make the same justifications—the ellipsis could be filled out to *from his behavior formerly* or to *from what it was formerly*—but it would not convince every ear. Perhaps this is because *formerly* is more evidently an adverb than *yesterday*, which is frequently a noun, and hence *formerly* strongly implies a verb, which militates against filling out the ellipsis with the verbless *from his behavior formerly*. In fact, the adverb seems to want to change into an adjective—*from his former behavior*. The mind has to make a little more effort to supply a verb by filling out *from* to the noun clause *from what it was formerly* than it would to supply a verb by filling out *than* to the adverbial clause *than it was formerly*. I am speculating, of course; I could prove by citation that usages such as *His behavior is different than formerly* have long been standard among well-educated users of the language, but I can only guess why that is the case.

Differently is an adverb, and whatever follows it needs a verb or an understood verb in it to match the verb that *differently* modifies in its own clause—that is, whatever follows it is a clause, even if the clause is an elliptical clause. Therefore *than* is appropriate. In *I do it differently than I did it a decade ago*, the verbs *do* and *did* are matched—which really means compared—by *differently than*. In *I do it differently than he*, the second clause is elliptical for *than he does it*, and the verb *do* and the understood verb *does* are matched.

I do it differently from him is, nevertheless, also correct. In Rule 3-20, I announce that *short compositions are handled differently from longer ones*. It is often possible to avoid *than* after *differently* when there is no verb in what follows—that is, when what follows is elliptical—and many writers and editors do avoid it. However, if *differently* is accepted as a comparative, as I think it should be, these sentences make a **false comparison.** The first matches *do* with *him*—a verb with a pronoun—and the second matches *handled* with *longer ones*—a verb with a modified pronoun. Furthermore, it is not so easy to fill the ellipsis in these sentences as it is in the earlier sentences involving *different. I do it differently from the way he does it* or *from how he does it* changes *him* to *he,* and the case of a word should not change when we fill in an ellipsis—if it does, the case must have been wrong to start with. *Short compositions are handled differently from the way longer ones are handled* similarly changes *longer ones* from being the object of a preposition to being the subject of a verb, and though there is no change in form of the phrase as there is with the pronoun *him* in the other sentence, the change in the function of the phrase is just as indefensible. The problems in sentences such as these do not seem to trouble anyone, and I wonder why; changes of case when an ellipsis is filled in and subtle false comparisons are exactly the sort of thing grammarians pounce on. Although the *Oxford English Dictionary* demonstrates that both *differently than* and *differently from* have been in use for centuries, I wonder if some modern uses of *differently from* result merely from fear of the criticized *different than*—I know that some "corrections" that I made routinely as a younger editor reflected this fear—and from failure to notice that *differently from* often makes a comparison that is false, or at least questionable, and forces a following pronoun into a case that cannot be defended by the routine analytical process of filling in an ellipsis.

Some readers who have stuck with my discussion this far may be so discouraged that they will resolve to avoid all criticsm by never using *different* with *than* and never using *differently* with either *from* or *than.* Probably most of the time they will find some acceptable way to express their meaning; for example, instead of writing *I do it differently from him* they could write *I do it in a way different from his* or *My way of doing it is different from his,* both of which are grammatically irreproachable. On the other hand, some readers may be so won over by my defense of usages with *than* that they will question all usages with *from,* especially *differently from.* I think neither the prejudice against *than* with *different* and *differently* nor my defense of the usage has to prevail alone;

there is a reasonable middle ground. I advise using *different from* and *differently from*, even when *from* can be attacked by analysis such as mine, as long as they seem natural, but not forcing them on elliptical sentences in which the ghost of an omitted verb cries out for *than*. Sometimes it helps to fill in enough of an elliptical clause to make it apparent that it is a clause and that *from* can't be used; see the discussion under **than**.

digression   a wandering from the point in speech or writing. Digressions are not always bad; see Rules 4-5 and 4-9.

direct, indirect   A *direct quotation* quotes someone's actual words and encloses them in quotation marks or otherwise sets them off. An *indirect quotation* may or may not quote the actual words and does not enclose them in quotation marks; the tense of verbs and the person of pronouns within it are usually made to conform to the tense and viewpoint of the enclosing sentence or passage. *She said, "I am going home"* contains a direct quotation; *She said she was going home* contains an indirect quotation. The terms *direct discourse* and *indirect discourse* are often used for the two types of quotation. See Rule 2-23.

A *direct question* is a sentence that is entirely a question, such as *What's cooking?* An *indirect question* is a question that is enclosed in a sentence that is not a question, such as *I wonder what's cooking.* See Rule 2-20.

direct object   the word or phrase directly affected by a **transitive verb.** *He gave me all the money* has the direct object *all the money*; the word *me* is an **indirect object.**

disinterested vs. **uninterested**   *Disinterested* means *impartial* or *without personal interest. Uninterested* means *indifferent* or *without any interest.* However, these words have shared their meanings for more than two centuries, and at present *disinterested* is used much more often than *uninterested* in both senses. *Disinterested* also sometimes suggests a former interest that has been lost, as in *After the chandelier fell on the mayor I tried to finish telling him my joke, but he was disinterested.* I recommend ignoring usage history and not using *disinterested* to mean *indifferent*, because many people who also ignore usage history think the usage is wrong. Other people, and I am one, have difficulty remembering which means which. In any case, it is often better to use *impartial*, *indifferent*, or some other word that has a commonly understood precise meaning.

distinguished   The word is often used to mean *eminent* or *respected*. The usage is occasionally criticized on the ground that when something is distinguished it has to be distinguished from something else. The phrase *distinguished scientist*, it could be argued, implies that the scientist is distinguishable from other scientists, presumably because of merit rather than lack of it, but it does not confine the adjectival participle *distinguished* to the meaning of the verb *distinguish* and hence might draw criticism. However, adjectival participles often achieve applications beyond those of the verbs they are based on. *Distinguished* might better be criticized simply for its overuse.

double negative   A double negative is wrong when, on analysis, it reverses the intended meaning, as in *I'm not going nowhere;* with the negatives canceling each other out, the sentence logically means *I'm going somewhere.* In fact, such a double negative is very rarely misunderstood—the double negative is intended and understood as an intensified negative, not a reversed one. It is nevertheless an immediate indication that the speaker's or writer's diction is substandard.

There are many words formed with the usually negative prefix *in* and a few words formed with the almost always negative prefixes *dis* and *un* that are not negative: *inflammable, disannul, unloose.* In these words the prefixes are intensifiers. The existence of such words may account for such condemned double-negative formations as *irregardless.*

The words *hardly* and *but* can carry a negative force and therefore often cause errors: *I haven't hardly any money; I haven't but a dollar to my name.*

A double negative is not wrong when the negatives are meant to cancel each other out, as in *He was not unfriendly* and *Not for nothing was he called Smirking Smith.* Triples can exist too: *The doctor said that tranquilizers were not only not indispensable but not effective at all when taken routinely.* Multiple negatives can express precise shades of meaning—*He was friendly* may be an overstatement—but they are wordy and the reader may have to reread them to untangle them; they should not be used indiscriminately.

double possessive   See **possessive case.**

due to vs. *because of*   Strictly, when *because of* is right, *due to* is wrong, and vice versa.

Due to is properly used after a **linking verb:** *The victory was due to forethought; His longevity was due to his diet.* Sometimes the verb is omitted in an elliptical clause, as in *The victory, though due to forethought, owed something to luck as well,* in which the filled-out clause would be *though it was due to forethought.*

Because of is used when there is no linking verb: *Victory was gained because of his forethought; He has lived a long time because of his diet.* However, *because of* rather than *due to* is preferable with a verb in **expletive** constructions: *It was because of forethought that we won.*

Due to is nevertheless very common without a verb, especially to begin a sentence: *Due to his diet, he has lived a long time.* This usage has been accepted by dictionaries, but many people still consider it an error, and it is easy to avoid—just never use *due to* when a linking verb is not present or understood.

Because of is common when there is a verb, as in *The defeat was because of our failure to plan ahead.* This also sounds wrong to many people, and it sounds childish as well. *The defeat was due to our failure to plan ahead* is preferable. *The defeat was because we had not planned ahead* is also childish; *We were defeated because we had not planned ahead* is much better. However, there is no reason to avoid all uses of *because* alone with a verb. *This was because we had not planned ahead,* for example, is unobjectionable.

each   should be considered singular in most constructions: *Each of the men has a hat.* However, when *each* is not the subject but merely modifies it, a plural subject takes a plural verb: *The men each have a hat.* See Rule 1-12.

each other vs. *one another*   These are considered interchangeable in most dictionaries, and they have been interchangeable in the language for centuries, but the distinction many people make between them is easy enough to maintain. *Each other* is used for two, *one another* for three or more: *John and Mary respect each other; John, Mary, and their children respect one another.* To my ear, *one another* when used for two is slightly troubling because the word *another* somehow suggests that there is more than one *other* for *one* to relate to, and *each other* when used for three or more is slightly troubling because there is more than one *other* for *each* to relate to.

The possessive forms are *each other's* and *one another's*, never *each others'* or *one anothers'*. A following noun is sometimes singular and sometimes plural, and in some cases it can be either: *They respect one another's right to privacy; They lied in one another's faces; They wore each other's hat or hats.*

either . . . or, neither . . . nor   These **conjunction** pairs, which are called **correlative** conjunctions, often cause problems because they are misplaced or misused in a sentence, as in *He was neither poor nor was he rich;* see Rule 1-5. They cause errors of agreement in person between subject and object, as in *Either they or he are wrong* and *Either he or they are wrong;* see Rule 1-11. They also cause errors of agreement in person between subject and object, and sometimes when there is no error the grammar still is jarring, as in *Either you or I am wrong,* which is correct but awkward; see Rule 1-10. Mismatched pairs—*neither . . . or* and *either . . . nor*—are, of course, errors.

elegant variation   use of a synonym to avoid repeating a word or use of a different grammatical construction to avoid repeating the same construction. It is called elegant only derisively; it is an amateurish device used in an attempt to seem elegant. Variation of some kinds is desirable in composition, but not elegant variation; see Rule 4-11.

ellipsis   omission of a word, or sometimes several words, that a listener or reader can be expected to supply to complete the meaning of a sentence. Ellipsis is not only permissible but often highly desirable to avoid tiresome repetition; see Rule 1-1. However, certain words should not be omitted even though they are easily supplied by listener or reader; see Rule 1-2. Sometimes words that can be omitted grammatically should nevertheless not be omitted because they are needed to prevent ambiguity; see Rule 1-3. Pronouns are often given the wrong case because they are in elliptical clauses and their grammatical function is not immediately evident; see Rule 1-6.

Points of ellipsis are the three period-like points that are used to show the omission of words in quoted material and, particularly in written dialogue, to indicate pauses and hesitations. For their proper use, see Rules 2-27 and 2-28.

Points of ellipsis are called *ellipses* by those who think that each point is an ellipsis and therefore that three of them together must be ellipses. Properly, an ellipsis is an omission, not part of a mark of punctuation. *Ellipses* will probably prevail, just as have the names of some other marks of punctuation that originally meant a part of a sentence rather than a mark. For example, *parenthesis* first meant an insertion in a sentence but now is used much more often to mean one of the marks of punctuation enclosing an insertion, and we speak of two *parentheses*. For the moment I advise against *ellipses*, except, of course, to mean two or more instances of ellipsis.

en dash a mark longer than a hyphen but shorter than an ordinary dash. In a given typeface it takes up as much space as a lowercase *n*; an ordinary dash, which is called an em dash by printers, takes up as much space as a lowercase *m*. Typewriters do not have a key for it, but the more elaborate word-processing systems, those that are used for desktop publishing, are beginning to include it. It is sometimes very useful; readers who have never heard of it benefit from it constantly.

The most helpful use of the en dash is to replace the hyphen in compounds in which one of the elements is two words, as in *New York–Vermont border* and *county clerk–elect*. The strong connecting effect of a hyphen would draw the second word away from the first word in the two-word element; the reader would momentarily perceive *York-Vermont* and *clerk-elect* as compounds. Those who frequently read typescript have probably noticed this effect of the hyphen. The en dash is also often used instead of the hyphen in ranges of numbers, as in *Figures 2–6* and *the years 1941–45*; it slightly improves readability.

I have seen advice to use the en dash in such compounds as *anti–blood-clotting agent*, to indicate that the agent counters blood clotting rather than clots anti-blood. I strongly advise against making this use of the en dash; it is extremely quirky and will just puzzle the reader's eye. Such multiword compounds are well served by the hyphen alone: *anti-blood-clotting agent*. There are several examples of multiword compounds in Rule 2-36.

equally as a **redundancy,** since *equally* and *as* have much the same meaning. In *equally as bad* and similar phrases, *equally* is misused to mean *just;* perhaps it is felt to be a more dignified word or a stronger intensifier than *just.* The misuse is very common and not new, and it may prevail, though dictionaries don't seem to have condoned it yet. See Rule 1-4.

etc.   the abbreviation of the Latin *et cetera* (meaning *and others*), used in English to mean *and so on.* It is a useful abbreviation and is acceptable in many types of writing, but it is annoying in writing that is intended to have much polish. It saves space, but there is usually no point in using such a device to save a few words. Spelling it out does not help; *et cetera* just surprises the reader, who is more accustomed to the abbreviation.

Etc. should not be used if the reader cannot actually continue the thought or series in some obvious way, and it is a more or less transparent evasion when writers use it because they themselves can't think of anything to add: *This book should appeal to dozens of special groups—worm farmers, etc.*

Etc. is often followed by a comma, as in *Stocks, bonds, debentures, options, etc., are the bursar's responsibility.* The comma separates the subject from its verb and thus is technically incorrect (see Rule 2-4), but it does sometimes improve readability; the eye seems to expect some punctuation after *etc.* if the sentence continues. For those who like to play by the rules, this is a good reason to minimize use of *etc.*

euphemism   a word or expression used in preference to a more direct one that the user fears would be harsh, disturbing, or rude. *Pass away* is a euphemism for *die; between jobs* is a euphemism for *out of work; expecting* is a euphemism for *pregnant.* Euphemisms are sometimes appropriate, but they very often suggest a self-conscious attempt to seem sensitive and refined.

even   can connect the elements of a compound subject, as in *Their position, even their lives, were now at risk.* See the last paragraph of Rule 1-11.

everyday vs. every day   *Everyday* should be used only as an adjective, as in *Arguments were an everyday occurrence. Every day* should be used as an adverb, as in *Arguments occurred every day,* and as a noun phrase, as in *Every day was a further test of her good nature.*

everyone*, *everybody These pronouns are singular, but they very often are followed by plural pronouns: *Everyone has taken off their shoes*. Many serious scholars of usage accept that the words naturally take singular verbs but plural pronouns. Nevertheless, I advise against allowing them to take plural pronouns; the usage draws heavy fire. See Rule 1-12.

Everyone is often misused for *every one*, as in *Everyone of them is going* and *There are five options, and everyone is unacceptable*. In the examples, *every* does not combine with *one* but merely modifies it, as does *each* in *each one*.

everytime There is no such word—it should be *every time* every time.

ex- causes problems when used with compound nouns, as in *ex-auto mechanic*; the hyphen connects *ex* and *auto* closely but doesn't get its connecting force through to *mechanic*. It can be replaced by *former*, which requires no hyphen: *former auto mechanic*. In printing, an **en dash** is often used instead of a hyphen in such situations: *ex–auto mechanic*. To my eye, the en dash only very slightly improves readability; I recommend using *former*.

exclamation point This mark of punctuation is sometimes misplaced when used with others; see Rule 2-22. Excessive use of exclamation points is amateurish and tiresome; so are doubled and tripled exclamation points.

expletive the word *it* or *there* used to represent a "true" subject or object that doesn't appear till later in the sentence. *It is clear that you dislike Bach* and *He made it clear that he dislikes Bach* both use *it* as an expletive. The first sentence can be reordered to avoid need for the expletive: *That you dislike Bach is clear*. The second sentence, in which the expletive represents the object, can simply drop the expletive, though many would consider it desirable: *He made clear that he dislikes Bach*. However, *There are few reasons for disliking Bach* cannot be reordered to avoid the expletive *There*; the sentence would have to be recast with a different verb: *Few reasons for disliking Bach exist*. For a discussion of grammatical problems that occur with expletive constructions, see **it is**, **there is**, **there are**.

It is raining is somewhat like an expletive construction, but here the *It* does not take the place of a later true subject or object. See **impersonal *it***.

Expletives are often desirable, as in *It was John who stole the cookies,* which uses the expletive construction to put an emphasis on *John* that would be missing in the straightforward *John stole the cookies.* Expletives are convenient in passive constructions, such as *It is generally believed that John stole the cookies.* However, a succession of sentences that use expletives is monotonous and should be avoided; see Rule 4-11.

false comparison   a comparison between elements in a sentence that cannot logically be compared. The error usually results from omitting a necessary word or phrase. In *Profits were not as high as the preceding year,* the word *in* has been omitted, so that in its literal meaning the sentence compares *Profits* and *the preceding year;* it should be *Profits were not as high as in the preceding year.* False comparison is not likely to mislead the reader but is nevertheless an error, unlike **ellipsis;** note that the correct version of the sentence above is elliptical—filled out it would be *Profits were not as high as they were in the preceding year.* See Rule 1-2 for discussion of other examples of false comparison.

false series   a series such as that in *They dined on turtle soup, sole, roast lamb, and drank appropriate wines,* in which the first three items in the series are objects of *dined* but the last is a complete predicate with its own verb, *drank.* Items in a series should be grammatically parallel. See Rules 1-5 and 2-6.

farther vs. further   *Farther* is used only in reference to physical distance: *Don't go farther than the corner; He lives on the farther shore.* However, the physical distance may be quite figurative; *Take this reasoning a step farther* has no real involvement with physical distance, but both the verb *take* and the noun *step* have associations of physical motion, and so *farther* can be used.

Further is used when there is no reference to physical distance: *He didn't discuss it further; There was no further discussion.* But *further* is also used in reference to physical distance; it could be used in all the examples for *farther* given above. Thus though *farther* is sometimes wrong, *further* can be used whenever it seems natural. I do often hold *further* to its more restricted application when editing poor writing, because imposing individually trivial editorial routines on such writing tends to improve it considerably.

feel bad vs. **feel badly**   *Feel badly* is an error unless *badly* really is an adverb modifying the verb, which it almost never is. In *I feel badly* it is linked by the verb to the subject, *I,* and thus it should be the adjective *bad,* not *badly.* Many well-educated people criticize the usage. It may sometimes be a **hyperurbanism,** resulting from fear of misusing adjectives, as in *He drives good,* and a notion that adverbs are more elegant than adjectives. See also **linking verb** and Rule 1-22.

fewer vs. **less**   *Fewer* is used in reference to a number of separate items: *There were fewer curtain calls on the second night; There were fewer than ten people in the audience. Less* is used in reference to an item that either is singular or is being thought of as a unit rather than a collection of separate items: *There was less applause on the second night; There was less than a hundred dollars left in her purse.* However, *less* has been encroaching on *fewer* for at least a millennium, according to one lexicographically sophisticated book on usage, and there are occasions when it seems at least as good as and perhaps better than *fewer* in reference to separate, or at least separable, items, as in *The experimental supercharger broke down after less than twelve laps.* Nevertheless I advise making the distinction when *fewer* does not seem unnatural; failure to make it is considered a sign of ignorance by many people.

figurative diction   diction that employs figures of speech, such as the **metaphor** and the **simile.** Figurative diction is vital in many kinds of poetry and is also important in many kinds of prose. It is not the opposite of **concrete diction,** since many figures of speech are highly concrete; *He turned his face to the wall* is more concrete than the straightforward *He gave up hope.* In fact, figures of speech are often used to express concretely something that otherwise would have to be expressed in **abstract diction,** and thus they make expression more vivid. However, they can be poorly chosen or overused; see Rule 4-11.

finite verb   A finite verb is one that is found in a **predicate**—that is, one that is performing the standard function of a verb. It is so called because it has a specific **person, number, tense,** and **mood,** which limit, or make finite, its meaning. In *They open the door,* the verb *open* is finite; in *He opened the door,* the verb *opened* is finite. In *He wants to open the door,* the word *open* is not a finite verb; it is an **infinitive.** In *Opening the door, he raised his eyebrows* and in *Opening the door was forbidden,* the word *opening* is not a finite verb; in the first sentence it is a **participle** and in the second it is a **gerund.** In the strictest sense, the term *verb* means a finite verb, though I sometimes use the term more loosely in this book. The term *verbal* is used for infinitives, participles, and gerunds.

first . . . second vs. **firstly . . . secondly**   Either may be used to introduce successive items in an argument. Sometimes they are mixed—*first . . . secondly* or the other way around—and the mixture is acceptable as long as it comes naturally and, on inspection, seems unlikely to trouble a reader. The forms without *ly* are brisker, and when there is a choice of using an adjectival or an adverbial form for a **sentence modifier**—that is, to modify an entire statement rather than just a verb or other word in the statement—the adjectival form often seems preferable, because a statement is a thing rather than an action or quality. See also *more important* vs. *more importantly.*

flourishes   words or phrases added to dress up a sentence. *I venture to say, Far be it from me to suggest that,* and *If I may be so bold* are familiar flourishes used to begin sentences. Very often a flourish is a **cliché;** see Rule 4-12. Nevertheless, flourishes can add humor or nuance; see Rule 1-4.

for   can begin a clause or sentence, either as a **conjunction** or as a **preposition.** The danger is that when it is a conjunction it may be momentarily misunderstood as a preposition, and vice versa. The following uses the conjunction: *He went bankrupt. For his creditors, who had been hounding him for months, would wait no longer.* The following uses the preposition: *He went bankrupt. For his creditors, who had been hounding him for months, he had only pennies in assets.* Both uses are correct, but they are unfair to readers; they have to wait to the end of the sentence to find out if they have guessed right on the meaning of *for.* If a sentence or clause begins with *for,* the next few words should make its meaning apparent.

Careless uses of *for* give ammunition to those who maintain, against centuries of good usage, that sentences should never begin with conjunctions; see Rule 1-1.

foreign words   are usually italicized unless they are proper nouns or are quite familiar to readers of English; see Rule 3-23. When a foreign phrase is used as an adjective, it should not be hyphenated as would be a corresponding phrase in English; see the discussion at the end of Rule 2-36.

formal   I have used the term in this book to characterize speech or writing in which informality is inappropriate, and it is probably clear enough to most readers. But in current usage the word *formal* may suggest pompous adherence to convention, and in these quite comfortable times informality is considered always a virtue. It is true that almost any category of speech or writing can have a somewhat informal character, from a eulogy to a Supreme Court decision; even the aggressively formal language of contracts has been deformalized, by law in some states. Nevertheless, some categories of speech and writing remain formal, requiring speakers or writers to demonstrate self-respect as well as respect for their subject, for those they address, and for the occasion or context. The standards of the day permit some informalities in formal contexts but not others. When I advise that a certain construction or usage should be avoided in formal writing, I do not mean it should be avoided by the pompous—I mean it should be avoided by all of us in contexts we consider formal or suspect our readers will consider formal. See also Rule 4-8.

forms of address   See Rules 3-14 to 3-16. For punctuation with words used in direct address, see Rule 2-10. See also **Ms.**, **Mrs.**, **Miss** and **reverend.**

fragment   a group of words that is not a grammatically complete sentence; see Rule 1-1.

ful **vs.** *fuls*   Words such as *cupful* and *handful* are sometimes given odd plural forms: *cupsful handsful.* The correct forms are *cupfuls* and *handfuls.* If it is really the container rather than the measure or quantity that is plural, the word *full* is used, not the suffix *ful* or *fuls. There were several bucketfuls of water on the floor* means that there was enough water to fill a bucket several times; *There were several buckets full of water on the floor* means that there were several buckets and they were full of water.

further   See *farther* **vs.** *further.*

gender   the classification of nouns or pronouns as masculine, feminine, or neuter. English has very few words that change in

inflection to indicate the different genders, but among these words are some of the most common pronouns, and consequently occasional errors do occur; see Rule 1-12. The masculine singular personal pronoun—*he, him, his*—has been used for centuries to refer to an antecedent that may be either male or female, as in *Everyone has his own tale to tell*, but sometimes it is obviously inappropriate, as in *Every divorced person has his own tale to tell*, and in any case in recent years there has been a strong trend away from this use of the masculine pronoun. See also **sexism.**

generic   A word that is generic represents or describes a whole group or class of things, not one specific thing. For example, the word *company* can refer to any company, and the word *chairman of the board* can refer to any chairman of the board. However, in *the Ajax Company* the word *company* becomes part of a **proper noun** phrase and is no longer a generic term; see Rule 3-12. In *The meeting was held in the absence of the Chairman of the Board*, the phrase *Chairman of the Board* refers to a specific office and a specific person, and the memos of the specific corporation involved would be likely to capitalize it, but it is still a generic term in its literal meaning, and in general usage—for example, in a newspaper account about the meeting—it ordinarily should not be capitalized; see Rule 3-14. Trademarked words such as *Kleenex* and *Plexiglas* are not generic terms, but many trademarked words, such as *Thermos*, have become generic terms and are commonly lowercased, and even those that remain trademarked, such as *Kleenex* and *Plexiglas*, are frequently used generically and lowercased, though they should not be; see Rule 3-12.

genitive   See **possessive case.**

genteelism   a word or construction used in preference to a plainer one because the user does not want to seem coarse. Often the user is innocent; a man who himself is not afraid of plain words may have had his vocabulary shaped by parents and others who were afraid of them, and words these mentors considered more elegant may have become part of his natural usage. *Luncheon* for *lunch, retire* for *go to bed*, and *parlor* for *living room* are likely to be perceived as genteelisms. The term is used scornfully, of course. However, those who are "careful" with their expression and consult books such as this one often share the motivation of those who use genteelisms—we all would like our expression to be admired, and why not? Sometimes a genteelism is actually an error; see **hyperurbanism.**

geographical regions and features   capitalization of names for, Rule 3-17; capitalization of directions such as *east* used to refer to regions, Rule 3-18. Geographical terms that are **generic** should ordinarily not be capitalized; see Rule 3-12.

gerund   a verb form that ends in *ing* and therefore looks like a **participle,** but that is used as a noun rather than as an adjective. *Smoking is a vice* contains the gerund *Smoking,* used as the subject of the sentence. *A smoking man is like a smoking chimney* uses *smoking* twice as an adjective; here *smoking* is a participle, not a gerund. However, even when an *ing* form of a verb is used as an adjective, it may be a gerund, since a gerund, like nouns in general, can modify another word. *Smoking section* uses *Smoking* as a gerund, not as a participle; the section may be smoky, but it is not smoking—it is a section for smoking.
     Gerunds are usually in the present tense, but occasionally they occur in the present perfect tense, with the auxiliary verb ending in *ing* and the base verb ending in *ed* if it is a regular verb: *Having smoked in the past makes one especially sensitive to the odor of tobacco.* The tense of a gerund has no effect on the tense of other verbs in the sentence; see Rule 1-15.
     A gerund can have a subject and an object: *She doesn't like his ignoring her.* The object is in the objective case, like the object of any verb. The subject is very often put in the objective case too, as in *She doesn't like him ignoring her,* but I recommend putting it in the possessive case when possible; see Rule 1-7.
     There are two types of gerunds. In *his cruelly ignoring her,* the gerund *ignoring* has two important properties of verbs—it is modified by an adverb and has a direct object. In *his cruel ignoring of her,* the gerund has only the properties of nouns—it is modified by an adjective and cannot have a direct object. See Rule 1-7 for a fuller explanation; see also Rule 2-34 for information on hyphenation of compound nouns formed with gerunds.

go   A strangely appealing use of *go* to mean *say* has become widespread in recent years: *So I go, "What do you mean by that?" and he goes, "If you don't know what I mean you must* *be pretty stupid,"* so I decked him. I have heard *went* as well as *go.* The usage somehow suggests a spirited exchange. It is, of course, highly informal.

got is used, unnecessarily but not incorrectly, in idiomatic constructions with *has* and *have: I have got to go, He has got a temper.* Such constructions get contracted to *I've got to go* and *He's got a temper,* then incorrectly reduced to *I got to go* and *He got a temper.* Actually, it is *got,* not *has* or *have,* that is dispensable; *I have to go* and *he has a temper* are correct.

got vs. gotten Both are correct past participles of the verb *get.* Either can be used in combination with *has* or *have,* with the meaning of *become* or *been: She has got tired of it; I have gotten fired.* In this construction, *gotten* is more common in the United States, *got* is more common in Britain.

Got and *gotten* are not always interchangeable. When the idea of possession is intended, *got* is used, merely intensifying the sense of *has* or *have,* and *gotten* cannot be used: *She has got a brother,* or, more likely, *She's got a brother.* When the idea of obtaining is intended, *gotten* is used, though *got* can be used and in Britain is more often used: *He has gotten a postponement.* Thus the choice of *got* or *gotten* can be significant. *He's gotten the money* can mean only that he has obtained the money; *He's got the money* almost certainly means that he's had it all along, except in Britain. When *had* rather than *has* or *have* is part of the construction—that is, when the tense is not present perfect but past perfect—there is no such distinction; both *got* and *gotten* indicate obtaining, not possession: *She had gotten the money from her father; She had got the money from her father.* Again, *gotten* is usual in the United States.

Got is the only form when obligation or necessity is meant: *She's got to find the money.*

grammar the system of inflections (changes in the form of a word, such as to show whether a noun is singular or plural) and syntax (the order of words in a sentence) that makes it possible to form sentences out of words. Strictly defined, grammar cannot be good or bad, right or wrong; it is the collection of conventions that exist in a language as it is actually spoken and written by its fluent users. The grammar of individual users of the language is nevertheless perceived as an indicator of their social and educational background, their intelligence, and their interest in and awareness of the sensibilities of those they address. I sometimes use the terms *grammar* and *grammatical* rather loosely in this book, as explained in the introduction to Chapter 1.

had better vs. better   See *better.*

had vs. had've, had of, hadda   *Had've,* as in *I wish he had've paid me,* is an error. *Had've* can only be a contraction of *had have,* which is not a proper English formation. *Had of* and *hadda* are just variants of *had've.* The forms may be a malformation of the contraction of *would have,* as in *I wish he'd've paid me;* the contraction *'d* is taken as representing *had* rather than *would. I wish he'd've paid me* and *I wish he would have paid me* are errors themselves, for the correct *I wish he had paid me;* see Rule 1-14.

half   causes hyphenation troubles in compounds. In compound nouns it usually is followed by a hyphen, as in *half-truth,* but it is not in some, as in *half brother,* and in others it combines solidly, as in *halftone;* see Rule 2-32. Hyphenation also varies in adjectival compounds such as those in *The half-asleep audience did not respond; The audience was half-asleep;* and *The money was half gone;* see Rule 2-35.

hang on to vs. hang onto, hold on to vs. hold onto   See *onto vs. on to.*

he or she vs. he/she, s/he   The formations *he/she* and its inflections and *s/he* should almost never be used; they are not words or valid compounds. If *he* is not permitted to mean either sex, it is better to use *he or she* or one of its inflections no matter how often this straightforward phrase must be repeated, or else to avoid the problem by using plural constructions whenever possible. See **sexism.**

hopefully   an adverb meaning *in a manner full of hope* or *in a hopeful manner. Hopefully he approached the two-dollar window* uses the word correctly. *Hopefully his loss will teach him a lesson* misuses it; it is a dangling construction, because *Hopefully* has nothing to modify except the verb *teach* or the whole sentence, and the word's meaning doesn't permit it to modify either. The misuse is only a few decades old but is very widespread, and some recent dictionaries accept it.

Hopefully is defended by some writers on usage as a **sentence modifier** meaning *let us hope that* or *it is to be hoped that,* just as *possibly* is a sentence modifier in *Possibly his loss will teach him a lesson*, meaning *It is possible that his loss will teach him a lesson*. The argument against this is that while the teaching of the lesson can be possible, it cannot be hopeful—it can only be hoped for. The primary meaning of the adjective *hopeful* is *full of hope*, and only a human being or some reasonably advanced animal can be full of hope. *Hopeful* can also mean *hope-inspiring*, as in *The outlook is hopeful*, which may seem to give sentence-modifying *hopefully* a boost, since *outlook* is not an animate being capable of feeling hope. In fact, *hopefully* can have this meaning too, as in *The outlook, hopefully enough, is better than it was last year*, in which it means that the improvement in the outlook is adequately hope-inspiring. However, in *Hopefully, his loss will teach him a lesson*, the adverb *Hopefully* does not mean *hope-inspiringly*, it means *I hope that* or *let us hope that*, or, if the speaker wants to keep *I* and *us* out of the statement, *it is to be hoped that*. One might perhaps claim that the possibility that his loss will teach him a lesson is hope-inspiring, but if so, the statement becomes rather tedious—it means that the possibility that his loss will teach him a lesson inspires the hope that his loss will teach him a lesson. That is not what it is intended to mean; it employs the primary meaning of *hope*. Of course, this kind of argument and counterargument is apt to have little effect on the evolution of the meaning of a word, especially if the evolution answers a need. Other words have broadened their application in the same way but seem to draw little criticism; see **thankfully.**

Some words that describe judgment or feeling, such as *regret*, have more than one adverb, one of which can be used somewhat as *hopefully* is misused: *Regretfully, he inspected his empty wallet* parallels the correct use of *hopefully*; *Regrettably, he has not learned his lesson* almost parallels the incorrect use. (*Regrettably* does not parallel *hopefully* completely, since whereas *Regrettably* in the example merely colors the flat statement *he has not learned his lesson*, the statement in *Hopefully, his loss will teach him a lesson* is only a possibility and is dependent on *Hopefully* for its meaning—*His loss will teach him a lesson*, without the modifying *Hopefully*, is quite a different thought. *Hopefully*, like *possibly*, mentioned in the preceding paragraph, not only modifies but governs the meaning of *his loss will teach him a lesson*.) Since no such word as *hopeably, hope-forably*, or *hopedly* exists in the language, the contested meaning of *hopefully* does seem to answer a need.

The correct constructions it replaces can be clumsy—they must be either a passive contruction with an expletive subject such as *It is to be hoped that,* an imperative construction such as *Let us hope that,* or a standard subject-and-verb construction such as *I hope that.* The expletive-and-passive construction is awkward, and often it is inconvenient to have to supply the human subject that *hope* requires as an active verb or the human object that the imperative *let* requires. But I think the convenience of sentence-modifying *hopefully* is one of the troubles with it. If it is really needed in the language, it is odd that the earliest *Oxford English Dictionary* citation for it is 1932 (in the dictionary's *Supplement*) and that it has become common only in the past thirty years. It allows a sloppy vagueness that seems more and more characteristic of public expression in this age when the media must be constantly fed words, words, any words—and therefore if it is now needed, the need itself could be deplored. If it is inconvenient in a given sentence to supply a human being to feel the hope in *hopefully,* the sentence very likely has a hazy intent and should be improved as a thought. If the fact that the possibility the sentence proposes is hoped for is incidental enough that it seems to deserve only an adverb rather than a clause, perhaps the fact is just a distraction and the sentence should be reworded to omit it; if the fact is not incidental but important to the statement, perhaps it would be better to make it more important grammatically and provide someone to feel the hope. Of course, arguments such as this, based on rhetorical considerations, and in this case on my own rather personal feeling that *hopefully* is rhetorically faulty, are no more likely to exterminate misuses of *hopefully* than is the argument based on semantic considerations in the preceding paragraph.

The best argument against using sentence-modifying *hopefully* is that so many condemn it so strongly. I dislike the usage myself partly because I encounter it almost invariably in bad writing, which is tedious to read or to edit; those whose writing is good or at least adequate are usually aware that the usage is condemned by many and therefore they avoid it. On the other hand, I find it objectionable in speech too, especially as a one-word reply replacing *I hope so* or *Let's hope so,* and here the guilt is not by association, because I hear it from people whose overall use of spoken language is excellent.

Perhaps sentence-modifying *hopefully* will prevail, like many another usage that was considered a barbarism when it first appeared. My guess is that it will be accepted within a generation; I don't hear it often from well-educated people my age, in their fifties, but I do hear it quite often from well-educated people only a decade younger. At present, it is perhaps the most controversial usage in the language, and many of those who condemn it—not all of whom are over fifty—are apt to consider it not only questionable or sloppy but despicable. I strongly advise avoiding their scorn.

however   Some editors, writers on usage, and English teachers object to *however* at the beginning of a sentence. However, that is usually the natural place for it when the sentence contradicts or qualifies the preceding sentence. In this book, I make far too frequent use of *however* at the beginnings of my sentences, so many of which follow sentences that must be immediately countered or qualified, but burying the word later in the sentence is not a good solution; it just postpones letting the reader know the intent of the sentence within the passage. I advise not hesitating to use *however* at the beginning of sentences, but also not committing my overuse.

hyperbole   exaggeration to strengthen meaning. *He raised a million objections* is a hyperbolic way of saying *He raised several objections* or *He was very critical. I almost keeled over* is hyperbolic for *I was surprised*; it is also a use of **metaphor,** since it is boats, not people, that keel over. Hyperbole is a standard method of emphasizing meaning; it may be imprecise but it is not intended to deceive, as other forms of exaggeration may be. Like any figurative diction, it can be overused; see Rule 4-11. It is often easy to puncture: "There are thousands of reasons why I can't make a donation." "Name ten." "Well . . ."

hyperurbanism   an error in grammar or usage that results from misunderstanding and misapplying a grammatical rule or stricture of usage. A child may be corrected repeatedly about the misuse of the objective case in sentences such as *Johnny and me were kicked out of class*, which is a common and even natural error in grammar, and conclude that *Johnny and I* is always better; later in life the adult may commit hyperurbanisms such as *The dean kicked John and I out of college*, which is an unnatural error in grammar—the speaker or writer makes it because of distrust of his or her own ear and an uneasy suspicion that the unnatural is more dignified and more apt to be correct than the natural. *He eats as an animal* is a hyperurbanism, caused by excessive fear of misusing *like. Whom shall*

I say is calling? is a hyperurbanism, caused by excessive admiration of the supposedly more elegant *whom* (see Rule 1-6).

The adjective *hypercorrect* is probably more common in reference to such errors than the noun *hyperurbanism*. I generally use *hyperurbanism* because it suggests the desire to appear citified and sophisticated rather than rustic and ignorant that is often behind such errors. *Hyperurbanism* also suggests disdain, which is a questionable advantage; disdain is rarely a pretty thing. See also **genteelism.**

hyphen   a mark used to connect the elements of some **compound** words and to indicate that a word has been divided at the end of a line. Some compound words, especially compound nouns, do not have the hyphen but are written as two or more separate words, and others are written as a single solid word. Although there are general principles that affect the formation of compound nouns (see Rule 2-34), so many compounds are exceptions to these principles that one must frequently rely on the dictionary.

Hyphens are not used with many prefixes, such as *un* and *pre*, that are not independent words. Instead these prefixes combine solidly with an independent word; see Rule 2-31. Hyphens are used with some other prefixes, such as *all* and *self*, that do exist as independent words; see Rule 2-32. Similarly, hyphens are routinely used with some suffixes, such as *free*, and not with others, such as *like*; see Rule 2-33.

Hyphens should be used between the elements of many compound adjectives. They are often omitted or misused. The principles governing them are quite complicated; adjectival combinations of some parts of speech require the hyphen, but combinations of others do not, and some combinations are hyphenated if they occur before the word they modify but not if they occur after it. See Rules 2-35 and 2-36.

Phrases that include numbers are often incorrectly hyphenated or incorrectly not hyphenated; for example, *a $10-loss* and *a ten dollar loss* are both incorrect. See Rule 2-37.

The hyphen to indicate division of a word at the end of a line should be positioned between syllables. Dictionaries generally use centered dots or other symbols to show where words should be divided.

ic* vs. *ical   *Geologic* and *geological* mean the same thing in most contexts, but *historic* and *historical* are different; a *historic* event is an important one, and a *historical* event is merely one that happened in the past. In general, an adjective ending in *ical* merely has a somewhat broader meaning than the same adjective ending in *ic*, but it may have the same meaning or it may have a distinctly different meaning. When in doubt, check the dictionary definition carefully; avoid errors such as *In classic times, slavery was common.*

When there is no apparent difference between the *ic* and *ical* form of an adjective, there is a tendency in the sciences and social sciences to use the *ic* form, which is shorter and seems more precise whether it is or not, and this can be annoying. In *The report includes parenthetic observations on biologic distinctions that may have influenced the data,* the rare forms *parenthetic* and *biologic* seem to be used only to rarefy the sentence, a questionable motive; the common *parenthetical* and *biological* would have exactly the same meaning in this context.

idiom   a usage or construction that is difficult to justify but is accepted as part of the language. In a sense, all language is idiom; literally the word means the language shared by any group.

imperative mood   the mood of verbs used to express commands and instructions. *Pay me immediately* and *Go straight till the next light* are imperative constructions. The second-person pronoun *you* is understood as the subject of the imperative verb. The verb form is almost always the same as the form that goes with *you* in the **indicative mood,** but in fact the imperative form is based on the infinitive—it just happens that for every verb except *be,* the infinitive form is the same as the form for the second person. *Be good* demonstrates that actually the infinitive form is used. The infinitive can also be seen in the occasional constructions that occur with the imperative in the third person, as in *Somebody hold the ladder or I'll fall;* the indicative form with the third-person pronoun *somebody* would be *holds.*

Let is used as an ordinary second-person imperative, as in *Let me go,* and also as a first-person-plural imperative, as in *Let us go* and *let's go.* See also **let's you and me** vs. **let's you and I** and the discussion of pronouns in apposition in Rule 1-6.

Although the imperative is not necessarily impolite—*Please accept this reward* and *Forgive me* are imperative—sometimes an imperative expression is softened by being put in the indicative mood or **subjunctive mood** and phrased, but not spoken or punctuated, as a question: *Will you attend to this imme-diately; Would you let me know as soon as possible.*

impersonal *it* a use of the pronoun *it* with no antecedent, as in *It is going to snow* and *It rained yesterday.* It is somewhat similar to an **expletive** construction. The impersonal *it* has been part of the language for many centuries, but in Gothic, one of the ancestors of English, it did not exist. If this short-coming had persisted we would be saying *Going to snow* and *Rained yesterday.*

imply* vs. *infer *Imply* means *hint* or *suggest; infer* means *draw a conclusion: He implied in his remarks that I was a crook; I inferred from his remarks that he considered me a crook. Infer* is often used for *imply*, and has been so used for several centuries, but this use is considered a misuse by a great many, who consider it a giveaway of ignorance. Arbiters of usage have been condemning it since early in this century. I advise observing the distinction.

independent clause a clause that could stand alone as a **sentence.** *I came in the door, and the burglar went out the window* contains two independent clauses. *As I came in the door, the burglar went out the window* contains only one independent clause, *the burglar went out the window;* the addition of *As* has made *I came in the door* a **dependent clause,** modifying the independent clause.

Sentences containing two or more independent clauses are called compound sentences; see Rule 2-1. For proper punctuation of compound sentences, see Rules 2-2, 2-12, and 2-13.

independent possessive See **possessive.**

indicative mood the most common mood of verbs, used to make straightforward statements or ask questions about facts. *I went to the party* and *Will you go to the party?* are both in the indicative mood. *Go to the party!* is in the **imperative mood.** *Would you go to the party if I were going?* has both its verbs in the **subjunctive mood;** it concerns not facts but possibilities and conditions.

indirect object a word or phrase indirectly affected by a verb. In *He gave me all the money,* the verb *gave* has the indirect object *me;* the **direct object** is the phrase *all the money.* A preposition is understood to precede the indirect object—usually the preposition *to*, though not always; in *We bought them candy*, the preposition *for* is understood to precede the indirect object *them*. When the preposition is supplied, which has to be done when the direct object intervenes, the indirect object becomes a prepositional phrase: *He gave all the money to me; We bought candy for them.*

An **intransitive verb** cannot have an indirect object, but may occur with a prepositional phrase that functions somewhat like an indirect object: *He seems honest to me.* (The intransitive verb *seems* in this example is of a special type; see **linking verb**.)

indirect quotation, indirect discourse, indirect question   See **direct, indirect.**

infinitive   the familiar base form of a verb that often is preceded by *to. I want to go* contains the infinitive *to go. I want to help solve the problem* contains the infinitive *to help* and also the infinitive *solve*, with the *to* omitted for the second infinitive. Some writers on usage have devised complicated rules to govern when *to* can be omitted, when it cannot be, and when it is optional, but one can almost always rely on the ear alone; errors are extremely rare. However, leaving out an optional *to* is sometimes undesirable. *I want to help, encourage, and to sustain the intellectually needy*, with *to* supplied for the third infinitive but not the middle one in the series, is faulty parallelism; see Rule 1-5.

Split infinitives, such as *to genuinely help*, with a modifier between *to* and the verb, are not errors but nevertheless are considered errors by many and should therefore be used sparingly; see Rule 1-20.

Infinitives do not function like ordinary verbs (see **finite verb**) but instead as nouns (*I want to go* uses *to go* as the direct object of *want*), adjectives (*He is the man to see* uses *to see* to modify the noun *man*), or adverbs (*I was happy to leave* uses *to leave* to modify the adjective *happy*). Nevertheless, infinitives can have subjects and objects—both of which are in the objective case, as in *I told him to call me.* The reason that the subject of an infinitive is always in the objective case is that it is always also the object of a verb, as *him* is the object of *call* in the preceding example, or the object of a preposition, as in *For him to call was rare*, in which *him* is the object of the preposition *For* as well as the subject of *to call.*

Infinitives also have tense: *To err is human; to have erred is also human.* The proper tense for the infinitive depends on the relationship of the time expressed by the infinitive to the time expressed by the main verb; see Rule 1-15. The present infinitive frequently expresses expectation, purpose, or compulsion, and thus its time can be future rather than present; *I expect to go; I am to go in the morning; I was to go in the morning.*

Infinitives also have voice; *It is difficult to lead, not so difficult to be led* contains the active infinitive *to lead* and the passive infinitive *to be led.*

We all use the infinitive impeccably in quite complicated constructions, as in *I saw him kiss her,* in which the infinitive *kiss* is part of an object predicate. But infinitives can be misused. For example, the infinitive of purpose, as in *I worked to earn my living,* should not ordinarily be used unless there really is some idea of purpose to express; *I worked all day to accomplish nothing* would be better as *I worked all day but accomplished nothing.* However, the addition of *only* subtracts the idea of purpose; *I worked all day only to accomplish nothing* is correct. As the term *infinitive* suggests, infinitives are virtually unlimited in their ability to contribute the essential meaning of a verb to a sentence.

Sometimes the role of an infinitive in a sentence is not clear. *He advised those who had not been trained to solve the problem* is ambiguous, because *to solve the problem* can go with either *advised* or *trained.* When a sentence contains more than one verb that an infinitive construction can follow, recasting the sentence may be the only way to prevent possible misreading. There is no easy way to make the example unambiguous, though the context may, of course, make misreading too unlikely to worry about.

inflection   A change in the form of a word to indicate its function and meaning. Some pronouns are inflected to indicate their **case** (*he, him, his*), **number** (*he, they*), **person** (*I, you, he*), and **gender** (*he, she, it*). Nouns are inflected to indicate number and case, though the subjective and objective cases are the same. Verbs are inflected to indicate person, though only in the present tense, and even in the present tense all but the third person singular are the same (*I cook, you cook, he cooks*). A few verbs, like *can,* aren't inflected at all to show person. The verb *to be* has more inflections for person than other verbs, with three forms in the present (*am, are, is*) and two forms in the past (*was, were*). Verbs are also inflected to show **tense** (*I cook, I* *cooked*), with auxiliary verbs helping to form many of the tenses (*I am cooking, I will cook*), and to show **mood** (*He cooks; I insist that he cook*). Adjectives are not inflected, except for the demonstrative adjectives *this* and *that*, which have the plurals *these* and *those*. The comparative and superlative adjective endings *er* and *est* are usually considered not inflections but suffixes, since they alter the basic meaning of an adjective rather than merely indicating its function.

Inflection is one of the two basic parts of grammar; the other is **syntax.**

initials   whether to use points with, Rule 3-10

interjection   one of the **parts of speech**; a word or phrase used to express feeling rather than meaning, usually as an exclamation. *Oh dear, it's raining* contains the interjection *Oh dear. I'd like to help, but, darn, I'm broke* contains the interjection *darn*. Interjections have no grammatical connection with a sentence they are part of; they are quite independent and can stand alone as complete sentences: *Oh dear! Damn! Hurray!* If they are connected to a sentence, they are almost always set off by commas or other marks of punctuation, like parenthetical constructions, which they basically are; see Rule 2-1. However, an interjection does not have to be set off if a writer wants to indicate a spoken delivery with no pauses around the interjection: *Oh I don't know about that; We could surrender, but oh the shame we would face.* Similarly, *I'd like to help, but darn, I'm broke* may suggest spoken delivery better than the earlier example with the comma after *but.*

into* vs. *in to   *Into* is a preposition, as in *She went into her office*, in which it is part of the adverbial prepositional phrase *into her office*. *In to* is an adverb plus a preposition, as in *He went in to lunch*, in which *in* directly modifies the verb *went* and *to* is a preposition with the object *lunch*. When the words are spoken, we can usually hear the difference. When *into* is misused for *in to*, the result is sometimes ludicrous: *He turned his uniform into the supply sergeant* states that the uniform was transformed into the sergeant, not handed over to him.

intransitive verb   a verb that does not have an **object**. A **transitive verb** transmits its action from a subject to an object: *The bat hits the ball.* An intransitive verb does not pass its action along: *The ball disappears.* Intransitive verbs do not require an object to complete their meaning.

Many verbs can be either transitive or intransitive. *The child is playing* uses the verb *play* intransitively; *The child is playing poker* uses it transitively. Other verbs, such as *lie* (meaning *tell a falsehood*), *sleep,* and *smile,* are always intransitive, except in a special construction in which they are given an object that repeats the verb in noun form: *He lied a terrible lie; He slept the sleep of the just; He smiled an ambiguous smile.* A few, such as *lie* (meaning *lie down*), cannot be transitive even in this special construction.

An intransitive verb can never be used in the passive voice. If an active verb is made passive, its object becomes its subject; *The bat hits the ball* becomes *The ball was hit by the bat.* But an intransitive verb has no object to be made its subject, and so the verb can't be made passive, since with very few exceptions (see **as follows vs. as follow**) a verb must have a subject. Even an imperative verb, as in *Go away,* has the understood subject *you.* See also **linking verb.**

introductory construction   a word, phrase, or clause that precedes the main clause of a sentence; see Rule 2-1. A comma after an introductory construction is usually helpful to indicate that the main clause is about to start, but this principle is sometimes misapplied: *In view of the circumstances, we chose to build a house* properly has a comma after the introductory construction, but *In view of the road, is a poor place to build a house,* which uses the prepositional phrase *In view of the road* not as an introductory construction but as the subject of the sentence, incorrectly has a comma between the subject and its verb; see Rule 2-4. *In view of the road, we saw a good site* uses the phrase *In view of the road* not as an introductory construction but as a modifier, and the basic problem is not the comma, although the comma is questionable, but the ambiguous position of the modifier, which makes it difficult to tell whether it modifies the verb *saw* or the noun *site;* see the discussion of inverted sentences in Rule 2-5. *We decided that, in view of the circumstances, we should build a house* uses the comma correctly after *in view of the circumstances,* which introduces the following clause, but questionably after *that;* see Rule 2-8.

inversion   in a sentence, a word order that is not the standard one. *"Not guilty" was the verdict* inverts **subject** and **comple-**

ment to put extra emphasis on *"Not guilty." Hurt in the accident were two bystanders* puts the subject at the end of the sentence and inverts the usual order of auxiliary verb and base verb; *Two bystanders were hurt in the accident* is the standard order. Inversion can create ambiguity (see Rule 2-5) and, since inverted sentences tend to sound unnatural anyway, can conceal various grammatical errors, especially errors of **agreement,** that would be automatically avoided in a straightforward sentence. Inversion is often used for no purpose other than to provide variety of sentence structure; such variety is desirable (see Rule 4-11), but inversion can be a poor way to achieve it.

italics   slanted, scriptlike type, as distinguished from roman type. In handwriting and in most typescript, italics are indicated by underlining; printers used in word processing often can produce italics. Italics have the effect of providing emphasis in writing just as rises in volume, pitch, or intensity provide emphasis in speech. They are often overused for this purpose; even two or three italicized words in a paragraph can create a gushy, gesturing effect that is annoying to the reader.

Italics are used for the titles of certain written works, musical compositions, and works of art; see Rules 3-19 and 3-20. They are also used for unfamiliar foreign terms; see Rule 3-23. They may be used instead of quotation marks in some circumstances, as I use them in this book for examples and for words under discussion; see Rule 2-26. They are almost always used for the names of specific ships, as in S.S. *United States*; note that initials preceding the name, such as S.S. and H.M.S., are not italicized. They are often used for the names of specific airplanes or spacecraft—*Air Force One, Voyager 2*—but roman may be used for these as well; different publishing houses and publications have different policies, and writers may decide their own policies as long as they think out a policy carefully and follow it consistently. Thus one might decide to use roman for Air Force One, which is actually the numerical Air Force designation for the President's plane rather than a true name, but to use italic for *The Spirit of St. Louis*.

it is, there is, there are   In these constructions, called **expletive** constructions, *it* or *there* temporarily takes the place of the "true" subject. In *It is true that there is no school today*, there are two such constructions. The true subject is the noun clause *that there is no school today*. The use of *It is* makes it possible to avoid the awkward *That there is no school today is true*. The use of *there* is essential; *No school is today* isn't English, though some centuries ago it was. The verb in such constructions can, of course, change tense as appropriate: *It was true that there had been no school that day.*

It is occurs in many familiar idioms in which there is no true subject, such as *It is cold.* The true subject—*the weather*, or perhaps *the temperature*, or perhaps *the day*—never occurs in the sentence, so these are not expletive constructions; they are uses of the **impersonal *it.***

It is can be followed by a true subject that is plural: *It is friends we need.* In this respect, it is like any construction with a **complement;** the verb *is* agrees in number with the grammatical subject, *It*, not the complement, *friends* (see Rule 1-11). But when a relative clause follows the true subject, the verb in the relative clause usually agrees in both number and person with the true subject, not with *It*, even though logically the antecedent of the relative pronoun is *It*: *It is friends that are needed; It is I that am friendless.* However, although *it is friends that is needed* and *It is we that is friendless* are wrong to everyone's ear, *It is I that is friendless*, in which I and *is* agree in number but not in person, has its defenders. Particularly in negative clauses, *is* may be more natural even when it disagrees in both number and person: *It is not I that is friendless, it is you that are friendless; It is not you that is friendless, it is I that am friendless.* When a negative and a positive subject share the verb, *is* can be clearly better even when it is wrong for the positive subject, which normally determines the person of the verb (see Rule 1-10): *Is it possible that it is I and not Kant who is boring?* Since there is disagreement on the point among writers on usage, we can often take our choice. See also ***what is* vs. *what are.***

There is and *there are* don't create this problem. If the true subject is singular, *is* is correct, and if the true subject is plural, *are* is correct: *There is no school; There are no classes.* Careless errors with the contraction *there's* are common, however: *There's eventually going to be objections* is a simple error of agreement, perhaps committed because *there're* is more difficult to pronounce. *There's plenty of objections* and *There's lots of objections* are similar errors, perhaps further encouraged because phrases with *plenty* and *lots* are sometimes singular: *There's plenty of discontent; There's lots of discontent.*

There is is often used when the true subject is a compound subject, and therefore plural, but its first element is singular: *There is a car and two chickens in his garage.* Although this

357

disagreement in number of verb and true subject cannot be defended logically, it sometimes seems preferable to careful agreement; *There are a right way and a wrong way of doing everything*, while strictly correct, is unnatural. The same disagreement occurs in inverted sentences, such as *In the garage was a car and two chickens*, where I think it is sometimes defensible; see the discussion of subjects joined by *and* that come after the verb in Rule 1-11. There isn't always a clearly right way or wrong way of handling *there is* and *there are*; expletive constructions in English are highly idiomatic, and idiom often ignores logic. Generally, *there are* will work when the true subject is plural; if it seems unnatural, we have the choice of recasting to avoid it or accepting *there is* as an idiomatic exception to the standard rules of agreement.

it is I vs. it is me   *It is I* is correct but often seems stilted. *It is me* is grammatically faulty, since *me* is being used as a subject **complement** and should be in the **subjective case,** but is accepted as idiom. Usually *it is me*, and especially the contraction *it's me*, should prevail, but the grammatically parallel *it is him* and *it is them* and their contractions are less often acceptable; see Rule 1-6.

its vs. it's   *Its* is the possessive form of the pronoun *it*: *The pen was missing its cap. It's* is the contraction of *it is* or *it has*: *It's snowing, though it's never happened here in September before.* One is often carelessly and sometimes ignorantly used for the other. For some reason, *it's* for *its* seems to occur more often than *its* for *it's*, though one would expect the careless to omit rather than add an apostrophe.

Jr., Sr.   These abbreviations should normally be preceded by a comma, and followed by a comma if the clause or sentence continues: *John Smith, Jr., was there.* This punctuation convention can be a nuisance when a name is possessive, as in *John Smith, Jr.'s, dog*; see Rules 2-29 and 3-11.

kind   The singular *kind* should not be used with the plural demonstrative adjectives *these* and *those*. Therefore *these kind of stories* is an error; the plural *stories* has been allowed to change *this kind* to *these kind*.

This kind of stories, though it seems to me as defensible grammatically as *this group of authors*, does not sound quite natural. When everything is plural—*these kinds of stories*—

there is no problem, but if the topic is one specific kind, not several kinds with something in common, the plural is il-logical; *I used to like stories about baseball, but these kinds of stories bore me now* is puzzling, because only one kind of story, stories about baseball, is mentioned. It is usually possible to make everything singular instead: *This kind of story bores me now.* When there is no alternative to using *this kind of* with a plural, it usually sounds natural enough: *I don't like this kind of beans.*

These kinds of story does not sound quite natural either, and it changes the meaning of *story* from a specific thing to a classification, but it too seems grammatically defensible, as is *these kinds of narrative.* If the topic is one kind, *this kind of* is correct; if it is two or more kinds, *these kinds of* is correct. The word that follows is singular or plural depending on just what word it is; some words seem more natural in the singular, others in the plural.

Some writers on usage believe that *kind of* and also *sort of* are perceived by users of the language not as combinations of noun and preposition but as adjectives—that *these kind of stories* is really *these stories* with *kind of* coming between the demonstrative adjective *these* and the noun *stories* to modify *stories*, just as an ordinary adjective such as *dreadful* does in *these dreadful stories.* Could be, but the usage will draw crit-icism nevertheless. A few others note that *kind* is derived from Old English *cyn*, meaning *kin*, and suggest that since *kin* is a plural, *kind* should be allowed to be plural too. I think this greatly exaggerates the effect that derivation both does have and should have on usage; words irresistibly change. *Kind* is sometimes a **collective noun** and hence plural, as in *There are good movies and bad movies, but the good kind are rarer*, but whatever its derivation it is usually unarguably singular. I advise never using *these kind.*

The *kind of* construction is somewhat overused. Often it is better to use an *of this kind* construction. *Stories of this kind bore me now*, when only one kind has been mentioned, and *Stories of these kinds bore me now*, when two or more kinds have been mentioned, are both correct, and both are natural.

Kind of is much too common as a vague qualifier, as in *I was kind of busy* and *I kind of had to cut her short.* It suggests that the speaker has no confidence in his or her own expression and feels apologetic; it should be avoided except in casual speech and the most casual writing. *Kind of a* is similarly unim-pressive in *He was kind of a solemn man.*

What kind of a story would you like to hear? would be criticized by some for unnecessarily using *a* before *story*, but the usage is common and not incorrect, even in formal writing; the little unstressed syllable may benefit an occasional carefully considered sentence.

kinship terms   when to capitalize, Rule 3-16; setting off with commas in direct address, Rule 2-10

lay **vs.** *lie*   These verbs are often confused; even many well-educated people make errors with them, especially in the past tense.

Lay is a **transitive verb** meaning *place or put*. Its past tense is *laid*, and its past participle is also *laid*. *I am going to lay the money on the table. He would not take the money, so I laid it on the table. "I have laid the money on the table," I said.*

Lie is an **intransitive verb** meaning *recline*; it is often used with the adverb *down* or with a prepositional phrase such as *on the bed*. Its past tense is *lay*—just like the present tense of the other verb, which is the source of much of the confusion—and its past participle is *lain*. *I decided to lie down. I lay on the bed for a while, then muttered to myself, "I have lain here long enough."* Among educated people the most common error is using *lay* for *laid*, as in *He lay the book on the table.*

leave **vs.** *let*   In some contexts, *leave* is obviously incorrect for *let* and should not be used: *Leave us go now; Leave me go; We should leave him sink or swim. Leave* is acceptable as idiom in some common constructions: *Leave me be; Leave him alone.* However, since *Let me be* and *Let him alone* are equally idiomatic, *leave* might as well be saved for contexts in which its basic meaning, *go away from* or *abandon*, applies.

Note that in *We should leave him to sink or swim* the addition of *to*, making *leave* unmistakably an **infinitive**, permits *leave* to have the meaning *abandon* and makes the sentence correct. In fact, *let* is never used with *to*—no one would say *Let me to go*—and there is good argument for considering the verb form that follows *let* to be not an infinitive at all but a **finite verb** in the **subjunctive mood**; see the discussion of pronouns in apposition in Rule 1-6. This perhaps accounts for the acceptability of *Leave me be* and *Leave him alone*; both can credibly be expanded to include infinitives—*Leave me to be* and *Leave him to be alone*—because both, with a little straining, permit *leave* to mean *abandon*. But *Leave us go now* and *Leave me go* cannot credibly be expanded to include infinitives; in these sentences it would take excessive straining to interpret *leave* as meaning *go away from* or *abandon*, which is to say that it means *let.* However, *let* is a very peculiar word, and analysis of its usages and limitations is difficult. For example, verbs following *allow* and *permit*, which have the same meaning as *let* in many sentences, are always infinitives with *to*—why is that?

less vs. fewer   See *fewer vs. less.*

let's you and me vs. let's you and I   *Let's you and me* is a contraction of *Let us, you and me,* in which the pronouns *you* and *me* are in **apposition** to the pronoun *us.* Since *us* is in the objective case, as the object of *let*, you and *me* must be in the objective case, and therefore *let's you and I* is wrong. In addition, a verb form usually follows the construction, as in *Let's you and me have a talk;* the verb form is generally considered to be an **infinitive,** and the subject of an infinitive, *you and me* in the example, should be in the objective case. However, *let's you and I* is heard among the well-educated, and though I advise against the usage, there are other ways of analyzing its grammar that support it; see the discussion of pronouns in apposition in Rule 1-6.

Let's you and him is clearly nonsense if the contraction is expanded to *let us you and him,* and *let's us* is baldly redundant, since the expansion is *Let us us.* The constructions are well established as colloquial idioms, however; *let's* has acquired a meaning beyond that of the uncontracted phrase.

None of the constructions, including the accepted *let's you and me,* is appropriate in anything but an informal or deliberately folksy context.

like   is sometimes used as a vague qualifier or modifier in speech, as in *She was like not interested in me at all, though I was trying to get a laugh out of her for like twenty minutes.* The word becomes a verbal tic and infests every sentence. The indecisive, apologetic overtones it gives sentences may have a kind of charm, as may the adolescents who use it, but using it amounts to an admission by the speaker that his or her expression is poor.

It was a vacation like I hadn't had in twenty years misuses *like; like* should be changed to *such as.*

It was a vacation like I had last year can retain *like,* but needs a pronoun to serve as its object: *like that I had last year* or *like the one I had last year.*

Careless use of *like* to introduce sentences can produce **false comparison,** as in *Like World War II, all of Europe was affected by World War I.* See Rule 1-5.

like for *as, as if,* or *as though* The word *like* can be several parts of speech, but usually it should not be used as a **conjunction**—that is, it should not be used to replace *as, as if,* or *as though.* Essentially, this means that *like* should not be used to introduce a **clause.** *He cleans his car like I brush my teeth* is wrong, because *like* is made to introduce a clause; *like* should be *as. He cleans his wife's car like she was holding a gun on him* is the same error; *like* should be *as if* or *as though* (and if that correction is made, *were* would be better than *was*; see Rule 1-17). Sometimes the error is less obtrusive, as in *She looks like I did at her age* and *She acts like she wants to be admired*; with certain verbs, including *look* and *act*, the faulty construction is exceedingly common.

Like is properly used as a **preposition,** as in *She looks like me at her age.* Note that the pronoun *me* is in the objective case, as the object of *like* (see Rule 1-9). I don't remember seeing an error as plain as *a gorgeous girl like I* in manuscripts I have edited, but I see errors such as *like my wife and I* as frequently as I see *between you and I* (see **hyperurbanism**). Note also that there is no verb in *like me at her age*—it is not a clause. The other examples can also be altered, if with some change in content, to make *like* correct: *He cleans his car like me brushing my teeth; He cleans his wife's car like a man with a gun trained on him; She acts like someone who wants to be admired.* The first example is not very graceful, but the grammatically identical *He cleans his car like a man brushing his teeth* is passable. In the last example a clause follows, but it is not the object of *like*; the object of *like* is *someone*, and the clause is a relative clause modifying *someone*.

Often when *like* means *as*, the clause following is elliptical and not so easily identified as a clause, as in *She takes to it like a duck to water*, which is incorrect if the clause is filled out: *She takes to it like a duck takes to water.* The verb is almost always omitted if it is the same as the verb in the preceding clause: *He played it like a pro* (plays it or would play it); *He eats like an animal* (eats). In fact, in these examples, and in general when a following clause is missing its verb, *like* is accepted. One might claim that the missing verb is not a **finite**

362

verb but merely a **participle** modifying the noun after *like*—
She takes to it like a duck taking to water, and so on—but that
seems farfetched; I believe that the missing verb is perceived as
a finite verb and that *like* is functioning as a conjunction.

When *like* is used to mean *as if* or *as though,* the verb is
always supplied (except in a few expressions such as *like
crazy*), as in the earlier example *He cleans his wife's car like
she was holding a gun on him,* and the usage, though common
in casual speech, clearly breaks the rule that *like* not be followed by a clause and is not accepted (but see the next paragraph). One test of whether *like* can be used is to see if *similar
to* or *similarly to* can replace it; if the answer is yes, *like* is all
right. Neither of these phrases can replace it when it means *as
if* or *as though,* but often one of them will work when it means
*as: She looks similar to me at her age; She takes to it similarly
to a duck to water.* A problem with the test is that to my ear,
and I think a good many other ears, a combination of adverb
and preposition such as *similarly to* never sounds quite right
but smacks of **false comparison.** In the example, it seems to
liken her taking to it to a duck rather than to a duck's taking to
water, and thus isn't completely convincing as a replacement
for *like.* See **different from vs. different than, differently from
vs. differently than** for more discussion of the point. The test
also rejects some acceptable usages discussed below.

It looks like it's going to rain and *It looks like we won't be
able to go* use *like* to mean *as if* or *as though,* and they follow
like with a clause. Yet both could be heard in the most verbally
sophisticated circles and seen in the best literature; it would be
foolish to condemn them. One difference between these examples and earlier ones is that they both use the **impersonal** *it* as a
subject (see also **it is, there is, there are**); the first example uses
it twice. Constructions with the impersonal *it* are often highly
idiomatic. Both examples also employ the verb *look,* which, as
already noted, seems to encourage *like* with a following
clause—perhaps partly because, unlike *appear* and *seem,*
which would have the same meaning, *look* cannot be followed
by *that* and a noun clause, and *like* seems a more convenient
alternative than *as if* or *as though.* At any rate, *it looks like*
must be accepted as capable of being followed by a clause.
However, *as if* and *as though* are also standard and natural with
look, and I advise using them rather than *like* in formal expression: *It looks as if it's going to rain; It looks as though we
won't be able to go.*

She looks like I did at her age and *She acts like she wants to be admired*, identified as errors in the first paragraph of this discussion, would actually be perceived as errors by only a few. *She looks like Mary used to*, with the subjective case following *like* not apparent, would be perceived as an error by fewer. Many other prepositions, such as *after*, can be conjunctions; why not let *like* be one, when so many well-educated people occasionally use it as one? There is no good reason, except a reason that for the purposes of this book must be considered sufficient. The use of *like* as a conjunction has become a shibboleth among the critical few, and they condemn it very strongly—at least whenever it does not get by them. Hence I advise avoiding the usages in the two examples, and also being a little wary of the *it looks like* construction discussed in the preceding paragraph.

She looks as I at her age and *He eats as an animal* are standard uses of ellipsis; the verbs in the clauses after *as* have been left out, which is permissible and often desirable. But these examples are not English. I have seen such sentences in manuscripts, and I think they must result from excessive fear of *like*; they are hyperurbanisms, committed by writers who do not trust their ears. Ellipsis does often suit the ear after *as*, as in *I had never seen as brave a man as he*, but it does not in the examples. All of us mistrust our ears once in a while, and when we ponder a grammatical point for any length of time, mumbling alternative phrasings, our ears lose their sensitivity. When in doubt about the propriety of *like*, one can use *as* but supply a verb, either the appropriate one or a form of *do*, which should make such sentences as the examples English again: *She looks as I did at her age; He eats as an animal does.* However, these sentences now show the effort that has gone into them. *She looks like me at her age* is far better and is also impeccable grammar. *He eats like an animal* is also far better, and is certainly acceptable as idiom.

linking verb   a special kind of **intransitive verb** that links its subject to a **complement**. In *The cat seems nervous*, the verb *seems* links *The cat* to the adjective *nervous*. In *He became president*, the verb *became* links *He* to the noun *President*. The most common linking verb is *be*, as in *The cat is gray*, but there are many others, such as *appear, remain,* and *grow*. Almost all can be used in other senses in which they are not linking verbs, but when they express some kind of being, seeming, or becoming, they are linking verbs.

Linking verbs are not complete in themselves (as are other

intransitive verbs: *He slept*) but require another word or phrase to complete their meaning, somewhat as a **transitive verb** requires an object to complete its meaning. But the complement of a linking verb is not an object; it should be in the subjective rather than the objective case: *The culprit was he*, not *The culprit was him*. There are idiomatic exceptions to this rule, especially in **expletive** constructions such as *It's me*; see Rule 1-6.

I feel badly is an error because *feel* is functioning as a linking verb in the sentence, and the pronoun *I* should not be linked with the adverb *badly*; see Rule 1-22. *I feel bad* is correct, linking the pronoun to an adjective—unless, of course, *badly* is actually meant to be an adverb, as in *I feel badly since my stroke and can no longer pick locks*, in which *feel* is not a linking verb.

literally   means *actually* or *without exaggeration*. In careless writing and speech it often has the opposite meaning—*figuratively*—or has no meaning at all beyond a vague and unnecessary intensification. *He was literally floored* and *He was literally caught red-handed* are misuses unless he actually collapsed on the floor and his hands were actually red. *He was literally flabbergasted* is a misuse because *flabbergast* doesn't have a true literal meaning; all *literally* does in the sentence is intensify *flabbergasted*, which is intense enough as it stands. Often *literally* actually weakens an expression instead of strengthening it.

Literally should be saved for contexts in which it indicates that an expression is intended in its literal rather than its figurative sense: *He was literally insane with anger and had to be confined in a psychiatric hospital; When the bride threw the groom rather than her bouquet down the stairs, the bridesmaids below were literally crushed.*

loan vs. *lend*   *Loan* is primarily a noun, *lend* only a verb. *Loan* has long been accepted as a verb, and the past-tense form *loaned* is much more common than *lent*. I advise using *loan* only as a noun and using *lend* and *lent* as verbs, just as a minor nicety.

long-drawn-out vs. *long, drawn-out*   The established phrase is *long-drawn-out*, as in *He made a long-drawn-out apology.* The phrase *long, drawn-out* seems more and more common and makes about the same sense, but is likely to be perceived as an error by those who are familiar with the older phrase.

malapropism   *Malapropos,* from a French phrase, means *inappropriate.* In his play *The Rivals* (1775), Richard Sheridan invented Mrs. Malaprop, who constantly and amusingly confuses somewhat similar words—for example, *allegory* and *alligator.* A malapropism is such a confusion. More loosely, a word that is not confused with another but is simply used inappropriately can be called a malapropism. The word **aggravate** may have been a malapropism when it was first used to mean *annoy,* about two centuries ago; now it is merely a questionable usage, and eventually it may be entirely acceptable. Malapropisms invite derision, and though sometimes the language evolves to accommodate them, it doesn't usually do so rapidly enough to benefit those who originate them.

may   See *can* vs. *may.*

mechanics   The mechanics of a language are the various principles and conventions that make it work—that make it more than a succession of independent words. In this book, Chapter 1, on grammar, Chapter 2, on punctuation, and Chapter 3, on miscellaneous matters such as capitalization and conventional uses for quotation marks and italics, are concerned with mechanics. Some of the mechanics of English, such as spelling, are not covered in the book. Chapter 4, on diction and composition, is largely concerned with matters that go beyond mechanics.

metaphor   a figure of speech in which something is spoken of in terms of something else, as in *Love is a shy flower. He sails close to the wind* is a straightforward statement if the context is sailing, but is a metaphorical statement if the context is business ethics. Metaphors are useful and often effective, but can be overused; see the discussion of figurative diction in Rule 4-11.

The metaphor should not be confused with the **simile,** which is similar but makes an explicit comparison: *Love is like a shy flower.* The term *metaphorical* is often misused to characterize any figurative diction. *When I said I almost fainted, I was not being metaphorical* is an error; *I almost fainted* may be **hyperbole** but is not metaphor. *I was not exaggerating* would be correct.

modifier   a word, phrase, or clause that modifies another word, phrase, or clause. Adverbs and adjectives are obvious modifiers, but the term is broad and includes phrases and clauses that have adverbial or adjectival functions; see **adjective** and **adverb**. Modifiers should not dangle without something to modify; see Rule 1-21.

momentarily can mean either *for a moment*, as in *He paused momentarily*, or *in a moment*, as in *The game will resume momentarily*, but the second usage is widely criticized. I advise bowing to the critics and using it only to mean *for a moment*.

mood The mood of a verb indicates whether the verb's sentence or clause concerns a matter of fact (the **indicative mood**), expresses possibility (the **subjunctive mood**), or is a command (the **imperative mood**). Sometimes the word *mode* is used instead of *mood*. See the discussion preceding Rule 1-17.

more, most *More* is a comparative form and *most* is a superlative form. If they are used with adjectives or adverbs that are already comparative or superlative, they are redundant. They are rarely misused when the words they modify are clearly comparative or superlative, as in *Truth is more stranger than fiction*, but even the well-educated sometimes misuse them with words such as *preferable*, which is not a comparative but does imply comparison. *Both usages are acceptable, but the first is more preferable* is an error, though correct uses of *more preferable* can exist: *Fame he considered preferable to riches, and honor more preferable still.*

Most should not be used to make a superlative out of an adjectival compound modifier that includes the word *well*, as in *the most well-known painter* and *the most well-respected lawyer*. Either *most* should be dropped and the modifier itself made superlative, as in *the best-known painter*, or the modifier should be stripped of *well*, as in *the most respected lawyer*. Similarly, *more* should not be used to make a comparative out of a modifier that includes *well*; *more well-known painter* and *more well-respected lawyer* should be *better-known painter* and *more respected lawyer*.

more important vs. ***more importantly***, ***most important*** vs. ***most importantly*** I advise using only *more important* and *most important* to introduce a sentence or clause, because those who condemn *more importantly* and *most importantly* do so very strongly. But the issue is not simple. Very often prejudices against specific usages arise from an excessively simple and rigid conception of grammar, but in this case one would expect to find simple and rigid critics on the other side of the argument.

An adverb can be a **sentence modifier,** as in *Fortunately, it did not rain,* and there is no reason why such an adverb cannot itself have an adverbial modifier, as in *Less fortunately, there was an attack by killer bees.* However, the function of a sentence-modifying adverb is in a way more adjectival than adverbial—it does not modify an action or a quality, as adverbs usually do, but a statement or the meaning of a statement, which can be thought of as a thing. Therefore, when there is a choice between using an adjectival form and using an adverbial form to modify an entire sentence, the adjectival form may be preferable.

More importantly is an adverb-plus-adverb combination very commonly used to modify entire sentences: *More importantly, we forgot to bring the beer.* But there is a choice with *more importantly;* the adverb-plus-adjective form is also common: *More important, we forgot to bring the beer.* This can be considered elliptical for *What is more important, we forgot to bring the beer.* In fact, there is lexicographical evidence that *what is more important* occurred in the language first, then *more important,* and finally *more importantly;* perhaps some of the prejudice against *more importantly* results from a feeling that *more important* is short for *what is more important* and that *more importantly* is merely a corruption. (Of course, all new usages are corruptions.)

Other combinations could defensibly drop the *ly* too—for example, *Less fortunate, there was an attack by killer bees* is acceptable—but I am not aware of any prejudice against *less fortunately.* Note that the *ly* is never dropped when the adverb can be read as modifying a verb in the sentence, as in *Less frequently, we hold our celebrations indoors,* in which *Less frequently* can be considered to modify either *hold* or the whole sentence.

Less importantly draws the same criticism as *more importantly. Importantly* is sometimes used alone as a sentence modifier—*important* is not, which is a point that anyone who is criticized for using *more importantly* might ask the critic to explain—but many find this use objectionable, as I do myself; somehow when it is not modified by *more* or *less* it seems to be a self-important jab in the reader's or listener's ribs.

more than, less than   When used with numbers, *more than* often implies that a considerable number will follow and *less* *than* often implies that a modest number will follow; see *several* **vs.** *a few.* *Less than* is sometimes used when *fewer than* is preferred; see *fewer* **vs.** *less.*

more than one   can take a singular verb, even though it is logically plural; see the discussion of subjects that look plural but may be singular in Rule 1-11.

Ms., Mrs., Miss   The title *Ms.*, which is not a true abbreviation but nevertheless usually has a period, has been in use for several decades in business correspondence to address a woman whose marital status is unknown. It is currently associated with feminism, because, like *Mr.*, it does not indicate marital status. Many women do not like it. It was often used archly, making it a sneer rather than a courtesy, in the early 1980s when I wrote the first edition of this book; I think in the 1990s it rarely has such overtones. However, I advise not using it for a woman whose marital status is known unless it is the woman's own preference. It should not, of course, be used with the husband's name: *Ms. John Brown* is pointless.

Mrs. should ordinarily not be used with a woman's given name; it can be thought of as meaning *wife of. Mrs. John Smith* is correct; *Mrs. Mary Smith* is not. However, a divorced woman may prefer *Mrs. Mary Smith* if she has retained her former husband's surname.

Mrs. should not be used with a maiden name or another name that a woman uses professionally and that is not her husband's name. If Mary Smith is an actress married to John Brown, she is Mrs. Brown but Miss Smith. Not just actresses but a great many women in the professions and business prefer to keep the name their colleagues know them by.

No title at all should be used if *Mr.* is not used for men in the same context. *The committee included John Brown, George Smith, and Miss Jane Jones* (or *Mrs. James Jones*) is discriminatory; if Brown and Smith don't need a tip of the hat, neither does Jones. Referring to a woman by her last name alone was formerly considered rude in most contexts and still bothers some people, but it is preferable to empty or unwanted courtesy.

music   For use of italics and quotation marks with the titles of musical compositions, see Rules 3-20 and 3-21.

myself, yourself, himself, herself, ourselves, themselves   These are reflexive or intensive pronouns; see **pronoun.** They should

369

not be used when ordinary pronouns will do. *She invited my wife and myself to dinner* has a hoity-toity flavor that is quite objectionable. Sometimes *myself* seems to be used because the speaker is not sure whether *I* or *me* is correct and thinks *myself* is safe.

neither . . . nor   See *either . . . or, neither . . . nor.*

nicknames   Quotation marks are sometimes used to enclose nicknames but are usually unnecessary; see Rule 2-26.

nominal   A word or group of words that functions as a noun in a sentence. Nouns themselves are nominals. In *His smiling at her suggested what he thought,* the gerund phrase *His smiling at her* is a nominal, acting as the subject of the verb in the sentence, and the clause *what he thought* is a nominal, acting as the object of verb. The term *substantive* means the same thing.

none   a pronoun that often means *not one* and is treated as a singular, as in *None of the men has retired.* However, it can also mean *not any* and be treated as a plural, as in *None of the trees in the forest are deciduous.* Often it can take either a singular or a plural verb with no significant change in meaning.

nonrestrictive   See **parenthetical construction.**

no one, nobody   These are singular pronouns and should not be the antecedent of a plural pronoun such as *their,* as in *No one clapped their hands.* The prohibition can be troublesome; see Rule 1-12.

nor   See *or* vs. *nor.*

no sooner . . . than vs. ***no sooner . . . when***   Since *no sooner* is a comparative construction, *than* must be used; *when* is incorrect. *No sooner had I hung up when the phone rang again* should be changed to *No sooner had I hung up than the phone rang again,* or else *No sooner* should be replaced by *Hardly* or *Scarcely,* which are not comparative and can be followed by *when.*

   No sooner did I hang up the phone than it rang again seems a questionable use of tenses to me, though I have not seen the usage criticized. *Did I hang up* is in the past tense—a variation on the usual past-tense form, *I hung up*—and thus in the same tense as *it rang again.* The sentence actually says, even if it may not quite mean, that the hanging up and the ringing again were simultaneous, which would seem to justify the same tense for the verbs. Perhaps I prefer the past perfect *had I hung up* because it admits that the hanging up and the ringing weren't quite simultaneous.

not often permits ambiguity, because, like other adverbs, it can be positioned in various places in a sentence and there can be more than one word available for it to modify (see Rule 1-20). *He was not imprisoned because of his beliefs* could mean either that his beliefs saved him from imprisonment or that he was imprisoned for some reason other than his beliefs. Negative statements of any complexity should always be examined closely; it may require considerable thought to make them entirely unambiguous.

not . . . but an **antithetical construction,** used to distinguish a negative element from a positive one. Often the negative element is set off with commas, as in *He went to college, not to play football, but to get a degree.* However, I advise omitting the commas in most cases; see Rule 2-7.

I did not bring but twenty dollars, in which *but* means *only*, is incorrect because it is a **double negative.** *I brought but twenty dollars* is correct, though quaint.

not only . . . but also a pair of phrases used as a **conjunction,** as in *Not only the students but also the principal was bored.* Note that the verb agrees with the subject after *but also*, not with the subject after *not only*; see Rule 1-11. Usually *also* can be omitted. Often the phrases are misused or mispositioned in a sentence, violating the principle of **parallel structure;** see Rule 1-5. For punctuation with the phrases, see Rule 2-7.

noun one of the **parts of speech;** a word that names a person, place, or thing. The thing named may be quite insubstantial; *truth* and *hallucination* are nouns. A primary function of nouns is to serve as subjects and objects in sentences. In *John ate fish in Japan*, the noun *John* is the subject of the verb *ate*, the noun *fish* is the object of the verb, and the noun *Japan* is the object of the preposition *in.* A noun in the **possessive case** functions as an adjective; in *John's trip*, the possessive noun *John's* modifies *trip.* Most nouns not in the possessive can also serve as adjectives, simply by being placed before another noun, as in *Bush proposal, California wine,* and *fish dinner.* However, excessive use of nouns as adjectives should be avoided; see the discussion of abstract diction in Rule 4-11. Strings of adjectival nouns modifying the same noun, as in *hard science replacement teacher shortage problem discussion* can be very difficult to read; see the discussion of adjective + noun and noun + noun adjectival compounds in Rule 2-36.

Noun phrases and *noun clauses* are so called not because they contain nouns—often they do not—but because they function as nouns. *His speaking so fast suggested he was nervous* contains the noun phrase *His speaking so fast,* acting as the subject of the verb *suggested,* and the noun clause *he was nervous,* acting as the object of the verb.

Proper nouns are those that name a specific person or place, such as *John* and *Japan,* or certain other specific things, such as *U.S. Senate, Ford Motor Company,* and *Nobel Peace Prize.* Proper nouns are capitalized.

Common nouns are all other nouns—those naming things, such as *fish, district,* and *peace.* Common nouns are not ordinarily capitalized, but when a common noun is used as part of a phrase with a proper noun, it is capitalized, as in *District of Columbia.* See also **generic** and Rule 3-12.

number in grammar, an **inflection** that indicates whether a word is singular or plural. The number of a verb and its subject should agree; see Rule 1-11. The number of a pronoun and its antecedent should also agree—a rule frequently broken, as in *Everyone clapped their hands;* see Rule 1-12.

numbers The treatment of numbers in written material is often inconsistent or otherwise faulty. A basic problem is when to spell out a number and when to use figures for it; see Rules 3-1 to 3-5. The plural of a number in figures usually requires no apostrophe; see Rule 3-6. Inclusive numbers joined by a hyphen or en dash are often misused, as in *from 1890–93;* see Rule 3-7. For other problems with numbers and hyphens, see Rule 2-37.

object a word, phrase, or clause in a sentence that is affected by the action of a verb in the sentence or by a preposition. In *The man with her writes books,* the pronoun *her* is the object of the preposition *with* and the noun *books* is the object of the

372

verb *writes.* Many verbs can have both a direct object and an indirect object; in *I gave him money,* the noun *money* is the direct object of *gave* and the pronoun *him* is the indirect object. The indirect object has a prepositional relationship to the verb, even though the actual preposition, which is usually *to* and sometimes *for,* does not appear. If the indirect object is separated from the verb, there is a preposition and what was an indirect object becomes its object: *I gave money to him.*

object complement   a noun or adjective that follows the object of a verb to complete the meaning. In *We elected him chairman,* the noun *chairman* is an object complement; in *The crash made him rich,* the adjective *rich* is an object complement. An object complement modifies a noun or pronoun, so it cannot be an adverb; see Rule 1-22.

objective case   the case of a noun or pronoun that is being used as the object of a verb or preposition. Only a few pronouns have a distinctive **inflection** for the objective case: *me, him, her, us, them, whom,* and *whomever.* Other pronouns and all nouns have the same form in the objective case as they have in the **subjective case.** Nevertheless, since the inflected pronouns are very common, mistakes are frequent; see Rules 1-6 to 1-9.

obligated* vs. *obliged   *Obligated* suggests duty, as in *I was obligated to finish writing the book. Obliged* suggests either constraint, as in *I was obliged by my tax situation to sell my stamp collection,* or gratitude, as in *I was obliged to the IRS for its mercy.* These past participles are sometimes confused, though confusion is rare with the base verbs, *oblige* and *obligate;* to *oblige* means to do someone a favor or force someone to do something, whereas to *obligate* means to make someone feel indebted or duty-bound.

of* vs. *have* or *'ve   *If you'd given me the figures earlier, I'd of been better prepared* is an example of a common error in writing. The word *of* is pronounced very much like the contraction *'ve* but should not be substituted for it; in the example, *I'd of* should be *I'd've* (see Rule 2-30). A novelist may sometimes use *of* instead of *'ve* in dialogue to indicate a contraction that is drawled or pronounced in a drawn-out way, but many readers doubtless suspect the novelist does not know better.

off vs. off of   *Off* is sufficient by itself: *He jumped off the roof; Please get this tick off me.* An added *of* is superfluous and should be avoided in all but casual speech and writing, but it is not wrong and may suit the cadence of a sentence: *How much money did you make off of that deal?*

one or two   can take a singular verb, as in *One or two has lost his place,* even though the plural *two* is closer to the verb; see the discussion of subjects joined by *or* and *nor* in Rule 1-11.

onetime vs. one-time   *Onetime* means *former* or *formerly,* as in *a onetime baseball player* and *a onetime great baseball player.* It is a contraction of *at one time,* just as **anytime** is a contraction of *at any time. One-time* indicates a single time or occasion rather than two or more, as in *Smith has won the trophy twice, but Jones is only a one-time winner.*

only   is frequently placed carelessly in a sentence so that it is not clear what it modifies; see the discussion of adverbs in Rule 1-20.

onto vs. on to   *Onto* is a preposition, as in *The key fell onto the sidewalk* and *He added the tax onto the bill.* It can usually be replaced by either *on* or *to: The key fell on the sidewalk; He added the tax to the bill.* Occasionally it cannot be replaced: *The bird watchers had unknowingly wandered onto the test site.*

On to is an adverb followed by a preposition, as in *We drove on to the gas station,* in which *on* modifies the verb *drove* and *to* is a preposition with the object *gas station.* Misuses can cause misreading. *We drove onto the bridge* means that we began to cross the bridge; *We drove on to the bridge* means that we continued driving until we reached the bridge.

Hang on and *hold on* are phrasal verbs (see under **verb**), combining a verb with an adverbial preposition. Thus *hang on to* and *hold on to* are almost always preferable to *hang onto* and *hold onto.* When *onto* seems preferable to *on to,* as in *She hung onto his words* and *He held onto his convictions,* it is likely that *onto* simply means *on* or *to: She hung on his words; He held to his convictions.*

or vs. nor   In some constructions, both *or* and *nor* are correct: *He cannot read or write; He cannot read nor write.* The second example, which is actually elliptical for *He cannot read, nor* *can he write,* no longer sounds natural unless special emphasis is intended for the word after *nor,* as in *He will not withdraw nor reduce his demands.*

In a **correlative** construction, *or* should be used after *either* and *nor* should be used after *neither: He refuses either to withdraw or to reduce his demands; He can neither read nor write.*

organization   in composition, the relationship and order of ideas. Some basic principles of organization are discussed in Rules 4-4 and 4-5.

out* vs. *out of   *Out* is sometimes sufficient by itself. In *He threw it out the window,* an added *of* would be superfluous, though it would not be wrong, and sometimes a sentence may benefit from the unstressed syllable. However, *of* is often required, as in *He drew the money out of his pocket* and *He made money out of that deal. Out of,* unlike *off of,* is not too casual for general or even formal writing.

parallel structure, parallelism   grammatical similarity between elements in a sentence or in a passage that play similar roles within the sentence or passage. For example, in *He liked swimming and sailing,* the two words *swimming* and *sailing,* joined by *and,* have similar roles because they are both objects of the verb *liked,* and they are grammatically similar because both are gerunds. In *He liked swimming and to sail,* the gerund *swimming* and the infinitive *to sail* still have similar roles, but they are not grammatically similar; the sentence is not, strictly speaking, faulty grammar, since both *He liked swimming* and *He liked to sail* are grammatically correct, but it is faulty parallelism. For parallel structure within a sentence, see Rule 1-5; see also the discussion of **elegant variation** in Rule 4-11.

parentheses   position of with other marks of punctuation, Rule 2-18. See also the discussion preceding Rule 2-18.

parenthetical construction   a construction used not to identify a word or phrase but merely to provide further information about it. A construction within parentheses is, of course, parenthetical; in *John (who won the tournament) is smiling,* the **relative clause** *who won the tournament* is a parenthetical construction. Instead of a pair of parentheses, a pair of commas or a pair of dashes can be used to set off a parenthetical construction: *Mary, who won the tournament, is smiling; Mary—who won the tournament—is smiling.* Parenthetical constructions are often called nonrestrictive, because they do not restrict the meaning of the words they modify. In *The woman who won the tournament is smiling,* the clause *who won the tournament* is no longer parenthetical; it is a **defining construction**, restricting the meaning of the word *woman.* Proper punctuation often depends on determining whether a construction is parenthetical or defining; see Rule 2-1.

participle   a form of a **verb** that is used as an adjective and in compound tenses of verbs. The present participle ends in *ing. The drinking man is laughing* contains the participle *drinking,* used as an adjective to modify *man,* and the participle *laughing,* used with the **auxiliary verb** *is* to form the present progressive tense of the verb *laugh.* The past participle usually ends in *ed,* but many common verbs form the past participle irregularly. *The elated man has drunk too much* contains the past participle *elated,* used as an adjective to modify *man,* and the irregular past participle *drunk,* used with the auxiliary verb *has* to form the present perfect tense of the verb *drink.*

Participles are versatile forms. Sometimes they have all the effect of a full clause, as in *He had an accident going home,* in which *going home* means *while he was going home.* Sometimes they seem to act as adverbs, as in *He didn't want to go staggering home,* in which *staggering* seems to modify *go,* describing the manner of the man's going rather than the man himself, and grammarians must come up with various ingenious ways of justifying their acceptability—for example, *go staggering* might be considered a special compound tense of the verb *stagger* that uses *go* as an auxiliary verb, or the usage might just be given an imposing name, such as *participle of attendant circumstance.* Fluent users of the language seem to use such constructions faultlessly and do not have to worry about what to call them.

Not all forms that look like participles are participles. In *The man drinking from the bottle should pay for more than the drunk portion,* the words *drinking* and *drunk* are participles. But in *The drunk man has been having a drinking bout,* the word *drunk* is not a participle but an ordinary adjective, and the word *drinking* is not a participle but a gerund. The man is not drunk in the sense that a bottle is drunk, he *is* drunk; the bout is not drinking in the sense that a man can be drinking, it is a bout *of* drinking.

When the present participle is used as an adjective, it is active in relation to the word it modifies: *an annoying man.* When the past participle is used as an adjective, it is passive in relation to the word it modifies: *an annoyed customer.* Thus the tense of an adjectival participle is primarily an indicator of active or passive rather than an indicator of time. However, the present participle does indicate time that is the same as the time of the main verb in the sentence, and the past participle with an auxiliary verb, as in *Having annoyed everyone, the man left,* does indicate time that is previous to the time of the main verb; see Rule 1-15. Loose use of the present participle to indicate action just before that of the main verb, as in *Crossing the room, he went out the door,* should be avoided; see Rule 1-16.

A *participial phrase* is an adjectival phrase (see **adjective**) that is based on a participle. *Diminishing in the distance, the road leading to the foothills seemed endless* contains the participial phrases *Diminishing in the distance* and *leading to the foothills,* both modifying *road.* Participial phrases are sometimes misused or misplaced in a sentence so that it is not clear what they modify; see Rule 1-20. Note that in *The guide advised following the road,* the phrase *following the road* is not a participial phrase; *following* is not a participle but a gerund, and the phrase is used not as an adjective but as a noun, the object of the verb *advised.* Also note that the *ing* form of a verb in a prepositional phrase, as in *We were committed to following the road,* has to be a gerund rather than a participle, because a preposition needs a noun—or something like one, such as a gerund—as an object; see **preposition.**

If a participle used as an adjective does not have anything to modify, it is a **dangling construction.** *Trudging toward the foothills, the road seemed endless* begins with a dangling participial phrase. See Rule 1-21.

parts of speech   Words are traditionally divided into eight parts of speech: **adjective, adverb, conjunction, interjection, noun, preposition, pronoun,** and **verb.** Some grammarians consider the interjection merely a special kind of adverb, and others consider *the* and *a* (or *an*) to be not just adjectives but a separate part of speech, the **article,** so the count may vary from seven to nine.

These classifications are accurate only when they are used to categorize a specific word in a specific sentence, because many words can be more than one part of speech. They actually characterize not a word itself but the relationship the word has to other words in a sentence. Thus the word *dog*, ordinarily thought of as a noun, can easily escape that classification; *dog food* uses it as an adjective, *dog her footsteps* uses it as a verb, and *dog-tired* uses it as an adverb.

passive voice   See **voice.**

perfect tenses   tenses of a verb used to indicate that the action of the verb has been completed—that is, has been perfected. They are **compound** tenses.

The *present perfect* indicates that the action is complete now, and it uses the present-tense form *has* or *have* (often contracted to *'s* or *'ve*) as an **auxiliary verb,** as in *He has arrived.* In older English, *is* or *are* was used as an auxiliary verb with an **intransitive verb,** as in *He is arrived*, and this usage survives in a few expressions, such as *The time is come.*

The *past perfect* indicates that the action was completed at some time previous to the time of some other verb in the sentence or passage, usually a verb in the past tense (see **tense**), and it uses the past-tense form *had* (often contracted to *'d*) as an auxiliary verb, as in *He had arrived when I arrived.* The past perfect is used less frequently than it once was but sometimes is essential or desirable; see Rule 1-14.

The *future perfect* indicates that the action will be completed at some future time and uses the future-tense form *will* along with *have*, as in *He will have arrived by the time I arrive.* Sometimes one of the auxiliary verbs is contracted: *He'll have, He will've.* Sometimes both are contracted: *He'll've. He will've* and especially *He'll've* look somewhat odd in print but are correct.

Fluent users of the language have little trouble with these forms in sentences that are in the **indicative mood,** as are all the examples. In response to *Where's Mom?* a child may say either *She went downtown* or *She's gone downtown*, but won't say *She's gone downtown an hour ago;* children understand when either the past tense or the present perfect tense will do and when only one will do, though in more complicated sentences they may occasionally use the simpler past when the present perfect or past perfect would be better, as in *Mom said* *to tell you she went downtown.* Fluent users do make errors in sentences in the **subjunctive mood;** see Rule 1-14.

period   the mark that ends a declarative sentence. In an interrogatory sentence the question mark replaces the period; in an exclamation the exclamation point replaces the period. A true period—that is, one that indicates a full stop, the end of a sentence—should not be used with the comma, semicolon, colon, dash, question mark, or exclamation point, but may be used with a closing parenthesis or bracket (see Rule 2-18) or with a closing quotation mark (see Rules 2-23 to 2-26).

The period that indicates an abbreviation, as in *Mr. Smith* and *Smith & Co.*, is not a true period; it is more properly called a point. Such a point can occur with all the marks of punctuation except the period itself. When an abbreviation with a point ends a declarative sentence, the single point serves both purposes; it is not doubled. I have been seeing such doubled points in manuscripts in recent years—perhaps writers who in early drafts have treated certain details inconsistently, for example by using both *Co.* and *Company*, are using their word processors to replace all instances of the full word with the abbreviation, resulting in doubled points when the full word is replaced at the end of a sentence.

The three points that indicate omissions and pauses are not true periods either but **points of ellipsis;** see Rules 2-27 and 2-28.

permanent compound   a compound word that is common enough to be found in dictionaries, such as the compound nouns *high school*, *place-name*, and *schoolteacher* and the compound adjective *well-known*. See also **temporary compound.**

person   in grammar, the form of a pronoun or a verb that indicates who is making the statement and whom it is being made about. *I am* contains a subject and verb in the first person; *you are* contains a subject and verb in the second person; *he is* contains a subject and verb in the third person. *We are* and *they are* are plural forms for the first and third persons. *You are* is the same in the singular and the plural; the singular form *thou art* was once standard.

A subject and its verb should agree in person (Rule 1-10), and a pronoun and its antecedent should agree in person (Rule

1-12). This agreement is so basic a part of the language that errors are rare, but they do occur.

phrasal verb, phrasal preposition, phrasal modifier   a verb, preposition, or modifier that is a phrase rather than a single word. *Phrasal verb* sometimes specifically means a combination such as *run down* in *Don't run down your colleagues*, in which *down* is not a preposition but an adverb that changes the meaning of the verb. In *Don't run down the corridors*, the verb *run* has its usual meaning and *down* is a preposition, so in this sentence *run down* is not a phrasal verb. Such grammatical terms are used more loosely by some writers on grammar than by others. *Window-shop* could be called a phrasal verb. Sometimes a verb in a compound tense (see **compound**), such as *have gone*, is called a phrasal verb, since with its **auxiliary verb** it forms a phrase; it is more likely to be called a verb phrase.

Out of and because of are common phrasal prepositions. A construction such as *in view of* is more likely to be called a prepositional phrase. *Out-of-order motion* uses the prepositional phrase *out of order* as a phrasal modifier; *run-down neighborhood* uses the past participle of the phrasal verb *run down* as a phrasal modifier. For advice on hyphenation of such modifiers, see the discussion of adjectival compounds that are prepositional phrases and the discussion of participle + adverb compounds in Rule 2-36.

place-names   capitalization of, Rules 3-17 and 3-18

plural   The **number** of a noun, pronoun, or verb can be either singular or plural. Problems of **agreement** in number can occur between subject and verb, often because it is not immediately apparent whether the subject is singular or plural; see Rule 1-11. Problems of agreement also occur between pronoun and antecedent; see Rule 1-12. Plural and possessive forms are often confused, especially when a plural is also a possessive; see Rule 2-29.

Plurals of lowercase letters usually require an apostrophe for clarity (*p's and q's*), but plurals of figures do not (*1900s*); see Rule 3-6.

An English noun typically forms its plural by adding *s* or *es*, but there are many exceptions, and sometimes more than one form is correct; when in doubt, use the dictionary to determine the correct or preferred form. One item not covered in dictionaries: A proper noun ending in *y*, such as *Mary*, does not form its plural as do common nouns ending in *y*—that is, by changing the *y* to *i* and adding *es*—but simply by adding *s*, as in *Last night there were four Marys at the party*. There are some exceptions, such as *the Rockies* and *the Ptolemies*. There are also a few common nouns ending in *y* that merely take *s*, such as *flybys*; these are likely to be in dictionaries.

When a possessive form used as a noun, such as *McDonald's* (the fast-food chain), is made plural, we usually pronounce the form with an *es* added—*McDonald'ses*—but this looks peculiar in writing. *There were two McDonald's on the same block* is acceptable. I advise against *McDonald'ses* unless there is some point in indicating pronunciation, as in dialogue. In most writing the problem can be avoided somehow: *There were two McDonald's restaurants*.

plus   The voguish use of *plus* to replace *and in addition* or some similar phrase, as in *They gave him a raise, plus he got a corner office*, is somewhat objectionable even in casual conversation, at least to my ear. English has many conjunctions and conjunctive constructions; it rarely needs to borrow *plus* from the chaste language of mathematics, which uses it so precisely, and corrupt it. Phrases such as *principal plus interest* are, however, acceptable, since they make use of the mathematical sense of the word. I frequently use phrases such as *apostrophe plus s* and *adverb + adjective* in this book; this borrowing of *plus* is conventional among writers on language. Perhaps we started the vogue that we now condemn.

point   the dot used as a **period** and for some other purposes, particularly to indicate abbreviations. *Point* can also mean any mark of punctuation, especially in Britain.

points of ellipsis   the three points—or four points, if a period is included—used to indicate omissions in quoted material and pauses in speech. See Rules 2-27 and 2-28.

political divisions and subdivisions   capitalization of, Rule 3-17

possessive case   the case of a noun or pronoun that possesses something else in the sentence. It is sometimes called the *genitive case*; the term *genitive* is somewhat broader than the term *possessive*, and in fact the case is used to show more than possession. Even the possession it expresses can be quite vague; although *John's hat* indicates simple ownership, *John's* *block* would usually indicate not that John owns the block but merely that he lives on it. *The dog's master* uses the possessive for the possessed rather than the possessor. *The doctor's discovery* would usually mean that the doctor discovered something and would be called a subjective genitive; in the case of Dr. Livingstone it would probably mean that H. M. Stanley discovered the doctor and would be called an objective genitive. *He is writing a children's book* uses the genitive of purpose; the children don't own the book, at least not yet, but it is being written for them. In many other possessive constructions the idea of possession is similarly far from simple ownership.

Nouns and some pronouns, such as *anyone*, typically form the possessive by adding an apostrophe plus *s* in the singular and just an apostrophe in the plural, but there are many complications and exceptions; see Rule 2-29. Some pronouns have distinctive possessive forms—*my, your, his, her, our, its*, and *their* and also some special forms discussed in the next paragraph.

The possessive case normally turns a noun or pronoun into an adjective, since the possessive noun or pronoun modifies the thing possessed, as in *the hamburger's aroma* and *his hamburger*. However, a special kind of possessive called an *independent possessive* functions like a noun, as in *My hamburger fell into the fire, so I ate John's,* in which *my* is an ordinary possessive pronoun but *John's* is the object of the verb *ate*. In the example, *John's* can also be thought of as short for *John's hamburger*, but the idea of the independent possessive is handy to explain the special forms that some of the personal pronouns have to indicate it: *mine, yours, hers, ours, theirs.* (These forms are also used as adjectives in sentences with a linking verb, such as *This house is hers.*) Note that the independent possessives do not have an apostrophe. Fluent speakers of English use them effortlessly and faultlessly, but in manuscripts I occasionally see the forms *your's, her's, our's,* and *their's*; they indicate a somewhat shaky understanding of the conventions of written English, though they were standard in past centuries. For more information on the independent possessive, see Rule 1-19 and the discussion of disagreement in case in Rule 1-12.

The preposition *of* can often replace the possessive case: *the government's role, the role of the government; the man's name, the name of the man.* However, when *of* is used, the possessive case often can be or must be used too: *John's friend, a friend of John's; my friend, a friend of mine.* (Note that it is apparent

382

from the last example, *a friend of mine*, that the possessive is like the independent possessive discussed in the preceding paragraph; *of* could not have an ordinary possessive such as *my* as its object.) This so-called double possessive is difficult to explain. One reason it has developed is that the word *of*, just like the possessive case, can express more than possession, but the relationships that *of* can express and those that the possessive case can express do not always overlap. (This explains why pairs such as *moment's thought* and *moment of thought* can have identical meanings; in the first the possessive *moment's* expresses the genitive, and in the second *of* expresses the genitive, but the genitives are of different kinds.)

One of the relationships that only *of* can express is the so-called partitive genitive, as in *some of the butter* and *slice of cake*, and another is a type of the so-called attributive genitive that describes what something is made of, as in *crown of gold*; it is obvious that possessive forms would not work in these phrases. In some situations, these exclusive functions of *of* would intrude, were it not for the double possessive, when some kind of ownership is intended—perhaps disturbingly, as in *a cake of the cook*, which carries the possible but unintended meaning that the cake is part of the cook or is made of the cook. To make it clear that ownership of some kind is intended, the possessive case is used along with *of*: *a cake of the cook's*. (Of course, the possessive case can be used without *of* if the possessive form is in the normal adjectival position, as in *the cook's cake*.) In many other situations, the special meanings of *of* do not intrude and the double possessive is not used. For example, *the arrival of the cook* cannot be *the arrival of the cook's*. Another reason that the double possessive has developed is that it sometimes makes a distinction in meaning. *His portrait* could mean either a portrait of him or a portrait owned by or perhaps painted by him. However, *a portrait of him* and *a portrait of his* separate these meanings; *of him* is an objective genitive and *of his* is a possessive genitive.

The double genitive seems to be used less often than formerly when it is considered optional, as in *Smith is an old friend of President Bush*. No unwanted meaning of *of* intrudes in the example. However, *Smith is an old friend of him* is not English; with personal pronouns we use the double possessive even when no unwanted meaning of *of* intrudes. I prefer to retain the double possessive in most optional situations and would make it *Smith is an old friend of President Bush's*. If the meaning is not that the President actually has Smith as a friend but merely that Smith has long felt friendly toward the President, who may not even know him, the possessive *Bush's* is not quite appropriate—Smith may own the President in a sense, but the President doesn't own Smith in that same sense, though one might argue that he unknowingly owns Smith because Smith feels friendly toward him. Since the possessive case and *of* both permit a variety of meanings, sentences that employ them can often be interpreted in a variety of ways, and the best course may be to recast the sentence and make its meaning unmistakable: *Smith and President Bush are old friends* if the friendship is reciprocal, *Smith has long felt friendly toward President Bush* if it is not.

precipitate vs. **precipitous**   *Precipitate* means *sudden* or *hasty*, as in a *precipitate decision*. *Precipitous* means *steep*, as in *a precipitous path*. The words are often confused, partly because suddenness and steepness can amount to the same thing and sometimes either word will do, as in *precipitate drop in value* and *precipitous drop in value*.

predicate   the part of a sentence or clause that expresses what is predicated—that is, set forth or asserted—about the **subject** of the sentence or clause. The predicate includes the **verb** and also any **object, modifier,** or **complement** of the verb. In many simple sentences in which the words are in the usual order, such as *The boy came slowly into the room*, everything that follows the subject, in this case *The boy*, is the predicate. In *Slowly into the room came the boy*, the usual order of words is altered and the predicate precedes the subject. In *The boy bearing the crown came slowly into the room*, the participial phrase *bearing the crown* modifies *The boy* and thus is part of the subject rather than part of the predicate. However, in *The boy came slowly into the room, bearing the crown*, the participial phrase *bearing the crown* modifies the verb *came* rather than *The boy*—it doesn't define the boy but adds more information about his coming into the room—and thus is part of the predicate. In *The boy, bearing the crown, came into the room*, the commas around the participial phrase make it apparent that it does not define the boy but just adds information about his coming into the room, and so again it is part of the predicate. In *The boy who was bearing the crown came into the room*, the relative clause *who was carrying the crown* defines the subject, *The boy*, and thus can be considered part of it. In *The boy, who was bearing the crown, came slowly into* *the room*, the relative clause still modifies the subject, but it does not define it, and so it can be considered a separate statement, neither part of the subject nor part of the predicate. If this effect of the commas is puzzling, see the discussion of defining and parenthetical constructions in Rule 2-1.

A *compound predicate* contains two or more verbs that have the same subject, as in *He sleeps too much and works too little.* Usually the elements of a compound predicate should not be separated by a comma; see Rule 2-3.

predicate appositive, predicate complement unfamiliar names for familiar constructions such as those in *He ended the day ruler of all he surveyed* and *He came home tired*, in which *ruler of all he surveyed* and *tired* describe the subject of their sentences but are not joined to the subject by a **linking verb,** as they are in *He was the ruler of all he surveyed* and *He was tired.* See also **appositive** and **complement.**

predominant vs. predominate *Predominant* is the adjective, and *predominate* is the verb. Therefore *predominantly*, not *predominately*, is the adverb. *Hardwoods predominate in the eastern woodlands; Hardwoods are predominant; The trees are predominantly hardwoods.* Historically, *predominate* was the adjective, and the verb *predominate* appeared later, but the adjective *predominate* and the adverb *predominately*, though accepted in modern dictionaries, are considered errors by many.

prefixes and suffixes Prefixes are added at the beginning of a root word; *unkind* has the prefix *un*, added to reverse its meaning. Suffixes are added at the end of a root word; *kindness* has the suffix *ness*, added to the adjective *kind* to make it a noun. Most common prefixes and suffixes combine solidly with the root word, but some require a hyphen; see Rules 2-31 to 2-33.

preposition one of the **parts of speech;** a word used to indicate direction, motion, or position or some logical or conceptual relationship. A preposition always has an object—which is a noun or pronoun or some construction acting as a noun, such as a gerund—and it relates that object to some other word in the sentence, usually a noun or verb. In *He went to France*, the preposition *to* relates its object, the noun *France*, to the verb *went.* In *The man in tweeds is English*, the preposition *in* relates its object, *tweeds*, to the noun *man.* There are

385

many prepositions in English; common ones include *with, without, for, against, on, under, between, of, during, among, through, by, above, below, after,* and *before.* There are also many compound prepositions, such as *far from, close to, out of,* and *because of.*

Some words that are prepositions can also act as a **conjunction.** *He bowed before me* uses *before* as a preposition, with the object *me; He appeared before I did* uses *before* as a subordinating conjunction, joining the clause *I did* to the rest of the sentence. Note that when *before* is a preposition, its object is in the objective case; see Rule 1-9.

Some words that are prepositions can also act as an **adverb.** *The ship beat up the coast* uses *up* as a preposition, with the object *the coast; The bosun beat up the mate* uses *up* as an adverb, modifying the verb *beat*—at a glance, *the mate* may look like the object of *up,* but actually it is the object of the verb-plus-adverb combination *beat up,* a **phrasal verb.** When a word that is usually a preposition does not have any apparent object, it is an adverb: *Let's see what turns up; Darkness closed in; The food ran out.* In *He got through by cheating, through* is an adverb and *by* is a preposition; *through* has no object, but *by* has the object *cheating.* In *He got by through cheating, by* is an adverb and *through* is a preposition.

A *prepositional phrase* is a phrase including a preposition, its object, and any modifiers of the object. A preposition can't ordinarily stand alone but has to be part of a prepositional phrase, since a preposition requires an object. However, the prepositional phrase can be elliptical, as in *That's the drawer I put it in;* without ellipsis, the sentence is *That's the drawer that I put it in* or *That's the drawer in which I put it,* with the pronoun *that* or *which* serving as object of *in.*

Note that it is permissible to end a sentence with a preposition, despite a durable superstition that it is an error. *He showed me where to stand at* is an error, but not because the preposition *at* is at the end; *at* shouldn't be in the sentence at all.

Prepositional phrases usually have adverbial or adjectival functions and sometimes can act as a noun. *Before breakfast is the time for prayers in the monastery* uses *Before breakfast* as the subject of the sentence (the usual function of a noun), *for prayers* to modify the noun *time* (the usual function of an adjective), and *in the monastery* to modify the entire sentence (one of the usual functions of an adverb). They often modify entire sentences as introductory constructions, as in *In view of the foregoing, please disregard our previous letter*. Adverbial and adjectival prepositional phrases are often carelessly positioned, making it unclear what they modify; see Rule 1-20.

presently   can mean either *soon* or, just as one would expect, *at present*. Some object to the *at present* meaning, though it has been in use for five centuries. See also **momentarily**, supposed misuses of which seem to raise more hackles.

progressive tenses   tenses of a **verb** used to indicate ongoing action and sometimes future or intended future action. They are **compound** tenses, combining the present **participle** and some form of the verb *to be* as an auxiliary. *I am attending college now* uses the *present progressive* to indicate ongoing action; *I was attending college then* uses the *past progressive* to indicate past ongoing action. *I am leaving tomorrow* uses the present progressive to indicate future action; *I had to pack, because I was leaving the next day* uses the past progressive to indicate action that was in the future at the time indicated by the main clause, *I had to pack*. Progressive **perfect tenses** can be formed: *I have been attending college for a year; I had been attending college for a year when the war began; I will have been attending college for a year when you graduate from grammar school*.

Progressive tenses of the verb *to go* are used with the infinitives of other verbs to indicate the future, as in *I'm going to pack* and *I was going to pack but I was interrupted*.

The progressive tenses cause those who learn English as a second language much trouble; they are unsure when the ordinary present and past tenses should be used and when not. Fluent speakers seem to have little trouble, though children are likely to simplify *I'm going to tell on you* to *I'm telling on you*.

pronoun   one of the **parts of speech;** a word that represents a noun. There are several types of pronoun.

Personal pronouns are *I, you, he, she, it, we*, and *they*, along with their possessive and objective forms—*my* and *mine* for the possessive, *me* for the objective, and so on. *Intensive pronouns* are special forms of personal pronouns used to add emphasis. In *John himself is going*, the pronoun *himself* is intensive.

Reflexive pronouns are the same as intensive pronouns in form but are used differently. In *John selected himself*, the pronoun *himself* is reflexive.

Reciprocal pronouns include *each other* and *one another;* they express a reciprocal, or returned, relationship, as in *They loved each other.*

Relative pronouns include *who, whom, whose, which,* and *that* when these words are used to introduce a **relative clause.** In *the man who selected himself,* the pronoun *who* is relative. Most relative pronouns also have indefinite forms (see below).

Interrogative pronouns include *who, whom, whose, which,* and *what* when these words are used to introduce questions, including indirect questions. In *I wonder who was selected,* the pronoun *who* is interrogative.

Indefinite pronouns include *someone, anyone,* and *one; either* and *each* unless they are adjectives; and the relative pronouns *whoever, whomever,* and *whichever.* They are called indefinite because it cannot be definite what they represent. *All* and *everyone* can be considered indefinite pronouns.

Demonstrative pronouns include *this, that, these,* and *those.* When these words are used as modifiers, as in *this book,* they are not pronouns but demonstrative adjectives.

Some pronouns, unlike nouns, have different forms for the **subjective case** and **objective case,** and some indicate the **possessive case** by changing form rather than adding apostrophe plus *s* or apostrophe alone, as nouns do. Mistakes in case are frequent; see Rules 1-6 to 1-9. A pronoun that is the subject of a verb should agree with the verb in **person** and **number;** see Rules 1-10 and 1-11.

If a pronoun has an **antecedent,** it should agree with the antecedent in person, number, and **gender;** see Rule 1-12. Often the meaning of a pronoun is unclear because there is more than one grammatically possible antecedent in the sentence; see Rule 1-13.

A pronoun can itself be the antecedent of another pronoun, as in *She blames herself.* However, a possessive pronoun, unless it is an independent possessive such as *mine* (see **possessive case**), functions as an adjective and thus cannot be the antecedent of another pronoun; see Rule 1-19.

proper noun   a noun that names a specific person, place, or thing and that is capitalized. *John, Boston,* and *Texaco* are proper nouns; *man, city,* and *corporation* are common or **generic** nouns. Exact definitions of the terms differ; some dictionaries limit it to nouns that cannot logically take a limiting modifier such as *this* or the articles *a* and *the,* but this rules out such nouns as *Christian* (derived from the proper noun *Christ*) and allows *France* to be a proper noun but not, apparently, *the United States*. A broader definition is more serviceable: Any noun that is customarily capitalized can be considered a proper noun, including common items identified by trademarks, such as *a Ford*. In addition, within a given piece of writing, any noun or noun phrase that the writer chooses to capitalize to indicate that it has a specific rather than a general meaning can be considered a proper noun. For example, *the Chairman of the Board* and similar titles are apt to be capitalized in a company's reports to stockholders.

The question of whether a given noun is proper or generic can therefore be restated. In practice, the question is merely whether or not to capitalize a given noun, which is covered in Rules 3-12 to 3-18.

provided* vs. *providing As conjunctions meaning *if* or *on the condition that*, both are now accepted by most dictionaries: *We'll raise your salary, provided you retire next month; We'll raise your salary, providing you retire next month. Providing* is nevertheless considered incorrect by many. It could be called a dangling construction, because in form it is a present participle and has nothing to modify—that is, nothing that can serve as its subject—when it means *if*. I advise using the past-participle form *provided*. Certain other present participles, such as *considering* and *regarding*, are similarly used and must be accepted because they cannot be replaced by past participles; see Rule 1-21.

punctuation the subject of Chapter 2; see the introduction to the chapter and Glossary/Index entries for the individual marks of punctuation.

quantum in physics, a unit of energy, such as the tiny amount of energy abruptly lost or gained by an electron in its change from one orbit or state to another. The special quality of a quantum is that it seems to be indivisible; there is no such thing as a fractional quantum. The term is commonly misapplied to mean a large change, as in *His rise from twenty-sixth to third in the seedings was a quantum leap.*

question mark often incorrectly used after indirect questions; see Rule 2-20. When it occurs with other marks of punctuation its position is always logical; see Rule 2-21.

quotation marks   used for direct quotations but not indirect quotations; see Rule 2-23. When a closing quotation mark is used with another mark of punctuation, its correct position may violate logic; see Rule 2-24. With certain exceptions, single quotation marks should be used only within double quotation marks; see Rule 2-25. Quotation marks can be used to set off unfamiliar terms, nicknames, and words used in a peculiar way, but this use can be overdone; see Rule 2-26. They are conventionally used to set off the titles of short stories, songs, and some other works; see Rule 3-21.

raise vs. rise   *Raise* is a **transitive verb** and hence has an object, as in *He raised the cup to his lips. Rise* is an **intransitive verb** and hence has no object, as in *He rose from his chair. Raise* is frequently misused for *rise*, as in *He raised to one elbow. He raised himself to one elbow* is correct, since the reflexive pronoun *himself* is provided as an object for *raised.*

reason is because   a common redundancy; it should be replaced by *reason is that.* The redundancy is particularly likely to occur when the elements of the phrase are separated, as in *The reason for the error may be partly because the redundancy seems to add emphasis,* but it is not rare even in the simplest sentences. Some accept it as an idiom. However, it is one of half a dozen or so expressions that the critical keep a constant lookout for, so I advise never using it.

redundancy   unnecessary repetition of meaning, as in *consensus of opinion,* which means simply *consensus.* Sometimes it constitutes a grammatical error, sometimes it is merely undesirable, and sometimes it is defensible. The term is often loosely used for phrases that are not actually redundant but merely wordy, such as *at the present time* for *now* and *a sufficient number of* for *enough.* Both redundancy and wordiness are discussed in Rule 1-4.

reflexive pronoun   See **pronoun.**

relative clause   a clause that begins with a relative pronoun, though the pronoun may not actually appear in the clause but be understood. *He is the man who robbed the bank* contains the relative clause *who robbed the bank. He is the man whom they arrested* contains the relative clause *whom they arrested;* as is frequently the case when the relative pronoun is the object rather than the subject of the verb in its clause and the clause is a **defining construction** rather than a **parenthetical construction,** the relative pronoun can be omitted: *He is the man they arrested.* However, such grammatically permissible omissions are not always desirable; see Rule 1-3.

Since a relative clause begins with a relative pronoun (whether actually present or understood), and since a relative pronoun cannot have as its **antecedent** anything but a noun or pronoun or some construction playing the role of a noun, a relative clause has the function of an adjective—it modifies the antecedent of the relative pronoun. Therefore relative clauses are often called adjectival clauses (see **adjective**).

Certain indefinite pronouns such as *whoever* are usually considered relative pronouns but cannot have an antecedent. It is moot whether clauses formed with such pronouns can be considered relative clauses. In *Whoever robbed the bank, they arrested the wrong man,* the *Whoever* clause doesn't relate to anything and certainly isn't adjectival. Such a clause can be considered an **absolute construction.**

restrictive   see **defining construction.**

retained object   the object in a passive sentence, such as *me* in *The letter was given me by him.* See **voice.**

reverend   the word is merely an adjective, like *honorable.* When it is used as a title of courtesy for the clergy, the proper forms are *the Reverend John Smith, the Reverend Mr. Smith,* and *the Reverend Mr. and Mrs. Smith.* The abbreviation *Rev.* can be used in any of these forms. The article *the* is required. *Dr.* can replace *Mr.* if the cleric has a doctoral degree, and in some churches *Fr.,* meaning *Father,* can replace *Mr.* Sometimes *Reverend* is modified: *Right Reverend* for a monsignor and in some Protestant denominations for a bishop, *Most Reverend* for an archbishop and a Roman Catholic bishop, *Very Reverend* for a dean.

Improper forms include *Reverend John Smith* (with no *the*), *the Reverend Smith, the Reverend,* and *the Reverend and Mrs. Smith.* They are probably used much more often than the proper forms. The improper forms are not new; in fact, in previous centuries *reverend* was used as a title in the same way *doctor* is, and the current correct forms are based on the relatively recent codification of forms of address in Great Britain. Furthermore, many members of the clergy do not object to

Reverend Smith or other improper forms, and some of them use these forms themselves. I advise using the current correct forms except in fictional dialogue; very few real people are careful to use the correct forms.

revision   an important step in composition, discussed in Rules 4-9 to 4-13. Revision can be harmful or overdone; see the discussion preceding Rule 4-9.

run-on sentence   See **comma fault.**

self-deprecating **vs.** *self-depreciating*   See *deprecate* **vs.** *depreciate.*

semicolon   a mark of punctuation that has functions similar to those of the comma but is stronger. It often either can be or should be used to separate independent clauses; see Rules 2-12 and 2-13. It is also often needed to separate items in a series when some of the items already contain commas; see Rule 2-14. Unlike the comma, the semicolon is positioned logically when it is used with a closing quotation mark; see Rule 2-24.

sentence   a group of words that begins with a capital letter and ends with a period, a question mark, or an exclamation point. Less evasive definitions are hard to defend; see the discussion preceding Rule 1-1. Some basic principles of good sentences are explained in Rules 1-1 to 1-5. For a discussion of types of sentences and sentence structure, including definitions of simple, compound, and complex sentences and parenthetical, defining, and introductory constructions within sentences, see Rule 2-1.

Sentences can be classified as declarative, interrogative, exclamatory, and imperative.

sentence modifier   an **adverb** that modifies everything else in its sentence, or sometimes everything in one clause in the sentence, rather than just a specific word or phrase. In *Unfortunately, the Red Sox won,* the adverb *Unfortunately* is a sentence modifier; it doesn't modify *won*—that is, it doesn't describe the manner in which the Red Sox won—but instead expresses a feeling the speaker or writer has about the whole statement. An adverbial phrase that begins a sentence is usually a sentence modifier, though often it can be understood either as a sentence modifier or as a verb modifier without any significant difference in meaning. In *After the sixth inning, the*

Yankees folded, it doesn't matter whether the adverbial phrase *After the sixth inning* is considered to modify *the Yankees folded* or just *folded*; the meaning is the same. Usually the term *sentence modifier* is used not for adverbial phrases, which very often modify whole sentences, but for single adverbs, which more often have specific words to modify and need a term to describe them when they do not.

Sentence modifiers typically come just before the sentence or clause they modify, but they can also be well buried in their sentences. *The season was nevertheless terrific* buries the adverb *nevertheless*, but the adverb modifies the whole sentence, not just the verb *was* or the adjective *terrific*. The sentence-modifying adverb in the example also acts as a buried **conjunction,** joining the thought of the sentence to some preceding sentence.

A sentence modifier is by nature a **parenthetical construction,** since it does not define anything in its sentence, and it is therefore usually set off by commas or other marks of punctuation (see Rules 2-1 and 2-5). It does not always have to be set off; in *The season was nevertheless terrific* and similar sentences in which its role is clear without parenthetical commas, adding commas may give it more emphasis than is desired. *The season was, nevertheless, terrific* may seem inappropriately measured and stately.

In a sentence with two or more clauses, a sentence modifier may be intended to modify only one clause, but faulty punctuation, faulty sentence structure, or both together may make it seem to modify more, as in *A moment later he left the room and reappeared only after dinner*, which would benefit from a comma after *room* and benefit still more from insertion of *he* after *and*; see Rule 2-3.

Adverbs that specify human feeling, such as *unhappily*, make somewhat illogical sentence modifiers, because a sentence itself is not animate. *Unhappily, the Red Sox won* could draw criticism; we would say that the Red Sox's winning was unfortunate, but we would not say it was unhappy. In a sense, *Unhappily* in the example is like a **dangling construction;** it has nothing appropriate to modify. This nicety is often violated as words evolve and expand their meanings; for example, the adjective *unhappy* can be applied to inanimate nouns, as in *unhappy occasion*, and no one would criticize the application. Similar freedom with adverbial sentence modifiers also generally goes unnoticed. But be very leery of one particular word: *hopefully.*

393

serial comma   the comma as used in a series of words, phrases, or clauses, such as *men, women, and children* and *He went, he saw, and he conquered.* A comma before *and* or another conjunction in a series of three or more items—the so-called final serial comma—avoids several problems; see Rule 2-6. A series of adjectives may or may not need to be separated by commas; see the discussion of adjective chains in Rule 1-20.

several **vs.** *a few*   *Several* suggests a considerable number, whereas *a few* suggests a modest number, even though the actual number may be the same. A woman with four things to do before she can leave her office is likely to say *I have several things to do, so I'll be home late* if she expects them to take a long time but *I have a few things to do, but I should be home early* if she expects them to take a short time. Though *a few* and *several* are not rigidly bound by their respective implications—in fact, they could be transposed in the examples without seeming odd—they should not be made to contradict their implications. I occasionally see *several* oddly used, as in *There were only several men among the women in the audience.*

Quite a few, of course, suggests an even more considerable number than *several* does.

sexism   The English language is conspicuously sexist in two principal ways: The word *man* occurs as a suffix in many long-established nouns denoting functions, titles, and occupations, such as *chairman*; and the masculine pronoun in the third person singular has for centuries been used when the antecedent could be either masculine or feminine, as in *Everyone has to live his own life.*

From the 1970s on, principles of sexual equality—which are hardly new to the world, but have in these years been widely and strongly expressed—have put pressure on the sexist features of English. English has bent, has flexed back and forth, continues to bend. As the 1990s begin, the flexing seems to have produced a bend away from sexism that may be permanent, to the degree that any language or the culture that employs it can be permanent.

Some words can have the word *woman* as a suffix, and nothing prevents replacing *man* with *woman* in almost any word, though *postwoman* and *radiowoman* do not please every ear. But many of those who object to sexism in language are far from satisfied by coinages of words of explicitly feminine gender. They would prefer gender to be removed from most words, because they believe the feminine gender indication is often patronizing or disparaging. They have a point. *Usherette* uses the diminutive suffix *ette* to indicate gender, suggesting a cute little thing. *Poetess* adds the *ess* feminine suffix to a word that can indicate either sex as it stands (the word *poet* actually comes from a Latin feminine, *poeta*). *Woman photographer*, *lady photographer*, and *girl photographer* add a modifier as if the noun would inevitably be taken as masculine unless so modified and seem to express a little surprise—why is the woman taking pictures instead of keeping house? Many object to *male prostitute* and *male nurse*, which are just backhand versions of the forehand slam *female doctor*. Some object even to *masseuse*, *heiress*, and *actress*, which are usually found in contexts in which gender is important. Perhaps some object to *empress* and *goddess*, in which the feminine endings are unlikely to have a belittling effect.

Often a noun ending in the suffix *man* can be replaced by another noun or compound that has no apparent gender. Thus, for example, *letter carrier* has largely replaced *postman*. *Radio operator* has very often replaced *radioman*. (Latin-derived words such as *operator* are actually masculine but have long been used for both sexes, though in a few cases the Latin feminine forms have been absorbed into English: *testatrix*, *aviatrix*.) A sometimes more troubling solution, using the word *person* as a suffix, seems to have worked for some words; for example, *chairperson* has become common (even though *chair* meaning one who presides has been available in the language for more than three centuries). New coinages such as *committeeperson* have begun to lose their abrasive unfamiliarity, and some may become genuine English words. It does seem questionable whether these genderless words really avoid sexism at present—they refer frequently to women but less frequently to men, and hence they can be perceived as indications of gender.

The pronoun problem has been even more troublesome. The careful use of *he or she, him or her, his or her*, and *himself or herself* is one solution. The three-word compound pronouns are no longer so troubling to eye and ear as they were a decade ago. But they are not a graceful solution when they must be repeated again and again in a passage. In addition, some have pointed out that for genuine equality *he or she* should be alternated with *she or he*—but *she or he* is still surprising and therefore graceless. A few writers alternate *he* and *she* as lone pronouns, writing *Every student must see his adviser monthly* and then a sentence or so later *A student who is failing must see her adviser weekly*; this is a poor solution, because even in the 1990s readers expect any lone feminine pronoun to have an explicit antecedent and will look in vain for one.

The most common and usually least conspicuous solution to the pronoun problem is to evade it by making any genderless word that will become the antecedent of a pronoun plural, so that *they, them, their*, and *themselves* can be used. This solution can be clumsy and is often a considerable strain on the writer, since not only do some common words, such as *anyone*, have no plural form (see Rule 1-12 for a discussion of the problems this causes), but a singular rather than a plural noun may be much more appropriate to the thought of a passage. Avoiding the problem in this way leads to annoying inconsistencies in number, because a much-repeated noun (such as *writer* in this book) must then be presented sometimes as a singular and sometimes as a plural, depending on whether pronouns are involved—unless, of course, the singular is ruled out completely, which is likely to be more annoying than the inconsistency.

I have known many writers, none of them male chauvinists as far as I could tell and some of them women, who were incensed at the idea that anyone would deny them the convenience of using the privileges that the masculine pronoun has enjoyed for centuries in English and its root languages, would require them to choose some imperfect alternative. Any solution to the gender problem causes some trouble—and the obligation to find some solution is the greatest trouble of all. It forces speakers and writers to keep the issue of sexual equality always in their consciousness, no matter how remote the issue from their subject.

But consciousness and unconsciousness are at the root of the problem of sexual inequality. It is undeniable that the language, like the cultures in which it has developed, is sexist, and that those who use it, both men and women, are sexist. Until recently, we—both men and women—spent little time thinking about sexism in language or in our culture; when we were conscious of it, we were complacent about it if male, resigned to it if female, and monkeying with the language was all but unthinkable. Now we are forced to think about sexism. Like many other men and many women as well, I do not like to be forced to think about it—but I must admit that the commotion about gendered nouns and personal pronouns has made me more aware of the pervasiveness of discrimination and less sexist in my own behavior and thinking. Quibbles about specific gendered words may be trivial, but the spirit behind the quibbles is not; the spirit should be respected, and during this period when both language and culture are changing in the direction of sexual equality, even the quibbles must be taken seriously.

Actually, in the years since I wrote this discussion for the first edition of this book, the language does not seem to have suffered greatly. Japes such as "So let's change *manhole* to *personhole* and *craftsman* to *craftsperson*" have died out; they trivialized the harm that antisexism poses to the language and merely pointed up the hidebound and language-reinforced discrimination that antisexists want to eliminate. The language has survived and will survive, has and will show grace under the antisexist pressure.

How careful should we be to avoid sexism in language? I think we should be very careful—but also careful not to let avoidance of sexism excessively distort our expression or distract a reader or listener. The line is a fine one, and it changes.

When I wrote the first edition of this book, the sexist conventions of English had already been under attack for several years, but they remained dominant in general writing; alternatives to them not only had all the shortcomings I have noted above but still annoyed a great many readers. Consequently I elected to retain the sexist conventions. In particular I routinely used masculine pronouns when the antecedent could be either masculine or feminine: *Each writer or speaker must consider his readers or listeners and devise his own policy.* I did this because I judged that the nature of the text required it. In many sentences I was forced into *or* constructions, especially *writer or speaker* and *readers or listeners*, as in the example, and I did not want to have to stir *his or her* into such sentences. I did not want to avoid the compound pronoun by using plurals, because I felt that the book was concerned with a matter essentially singular—each person's use of language. *Writers and speakers must devise their own policies* seemed—and still seems—comparatively weak and diffuse to me.

When I was revising the book in 1989 and 1990, I modified my judgment—as I advise anyone who is still sticking to the sexist conventions to do. I believe that readers of the 1990s are likely to find *he* with an indefinite antecedent at least as glaring and troublesome as readers of a decade ago found *he or she.* Only rarely have I retained the sexist diction of the first edition—a reader who wants to examine these instances and judge whether I should have avoided them too can find a few in Rules 4-5 and 4-8, and there are perhaps half a dozen others in the book.

I fear that some of the hundreds of changes I have made in the diction of the first edition have slightly weakened my expression. However, surprisingly often I found that in removing the sexism I could strengthen my expression, for the chore, tedious as it was, focused my attention in productive ways.

I also feel a kind of resentment. I was forced by the times to make these changes, to adopt diction that still annoys many readers (to whom I apologize). I do not like being forced—I do not like having to observe this new and pervasive stricture of good English. But then my book is full of strictures that I urge on my readers, and it is only fair that I, for whom the traditional strictures are for the most part second nature, experience a bit of the resentment some of these strictures may arouse.

In any case, I do not resent the principle of sexual equality and its current vitality. I have heard some large doubts expressed. Does the antisexist impulse in English presage a kind of Orwellian Newspeak in which evident truths, such as the existence of two sexes in the species, are ignored or denied? Is the blurring of sexual roles that the antisexist pressure on English presumably reflects an indication that our culture has become old, tired, epicene? Well . . . who knows? I am hopeful that our culture will survive for some time, and I am certain that our language will accommodate rather than obstruct its evolution.

shall* vs. *will An elaborate distinction was once made between these two forms. To express merely the future, *shall* was used in the first person (that is, with *I* and *we*) and *will* was used in the second and third persons (with *you, he* and *she,* and *they*). To express necessity or determination, *will* was used in the first person and *shall* in the second and third persons. The negative contraction of *shall* was *shan't,* which is very rare today. *I shall probably stay up late; I'm tired but I will keep going until I finish. You will probably turn in early, but you shall give me a hand first, or I shan't be able to finish.*

Will has almost completely displaced *shall* in American English. Very few Americans sense the distinction, and very few ever use *shall* except in questions, as in *Shall we go?* It is still used in contracts and other legal documents, in which it does quite properly express compulsion or obligation but is perceived by most of us as just another lawyerly stiffness: *In such circumstance the property shall revert to Mortgagee.* The British also often use *will* where their writers on grammar prescribe *shall*. Many decades ago, the famous usage arbiter H. W. Fowler and his brother devoted twenty pages to the subject in *The King's English*, beginning their discussion by noting that only southern Englishmen used *shall* and *will* properly and that their usage was so complicated that "those who are not to the manner born can hardly acquire it."

Those who do use *shall*, perhaps admiring its archaic flavor, may misuse it, as in *You shall probably turn in early.* This merely seems a little stilted to most of us, but to well-educated English people and to Americans who do feel the distinction between *shall* and *will*, such a misuse is gross; it suggests the speaker or writer is ill-educated and laughably pretentious. Even in England, *will* is acceptable where *shall* was once pre-scribed, but *shall* where *will* is prescribed is wrong both there and here.

should   *Should* and *would* once followed, and in Britain sometimes still follow, the same rules as *shall* and *will*. Thus in Britain, *The headmaster told me I should be a rich man someday* means that the headmaster said to me, "You will be a rich man someday." Americans use *would* instead of *should* in such sentences regardless of person. We do, like the British, use *should* in all persons to mean *ought to*, as in *The headmaster told me I should study more* and *I told the headmaster he should get off my back.*

Both we and the British also use *should* in all persons as an **auxiliary verb** to express future conditions, as in *If I should oversleep, please wake me* and *If fire should break out, leave the building immediately*, but we much more often use the present tense of the verb—*If I oversleep; If fire breaks out*—unless we intend to imply that the future condition is highly unlikely. When *should* is used in an *if* clause, *would* is usually preferable to *will* in the following clause: *If fire should break out, the building would go up like timber.* Sometimes *will* is preferable: *If I should oversleep, my wife will wake me.* See also the discussion of *were* in future conditional clauses in Rule 1-17.

simile   a figure of speech in which something is said to be like something else, as in *Love is like a shy flower.* See **metaphor.**

simple sentence   a sentence that has only one clause, unlike a compound sentence (see under **compound**), which has two or more independent clauses, or a **complex sentence,** which has at least one dependent clause. Simple sentences may actually be quite complicated; see Rule 2-1.

simplistic   means *excessively simple* or *oversimplified*, as in *His simplistic theory ignored several inconvenient facts.* It should not be used to mean merely *simple;* simplicity is often a virtue.

since   See *as* for *because* or *since.*

singular   The **number** of a noun, pronoun, or verb can be either singular or **plural.** Problems of **agreement** in number can occur between subject and verb, often because it is not immediately apparent whether the subject is singular or plural; see Rule 1-11. Problems of agreement in number also occur between pronoun and antecedent; see Rule 1-12.

slant, slash   a **diagonal;** see Rule 2-38.

so . . . as   See *as . . . as* vs. *so . . . as*

solecism   an error in grammar. The word is derived from Soloi, an ancient Greek colony whose inhabitants eventually developed their own dialect of Attic Greek.

solidus   a **diagonal;** See Rule 2-38.

someone, somebody   These are singular pronouns and should not be the antecedent of a plural pronoun such as *their,* as in *Someone forgot to wipe their shoes.* The prohibition can be troublesome; see Rule 1-12.

sometime vs. *some time*   See *anytime, sometime.*

sort   See *kind.*

spelling variants   This book does not deal with incorrect spelling; anyone in doubt about the spelling of a word should consult a dictionary. However, sometimes more than one spelling of a word is correct, and a choice has to be made.

American dictionaries of desk size and larger often give two spellings of the same word: *honor, honour; civilize, civilise; connection, connexion; judgment, judgement; leaped, leapt; offense, offence; theater, theatre; program, programme; traveler, traveller; gray, grey.* Each dictionary has some way of indicating which spelling it considers primary, as explained in the dictionary's introduction; usually the spelling given first is primary. Often the secondary spelling is one common in Great Britain and its current and former possessions, but uncommon in the United States. There is little point in using any spelling but the primary one. Some people consider British spellings chic, like British haberdashery, but such spellings are apt to be perceived as amateurish or pretentious if the writer is American.

Toward, backward, and some other words ending in *ward* are often heard and seen with an *s: towards, backwards.* The *s* is not wrong, and probably almost all Americans use it in both speech and writing some of the time. Many American book, magazine, and newspaper editors routinely take the *s* out—which is justifiable, except in carefully reported or composed dialogue, because very few Americans always use the *s;* their inconsistent use of it is unnoticed in speech but is apt to be noticed in writing, and such small inconsistencies are better avoided.

Simplified spellings such as *thru* and *tho* are acceptable only in casual notes. Some others, such as *cigaret* and *employe,* have been pushed by major newspapers and magazines but have failed to displace older spellings; they are correct, in the sense that dictionaries include them, but they annoy many readers. A few, such as *omelet* and *catalog,* are accepted and have become at least as common as the longer spellings.

split infinitive an infinitive with some interruption between *to* and the verb itself, as in *to humbly ask.* It is not a true error, though it was formerly regarded as one and is still offensive to some; see Rule 1-20.

squinting modifier a modifier, usually an adverb, that is positioned in such a way that it could be understood to modify either what precedes or what follows, as in *It was impossible completely to follow his logic.* See Rule 1-20.

Sr. See *Jr., Sr.*

style Generally the word *style* means *manner,* and style in language means the choice of diction and tone that makes one person's expression different in manner from another's. Among those involved professionally in writing, *style* also means rules and conventions for capitalization, use of italics, and other details of written English. Style in this special sense is the subject of Chapter 3.

subject a word or group of words in a sentence or clause that is responsible for the action of the verb or, if the verb is passive, is affected by the action of the verb. In *I gave him money* and *I was given money,* the pronoun *I* is the subject. A verb must have a subject, though in the imperative mood the subject is not usually expressed but understood—*Give him the money* has the understood subject *you*—and there are a few idioms with subjectless verbs (see *as follows* vs. *as follow*).

A verbal—that is, an **infinitive,** a **participle,** or a **gerund**—can be said to have a subject, though the relationship between subject and verbal is not exactly like the relationship between subject and verb. In *My giving him the money stored in the vault enabled him to satisfy his clamoring creditors,* the gerund *giving* has the possessive pronoun *My* as its subject, the past participle *stored* has the noun *money* as its subject, the infinitive *to satisfy* has the objective pronoun *him* as its subject, and the present participle *clamoring* has the noun *creditors* as its subject. A participle almost always requires a subject, since it is either an adjective that requires something to modify or else part of a compound tense of a verb; see Rule 1-21 for a few exceptions. Gerunds and infinitives often do not require a subject, since a gerund functions as a noun itself and an infinitive can function as a noun or as an adverb.

subject complement a noun, pronoun, or adjective that follows the subject of a verb to complete the meaning. It is usually connected to the subject by a **linking verb.** In *He became chairman,* the noun *chairman* is a subject complement linked to the subject, *He,* by the linking verb *became,* and in *He is rich,* the adjective *rich* is linked to the subject by the linking verb *is.* A subject complement should be in the subjective case, like the subject, and therefore *The best player is her* is an error, though certain violations of this rule, such as *It's me,* are accepted; see **complement** and Rule 1-11.

subjective case the case of a noun or pronoun that is being used as the subject of a verb. Nouns and many pronouns have the same form in the subjective case and **objective case,** but the pronouns *I, he, she, we, they, who,* and *whoever* have different forms for the objective—*me, him,* and so on—and frequently the wrong case is used for these pronouns. See Rules 1-6 to 1-9.

subjunctive mood the mood of verbs that is used to express possibility rather than actuality—that is, to express what something might be or do, should be or do, or must be or do rather than what something actually is or does. See the discussion preceding Rule 1-17.

Subjunctive forms usually look like past-tense forms of the **indicative mood.** In *Last summer I would cut the grass every Saturday,* the verb phrase *would cut* is indicative, a special compound past tense of *cut* that expresses repeated or habitual action. But in *I would cut the grass today if we had a lawn mower,* the verb phrase *would cut* is subjunctive, because it does not indicate past action but possible present or future action, and the verb *had,* which looks like the past tense of *have,* is also subjunctive—it too does not relate to the past but to an imagined present. When the intended meaning is both subjunctive and past, the subjunctive form sometimes changes and sometimes does not. In *I would have cut the grass yesterday if we had a lawn mower,* the verb phrase *would cut* changes to *would have cut* to indicate the past, but the verb *had* does not need to change—one could say that the situation expressed by its clause is imaginary and therefore not bound by time. The verb *had* can change, however; in *I would have cut the grass yesterday if we had had a lawn mower, but we didn't get one till today* it changes to *had had,* because the situation that was imaginary yesterday is not imaginary today. The wrong tense is sometimes used for the imagined-situation clause, as in *I would have cut the grass if you would have lent me your lawn mower;* see Rule 1-14.

There are certain distinctive subjunctive forms. *He holds his temper* and *He is polite* contain the indicative forms *holds* and *is; I insist that he hold his temper* and *I insist that he be polite* contain the subjunctive forms *hold* and *be,* which are the same as the form of the present infinitive. They keep this form regardless of the tense of the main verb: *I had insisted that he be polite, but he lost his temper.* In certain subjunctive constructions, *were* is used with the first person and third person singular instead of *is, am,* or *was. I am glad that I am rich and he is not* is indicative; *I would be glad if I were rich and he were not* is subjunctive. See Rule 1-17.

subordinate clause a clause that is dependent on another clause or some word or phrase in another clause; see **dependent clause.**

substantive a word or group of words that functions as a noun in a sentence; a **nominal.** A noun itself is normally a substantive, but most nouns can also be **attributive**—that is, they can function as adjectives and modify another noun, as does the noun *government* in the phrase *government job.*

such as can be followed by a subjective pronoun that is the subject of a supplied or understood verb, as in *a man such as he is* and *a man such as he,* or by an objective pronoun, as in *a man such as him.* Often it is sensible to choose the construction that agrees with the role, subjective or objective, that the preceding word plays in the sentence—*A man such as he could never be elected; No one would vote for a man such as him*—but this agreement is not required.

superlative See **comparative and superlative.**

suspension points another term for **points of ellipsis.** Their use is discussed in Rules 2-27 and 2-28.

syllepsis the use of a single word in two applications at once in such a way that the word's form is proper for one application but not for the other. (The word *syllepsis* is straight from Greek and means a gathering together; in English it means a gathering of grammatical applications.) In *He either has or will go,* the verb *go* is intended to be understood after *has* but is in the wrong tense to be so understood, since without the omission the sentence would be *He either has gone or will go.* In *I regret, and my wife too, that we cannot come,* the noun *wife* requires the third-person form *regrets.* In *He's an idiot under those fine manners and intellectual bearing,* the singular phrase *intellectual bearing* requires the singular demonstrative adjective *that.* Syllepsis is sometimes called **zeugma,** but zeugma more precisely describes use of a word in two distinct meanings. Syllepsis is sometimes permissible; see Rule 1-10 and the discussion of omission of verb forms in Rule 1-2.

syntax the arrangement of words to form sentences. The alphabetical word list *all are in made meaningful of order sentences some up words* does not make a sentence, but when these words are arranged according to syntactical conventions they do make a sentence: *All sentences are made up of words in some meaningful order.* Syntax can thus be considered word order. Syntax is one of the two basic parts of grammar; the other is **inflection,** which means change in the form of a word to indicate its meaning and function. English could get by as a language without any inflections—it very nearly does in some dialects—but it could not be a language without syntax.

Errors in syntax include failures to make elements of a sentence parallel in structure when they are parallel in meaning (see Rule 1-5) and failures to position modifiers unambiguously (see Rule 1-20).

telephone conversations One side of a telephone conversation can be difficult to punctuate; see a suggestion in Rule 2-28.

temporary compound a compound word that is formed of two or more words that ordinarily stand alone, that is not common enough to be listed in dictionaries, and that is compounded because of the role it plays in a specific sentence. *Motorboat* is a **permanent compound,** common enough to be found in dictionaries. *Small boat* is not in dictionaries, nor is it a temporary compound—it is not a compound at all but merely an ordinary noun phrase, a noun modified by an adjective. However, in the phrase *small-boat regulations*, the noun phrase has temporarily become a compound modifier; it is a temporary compound. Many compound modifiers are common enough to be listed in dictionaries, such as *well-known*, and these can be considered permanent compounds, but the language permits the formation of an unknowable number of temporary compounds, just as it permits the formation of an unknowable number of sentences.

Temporary compounds sometimes require a hyphen, as does *small-boat* in the phrase *small-boat regulations*, and sometimes do not. The principles governing hyphenation of compounds are quite complex, and usage varies considerably. See Rules 2-31 to 2-37 and the discussion preceding Rule 2-31.

tense the form of a verb that expresses the time of action of the verb. The basic tenses of a verb are present, past, and future—*I cook, I cooked, I will cook*—but there are many others; see the discussion preceding Rule 1-14. When there are two or more verbs in a sentence, often their tenses must be in an exact relationship to one another; *I arrived just as he will leave and she greets me* clearly misuses tenses. Just as often there is a choice of tenses, and sometimes the choice affects the meaning and sometimes it doesn't; see Rule 1-14.

Participles, infinitives, and gerunds have tenses, which are sometimes misused; see Rules 1-15 and 1-16.

The past tense in English is typically formed by adding *ed* to the basic verb, or just *d* if the verb ends in *e*: *cooked, served.* (If the basic verb ends in a single consonant preceded by a single vowel, the consonant is usually doubled if the basic verb has only one syllable or if its last syllable is stressed: *bat, batted, abet, abetted,* but *target, targeted.*) However, a great many verbs, including some of the commonest ones, have irregular forms for the past tense, and some have still other forms for the past participle, which is used to form other tenses: *I drink, I drank, I had drunk.* Some verbs have both a regular and an irregular form for the past: *leaped, leapt.* The verb *spit* in its more common sense has two irregular forms for the past, *spit* and *spat;* when it means *to fix on a spit,* it has the regular past-tense form *spitted.* If in doubt, consult a dictionary; when there is more than one form, a dictionary usually indicates a preference.

See also **perfect tenses** and **progressive tenses.**

than   a word used to introduce the second element of an unequal comparison, as in *John is taller than Mary.* It is always associated with a comparative modifier, such as *taller* in the example, or with one of a few other words that contain the idea of comparison, such as *different* and *differently, other, rather,* and *else.* When *than* is not associated with a comparative modifier, it is being misused, as in *Scarcely had we sat down to dinner than the phone rang,* which should be either *Scarcely had we sat down to dinner when the phone rang,* replacing *than* with *when,* or *No sooner had we sat down to dinner than the phone rang,* replacing the adverb *Scarcely,* which is not comparative, with the comparative *No sooner.*

Than is almost always a conjunction introducing a clause, even though the clause is very often elliptical. *John is taller than Mary* is elliptical for *John is taller than Mary is tall;* we would not, of course, fill out the ellipsis completely, but we would often make it *than Mary is.* Because of ellipsis, sentences with *than* are frequently ambiguous. *John praises Mary more than Jane* can mean either that John praises Mary more than he praises Jane or that John praises Mary more than Jane praises Mary. The ellipsis is not usually a problem, because the context generally makes it clear which meaning is intended. When ellipsis does cause problems, they are difficult for writers to catch, because they already know what their meaning is; see Rule 1-3.

When *than* is followed by a personal pronoun, the case of the pronoun is determined by its function in the *than* clause—that is, by whether it is subject or object. Thus *John loves money more than she* and *John loves money more than her* are different statements; when the elliptical *than* clauses are filled in, the statements become *John loves money more than she loves money* (or, in normal diction, *than she does*) and *John loves money more than he loves her*. Unfortunately, however, this explanation is too simple. In fact, *than* is often used as a preposition, followed by the objective case, as in *John is older than her*, and many modern dictionaries accept the usage. If *than* is considered only a conjunction, as many writers on usage insist it should be, *her* is obviously wrong; the partly expanded form would be *John is older than her is*. The objective case is particularly likely to be used after *than* when the first element of the comparison—that is, the one before *than*— is functioning as an object rather than a subject, as in *John has dated girls taller than her*. Logically this is incorrect; it does not mean *John has dated girls taller than he has dated her*, it means *John has dated girls taller than she is*. But there is no denying that objective pronouns are commonly found after *than* when the subjective would be required if *than* were being used as a conjunction. And careful use of the subjective case may sound quite stilted, as it does in *It's I*.

It is, of course, somewhat pigheaded to insist that *than* cannot be used as a preposition when it is so used by virtually everyone in casual speech and by most people in writing. The issue is much the same as that over use of *like*, which is officially a preposition, as a conjunction (see **like for as, as if, or as though**). Yet the intent of this book is to protect the reader from pigheaded as well as clearheaded criticism, so I advise avoiding all prepositional uses of *than* except in casual speech, and perhaps being a little careful even then. If the subjective case sounds stilted, as perhaps it does in *John has dated girls taller than she*, enough of the elliptical clause can be supplied to make it obvious that *than* is functioning as a conjunction and that the subjective case is required. Usually this means simply adding a form of the verb *do, be,* or *have.* As a happy by-product, this may prevent ambiguity and may expose inferior phrasing. *John has had older partners than her* thus becomes either *John has had older partners than she is* or *John has had older partners than she has,* depending on which is meant, and it is apparent that the word order of the first sentence can be improved: *John has had partners older than she is.* The subjective pronoun may sound stilted standing alone, but it doesn't sound stilted when a verb is provided for it.

Than whom, as in *He has dated Mary, than whom no one is taller,* is a special case. Clearly it should be *than who,* once the grammatical relationships are unscrambled—*no one is taller than she is,* with *whom* replaced by the personal pronoun appropriate for the antecedent, *Mary.* But *than whom* is correct, not just in modern dictionaries and books on grammar but in older ones as well. *Than whom* is rare, and when I see it, the context is usually somewhat arch in tone, as the example is.

than any vs. **than any other** In a comparison with *than any,* the first element is often part of the second element, as in *John has lost more at the track than any gambler in town.* If John is one of the gamblers in town, this sentence is illogical; John can't have lost more than he himself has lost. The addition of *other,* or some other qualifying word that leaves John out, makes the sentence logical: *John has lost more at the track than any other gambler in town.*

However, *other* should not appear if the second element in the comparison already has an adequate qualifier—that is, a qualifier that excludes the first element—or if the second element does not include the first element anyway. *The new chairman is ruder than any other previous chairman* has an unnecessary and illogical *other,* since *previous* excludes the new chairman. So does *Poor John has lost more in his company retirement plan than any other gambler in town;* John is apparently not one of the gamblers in town.

thankfully The word means *in a thankful manner,* as in *He wrote thankfully to his benefactor.* It is also used occasionally as a **sentence modifier,** as in *Thankfully, it did not rain.* Thus in common usage it has broadened its application, unlike, for example, *gratefully;* no one would say *Gratefully, it did not rain.* Sentence-modifying *thankfully* is occasionally condemned, since a sentence, such as *It did not rain,* cannot be thankful—it takes something animate to be that—but it has drawn nowhere near as much attention as *hopefully* (which I discuss at length). *Thankfully* does not govern the meaning of the sentence it modifies, as *hopefully* does—*Hopefully, it will not rain* is a very different statement from *It will not rain*, but *Thankfully, it did not rain* is the same statement as *It did not rain* with a modifier added to indicate the speaker's feeling about it—but in other respects it invites criticism the same way *hopefully* does. It is easy to avoid the usage, since the common adverb *fortunately*, which can be a sentence modifier, is available.

that When used as a **conjunction** to introduce a clause, as in *We hope that you will win*, the word usually can be omitted and often is better omitted, but it should not be omitted if ambiguity results; see Rule 1-3. It can also often be omitted as a relative **pronoun;** see *that* vs. *which*. Sometimes instead of being omitted it is wrongly repeated, as in *He said that after the competition was over and the winner had been announced that he would award the prize*, in which the long construction between the two appearances of *that* makes the repetition not immediately apparent; see Rule 1-4. Sometimes it is mispositioned, as in *He said after the winner had been announced that he would present the prize*, which is incorrect unless it was actually after the announcement that he said what he did.

That should not be used before a direct quotation that begins with a capital signaling the beginning of a sentence. *He said that "War is unlikely"* should be either *He said, "War is unlikely"* or *He said that "war is unlikely."* See Rule 2-23.

That as a relative pronoun can refer to a person, as in *the child that I saw.*

But that, as in *I don't doubt but that she is rich*, is questionable but nevertheless common in good writing; see *but.*

That is often used to introduce **appositive** constructions, as in *That bane of the lexicographers John Malaprop was there.* This is a defining construction, and therefore the appositive *John Malaprop* should not be set off with commas, as in *That bane of the lexicographers, John Malaprop, was there*, but much more often than not such appositives are set off. It must be admitted that such constructions can be difficult to read without the commas, but I recommend omitting the commas if their absence does not make a sentence entirely unreadable. Usually the elements of such a construction can be transposed to make the appositive a **parenthetical construction,** which is properly set off with commas: *John Malaprop, that bane of the lexicographers, was there.*

that vs. which   As relative pronouns, *that* and *which* can be kept strictly apart in their application. *Which* can be confined to introducing a **parenthetical construction,** which means using it only when a comma is appropriate preceding the construction, as in *I'm returning this book, which I enjoyed.* *That* can be confined to introducing a **defining construction,** which means using it only when a comma is not appropriate preceding the construction, as in *I'm returning a book that you lent me.* However, although *that* is indeed very rarely used for parenthetical constructions, *which* has long been used for both types, and the "rule" that it should not be used for defining constructions is merely an invention of usage arbiters who wanted to make the language neater than they found it. *I'm returning this book, which you lent me* is correct, but *I'm returning a book which you lent me* is also correct. *I'm returning this book, that you lent me,* in which *that* introduces a parenthetical construction, seems unnatural and is considered incorrect, but *that* was so used in previous centuries. A parenthetical *that* sometimes creeps in when there are two parallel relative clauses, perhaps because the speaker or writer thinks it is desirable not to use the same pronoun twice: *I'm returning this book, which you lent me and that I liked very much.* It is better to repeat *which* or omit the second pronoun entirely, if it can be omitted, as it can be in the example. In *I'm returning this book, which you lent me and which pleased me very much,* the second *which* should not be omitted, because the first *which* should not be made to serve as both the object of *lent* and the subject of *pleased;* see the discussion of omission of relative pronouns in Rule 1-2.

There is something to be said for making a strict distinction between *that* and *which*—that is, using *which* only for parenthetical constructions. The consistent use of the pronouns can add precision and clarity to expression, and it reinforces the punctuation of sentences—when there is no comma the pronoun is *that,* when there is a comma the pronoun is *which,* and the reader probably benefits somewhat from the consistency. Also, for whatever reason, some writers greatly overuse *which,* producing a rather itchy effect; *The books which last are those which reflect the cultures which produce them* is inferior to *The books that last are those that reflect the cultures that produce them,* because repetitions of *that* are less noticeable

410

than repetitions of *which*. Nevertheless, *which* occasionally may seem better for a defining construction, and it is necessary for some, as in the combination *that which*, in which *that* is a demonstrative pronoun and *which* is a defining relative pronoun; imposing the strict distinction would result in *that that*, a doubling that is not always objectionable but is objectionable when the meaning is *that which*. Also, *that* cannot be used as a relative pronoun directly after prepositions; *This is the room in that I work* is not English. *This is the room that I work in*, with the preposition following the pronoun, is correct.

That can often be omitted when it is the object of a relative clause, as is explained in Rule 1-2: *I'm returning the book you lent me*. If the relative clause is separated from its antecedent, *that* is usually desirable—*I'm returning the book, the one on economics, that you lent me*—but it is almost always better not to separate a relative clause and its antecedent in the first place, and in the example the separation is easy to avoid: *I'm returning the book you lent me, the one on economics*.

the   whether to consider part of the title of a published work, Rules 3-19 and 3-20; whether to capitalize within a title, Rule 3-22

there is, there are   See **expletive** and *it is, there is, there are.*

these kind of, these sort of   See **kind.**

this, these   *This* can be a demonstrative pronoun, as in *It rained yesterday, and this kept us from going*. Its particular usefulness is that its antecedent can be an entire preceding clause or sentence, or even an entire passage. Its use when it does have a specific word as its antecedent and is therefore merely displacing the pronoun *it* or sometimes even *he* or *she*, as in *I offered him a dollar, and this was rudely rejected* and *The headwaiter approached me, and this was a lordly man*, is sometimes criticized. However, though *this was rudely rejected* could just as well be *it was rudely rejected*, replacing *this was a lordly man* with *he was a lordly man* removes an intended irony. I advise letting *this* represent a single word when it seems to communicate something that *it* or *he* or *she* does not. *These* is similarly used, sometimes pointlessly, as in *The place was full of waiters, but these were all chatting in a corner*, and sometimes justifiably, as in *The place was full of waiters, and these were an insolent crew.*

411

Frequently *this* or *these* is necessarily used because there is no preceding word to serve as its antecedent. In *I've had bad food here before, but this is terrible,* the word *this* does not refer to *food* in the preceding clause but to some other food now being judged, and in *Waiters are often rude, and these were no exception,* the noun *Waiters* means waiters in general whereas *these* means specific waiters. In such a construction, *this* or *these* is not actually a demonstrative pronoun but a demonstrative adjective with the word it modifies understood: *this food, these waiters.*

till vs. 'til   *Till* is a word meaning *until,* and *'til* is a contraction of *until.* They are synonymous, and both are correct, but one almost never sees *'til* in print and there seems no reason to use it.

time of day   See Rule 3-5.

titles   of books, independently published poems, plays, movies, musical compositions, paintings, sculptures, and other works of art, Rule 3-20; of newspapers and periodicals, Rule 3-19; of officials, Rule 3-14; of parts of books, short stories, essays, features in periodicals, and short musical compositions and parts of longer ones, Rule 3-21

tone   the manner in which a writer or speaker addresses a reader or listener. In a spoken address, both tone of voice and choice of words affect overall tone; in writing, choice of words—that is, diction—determines tone. See Rules 4-6 to 4-8.

too   has the distinct meanings *excessively* and *also* and has a function in various idioms. In its *excessively* meaning it is sometimes used unnecessarily, and sometimes an idiom uses it illogically. *John is too pigheaded* has an unnecessary *too; too* pigheaded for what? *John is too pigheaded to give in* is a better use. *He was too dishonest to be a judge* cannot do without the *too* because the idiom requires it, but taken literally the sentence implies that some degree of dishonesty is acceptable in a judge, which the writer may not believe. The idiom has to be accepted, but *His dishonesty made him unfit to be a judge* would be more precise.

In its *also* meaning, *too* is often set off with commas, as in *You, too, are an Aries.* Parenthetical constructions are generally set off with commas, and *too* is essentially parenthetical in the example. However, an overriding principle of modern punctuation is to use none when it performs no helpful function and cannot be heard when the sentence is spoken. I advise not setting off *too* unless setting it off is helpful in some way. *You too are an Aries* is smoother.

trademarks   should be capitalized; see Rule 3-12. The most convenient reference work for checking trademarks is the *Trade Names Dictionary* (Gale Research Inc.), which most public libraries have.

Owners of trademarks are obliged to use special symbols with them—an *R* or *TM* within a circle—in their advertisements; if they don't, they may lose their legal right to exclusive use of a trademark. The general writing public is under no such obligation.

transitive verb   a verb that has an **object.** A transitive verb transmits its action from a subject to an object, as does the verb *hits* in *The bat hits the ball.* Some verbs do not pass their action along and cannot have an object, like the verb in *The ball disappears*, which is an **intransitive verb.**

transpire   means *become known* or *come to light*, as in *It transpired that he had been the culprit all along*, but it is often used to mean *happen*, as in *Something funny transpired on my way to the office.* The second meaning is accepted by dictionaries, and it must be admitted that the *become known* meaning is none too pure either; the word was coined in the early seventeenth century to describe the movement of vapor through a membrane such as the surface of a leaf (its Latin roots combine to mean *breathe through*), and it still has that meaning in technical contexts. Nevertheless I advise not using the word to mean *happen*; in this meaning it often seems pretentious or pointlessly whimsical, and the usage is apt to be considered a sign of ignorance by those who are aware of the *become known* meaning.

try and **vs.** *try to*   *Try and* is solidly established in such constructions as *Try and stop me* and *I'm going to try and reach her at home.* It means *try to.* It cannot be considered an error—it's an idiom—but it is decidedly informal. Some are critical of *try and*, and I advise making little use of it; *try to* does not sound stilted in even the most casual speech.

uninterested   See *disinterested* **vs.** *uninterested.*

unique   should not be given a comparative or superlative form (*more unique, most unique*); see **comparative and superlative.**

unlike   Errors with *unlike* are very much like errors with *like*. Neither should be used as a conjunction (see *like* **for** *as*, *as if*, **or** *as though*). *Unlike in the War of 1812, the British had little at stake* and *Like in the War of 1812, the British had a great deal at stake* are both wrong, and for the same reason. However, the second sentence can easily be corrected by changing *Like* to *As*, but there is no easy repair for the first sentence. The language has no word that means the opposite of *as*, so some awkward phrasing is necessary, perhaps *As was not the case in the War of 1812, the British had little at stake*, or else a complete recasting, such as *Unlike the War of 1812, this war was not a threat to British interests.*

Often a second error is committed at the same time: *Unlike the War of 1812, the British had little at stake*, with the preposition *in* missing, is a false comparison; see Rules 1-2 and 1-5.

Perhaps because of the difficulty of finding alternatives that are graceful as well as correct, errors with *unlike* are committed by many who would not misuse *like*, and these errors get by editors too; I see them frequently in books and periodicals, not just in manuscripts. Yet they must be considered rather serious errors, because they indicate a dim comprehension not only of the proper role of the word but of the structure of sentences in which it is used.

upon vs. on   When *upon* can be replaced by *on*, as most of the time it can be, *on* is usually better. *I put the book upon the table* is slightly ponderous for *I put the book on the table.* However, *upon* is as common as *on* in many expressions, as in *Upon reflection I picked it up again*, and sometimes comes more naturally, as in *His schemes, built upon one another for so long, tumbled in disarray.* The *up* in *upon* is usually not significant; when it is, and would be stressed in speech, *up on* should be used: *The moon shone upon the mountain*, but *We could see a distant campfire up on the mountain.*

usage   means *manner of use* or *instance of use*, though it often merely means *use*. *I object to his use of my typewriter* suggests that I object to his using it at all; *I object to his usage of my typewriter* suggests that I think he misuses or abuses it—I object to his manner of use. In discussing language, *usage* of a word or construction means not just that it is used but that it is used in a specific way. Usage can thus be good or bad, acceptable or unacceptable. Whether a usage is acceptable often depends on the context, for there are levels of usage—informal, colloquial, slangy, vulgar—between the clearly correct and the clearly incorrect. The most convenient way to determine usages of a specific word and the degree of acceptance of a specific usage used to be to read the word's dictionary definition carefully. But some modern dictionaries, among them the Merriam-Webster dictionaries, which are very widely used in book publishing, make few attempts to distinguish correct and incorrect usage and levels of usage; they do include occasional usage labels such as "colloquial" and "vulgar," but their intent is to describe how the language is used rather than prescribe how it should be used.

Webster's Third New International Dictionary, which is almost entirely descriptive, was attacked when it appeared in 1961 and for years thereafter by those who had long valued the preceding edition for its numerous distinctions and prescriptions. The desk-size *Webster's Ninth New Collegiate Dictionary*, which appeared in 1984, is based on the unabridged *New International* but does include comments rather peremptorily defending a few of the most disputed usages. The *Random House Dictionary* includes more comments, which are less peremptory but also largely in defense of disputed usages. The *American Heritage Dictionary* has many usage notes; some are based on the opinions of a panel of more or less expert users of the language rather than on scholarship or knowledgeable linguistic judgment, so they have little lexicographical authority, but they do alert the reader to the strength of prejudices against many usages that lexicographers must accept as established. *Webster's New World Dictionary* (published by Simon & Schuster, not Merriam-Webster), which has long been the first authority for many newspaper and magazine editors, provides little comment.

This change in the nature of dictionaries reflects a controversy over language study and over educational goals and standards that has been in progress for many decades, and, inconvenient as the change has been for writers and editors, there is much to say in its favor. Edward Finegan's *Attitudes Toward English Usage: The History of a War of Words* (Teachers College Press, 1980) is a good account of the controversy on its several fronts.

There are, of course, a great many specialized dictionaries and handbooks of usage. *Webster's Dictionary of English Usage*, brand-new from Merriam-Webster in 1989, is an excellent supplement to any dictionary, including a prescriptive one; it is based, in lexicographical fashion, on citations of actual past and present usage from the huge Merriam-Webster files, but it also reflects careful and critical study of the opinions of dozens of writers on usage, and thus even when it supports a disputed usage—as it most often does—it gives the cautious reader adequate, if sometimes breezily skeptical, explanation of the grounds for the dispute. Among the many books on usage written by a single author or pair of authors rather than a team, an older one, *A Dictionary of Contemporary American Usage*, by Bergen and Cornelia Evans (Random House, 1957), is excellent. Being scholarly rather than opinionated, it is too permissive for some; for example, with little discussion it accepts plural pronouns with *everyone* as their antecedent. H. W. Fowler's classic *A Dictionary of Modern English Usage*, first published in 1926 and revised in 1965 by Sir Ernest Gowers (Oxford), is both scholarly and opinionated. Its discussions are acute and often amusing, but compressed and sometimes difficult to follow, and some of the errors they cover, drawn from British journalism and other public writing, are uncommon here, perhaps because British journalists favor long sentences and complicated constructions more than most Americans do. Another classic, *The Elements of Style*, by William Strunk, Jr., and the splendid E. B. White, has deservedly been a best-seller for decades, but it is not a general reference book; although it has expanded from edition to edition, it remains a brief and highly generalized attempt to prevent college students from committing the most common errors and from assuming absurd personae as writers.

Many recent books are more opinionated than scholarly, and their value depends somewhat on what the reader thinks of the writer and of the writer's attitude toward language. Some are good company, but some seem overanxious to find things in current usage to deplore; they might be said to uphold the Princess's English, because they complain about ever smaller peas under the mattresses of generally accepted usage. Their air of moral indignation is not entirely inappropriate, since there is something shameful in the laziness and thoughtlessness of much public expression, but it makes their readers overanxious. Quite unlike them is the very widely read William Safire, whose good-natured and witty *New York Times*

Magazine column—which is very often about neologisms these days but occasionally discusses basic usage issues—deserves its long life; several collections of letters to Safire it has generated have been published (Times Books), and they are fascinating proof of the diversity of opinion, both informed and uninformed.

The modern books that I have found most useful as an editor are by other working editors whose prescriptions and opinions reflect the realities and responsibilities of their functions, such as Roy H. Copperud and Theodore M. Bernstein. Some other books are equally levelheaded and dispassionate but do not seem to be based on much experience coping with actual text that must somehow be improved. A few books are hilarious combinations of strong opinion and weak background, but even they are likely to contain worthwhile insights and to display an exemplary sensitivity to language. Almost any one-man effort, including mine, is bound to originate or perpetuate at least an occasional questionable idea about what the language is and what it should be. Those who take usage and its prescribers too seriously should read Jim Quinn's *American Tongue in Cheek* (Pantheon, 1980), which humiliates a few of us prescribers specifically and all of us in general—but they shouldn't take its antiprescriptive attitude too seriously either.

used to, use to   a construction that indicates continual or habitual action in the past, as in *We used to play tennis.* In negative statements, *use to* is used, as in *We didn't use to play it as much as we do now*; it is correct but seems clumsy to many.

verb   One of the parts of speech; a word that expresses an action or state of being. Every sentence, except some exclamations and elliptical sentences (see **ellipsis**), should have a verb. *He saw that it was good* contains the verbs *saw* and *was.*

A verb that has an **object** is a **transitive verb**; a verb that does not have an object is an **intransitive verb.** A transitive verb can be either active or passive; see **voice.** An intransitive verb may be of a special type called a **linking verb.**

A verb can change its form to indicate its **tense,** its **mood,** and its **number.** Such a change is called an **inflection.**

A *verbal* is one of three special forms of a verb: a **gerund,** an **infinitive,** or a **participle.**

A *verb phrase* is a verb form that includes both a basic verb and an **auxiliary verb,** which is usually a form of *be* or *have.* A *phrasal verb* is a verb combined with an adverbial preposition; in *He messed up the report*, the combination *messed up* is a phrasal verb.

A *verb root* is the basic form of a verb; it can be thought of as the infinitive without *to*. Thus *be, have, go,* and *come* are verb roots. Verb roots are used in various compounds that are not verbs, such as *have-not* and *go-between*.

very vs. very much   The adverb *very* is not used alone to modify a verb—we do not say *I very love her* but instead say *I very much love her* or *I love her very much*. When a participle is used in a compound tense, the same restriction applies; we do not say *She is very enjoying her trip* or *She was very loved by her fans* but instead insert *much*, or else replace *very* with *much*.

However, often past participles are perceived more as adjectives than as verb forms, and so we do use *very* with them. We would quite properly say *She was very tired*, using *tired* as an adjective linked to *She* by the verb *was*. This can lead to uses of *very* that don't bother every ear but are considered errors. *She was very tired by our visit* uses *was* as an auxiliary verb and *tired* as a passive verb—*by our visit*, supplying an agent for *tired*, makes it clearly a verb—and *very* now is wrong; the insertion of *much* is required. Certain participles seem to reject *very* even when they are clearly adjectival. In *very belabored point*, the participle *belabored* seems to retain its force as a verb and hence to reject *very*—or so my ear tells me; people's ears differ at any given time, and over time a given participle may become more adjectival than it was.

We must trust our own ears on participles that are grammatically adjectival, and perhaps must expect that people a generation older may occasionally wrinkle their noses at a use of *very* with a grammatically adjectival participle that to our ears but not to theirs is adjectival in spirit as well. When we don't trust our own ears, we can insert *much* in doubtful cases, but we should not have so little trust in our ears that we change *She had a very tired expression* to *She had a much tired expression*. Some participles, including *tired*, are likely to be listed as adjectives in dictionaries, and it is safe to use *very* with them as long as they are not followed by a *by* construction that requires them to be perceived as passive verb forms.

virgule   a **diagonal,** as in *and/or*; see Rule 2-38.

virtually   means *almost entirely* or *nearly.* Some people think it should mean *veritably*, and that its standard use is an error in the same way **literally** is an error when it means *figuratively.* However, *virtually* and *veritably* have different roots and different histories.

voice   the form taken by a **transitive verb** to indicate whether the subject of the verb is the verb's agent—that is, is acting—or is the verb's recipient—that is, is being acted upon. In the *active voice*, the subject is the verb's agent; in *I hit the ball*, the pronoun *I* is both subject and agent. In the *passive voice*, the subject is the verb's recipient, and the agent is indicated by a participial phrase with *by*; in *I was hit by the ball*, the pronoun *I* is still the subject, but *the ball* is the agent.

A sentence in the active voice means the same as a sentence in the passive voice if the object of the active sentence is made the subject of the passive sentence and the subject of the active sentence is replaced by a prepositional phrase with *by*: *I hit the ball* means the same as *The ball was hit by me*, and *The ball hit me* means the same as *I was hit by the ball*. Note that the subject of the active verb does not become the object of the passive verb; it remains the agent of the verb. In the passive examples above, there is no object.

If a sentence in the active voice has both an **indirect object** and a **direct object,** either the direct object or the indirect object can become the subject of the equivalent passive sentence. The one that does not become the subject is called the retained object. Thus *He gave me the letter* can become either *The letter was given me by him*, with the indirect object *me* retained, or *I was given the letter by him*, with the direct object *letter* retained. The second version, in which it is the indirect object that becomes the subject, is difficult to explain grammatically, because the *to* that is implicit in an indirect object somehow loses its effect and the *me* that *to* would have as an object becomes *I*. Standard rules of grammar would seem to require *To me was given the letter by him*. That's what it would have to be in Latin—but despite the efforts of nineteenth-century rulemakers, English is not Latin. Use of the indirect object as the subject may occasionally be criticized in Britain but seems to be universally accepted here.

A passive verb must be a transitive verb—that is, one that has an object when it is in the active voice—because if it had no object in the active voice, there would be nothing to become its subject in the passive voice, and a verb must have a subject except in certain idioms (see **as follows** vs. **as follow**).

The passive voice is wordier than the active voice, and it is often comparatively clumsy. When it is used excessively, it makes expression seem vague and evasive. However, it has many legitimate uses; see Rule 1-18.

were vs. was   *Were* is used instead of *was* with *I* and *he, she,* and *it* in certain subjunctive constructions; see Rule 1-17.

what is vs. what are   In some constructions, *what* combines the functions of the demonstrative pronoun *that* or *those* and the relative pronoun *which*. For example, the cumbersome *That which is important is the money* becomes *What is important is the money*, and the cumbersome *Those which are welcome are large donations* becomes *What are welcome are large donations*. As may be apparent in the second example, *what are* is often somewhat troubling; *what* is accepted by grammarians as a plural relative pronoun as well as a singular one, but nevertheless it seems happier in singular constructions.

There is a strong tendency to mix singular and plural verbs, as in *What is welcome are large donations*, and the tendency is stronger when some verb other than *is* follows *what* and there are several words between the first and second verb, as in *What warms the cockles of our hearts are large donations*. The advice of most writers on grammar and usage, including me in the first edition of this book, is to resist this tendency and allow ourselves only either *What warm the cockles of our hearts are large donations* or *What warms the cockles of our hearts is large donations*, with the verbs agreeing in number. In the singular-verb version, which I think is preferable, it is entirely correct for *is* not to agree in number with *donations*, since *donations* is merely the **complement** in the construction, not the subject, and it is the subject that determines the number of the verb (see Rule 1-11). *What* in the sentence represents a singular idea—a kind of donation—and since this singular idea is the subject of both verbs, it seems natural to make both verbs singular rather than to make both plural. Even in *What warm the cockles of their hearts are gems, coins, and banknotes*, in which the complement has three plural elements, I would prefer to make the two plural verbs singular, because I think *What* represents a singular idea, a greed, rather than all the items in the complement.

I have seen some sentences in which plural verbs seem irresistibly right, such as *What have always been censured as*

Shakespeare's conceits are completely justifiable, a quotation from Coleridge cited by the great grammarian George O. Curme, but I think they are rare, because much more often the idea of the subject is singular. Note that in this example it is not a plural complement that draws the verbs to the plural, for the complement is merely a modifier; the verbs are plural because the subject is a plural idea, and singular verbs would be unnatural. *What are called diamonds are often merely zircons* and *What are called diamonds are often merely paste* similarly require plural verbs.

Plural verbs can result in terrible sentences, like the following from a weekly newsmagazine: *What really bother George Bush most about Richard Gephardt are neither his accusations of presidential timidity nor his proposal to send direct U.S. aid to the Soviet Union, but what the President considers the Missouri Democrat's "cheap shot" attempts to stir up class animosities.* The writer, or more likely the copy editor, probably traced the opening *What* through its negative complements (one of which is plural) and the second *what* to the plural *attempts*, and concluded that since *attempts* is the complement of the second *what*, that *what* must be plural, and since that *what* is the positive complement of the opening *What*, the opening *What* must be plural—hence the plural verbs *bother* and *are*, bother the eye though they may. I think *bothers* and *is* would be much more natural. The sentence concerns three aspects of Gephardt's behavior, and the idea, if not the phrasing, of each aspect can be considered singular.

Moreover, sentences in which the verbs are mixed, such as *What warms the cockles of our hearts are gems, coins, and banknotes*, occasionally seem worth defending to me now, as they did not a few years ago. Perhaps *What* is thoughtlessly allowed to have the singular verb it seems to prefer or perhaps *are* is illegitimately and lamentably drawn into agreement with the plural complement, but I see such mixtures of singular and plural verbs in the best literature and the best of the manuscripts I edit, and I have tried to think of some grammar-based argument in favor of the mixture. One possibility is to consider such sentences to be in the reverse of standard order, with the complement preceding the subject; for more on this wily reasoning see the discussion of subjects and complements of different number in Rule 1-11. In its "real" order, the example becomes *Gems, coins, and banknotes are what warms the cockles of their hearts*, and since *what* is now merely the complement instead of the subject, its verb does not have to agree with the preceding verb. It might be argued that *what* still has a plural **antecedent,** and ordinarily a relative pronoun should agree in number with its antecedent (see Rule 1-12). But *what* is not an ordinary relative pronoun here, it is a combination of a demonstrative and a relative pronoun, and certainly it seems more like a combining of *that which* than a combining of *those which,* so I would argue that it is singular.

Another line is to examine whether the two verbs really have the same subject; if they do not, perhaps there is no reason they should have the same number. Certainly *What* is the subject of *warms.* But the subject of *are* is really the whole clause *What warms the cockles of their hearts,* not just *What.* The clause is something like a noun clause (see under **noun**). However, a clause used as a noun is always singular—a clause is a statement, a unit of thought, no matter how many plurals occur in it, and if it is used as the subject of a sentence, it always takes a singular verb, as in *That their parents refuse to give them their blessings does not seem to have discouraged them,* in which all the words up to *does* are a noun clause. Thus though this argument supports my feeling that it is almost always better to use two singular verbs than two plural verbs, and perhaps strengthens my argument that *what* is correctly singular when the order of clauses is changed to make it the complement rather than the subject, it undermines my effort to prove that the second verb in a *what is* construction should be allowed to agree with a plural complement. I'll continue to think about it.

My advice now is to take note of the condemnation of mixed singular and plural verbs and to make both verbs singular whenever *what* represents a singular idea rather than something plural—but perhaps occasionally to allow a mixture; if it really seems better it probably is better, and the reader is unlikely to notice that a rule has been bent.

when and **where** in definitions   *Overacting is when the actor tries too hard* and *A solecism is where you make some mistake in grammar* are childish constructions. Adults sometimes switch them around and complicate them, but they remain childish: *When you make some mistake in grammar it's called a solecism.* Actually, when you make some mistake in grammar you probably get away with it and the mistake isn't called anything, let alone a solecism, so the literal meaning of the sentence is false. Sometimes the *when* or *where* construction is an unnecessary complication and can just be eliminated: *A solecism is a mistake in grammar.* Sometimes a *what* construction can replace a *when* or *where* construction: *Overacting is what an actor does when he tries too hard.*

When and *where* are, of course, quite correct in constructions that employ them to define a time or place, as in *Teatime is when we bring out the decanters* and *Jerez is where sherry originated.*

where is too often used as an all-purpose word to introduce a clause, as in *I see where Prince Charles used "hopefully" as a sentence modifier the other day*, in which the conjunction *that* would be better, and *It was the kind of discussion where everyone talks and no one listens*, in which the preposition-and-relative-pronoun combination *in which* would be better. *Where* cannot, of course, be prevented from extending its applications beyond those involving physical location if that is the will of users of the language, as it long has been, but at least in formal writing it should not replace *that* or *in which*.

whether vs. *whether or not*   When *or not* can be omitted, it might as well be. In *I don't know whether or not to go*, it can be; in *I am going whether or not he goes* (or *whether he goes or not*), it cannot be.

Errors occur in long sentences with *whether or not*, as in *I am going whether or not John, who said he had the minutes of the last meeting prepared and I could take them, goes or not.* This reduces to *I am going whether or not John goes or not*, which is a **redundancy.** The sentence does require one *or not* but shouldn't have two.

which vs. *that*   See *that* vs. *which*.

while means *during the time that*, as in *John slept while his children cleaned the house*, and also *whereas* and sometimes *but*, as in *While some children are lazy, some parents are too* and *John is lazy, while his children are quite energetic.* Too often it is used when neither of these meanings applies, as in *John is a popular fellow, while his wife is one of the best hostesses in town*, in which it means simply *and*, the most common conjunction. I advise not using *while* when *and* is meant.

who is sometimes used with something inanimate as its **antecedent,** as in *The report praised General Motors, who had quickly admitted responsibility and promised to recall their* *who, whom; whoever, whomever*

1928 models. In the example, the usage is encouraged by the verbs that follow, because it is difficult to imagine something inanimate admitting and promising, and the *who* then encourages the plural pronoun *their.* The usage would be acceptable in Britain (see the discussion of subjects that look singular but may be plural in Rule 1-11), but the dominant American practice is to consider corporations, government bodies, and such things impersonal and singular, even with verbs that imply an animate subject. If *General Motors* is replaced by *the management of General Motors*, the subject is still impersonal and singular; a term that specifically denotes people, such as *the directors*, is needed to make the subject personal and plural.

who, whom; whoever, whomever   There is no question that *who* and *whoever* are the correct forms for the *subjective case* and *whom* and *whomever* are the correct forms for the **objective case.** Nevertheless, *who* and *whoever* are often used when strict grammar calls for the objective case, and such usage is acceptable in speech and most writing; see Rules 1-8 and 1-9. However, the opposite flouting of grammatical rules—using *whom* or *whomever* when the subjective case is called for, as in *For whomever kills the dragon there will be a crown*—is not acceptable; see the discussion of pronouns as part of their own clauses in Rule 1-6.

Than whom, as in *John, than whom there is no more skillful sailor, capsized*, is correct, even though the subjective case seems clearly called for unless *than* is accepted as a preposition, which ordinarily it is not—it is accepted only as a conjunction. See also **than.**

whose* vs. *of which   *Whose* seems to be based on the pronoun *who*, which should be used only when its **antecedent** is human or at least something animate, and therefore the rule used to be that *whose* should not be used with an inanimate antecedent. Such usages as *These are the organizations whose members generally vote twice* and *Show me a street whose inhabitants don't love it* were condemned. The correct forms of the examples would be *These are the organizations of which the members generally vote twice* and *Show me a street the inhabitants of which don't love it*, which to modern ears seem in far worse trouble than could be caused by using *whose* to represent a thing rather than a person. *Whose* with an inanimate antecedent is now accepted.

Nevertheless, *whose* still seems inelegant to some people when it can be avoided easily, and sometimes it is still incorrect. It should not be used as an interrogative pronoun with something inanimate as its referent, as in *Whose climate is better, Florida's or California's? I met that author whose book I read* is a conventional use of *whose* with a person as its antecedent, but *I read that book whose author I met* is clumsy; it should be changed to *I read that book by the author I met* or some similar rewording.

whose vs. who's   These words are so often confused in manuscripts that something worse than mere carelessness must often be the problem. *Who's* is the contraction of *who is* or *who has,* as in *I wonder who's here* and *I wonder who's been invited. Whose* is the possessive form of *who,* as in *I think I know whose woods these are* and *Whose woods are these?*

word order   the principal method by which individual words are made into meaningful sentences in English. See **syntax.**

worth   In constructions such as *ten dollars' worth,* the apostrophe is often omitted. It is required, as is evident from some other phrases such as *his money's worth.* Some may omit the apostrophe because they think the idea of possession is rather remote in such constructions, but it often is remote in other possessive constructions as well; see **possessive case.**

would have vs. had   *Would have* is more and more common where *had* is required, as in *I wish you would have done it* and *I would have done it if you would have asked me.* The examples should be corrected to *I wish you had done it* and *I would have done it if you had asked me.* See the discussion of problems with subjunctive tenses in Rule 1-14.

your vs. you're   Like *whose* and *who's,* these words are confused surprisingly often. *Your* is a possessive pronoun, as in *This is your life. You're* is the contraction of *you are,* as in *You're going to have to live your own life.*

I sometimes see the error *your's.* It should be *yours,* a special form that the pronoun *you* has when it is an independent possessive; see **possessive case.**

zeugma   the use of a word, often a verb, in two senses, as in *He took his hat and his leave*, in which the verb *took* has a distinctly different meaning with one of its objects than it does with the other. In *I was repelled by his threadbare clothes and manners* the adjective *threadbare* is used literally with *clothes* and figuratively with *manners*. Zeugma is sometimes loosely called **syllepsis;** see the discussion of omission of verb forms in Rule 1-2. Zeugma is often accidental, as in *She wore a rusty black dress, a feather boa, and an alligator handbag;* since *wore* has no legitimate application to *handbag*, this zeugma is an error. When it is used deliberately, it is usually for humorous effect. M. H. Abrams in his *A Glossary of Literary Terms* includes a sardonic zeugma from Byron: *The loud tempests raise / The waters, and repentance for past sinning.*

ABOUT THE AUTHOR

EDWARD D. JOHNSON was born in 1935. He was graduated from Exeter and Harvard, and since 1960 he has been a book editor. He has worked for Simon & Schuster, Alfred A. Knopf, and several other publishing houses; he is currently a free-lance editor.